Second Edition

Strategic Human Resources Planning

Second Edition

Strategic Human Resources Planning

Kenneth J. McBey
York University

Monica Belcourt
York University

Series Editor: Monica Belcourt

Australia Canada Mexico Singapore Spain United Kingdom United States

Strategic Human Resources Planning
Second Edition

by Monica Belcourt and Kenneth McBey

Editorial Director and Publisher:
Evelyn Veitch

Acquisitions Editor:
Anthony Rezek

Marketing Manager:
Don Thompson

Senior Developmental Editor:
Karina Hope

Permissions Coordinator:
Nicola Winstanley

Production Editor:
Wendy Yano

Copy Editor:
Wendy Thomas

Proofreader:
Carol J. Anderson

Indexer:
Edwin Durbin

Production Coordinator:
Renate McCloy

Creative Director:
Angela Cluer

Interior Design Modifications:
Erich Falkenberg

Cover Design:
Johanna Liburd

Compositor:
Carol Magee

Printer:
Transcontinental

Printed and bound in Canada
5 6 7 8 09 08 07 06

For more information contact Nelson, 1120 Birchmount Road, Toronto, Ontario, M1K 5G4. Or you can visit our Internet site at http://www.nelson.com

National Library of Canada Cataloguing in Publication Data

Belcourt, Monica, 1946–
Strategic human resources planning/Monica Belcourt, Kenneth McBey.—2nd ed.

(Nelson series in human resources management)
Includes bibliographical references and index.
ISBN-13 : 978-0-17-622459-2
ISBN-10 : 0-17-622459-9

1. Manpower planning. I. McBey, Kenneth James, 1956– II. Title. III. Series.

HF5549.5.M3B45 2003 658.3'01
C2003-904435-1

To my son Marc, for his cool calm and engaging wit.
M.B.

With love to Betty-Anne, Robert, June, Roderick, Donald, and Jim.
Nulli Secundus!
K.M.

Brief Contents

About the Series xv
About the Authors xvii
Acknowledgments xix
Preface xx

Part I	**Introduction 1**
Chapter 1	Concepts of Strategy and Planning 3
Chapter 2	Aligning HR with Strategy 21
Chapter 3	Environmental Influences on HRM 53
Chapter 4	Evaluation of HR Programs and Policies 77
Part II	**HR Planning 109**
Chapter 5	Job Analysis 111
Chapter 6	HR Management Systems 137
Chapter 7	The HR Forecasting Process 159
Chapter 8	HR Demand 181
Chapter 9	Ascertaining HR Supply 203
Chapter 10	Succession Management 231
Part III	**Strategic Options and HR Decisions 263**
Chapter 11	Downsizing and Restructuring 265
Chapter 12	Strategic International HRM 299
Chapter 13	Mergers and Acquisitions 327
Chapter 14	Outsourcing 355

Index 372

Detailed Contents

About the Series xv
About the Authors xvii
Acknowledgments xix
Preface xx

Part I Introduction

Chapter 1 Concepts of Strategy and Planning 3

Chapter Goals 3
A Need for Strategic HRM 4
Strategy 5
Strategic Types 8
Models of Business Strategies 14
Summary 17
Key Terms 17
Suggested Websites 18
Discussion Questions 18
Exercises 18
Case: Aldo Shoes Limited 19
References 19
Endnotes 20

Chapter 2 Aligning HR with Strategy 21

Chapter Goals 21
Strategic HRM 22
The Risks 26
Linking HR Processes to Strategy 27
HR Strategy by Division 35
Characteristics of an Effective HRM Strategy 35
The Strategic HR Planning Model 37
Summary 38
Key Terms 39
Suggested Websites 39
Discussion Questions 39
Exercises 39
Case: A New Vision of HR 40
References 41
Endnotes 43

Appendix HR Alignment with Two Strategies 45

Chapter 3 Environmental Influences on HRM 53

Chapter Goals 53
Environmental Scanning Sources and Methods 54
Sources of Information 55
Techniques for Scanning 56
Challenges in Environmental Scanning 59
Environmental Factors 60
Stakeholders 67
Environment Scanning: A Case Application 70
Summary 70
Key Terms 71
Suggested Websites 72
Discussion Questions 72
Exercises: The Nominal Group Technique 73
Case: Work–Life Family Balance 73
References 75
Endnotes 76

Chapter 4 Evaluation of HR Programs and Policies 77

Chapter Goals 77
The Scorecard 78
The Importance of Evaluating HRM 78
The 5C Model of HRM Impact 81
Approaches to Measuring HRM Practices 91
Challenges in Measuring the Impact of HRM 96
Summary 97
Key Terms 97
Suggested Websites 98
Discussion Questions 98
Exercises 99
Case: Measuring HR Impact at Wells Fargo 99
References 100
Endnotes 102

Appendix HR Accounting Methods 104

Part II HR Planning

Chapter 5 Job Analysis 111

Chapter Goals 111
Introduction 112

Job Analysis 112
Problems Associated with Job Analysis 115
The Process of Job Analysis 116
Specific Job Analysis Techniques 124
Competency-Based Approaches 126
Summary 129
Key Terms 129
Suggested Websites 130
Discussion Questions 130
Exercise 130
Case: Madness at Moosehead U 131
References 132
Endnotes 134

Chapter 6 HR Management Systems 137

Chapter Goals 137
Three Stages of HRMS Development 139
Selection and Design Criteria for HRMS 141
Criteria for Data Inclusion in the HRMS 146
Core HRMS Data Entries 147
Summary 153
Key Terms 154
Suggested Websites 154
Discussion Questions 154
Exercise 155
Case: HRMS at Canada Bread Limited 155
References 156
Endnotes 157

Chapter 7 The HR Forecasting Process 159

Chapter Goals 159
Forecasting Activity Categories 160
Benefits of HR Forecasting 161
Key Personnel Analyses Conducted by HR Forecasters 163
Environmental and Organizational Factors Affecting HR Forecasting 166
HR Forecasting Time Horizons 167
Determining Net HR Requirements 168
Summary 175
Key Terms 175
Suggested Websites 176
Discussion Questions 176
Exercise 176

Case: Sun Microsystems 177
References 177
Endnotes 179

Chapter 8 HR Demand 181

Chapter Goals 181
Index/Trend Analysis 182
Expert Forecasts 184
Delphi Technique 185
Nominal Group Technique 188
HR Budgets: Staffing or Manning Table 190
Envelope/Scenario Forecasting 191
Regression Analysis 194
Summary 198
Key Terms 198
Suggested Websites 199
Discussion Questions 199
Exercise 199
Case: Recruiting with Bells and Whistles 200
References 200
Endnotes 202

Chapter 9 Ascertaining HR Supply 203

Chapter Goals 203
Skills and Management Inventories 204
Succession/Replacement Analysis 205
Markov Models 210
Linear Programming 213
Movement Analysis 214
Vacancy Model 218
HR Supply and Retention Programs 221
Summary 224
Key Terms 225
Suggested Websites 225
Discussion Questions 225
Exercise 225
Case: Ontario's Faculty Shortage Crisis 226
References 228
Endnotes 230

Chapter 10 Succession Management 231

Chapter Goals 231
Importance of Succession Management 232

Evolution of Succession Management 235
Succession Management Process 238
Employee Role in Succession Management 250
Succession Management's Soft Spots 252
Succession Management at Air Canada 255
Summary 257
Key Terms 258
Suggested Websites 258
Discussion Questions 258
Exercise 258
Case: Acceleration Pools at PepsiCo 259
References 260
Endnotes 262

PART III STRATEGIC OPTIONS AND HR DECISIONS

CHAPTER 11 DOWNSIZING AND RESTRUCTURING 265

Chapter Goals 265
The Downsizing Phenomenon 266
Defining Downsizing and Restructuring 266
How Common Is Workforce Reduction and Restructuring? 269
Why Do Organizations Downsize? 270
The Downsizing Decision 271
The "Survivors" of Downsizing 275
Financial Performance and Downsizing 278
Consequences of Downsizing 279
Effective Downsizing Strategies 280
HRM Issues 285
Summary 290
Key Terms 290
Suggested Websites 291
Discussion Questions 291
Exercises 291
Case: A Downsizing Decision at the Department of Public Works 292
References 294
Endnotes 297

CHAPTER 12 STRATEGIC INTERNATIONAL HRM 299

Chapter Goals 299
Strategic International Human Resource Management 300
Corporate International Business Strategies 301
Strategic IHRM Fits with Corporate International Business Strategies 302

Strategic IHRM Flexibility 304
International Staffing and Career Development 304
Other Issues in Strategic IHRM 314
Summary 318
Key Terms 319
Suggested Websites 319
Discussion Questions 319
Exercises 320
Case: An International Career Move 320
References 321
Endnotes 324

CHAPTER 13 MERGERS AND ACQUISITIONS 327

Chapter Goals 327
Big Is Beautiful 328
Definitions 328
The Urge to Merge 330
Cultural Issues in Mergers 336
HR Issues in M&As 339
Summary 346
Key Terms 347
Suggested Websites 347
Discussion Questions 347
Exercise 348
Case: The City of Toronto—Courage in the Face of Chaos 348
References 351
Endnotes 352

CHAPTER 14 OUTSOURCING 355

Chapter Goals 355
Outsourcing 356
Management of Outsourcing 363
Summary 366
Key Terms 366
Suggested Websites 366
Discussion Questions 367
Exercise 367
Case: Calgary Health Region 368
References 369
Endnotes 370

Index 372

About the Series

More than ever, Human Resources Management (HRM) professionals need the knowledge and skills to design HRM practices that not only meet legal requirements but also are effective in supporting organizational strategy. Increasingly, these professionals turn to published research and best practices for assistance in the development of effective human resources (HR) policies and practices. The books in the *Nelson Series in Human Resources Management* are the best source in Canada for reliable, valid, and current knowledge about practices in HRM.

The texts in this series include:

- *Managing Performance through Training and Development*
- *Management of Occupational Health and Safety*
- *Recruitment and Selection in Canada*
- *Strategic Compensation in Canada*
- *An Introduction to the Canadian Labour Market*
- *Research, Measurement and Evaluation of Human Resources*

The *Nelson Series in Human Resources Management* represents a significant development in the field of HRM for many reasons. Each book in the series (except for *Compensation in Canada*) is the first Canadian text in its area of specialization. HR professionals in Canada must work with Canadian laws, statistics, policies, and values. This series serves their needs. It also represents the first time that students and practitioners have had access to a complete set of HRM books, standardized in presentation, that enables them to access information quickly across many HRM disciplines. The books are essential sources of information that meet the requirements for the Knowledge exam for the academic portion of the HR certification process. This one-stop resource will prove useful to anyone looking for solutions for the effective management of people.

The publication of this series signals that the field of human resources management has advanced to the stage where theory and applied research guide practice. The books in the series present the best and most current research in the functional areas of HRM. Research is supplemented with examples of the best practices used by Canadian companies that are leaders in HRM. Each text begins with a general model of the discipline, then describes the implementation of effective strategies. Thus, the books serve as an introduction to the functional area for the new student of HR and as a validation source for the more experienced HRM practitioner. Cases, exercises, and references provide opportunities for further discussion and analysis.

As you read and consult the books in this series, I hope you share my excitement in being involved in the development of a profession that has such a significant impact on the workforce and in our professional lives.

Monica Belcourt
Series Editor
April 2003

About the Authors

Monica Belcourt

Monica Belcourt is a professor of Human Resources Management at York University. Her research work is grounded in the experience she gained as director of personnel at CP Rail, director of Employee Development at the National Film Board, and as a functional HR specialist for other organizations. Dr. Belcourt alternated working in HRM with graduate school, earning an M.A. in psychology, an M.Ed. in adult education, and a Ph.D. in management. She also holds the designation of Certified Human Resource Professional (CHRP). She has taught HRM at Concordia University, Université du Québec à Montréal (UQUAM), McGill University, and York University. At the latter, she founded and managed the largest undergraduate program in HRM in Canada. She is the academic editor of the *Nelson Series in HRM*.

Dr. Belcourt is the founding director of the International Alliance for Human Resources Research (www.yorku.ca/hrresall), a catalyst for the discovery, dissemination, and application of new knowledge about HRM. Under her leadership, IAHRR has launched The Research Forum, a column in the *Human Resources Professional*; the Applied Research Stream at the annual HRPAO conference; and the best theses awards program.

Professor Belcourt is active in many professional associations and not-for-profit organizations, and is currently the president of the Human Resources Professionals Association of Ontario (www.hrpao.org). She is a frequent commentator on HRM issues for CTV's *Canada AM*, CBC, *The Globe and Mail*, and other media.

Kenneth McBey

Kenneth McBey is a professor of Human Resources Management at York University. His research and teaching draw on his career as an infantry officer in the Canadian army, where he rose to the rank of Lieutenant-Colonel and commanding officer of the 48th Highlanders of Canada. Throughout his military career, Dr. McBey held a wide variety of command and staff appointments, including those in human-resource related areas such as recruiting, operations and training, personnel officer (adjutant), and compensation. This real-life testing of HR theories has proved to be of invaluable assistance to his work in the academic realm. Professor McBey earned an Honours B.A. in political economy and a B.Ed. from the University of Toronto, and an M.B.A. and Ph.D. in management from York University.

Dr. McBey has served as coordinator of York University's Human Resources Management program, and he teaches a wide variety of courses, including Human Resources Planning, Leadership and Management Skills,

Recruitment, Selection and Performance Appraisal, Organizational Behaviour, and Organizational Theory. He has been a visiting professor at the Aberdeen Business School and the Graduate Programmes in Human Resources and in Management at the University of Aberdeen, Scotland.

Professor McBey is active in a wide variety of community and voluntary associations, and he serves on the boards of several not-for-profit organizations. He was recently awarded the Queen's Golden Jubilee Medal by the Government of Canada for making a "significant contribution to his fellow citizens, community and to Canada." Among Professor McBey's other honours and awards are the J. Reginald Adams Gold Medal from the University of Toronto, the Canada 125th Anniversary Medal for outstanding service to Canada, the Canadian Forces Decoration (C.D.), and appointment to the Order of St. John by Her Majesty Queen Elizabeth II.

ACKNOWLEDGMENTS

The authors wish to acknowledge the contributions of two of Canada's experts in HRM: Professor Terry Wagar of Saint Mary's University, and Professor Xiayun Wang, of the University of Manitoba. Each drew on personal research and experience to write outstanding chapters in their areas of expertise. We thank Professor Wagar for his chapter "Downsizing and Restructuring," and Professor Wang for building on the work of Professor Sharon Leiba-O'Sullivan, of the University of Ottawa, for her chapter "Strategic International HR."

The authors wish to thank the following reviewers who made helpful comments for this revision: Brian Harrocks, Algonquin College; Suzanne Kavanagh, George Brown College; M.F. Mandl, British Columbia Institute of Technology; Gloria Miller, University of Regina; David Morrison, Durham College; Ash Patel, Seneca College; Sherry Price, Okanagan University College; Carol Ann Samhaber, Algonquin College; and Ted Mock, of the University of Toronto. The team at Nelson—Anthony Rezek and Karina Hope—contributed enormously through their professionalism and dedication.

Above all, we wish to thank our colleagues across Canada who have supported the HRM Series by contributing their research, their experience, and their input to enable HRM students to read about the HRM landscape in this country.

Finally, we continue to owe much of our career success to the support of our families. I, Monica, thank Michael, my husband, and my sons, Marc and Brooker, who provide the affection and humour that vitalize a project like this. I, Kenneth, acknowledge the loving support of my family and the active interest and involvement of students in my Human Resources Planning courses for the evolution of this text.

Monica Belcourt
Kenneth McBey
York University

PREFACE

The fundamental premise of this text is that different organizational strategies require different human resources management (HRM) policies and practices. *Strategic Human Resources Planning*, second edition, is designed to help human resources (HR) managers plan and make decisions about the allocation of resources for the effective management of people in organizations, within a given strategy.

There is a growing perception that human resource planning should be more than just demand and supply forecasting. HR professionals should be business partners in strategy formulation and implementation and should be concerned with the implications of strategic decisions on HRM practices. A decision to expand internationally affects selection, compensation, and other functional areas. Strategic decisions to merge or downsize have HR implications beyond simple forecasting ones. All these strategic options will lead to questions about the best types of compensation, selection, and training to ensure the success of the chosen strategy. This text attempts to answer these questions, without neglecting traditional and important HR forecasting processes. It provides tools for HR planning and forecasting and tries to match corporate strategies with specific HR practices.

STRUCTURE OF THE TEXT

The text is organized in a way that introduces the reader to the concepts of strategy formulation and implementation, within an HR context. Part I outlines the fundamental building blocks of strategic HR with an introduction to the concepts and their links to HR planning, how trends and issues are identified, and how organizations determine if implementation of strategies, policies, and plans are successful. Chapter 1 lays the groundwork by introducing the concepts of both corporate and business strategies. We spend some time explaining strategic choices, because it is imperative that, as HR managers become business partners, they understand commonly used business terms. This will help them to participate fully in strategic discussions and to explain the impact of their HR programs on the organization. Strategy seems to imply that only corporate-wide plans are made, and these are used to manage and control the various units that exist within an organization. But many large organizations operate several businesses, each with its own strategy. For example, Bata operates two "divisions" or businesses, one that focuses on production and the other on retailing. Each has a different business strategy, although the overall corporate strategy is growth. Two types of business-level strategies are discussed. Chapter 2 continues the introduction to strategy by embedding HRM strategy within an organizational strategic framework. A model of strategic HR planning is introduced in this chapter to orient the reader and to provide the structure for the text.

The environmental factors that influence strategic choice, particularly within an HR context, are discussed in Chapter 3. We look at the sources of information about the environment and the methods HR strategists use to scan the environment. A critical part of strategic planning is the ability to measure results and to determine if goals have been met. Chapter 4 provides a framework for understanding how HR processes, practices, and policies can affect organizational outcomes. It also provides the tools for measuring HRM outcomes.

Part II focuses on the more traditional aspects of HR planning: forecasting supply and demand. A critical component of strategy is matching employee capabilities with organizational objectives. The ability to assess current skills is a fundamental part of strategic planning for human resources. Part II provides a comprehensive set of tools that enables the HR professional to develop the numbers and methods needed to support organizational objectives. The critical role of job analysis within a planning context is discussed in Chapter 5, and the use of systems to manage data is outlined in Chapter 6. Chapter 7 explains the techniques used to forecast demand for human resources. Chapter 8 focuses on the use of methods for analyzing demand, while Chapter 9 looks at the methods used for determining supply. Managerial succession planning and career development, discussed in Chapter 10, are important considerations for ensuring that the organization has a stock of replacements for its leaders.

Part III examines the types of strategic orientations that firms may choose. Company-wide strategies, sometimes referred to as corporate strategies, are focused on overall strategy for the company and its businesses or interests. Examples of corporate strategies include decisions to merge or to establish the organization in international markets. Strategies at this level are usually also focused on long-term growth and survival goals. We discuss four major decisions facing organizations: restructuring, international operations, mergers and acquisitions, and outsourcing.

Chapter 11, written by Professor Terry Wagar of Saint Mary's University, discusses restructuring and downsizing. We then turn to an area of increasing importance in the strategies of organizations—growth through international initiatives. In Chapter 12, Professor Xiaoyun Wang of the University of Manitoba, discusses the growth option of seeking new customers or markets by locating internationally. HR managers state that globalization of their businesses is the number-one trend affecting their organizations. Operating a business in a foreign country, particularly one that is not North American or European, poses singular problems for the Western HR manager.

In Chapter 13, we examine another high-growth area—mergers and acquisitions. An acquisition occurs when one company acquires another, whereas a merger is typically seen as two organizations merging to achieve economies of scale. Both acquisitions and mergers lead to issues of integration of common functions, elimination of duplication or underproductive units, and a meshing of cultures and practices. Finally, the hot issue of outsourcing is explored in Chapter 14, with a thorough analysis of the risks and benefits of the outsourcing decision.

HRM issues such as HR planning, compensation, selection, training, performance evaluation, and labour relations are discussed within the overall strategies of restructuring, international initiatives, and mergers. By the end of Part III, readers will have an understanding of how specific strategic decisions can be matched with HR policies and practices.

New to this edition are the inclusion of related websites, with descriptors to assist students in searching for more and current information. Every chapter includes not only discussion questions, but excercises and cases. Text boxes showcase real-life applications of the content. For instructors, new to this edition are an Instructor's Manual and Power Point slides that can be downloaded directly from www.hrm.nelson.com.

Monica Belcourt
Kenneth McBey
April 2003

Part I

Introduction

1

CONCEPTS OF STRATEGY AND PLANNING

CHAPTER GOALS

Air Canada, an organization with 40 000 employees, was facing crucial strategic decisions because of a drop in passenger traffic due to unstable political conditions around the world, increased competition from low-cost carriers, heavy debt, and declining revenues. At the time of this writing, Air Canada had sought bankruptcy protection. To forestall this end, Air Canada made a number of strategic decisions. One early strategy was to acquire its competition, Canadian Airlines. Then, in order to focus on its key business, Air Canada attempted to divest some of its assets, by selling 35% of Aeroplan to Onex Corporation, an investment firm. Another business strategy was to create multiple brands such as Tango and Zip in an attempt to compete with the low-cost carriers. A third strategy was to try to increase its market share of international business travel because the domestic airline market was stagnant. A fourth strategic decision was to downsize by laying off 10% of its employees in an attempt to reduce its $3-billion annual labour expense. If Air Canada operated under the same work rules and pay scales as the low-cost carriers, it would be profitable. Air Canada therefore attempted to turn around its decline by demanding wage concessions from its unions.

The Air Canada example highlights the strategic decisions made by organizations in their attempts to survive and become profitable. The types of strategic decisions made by Air Canada (acquisitions, divestiture, downsizing, and going international) and its business strategies will be introduced in this chapter. Each strategic choice has implications for the management of human resources. We start in this chapter by establishing a common understanding of strategy, its importance, and its link to HRM (human resources management).

After reading this chapter, you should be able to do the following:

1. Discuss why managers need to examine the human resource implications of their organizational strategies.
2. Understand the various terms used to define strategy and its processes.
3. Describe organizational strategies, including restructuring, growth, and maintenance.
4. Define business strategy and discuss how it differs from corporate strategy.
5. Discuss three approaches to business strategies: the Boston Consulting Group approach, the Miles and Snow approach, and Porter's generic competitive strategies.

A Need for Strategic HRM

Read any Canadian newspaper and you will see stories such as these:

- IBM and Apple established a joint venture to develop an object-oriented operating system to compete with Microsoft. The social-engineering challenge (to get two cultures working together) was greater than the technical-engineering challenge.
- The cities of Toronto, East York, Etobicoke, York, North York, and Scarborough merged into one megacity (called Toronto). Five years later, the predicted savings of merging the cities have not been realized.
- Forty employees of the Ontario solicitor general's office took advantage of early retirement packages only to be hired as private consultants to do the same work for double the pay. In one case, an employee's daily compensation rate went from $735 a day to $2600 a day. The amount of money spent on consultants increased from $271 million in 1998 to $662 million in 2002.[1]

What is the common theme in these stories? All these organizations had adopted a strategy but had problems with the HRM implications. In most cases, unless the HRM strategy is appropriately formulated and skilfully implemented, the success of the organizational strategy is at risk.

We have written this book with the hope that we can provide some answers to those human resources (HR) professionals who have questions about the proper alignment of human resources policies with organizational strategies. Managers who have implemented any kind of change within their organizations realize the importance of matching the HRM practices with organizational goals. There is a growing acknowledgment that the strategic management of people within organizations affects important organizational outcomes such as survival, profitability, customer satisfaction levels, and employee performance. Our goal is to help readers understand strategy and the HRM programs and policies that enable organizations to implement that strategy. We discuss strategy at some length because HR professionals have been criticized for not understanding or using the language of business when discussing the value of HR programs. HR managers have to use strategy terms to show how their HR practices support organizational strategies. The next sections present a discussion of strategy and outline the types of strategies most frequently used by organizations.

STRATEGY

Strategy is the formulation of organizational missions, goals, and objectives, as well as action plans for achievement that explicitly recognize the competition and the impact of outside environmental forces. Strategy is the plan for how the organization intends to achieve its goals. The means it will use, the courses of action it will take, and how it will generally operate and compete constitute the organization's strategy.[2]

strategy the formulation of organizational missions, goals, objectives, and action plans

We have presented one definition of strategy, but there are many other definitions. A sampling of these is found in Box 1.1.

Mintzberg has developed a useful framework for understanding strategy, incorporating many of the meanings found in Box 1.1. The five Ps of strategy he described are:

Plan: an intended course of action a firm has selected to deal with a situation

Purpose: a consistent stream of actions that sometimes are the result of a deliberate plan and sometimes the result of emergent actions based on reactions to environmental changes or shifting of assumptions

Ploy: a specific manoeuvre at the tactical level with a short time horizon

Position: the location of an organization relative to its competitors and other environmental factors

Perspective: the gestalt or personality of the organization[3]

In this text, we consider strategy as both a purpose and a plan. This perspective views strategy as a rational process in which ends are defined in measurable terms and resources are allocated to achieving those ends. In this context, organizations would set objectives such as "achieves 25% market share by 2007" or "be the best health-care facility in the province." The organization then develops plans, which include HRM programs, to achieve those goals.

BOX 1.1 Descriptions of Strategy

Concepts of strategy can be confusing. Here is a guide to some common terms used throughout the text and in the organizations where you work:

Strategy: a declaration of intent

Strategic intent: a tangible corporate goal, a point of view about the competitive positions a company hopes to build over a decade

Strategic planning: the systematic determination of goals and the plans to achieve them

Strategy formulation: the entire process of conceptualizing the mission of an organization, identifying the strategy, and developing long-range performance goals

Strategy implementation: those activities that employees and managers of an organization undertake to enact the strategic plan, to achieve the performance goals

Objectives: the end, the goals

Plans: the product of strategy, the means to the end

Strategic plan: a written statement that outlines the future goals of an organization, including long-term performance goals

Policies: broad guidelines to action, which establish the parameters or rules

Senior management typically sets the goals and has them approved by the board. These objectives are then negotiated and revised as they filter throughout the organization. The top management team determines these objectives through a process of environmental analysis (which is discussed in Chapter 3) and discussions.

Execution of strategy is as important as the careful crafting of strategy. Strategy formulation and implementation achieve the following:[4]

1. Define the vision, and thus provide the organization with a sense of purpose, a mission, and a clear direction.
2. Convert this vision into measurable objectives and performance targets.
3. Determine the plan to achieve the strategy.
4. Implement the plan in ways that are both effective and efficient.
5. Measure the results against goals and revise plans in light of actual experience, changing conditions, new ideas, and new opportunities.

Strategic planning requires thinking about the future. In a perfect world, the strategic planner would establish an objective for five to ten years and then formulate plans for achieving the goals. Other experts do not perceive strategy in such a simplistic, linear fashion. They assert that the future is not that predictable. Planning for the long-term future (i.e., more than ten years) is difficult and would be more appropriately judged as a best guess. The airline industry could not have predicted the catastrophic events of September 11, 2001, or the 2003 SARS crisis in Toronto and their impact on airline travel.

Because of this, many planners look at a relatively shorter period of time, a more predictable term of three to five years. Because of the uncertainty, these plans are formulated to be somewhat flexible, so they can respond to changes in the environment. Thus, strategic planning must be viewed as a dynamic process, moving and shifting and evolving as conditions warrant changes. The process of subtly redirecting strategy to accommodate these changes is called logical incrementalism.[5] Rather than calling for a straight path to the goal, this strategy calls for a series of actions to react to changes in competitor actions or new legislation. Another name for this reactive process is **emergent strategy**. This cumulative process can look like a dramatic revolutionary change to those on the outside, but to those on the inside, the strategy has been incrementally implemented.[6] Firms can wait passively for these changes to occur and then react, or they can anticipate these moves and adopt a proactive stance.

emergent strategy
the plan that changes incrementally due to environmental changes

Writers on strategy sometimes distinguish between intended strategy and realized strategy. The **intended strategy** is the one that was formulated at the beginning of the period. The **realized strategy** is, of course, what actually happened.

intended strategy
the formulated plan

realized strategy
the implemented plan

You may be asking yourself, Why develop a strategy if the organization must continually change it to accommodate unforeseen changes? Think of strategy as a game plan or a flight plan. A pilot's flight plan appears relatively simple: fly from Toronto to Edmonton. However, before departure, the pilot is aware of the environment and the capacities (or competencies) of the plane. Based on these external and internal factors, the pilot develops a strategy for a safe flight. While on the voyage, however, environmental changes, such as strong winds or a blizzard, may require the pilot to modify the plan. Even internal factors, such as a passenger suffering a heart attack, may necessitate changes to the plan. But the plane and/or its passengers will somehow, at some time, arrive in Edmonton. This is what is meant by incremental adjustments to the strategy, adjustments that do not require changing the focus of the desired result. There is no strategy so finely crafted that adjustments aren't needed. The general rule is that, unless there is a crisis, it should not be necessary to make quantum leaps in strategies. Thus, these strategies should withstand the time test and be durable for several years.

A good strategy recognizes the complexity of these realities. To be effective, strategic management anticipates future problems, provides an alignment with external contingencies and internal competencies, recognizes multiple stakeholders, and is concerned with measurable performance[7]—just like the flight plan.

The fundamental premise of this book is that different organizational strategies demand different human resource policies and practices. Therefore, before we can discuss HRM strategies, you need to understand the different types of strategies that organizations formulate and implement.

Strategic Types

Strategies are not idiosyncratic—that is, unique to each organization that develops one. Many executives and senior managers put in an incredible number of hours forging the strategy for the firm, and they believe the strategy they developed, with much sweat and tears, is unique to their organizations. Do pure, unique organizational strategies exist? In one sense, they do, because organizations are extremely complex and no two are identical. In another sense, they do not, because it is possible to group strategies into categories or generic types. In the same way we can group our friends into personality categories of introvert and extrovert, we can group organizations by strategy. By their simplicity, these typologies, or classification schemes, aid our understanding. The more we add variables to approximate the reality of an organization, the more the typology becomes unwieldy.[8] Organizational theorists use classification schemes not only to help us understand how organizations work but also to enable us to test the concepts, leading us to better information about how to manage.

These identifiable, basic strategies can be classified into corporate strategies and business strategies.

Corporate Strategies

corporate strategy organizational-level decisions that focus on long-term survival

Company-wide strategies, sometimes referred to as **corporate strategies**, are focused on overall strategy for the company and its businesses or interests. Examples of corporate strategies include decisions to compete internationally or to merge with other companies. Strategies at this level are usually focused on long-term growth and survival goals and will include major decisions such as the decision to acquire another company.

Grouped within corporate strategies are three options: restructuring, growth, and maintenance.

Restructuring Strategies

When an organization is not achieving its goals, whether these goals are business goals of profitability or social goals of helping rehabilitate prisoners, corporate strategy becomes one of trying to deal with the problem. Restructuring options include turnaround, divestiture, liquidation, and bankruptcies.

Turnaround

turnaround strategy an attempt to increase the viability of an organization

A **turnaround strategy** is one in which the managers try to restore money-losing businesses to healthy profitability or government agencies to viability. Turnaround methods include getting rid of unprofitable products, layoffs, making the organization more efficient, or attempting to reposition it with new products. See Box 1.2 for a description of McDonald's turnaround efforts.

BOX 1.2 Turnaround Efforts at McDonald's

Burger chain McDonald's has, for several decades, been a success story. Each year saw increases in outlets, people served, profits, and shareholder value. In 2002, McDonald's had 30 000 outlets, served 46 million people a day in 118 countries, and generated $40 billion sales. But in 2003, restaurant sales were down nearly 5% and profits were down by 11%. McDonald's had made several attempts to revive its success. One effort focused on making its food healthier by offering salads. Related to this introduction was an alliance with Paul Newman, actor and philanthropist, to introduce Newman's Own salad dressings to their light menu. The company also introduced a food and nutrition website, which allowed customers to calculate the nutrients in their meal choices. But as one critic pointed out, this healthy eating effort was doomed because no one goes to fast-food restaurants for healthy food (except perhaps for the five-foot-ten, 272-pound New Yorker who sued the company because he was led to believe that the food was good for him). Another effort attempted to tap regional food interests; grits were introduce in some southern U.S. restaurants, for example. A third attempt was to diversify; McDonald's bought interests in Donatos Pizzeria and Chipotle Mexican Grill. Finally, like other companies with declining market share, McDonald's restructured by eliminating several hundred administrative jobs and dropping a $300-million (U.S.) plan to renovate older restaurants.

Source: Adapted from D. Goold, "McDonald's Woes a Matter of Taste," *The Globe and Mail*, November 28, 2002, p. B9; www.McDonalds.com; "McDonald's Said Ready for More Restructuring," *The Globe and Mail*, March 24, 2003, p. B1.

Divestiture

Divestiture refers to spinning off a business as a financially and managerially independent company or selling it outright.[9] In the opening example, Air Canada attempted to divest itself of its Aeroplan business and then put its maintenance division and its low-cost carrier Jazz on the market. Sometimes fit is the problem, not finances. One pharmaceutical company divested itself of a cosmetics business. The scientists in the pharmaceutical company had no respect for the frivolous cosmetic unit because they had been trained to apply their scientific knowledge to discovering miracle drugs, not making pretty faces.

divestiture the sale or removal of a business

Liquidation

The least attractive alternative is **liquidation**, in which plants are closed, employees are released, and goods are auctioned off. There is little return to shareholders under this option. But an early liquidation may allow some resources (including human resources) to be salvaged, whereas a bankruptcy does not.

liquidation the termination of a business and the sale of its assets

Bankruptcy

Bankruptcy occurs when a company can no longer pay its creditors, and, usually, one of them calls a loan. The company ceases to exist, and all its assets are divided among its creditors. The insurance company Confederation Life was a very public example of a company that went bankrupt, owing its creditors $740 million.

bankruptcy a formal procedure in which an appointed trustee in bankruptcy takes possession of a business's assets and disposes of them in an orderly fashion

Restructuring strategies, like growth strategies, have profound effects on human resource issues. Restructuring strategies demand HR strategies that include managed turnover, selective layoffs, transfers, increased demands on remaining employees, and renegotiated labour contracts. These strategies are described in Chapter 11.

Growth Strategies

Many organizations in the private sector target growth as their number one strategy. By this they mean growth in revenues, sales, market share, customers, orders, and so on. To a large extent, the implications of a growth strategy for HR practices are profound. A firm in a growth stage is engaged in job creation, aggressive recruitment and selection, rapidly rising wages, and expanded orientation and training budgets, depending on how the organization chooses to grow.

Growth can be achieved in several ways: incrementally, internationally, or by mergers and acquisitions.

Incremental Growth

Incremental growth can be attained by expanding the client base, by increasing the products or services, by changing the distribution networks, or by using technology. Procter & Gamble uses all these methods:

- expanding the client base (by introducing skin-care lotion and hair conditioner for babies),
- increasing the products (by adding Pringles potato chips to a product mix of cleaning and health-care products),
- changing the distribution networks (by adding drugstores to grocery stores), and
- using technology to manage just-in-time customer purchasing.

These are incremental ways of achieving growth.

International Growth

Seeking new customers or markets by expanding internationally is another growth option. The doughnut company Krispy Kreme is an example of a company going international, as described in Box 1.3. Operating a business in a foreign country, particularly one that is not in North America or Europe, poses singular problems for the Western HR manager. The HR implications for an international strategy are described in Chapter 12.

Mergers and Acquisitions

acquisition the purchase of one company by another

Quantum leaps in growth can be achieved through acquisitions, mergers, or joint ventures. An **acquisition** occurs when one company buys another,

BOX 1.3 Growth in Doughnuts

Krispy Kreme doughnuts are invading Canada as part of an international growth strategy that is resulting in an average growth of about 10% a year. Each store, equipped with a $300 000 doughnut-making machine, can produce 3000 doughnuts per hour, for a total of nearly 2 billion a year. Tim Hortons, with 2200 stores, produces about 1.5 billion doughnuts a year, about 44 doughnuts per year for every man, woman, and child in Canada. The most amazing thing about Krispy Kreme's success is that it does no advertising, but relies on word of mouth.

Sources: K. Libin, "Holey War," *Canadian Business*, August 21, 2000, pp. 34–40; www.krispykreme.com; www.timhortons.com.

whereas a **merger** typically is seen as two organizations merging to achieve economies of scale. Acquisitions and mergers have an obvious impact on HR: they eliminate the duplication of functions, meld benefits and labour relations practices, and, most importantly, create a common culture. The complexity of merging two companies is outlined in Chapter 13. Box 1.4 describes a difficult merger.

merger two organizations combine resources and become one

Maintenance Strategies

For many reasons, some executives wish to maintain the status quo. They do not wish to see their companies grow. The executive team is content to keep market share, doing what it has always been doing (this is a neutral or even a do-nothing strategy). HRM practices remain constant, as they are assumed to be effective for current strategy. We have not included chapters on the maintenance strategy because the HRM issues would, by definition, be subsumed under another generic strategy.

BOX 1.4 Merger Misery

Minacs Worldwide Inc., a company that operates in-bound customer contact centres (i.e., call centres), was a Canadian success story. More and more companies were using its services as they turned to outsourcing their call centres. Minacs had experienced growth rates of 50% over five years and, in 2002, employed 4500 people in 20 countries and generated sales of $250 million. The company expected to double sales and profits very quickly with the purchase of Phoenix Group, a U.S.-based call centre. But the purchase resulted in heavy losses. Although the two cultures seemed similar, the integration proved very difficult and time-consuming due to differences in accounting systems, pricing methods, and efficiency levels. The losses led to layoffs, the consolidation of offices, debt restructuring, and a severe drop in share value.

Sources: O. Bertin, "Minacs Worldwide Dials Back in after Disastrous US Purchase," *The Globe and Mail*, March 6, 2003, p. B17; www.minacs.com.

Executives in other companies, recognizing that the current profitable situation will not last forever, choose to milk the investment. This *harvest* strategy can also be seen as a retrenchment strategy because no investment or efforts will be made to make the business grow; therefore, the goal will be restructuring.

You may assume that businesses choose one strategy and pursue it but in fact businesses can pursue several strategies over time or concurrently. Read in Box 1.5 about the strategies implemented by Cara Operations Ltd.

Business Strategies

Strategy, as discussed, seems to imply that only corporate-wide plans are made and these are used to manage and control the various units that exist within an organization. But many large organizations operate several businesses under the same or different names. Each of these businesses within the organization might have its own strategy. For example, Alcan Aluminum Ltd. operates two "divisions" or businesses, one that focuses on primary metals and the other on fabrication. Each has a different business strategy, although the overall corporate strategy is growth.

business strategy plans to build a competitive focus in one line of business

Business strategy focuses on one line of business (in a diversified company or public organization), while corporate strategy examines questions

BOX 1.5 Multiple Strategies

The mission statement of Cara Operations Ltd. declares that its aim is to be Canada's leading integrated restaurant company. Cara owns or controls such food outlets as Harvey's and Swiss Chalet. In 2002, Cara outlets served 100 million customers in 1200 restaurants; 18 million customers were served in the company's 83 airport-based food and concession outlets; and 26 million meals were served to airline passengers. Cara is an example of a company employing multiple corporate strategies—through acquisition, divestiture, and going international—to achieve increased sales and profitability.

- *Acquisitions*—Cara began an aggressive acquisition strategy in 1999 when it bought 61% of Kelsey's, a Canadian company that owned 74 restaurants including Kelsey's, Montana's, and Outbacks. In 2002, Cara bought the Second Cup coffee chain and acquired a 74% stake in Milestones, a chain of up-scale restaurants.
- *Divestiture*—In 2000, Cara sold its Beaver Food Catering business, and, in 2001, it sold its health-care institutional food-services division.
- *International*—In 2003 Cara began to export its Second Cup concept to the Middle East, starting in Dubai.

Sources: Adapted from www.cara.com; and "Case Study: Cara Operations Ltd.," *National Post Business*, October 2002, pp. 47–50.

about which competitive strategy to choose. Corporate strategies focus on long-term survival and growth. Business-level strategy concerns itself with how to build a strong competitive position. Organizations try to become (or remain) competitive based on a core competence, which can be defined as a specialized expertise that rivals don't have and cannot easily match. As Thompson and Strickland[10] note, business strategy is the action plan for managing a single line of business. Business strategy is concerned with competitive position.

The next section introduces the concept of the business strategy and differentiates it from corporate strategies.

Corporate strategies are concerned with questions such as these: Should we be in business? What business should we be in? Business strategies are concerned with questions such as these: How should we compete? Should we compete by offering products at prices lower than those of the competition or by offering the best service? Business strategy is concerned with how to build a competitive position, and with the best way to compete in that line of business. Businesses compete for customers. Air Canada was struggling with its business strategy when it attempted to segment the market by creating a series of sub-brands—discount, high end, and charter. The discount airline Zip was created to compete directly with WestJet. Businesses try to demonstrate to the customer that their product or service is better than their rivals' because they have lower prices or more innovative services.

Business strategy is all about means and ends. These strategies focus on the best ways to compete in a particular sector. Organizations try to become (or remain) competitive based on their core competence. Wal-Mart's core competence is inventory management, resulting in low prices. Kimberly-Clark is the best in the world at producing paper-based consumer products, choosing to specialize in category-killer brands (where the name of the product is synonymous with the name of the category—e.g., Kleenex).[11]

A business strategy is the action plan for managing a single line of business. It is entirely possible that there is one corporate strategy and many business strategies. For example, the overall corporate strategy for the Royal Bank might be growth, but the business strategy for its bank business might be to provide a unique kind of banking, and for its insurance business, to be a low-cost provider of insurance.

In the next section, we will describe three popular approaches to understanding business strategies. (No one has developed generic strategies for not-for-profit organizations, so this discussion focuses on private, for-profit firms.) We will spend some time describing these models because HR professionals are expected to understand the language of business and to be able to discuss HR programs using the terminology of strategic planning. This exposure to strategic models and terms will enable HR practitioners to participate more fully during strategic planning discussions. By learning the models and terms used by managers in business, HR managers will be able to propose or defend HR programs in ways that other managers will understand.

Models of Business Strategies

There are three popular models for analyzing businesses: the Boston Consulting Group model, the organizational types model proposed by Miles and Snow, and Porter's five forces model.

Boston Consulting Group Model

Organizations with multiple businesses need a technique for analyzing the strategies of the different business units. The most frequently used method is called portfolio matrix analysis. In this method, indicators such as industry growth rate, market share, long-term industry attractiveness, and competitive strategy or stage of product/market evolution are placed on a graph. One popular matrix is that developed by the Boston Consulting Group (BCG).[12] Figure 1.1 illustrates the grid; industry growth rate is on the vertical axis and relative market share is on the horizontal axis.

To place a business unit on the grid requires some analysis. For example, to position a firm on the high end of the industry growth rate, the firm must be competing in a sector in which the growth rate is around twice the real GNP growth rate, plus inflation. In other words, the industry is growing faster than the economy as a whole.

Then, to position a firm on the horizontal axis, one analyzes the business's market share in comparison to the market share held by the largest competitor in the sector. For example, if Reebok has 20% of market share, and Nike has 30%, then Reebok's relative share would be 2:3. (Market share is measured in unit volume, not dollars.)

An analysis of the grid follows.

FIGURE 1.1 THE BCG GROWTH IN SHARE BUSINESS POSITION

		Relative Market Share	
		High (above 1.0)	Low (below 1.0)
Industry Growth Rate	High	Stars	Question marks
	Low	Cash cows	Dogs

Stars: Stars are found in the upper left-hand quadrant. These businesses offer excellent profit and growth opportunities, and parent companies will pour cash into expanding them. In some cases, stars can generate enough cash to fund their own expansion. Microsoft does this better than most companies.

Question marks: Businesses in the upper right-hand quadrant of the matrix are labelled question marks or problem children. This is because the industry growth rate suggests lots of opportunity, but the firm has a limited market share and does not seem to be capitalizing on the opportunity. The questions to be asked are these: Does the firm have the strength to compete? Does the parent company have the cash (or resources) to make it competitive? The firm is left with two options: divest or invest and expand aggressively.

Dogs: Dogs, found in the lower right-hand quadrant, have no potential and cannot generate enough cash to fortify and defend themselves. Profits are marginal in an industry where competition is tough, and so the strategy is almost always "close," through harvesting, divesting, or liquidating. Eaton's is a recent example of a major retailer divesting in a brutally competitive market where margins are thin.

Cash cows: Cash cows are firms with a relatively high market share in a low-growth market. This type of business typically generates more cash than is needed to grow or reinvest. The strategy is a defensive one: keep the cow healthy to subsidize the stars or deal with the problem children. It may be profitable because its products are less expensive than those of competitors or its services are unique in the industry.

Another way of understanding business strategy is by grouping organizations into types based on how they approach businesses in stable or turbulent environments.

Miles and Snow's Organizational Types

Another approach to examining business strategy was proposed by Miles and Snow.[13] They identified four organizational types:

1. *Defender:* The defender type competes in a relatively stable and predictable environment and pursues low-cost operations, focusing on efficiency through standardized jobs, formalization, and centralization. A manufacturer of toasters would fall into this category.
2. *Prospector*: The prospector operates in a dynamic environment. Innovation and adaptation are critical to success. Any company operating in the telecommunications sector, such as Clearnet, would exemplify this organizational type. Such companies achieve innovation and adaptation through heavy investments in research and development, and through organic

structures that are highly decentralized to allow for rapid and intelligent responses to the changing environment.

3. *Analyzer:* Miles and Snow's third type, the analyzer, is a combination of the defender and the prospector, attempting to achieve efficiency with an interest in new markets and products. These companies scan competitors' actions and react promptly by developing better ways to get products to market. The Bay, in its attempt to outmanoeuvre Wal-Mart, is a good example of a company with this strategy.
4. *Reactor*: The reactor type of company has no apparent strategy, and, indeed, Miles and Snow see it as an imperfect type that lacks a consistent response to changing conditions. Research has shown that reactors are always ineffective, that an organization with a strategy is better off than one without one.[14]

Finally, we introduce a model that has received a lot of recognition in the field of strategic management.

Porter's Model

Michael Porter[15] made a major contribution to the field of strategic management by grouping the many ways in which organizations can compete into five generic competitive strategies:

1. *Low-cost provider strategy:* The goal here is to provide a product or service at a price lower than that of competitors while appealing to a broad range of customers. Fast-food businesses use this strategy almost exclusively. A range of customers from toddlers to seniors consumes the cheap hamburger, a good, basic product with few frills. A company competing on this basis searches continually for ways in which to reduce costs.
2. *Broad differentiation strategy*: An organization employing this strategy seeks to differentiate its products from competitors' products in ways that will appeal to a broad range of buyers. The company employing this strategy searches for features that will make its product or service different from that of competitors and that will encourage customers to pay a premium for it. Thus, Burger King will introduce the Whopper with "frills," for which people will pay an extra dollar.
3. *Best-cost provider strategy:* The goal here is to give customers more value for the money by emphasizing a low-cost product or service and an upscale differentiation. The product has excellent features, including several upscale features that are offered at low cost. East Side Mario's offers hamburgers but presents them on a plate, with extras such as potato salad, served by a waiter in an attractive setting featuring such things as focused lights and art on the walls.
4. *Focused or market niche strategy based on lower cost*: The goal here is to offer a low-cost product to a select group of customers. Red Lobster uses this

approach, selling fish and seafood at reasonable prices to a narrow market segment.

5. *Focused or market niche strategy based on differentiation*: Here, the organization tries to offer a niche product or service customized to the tastes and requirements of a very narrow market segment. For example, Black and Blue is a very expensive restaurant in Toronto that specializes in steaks and permits cigar smoking, thus appealing to the older, usually male, business customer.

Under Porter's schema, business strategy concerns itself with the product and market scope. What particular goods and services are to be provided? What distinguishing features or attractive attributes will characterize these products and services? Typical product characteristics include cost, quality, optional features, durability, and reliability. Market dimensions refer to the characteristics of the target market—size, diversity, buying patterns, and geographic regions.

The strategy language used in these three models has been adopted by businesses. An understanding of the concepts of each is the essential first step to creating an HR strategy that makes sense for the organization.

Summary

It is important that HR professionals appreciate the role of strategic planning in their organizations and understand the language and terminology of strategic planning. A strategy is a planned process whereby organizations can map out a set of objectives and methods of meeting those objectives. A strategy may be intended—one that is formulated at the beginning of the process—or realized—what actually happens. The strategy may also be emergent—that is, it is reactive, changing as necessary to deal with environmental changes. Corporate or company-wide strategies are concerned with the long-term view of the organization. Business strategies focus on one line of business, building a strong competitive position. Three popular models of business strategies are available for analyzing businesses: the Boston Consulting Group model, Miles and Snow's organizational types, and Porter's model. By understanding strategy language and models, the HR professional can work with other executives to implement HR practices that enable strategy.

Key Terms

acquisition, 10
bankruptcy, 9
business strategy, 12
corporate strategy, 8

divestiture, 9
emergent strategy, 7
intended strategy, 7
liquidation, 9
merger, 11
realized strategy, 7
strategy, 5
turnaround strategy, 8

Suggested Websites

www.strategyclub.com The Strategic Management Club Online website has excellent links for references on strategic planning.

www.systemsthinkingpress.com Explores strategic management theories from a variety of perspectives.

www.ist.unomaha.edu/aboutus/cist_strategic_plan.pdf Contains examples of strategic plans of universities.

www.smsweb.org Articles from the professional society for the advancement of strategic planning.

www.planware.org/strategy.htm#1 Explains in detail how to develop a strategic plan and compares it to a business plan.

Discussion Questions

1. Using a real company as an example, describe the differences between corporate strategy and business strategy.
2. Identify companies currently operating under these corporate strategies: divestiture—turnaround, divestiture, liquidation, and bankruptcy; growth—incremental, international, and mergers and acquisitions.
3. The focus in this chapter (and in strategy literature) is on private companies. Check the websites of government departments, and identify at least ten strategies (often called plans or mission statements). Can you identify any that correspond to some of the models of business strategies? Can you create a model or typology for public-sector organizations? To start, you could consult J. Tomkins, "Strategic Human Resources Management in Government: Unresolved Issues," *Public Personnel Management*, vol. 31, no. 1 (2002), pp. 95–110.

Exercises

1. Identify two companies working in the same sector (hotels, restaurants, and schools are good choices). Compare and contrast the practices of a company

using a low-cost provider strategy with one using a differentiation strategy. For example, contrast the MBA schools at Queen's University or the Ivey School of Business at the University of Western Ontario with those at the University of Athabasca or Concordia University.

2. In describing the Porter model, examples from restaurants were used to illustrate the five types. Pick another sector and identify five companies that best exemplify each of the five business strategies.

Case: Aldo Shoes Limited

The Canadian shoe market is worth $1.8 million. The dominant shoe retailers are Wal-Mart (9.1% of market share), Payless (8.8%), Aldo (8.8%), Sears (8.0%), and the Bay (6.9%). Aldo has a variety of brands catering to the niche markets of young spirited consumers (Aldo), sophisticated men and women (Pegabo), private labels (Simard, Calderone), comfort shoes (Feet First), and family-focused, large selection (Globo). Aldo is considered a dominant player because when all its brands are included, its market share is an impressive 25%. It has achieved high growth rates since its founding in Montreal in 1972; in 2002 it had revenues of $650 million with over 600 stores. The company's growth strategies included plans to expand internationally (United States, England, and the Middle East) with future plans for Scandinavia, Australia, Singapore, and Western Europe. Its business strategy was to achieve growth through the creation of private labels—seven to date.

Adapted from www.aldoshoes.com; J. McCann, "Best Foot Forward," *National Post Business*, October 2002, pp. 53–61.

Question

Aldo has grown rapidly through multi-branding (differentiation) and international sales. What are the advantages and disadvantages of achieving more growth through mergers and acquisitions? Using the three business strategy models, attempt to label Aldo's business strategy.

References

Anthony, W.P., P.L. Perrewe, and K.M. Kacmar. 1993. *Strategic Human Resources Management*. Fort Worth, Texas: Harcourt Brace Jovanovich.

Collins, J. 2001. *Good to Great*. New York: Harper Business.

Duane, M.J. 1996. *Customized Human Resource Planning*. Westport, Conn.: Quorum Books.

Lengnick-Hall, C., and M. Lengnick-Hall. 1990. *Interactive Human Resource Management and Strategic Planning*. New York: Quorum Books.

Mallan, C. 2002. "Rehired at Twice the Rate of Pay." *Toronto Star*, December 4, p. A1.

Miles, R.E., and C.C. Snow. 1978. *Organizational Strategy, Structure and Process*. New York: Free Press.

Mintzberg, H. 1988. *In the Strategy Process*. Englewood Cliffs, N.J.: Prentice Hall.

Porter, M.E. 1985. *Competitive Advantage*. New York: Free Press.

Quinn, J.B. 1980. *Strategies for Change: Logical Incrementalism*. Homewood, Ill.: Richard D. Irwin.

Rollo, J.A. 2002. *Strategic Human Resource Management*. Cincinnati Ohio: South Western Thomson Learning.

Smith, G.S, J.P. Guthrie, and M. Chen. 1989. "Strategy, Size and Performance." *Organizational Studies*, Vol. 10, No. 3: 63–81.

Thompson, A.A., and A.J. Strickland III. 1995. *Crafting and Implementing Strategy*, 6th ed. Chicago: Irwin.

ENDNOTES

1. Mallan, 2002.
2. Anthony et al., 1993.
3. Mintzberg, 1988.
4. Ibid.
5. Quinn, 1980.
6. Collins, 2001.
7. Lengnick-Hall and Lengnick-Hall, 1990.
8. Duane, 1996.
9. Thompson and Strickland, 1995.
10. Ibid.
11. Collins, 2001.
12. Thompson and Strickland, 1995.
13. Miles and Snow, 1978.
14. Smith et al., 1989.
15. Porter, 1985.

2

ALIGNING HR WITH STRATEGY

CHAPTER GOALS

Both the Coca-Cola Company and PepsiCo manage their employees in unique ways that match their strategies. Coke hires liberal arts graduates (and rarely MBAs) with no corporate experience and trains them extensively. Employees are committed to the company because they can count on lifetime employment, seniority-based salary increases, and promotion from within. In this family culture, decision-making is centralized. The company's human resource management practices produce career managers who have been thoroughly socialized into understanding the company trademark, which is the most recognized in the world, and its value.

Pepsi is not Coke. Pepsi succeeds by targeting market niches where Coke is not dominant and finding new markets through diversification. The human resource management practices have to produce employees who are innovative. Its people-management process consists of hiring experienced employees, many with advanced degrees, and fast-tracking those employees who demonstrate early successes. In this individualistic culture, there is almost no job security and no guaranteed promotion from within. What Pepsi achieves is a continuous flow of new ideas (from experienced and intelligent employees) and the ability to change quickly (with hiring and firing policies).[1]

Those two succinct examples neatly illustrate the concept of aligning HR practices, policies, and philosophies with organizational strategy—strategic HR.

After reading this chapter, you should be able to do the following:

1. Understand the importance of strategic HR planning.
2. Identify the risks associated with not planning.
3. Discuss approaches to linking strategy and HR, including the barriers to becoming a strategic partner.
4. List the characteristics of an effective HR strategy.
5. Delineate the steps in the strategic HR planning model.

Strategic HRM

Human resources management can be viewed as an umbrella term that encompasses the following:

- Specific HR *practices,* such as recruitment, selection, and appraisal
- Formal HR *policies* that direct and partially constrain the development of specific practices
- Overarching HR *philosophies,* which specify the values that inform an organization's policies and practices

strategic HRM
interrelated practices, policies, and philosophies that facilitate the attainment of organizational strategy

Strategic HRM is a set of distinct but interrelated practices, policies, and philosophies whose goal is to enable the achievement of the organizational strategy. Ideally, these practices, policies, and philosophies form a system that attracts, develops, motivates, and trains employees who ensure the effective functioning and survival of the organization and its members.[2]

While managers recognize implicitly that marketing strategy must support the business strategy, there is not the same sense among managers that HR programs can be designed to support the organizational strategy. And yet, human capital issues are at the top of the CEO agenda, with more than half of the top priorities (attraction, retention, innovation) needing HR input.[3] As Ulrich states:

> *The truth is that HR has never been more necessary. The competitive forces that managers face today and will continue to confront in the future demand organizational excellence. The efforts to achieve such excellence—through a focus on learning, quality, teamwork and re-engineering—are driven by the way organizations treat their people. These are fundamental HR issues. To state*

it plainly: Achieving organizational excellence must be the work of HR.[4]

The term **human capital**, which will be used throughout the text, refers to the collective sum of the attributes, experience, knowledge, and commitment that employees choose to invest in their work. This intangible asset comprises the knowledge, education, vocational qualifications, professional certifications, work-related experience, and competence of an organization's employees.[5]

human capital the sum of employees' knowledge, skills, experience, and commitment invested in the organization

Workforce management issues are often cited as a threat to an organization's ability to execute strategy. We hope that, by the end of this book, you will understand that HRM strategy must match the business strategy. But first, let us try to understand what we mean by HRM strategy.

A more traditional perspective of the HR planning concept implied that the organization was concerned only with possible problems of labour surpluses and shortages. The goal was to determine the knowledge, skills, and abilities (KSAs) required within broad organizational outcomes such as growth or decline. Much emphasis was placed on the statistical techniques for analyzing resource supply and demand forecasting while ignoring managerial realities and support for the process.[6] This is now regarded as a narrow, linear approach to HR planning.

Despite the apparent link between planning and strategy, there is some concern that HR planning has been preoccupied with resource supply and demand forecasting without considering the different HR practices required by fundamentally different strategies. For example, a company that decides to grow through the development of international businesses has different personnel requirements than a company that decides to grow through mergers and acquisitions. Under traditional HR planning models, both strategies would require the acquisition and absorption of large numbers of employees, but the prescriptions for supplying labour effectively would differ radically.

In this book, we are suggesting an approach to HR strategy that calls for tailoring human resource policies and practices to the organizational needs of the future. Some writers have recognized the need to do this in specific functional areas, such as matching compensation strategies to the different phases of a business.[7] However, there is a disturbing lack of understanding of the need to align all HR functional practices with corporate strategy. The proliferation of bankruptcies, mergers, and restructuring has affected our view of employees in a profound way and highlighted the need for the input of HR professionals in formulating policy. The next section explains why HR strategy is so important to the achievement of organizational strategies.

The Importance of Strategic HR Planning

Executives are demanding that the HR department move from articulating perceived value ("training builds employee skills") to demonstrating real value (an external client can see the economic value). As a game player on the corporate team, the focus of HR must be on scoring points, not just coaching, training, or counting the number of players. The value of HR will be seen in its ability to deliver the behaviours needed to enable the organization's strategy. There are at least two reasons why strategic HR planning is so important: (1) Employees help an organization achieve success because they are strategic resources and (2) the planning process itself results in improved goal attainment.

Employees as Strategic Resources

Michael Porter has argued strongly that an organization's employees can provide a firm with a competitive advantage. Employees who provide superior performance because of their skills or flexibility will enable a company to beat its competitors through superior service or the development of unique products. This is a resource-based view of the organization. Classical economists describe three types of resources or inputs used in the production of goods and services: land, capital, and labour. Labour, or human capital, can be described as the mental and physical talents of employees. Other terms that describe these talents include KSAs, competencies, and human assets. The advantages of an organization with effective HR practices may come not from having better resources but from making better use of these resources by achieving higher productivity per worker and by matching the capabilities of employees with the strategy.[8]

HR programs represent an investment in human capital. This human capital is difficult to duplicate or imitate. Let us describe the value of human capital. If IBM introduces a new software package in January, Microsoft can probably imitate or duplicate this package by February of the same year. However, if IBM technical support people are trained and motivated to provide "knock-your-socks-off service," Microsoft will have a difficult time imitating this service by February of the next year. Indeed, Porter estimates that it takes approximately seven years to duplicate a competitive edge in human resources. The less a resource can be imitated, the more durable the source of competitive advantage. HRM can offer this kind of durable, competitive advantage. The competition can't just buy these human resources because their effectiveness is embedded in the systems and culture that allow them to work productively.[9] The HRM process that creates this human capital can't be bought or imitated.

As researchers have noted, "In the new economic paradigm, as the demands for continuous change make innovation, adaptability, speed and efficiency essential features of the business landscape, the strategic importance of intellectual capital and intangible assets have increased substantially. While these assets are largely invisible ... the sources are not. They are found in the human capital of the firm's employees."[10]

Like other resources, human resources can deteriorate. Skills and knowledge can become obsolete unless either the individual or the employer invests in further education and training. If these investments in training are not made, and the skills become obsolete, the value of that company's human resources is decreased. Higher investments in training result in higher-value human capital. Thus, human capital has to be replenished.

The value of employees as a resource must be placed within a strategic framework. In other words, a strategy itself can become obsolete, making current employee skills obsolete. Suppose, for example, the current workforce is valuable because of manual skills, but the market for the company's manufactured products is declining. Environmental analyses suggest that the corporation enter the high-tech field, with its demand for flexible, knowledgeable workers. By changing the strategy, the "value" of the current workforce is diminished. A corollary to this is that employees can expect to face different HRM practices throughout their lifetimes, and even within a single organization. Employees may be asked to exhibit different behaviours, depending on strategic goals, and these behaviours will be motivated by different HRM practices.[11] Organizations with different business units are likely to have different HRM policies for each business unit to optimize employee performance.

To summarize, human assets offer organizations a competitive advantage. Box 2.1 describes how Sears used data from their own studies to improve the workplace for their employees. These assets must be managed and matched to the organizational strategy. An organization that manages its human resources strategically is more likely to survive and profit. A second advantage of managing human resources well is that the possibility of achieving organization goals is increased.

Improved Goal Attainment

Strategic HRM can improve an organization's performance. The goals of these HRM strategies are to shape employee behaviour so that it is consistent with the direction the organization identifies in its strategic plans. Organizations

BOX 2.1 Sears: A Compelling Workplace

Sears was one of the first organizations in the world to document the relationship between employee behaviour and the firm's performance. The company pioneered studies that defined and empirically verified the correlation between individual sales associates' behaviours, customer satisfaction, and ultimately financial performance. Sears executives have embraced a business strategy that relies on employees as the source of competitive advantage. Sears has only three strategic imperatives: to make its stores and business

- a compelling place to work,
- a compelling place to shop, and
- a compelling place to invest.

In order to implement the first imperative, the company made sure employees received performance feedback from customers, so that they could see the direct relationship between their behaviour and profits. The executives so fully support the human capital perspective that they fund the training of over 20 000 managers (including teams of managers) every year at Sears University.

Sources: Becker, B.E. and M.A. Huselid. 1999. "Overview: Strategic Human Resources Management in Five Leading Firms." *Human Resource Management*, Vol. 38, No. 4 (1999), pp. 287–301.

with clear strategies provide direction and meaning to employees and mitigate the need for control by substituting a consistency of purpose—in other words, a mission. This articulated vision for the future may result in a more effective organization through increased motivation and performance, lowered absenteeism and turnover, and heightened stability, satisfaction, and involvement.[12]

To summarize, strategy formulation is important to the attainment of organizational goals in order to align all HR functional strategies with overall strategy and to focus employees on important missions and goals of the organization. Research and observations have demonstrated that developing HR practices that support the strategy leads to improved strategy implementation.[13]

THE RISKS

Is there a downside to strategic HR planning? The strategic management of human resources seems beneficial, but some researchers point out that there are costs.[14] Research shows that these costs include the increased time and energy involved in making decisions, greater potential for information overload, impossible commitments to employees, and an over-concern with employee reactions that may be incompatible with industry conditions. In other words, the strategic management of employees is hard work. As anyone who has gone through the strategy formulation and implementation process understands, the strategy formulation phase is relatively easy. Motivating employees to commit to the strategy and implement it is far more difficult; this text offers guidelines on how to do this. A further difficulty is that any HR plan for the future may raise employees' expectations that they have jobs for life and will be trained for those jobs. The reality is that conditions change, and that the plan may be changed, resulting in job losses.

Another problem, some would argue, is that organizations that commit to one strategy become blinded to changes in the environment and lose their flexibility. However, as we have seen, incremental adjustments based on environmental scanning are part of strategy implementation. The risk of not having a strategy seems greater.

There are risks to not developing a strategy. Organizations that do not actively scan the environment (methods for doing so are discussed in Chapter 3) face the danger of being out of touch with reality. Today's operating decisions may be based on yesterday's conditions. Comfortable with past success, the managers in these organizations focus on resolving internal problems, such as making better horse carriages when automobiles are on the horizon.

An example of a company that was not in touch with reality was Consumers Distributing. Consumers Distributing did not develop a strategy to match or surpass the changing distribution networks and customer-service levels of their competitors. The company, now bankrupt, continued to require customers to come to the stores and stand in line, often for out-of-stock items. Meanwhile, their competitors were offering electronic purchasing or were providing greeters at the door of the store who helped the customers find anything they wanted, all for a competitive price. MacMillan argues that firms that develop strategies gain an advantage and control their own destinies.[15] An apt cliché is "an organization that fails to plan, plans to fail."

Therefore, strategic HR planning is important to optimize the use of the organization's human resources and to focus behaviour on the important goals of the organization.

Linking HR Processes to Strategy

Strategic HRM must facilitate the formulation and implementation of corporate and business-level strategies. Senior managers must focus on issues such as: What are the HR implications of adopting a strategy? What are the internal and external constraints and opportunities? Exactly what policies, practices, and philosophies contribute to the successful implementation of the strategy?

The basic premise is that every HR policy and practice must directly support the organization's strategy and objectives.[16] This does not happen as frequently as it should. In the worst-case scenario, HR plans are developed as an afterthought and separately from organizational strategy. They are not relevant to the business and are seen as important only by the HR people. No other unit or level is committed to these plans.

While it has long been recognized that HR policies and practices must be linked to the firm's overall strategy, there has been little research that offers prescriptions on exactly how to do this. Aligning HR strategy with business strategy can be done in one of these ways:

1. Start with organizational strategy and then create HR strategy.
2. Start with HR competencies and then craft corporate strategies based on these competencies.
3. Do a combination of both in a form of reciprocal relationship.

Let us examine each approach.

Corporate Strategy Leads to HR Strategy

A traditional perspective of HR planning views HRM programs as flowing from corporate strategy. Corporate strategy drives HR strategy. In other words, personnel needs are based on corporate plans. If a firm decides to compete on the basis of offering low-cost products, HR policies and practices must align and be based on low labour costs. McDonald's is a good example of a firm that follows this strategy. This model assumes that people are more adaptable than strategy and that cause-and-effect relationships are unidirectional.[17] Square workers are forced to fit into round holes, with little consideration for their ability to adjust. If the workers can't adjust to a new strategy, they are terminated in a massive restructuring.

Given their investment in thousands of employees, larger organizations seem to prefer this approach (making the resources fit the strategy), despite the literature showing the difficulty and time-consuming nature of organizational change. Within this approach, employees are considered means to an end, not part of the strategy formulation equation.

But another perspective reverses this view, suggesting that employee competencies determine the business strategy.

HR Competencies Lead to Business Strategy

A competing view states that an organization cannot implement a strategy if it does not have the human resources necessary. In the late 1990s, companies were scrambling to find high-tech workers in order to enable them to launch web-based services and products. Box 2.2 describes the value that "Silicon Valley" organizations place on employees.

The critical question is, Is it easier to change HR to fit the strategy or should you change the strategy to fit the human resource pool? Small businesses seem to choose the latter course. The owners of very small businesses are nimble and quickly recognize that, if an employee has a certain capability, it can be exploited to develop new products or services. Diversity management efforts are currently building on this theme. For example, if the number of employees who speak Mandarin reaches a sufficient number within an organization, the observant executive will start to explore Asian markets.

This "skills determine strategy" outlook relies too heavily on employee capabilities and not enough on environmental analysis. Nor is consideration given to changing HR practices in training or compensation to facilitate this change in strategy.

These perspectives represent two extremes on a continuum between organizational strategy and HR practices. The reality is closer to the concept of reciprocal interdependencies.[18]

BOX 2.2 Hoarding Employees

When companies face falling sales, revenues, and profits, one predictable strategy is to begin to lay off employees. However, Sun Microsystems, when faced with declining growth, refused to lay off employees. Instead, managers were summoned to the headquarters in Palo Alto, California, and urged to find other ways to cut expenses. After having faced acute labour shortages in the high-tech sector, this company was determined to keep employees who would be difficult to replace when the markets recovered. Known as labour hoarding, this strategy is an unusual one in North America and reflects an understanding that a firm's employees are its chief asset.

Source: Adapted from G. Smith, "Firm Hoards Workers Despite Pinch," *The Globe and Mail*, July 9, 2002, p. B1.

HR Strategy and Corporate Strategy

An emerging perspective sees HR strategy as contributing to business-level strategy, and vice versa. Increasingly, in large firms, senior HR vice-presidents are asked not only to review business plans to ensure consistency with HR strategy, but also to provide input to this strategy based on HR strengths and weaknesses.

In this context, an organization chooses a business strategy, such as being a leader in innovative products, based on its in-house, highly educated, trained employees who have been socialized to value creativity. Bill Hewlett and David Packard's single founding concept for Hewlett-Packard (HP) was "who"—not "what." They wanted to build a great company together. They stumbled for months searching for what that company would be.[19] Simply phrased, an organization develops its employees and then capitalizes on their skills; the employees then learn new skills, and so it continues. In many ways, HR strategy generates the business strategy, and business strategy determines HR strategy. This concept of reciprocal interdependence is widely accepted in the HR strategy literature.[20]

HR Becomes a Business Partner

The key point here is the concept of *concurrent strategy formulation*. Strategy development, based on environmental analysis, is conducted at the same time that HRM issues are considered. HR issues do not solely determine strategy, nor does strategy unilaterally determine HR practices. The HR senior management team moves from outsider status to insider status. The implications are not trivial. HR managers must understand the numbers language of business or the outcome expectations of nonprofit organizations. They must be able to understand analyses presented by marketing, financial, and operational managers. Cost–benefit assessments of options within the HR domain will have to be prepared and defended. Entrepreneurial instincts will have to be sharpened, as HR managers will be expected to engage in scanning human resource capabilities for business opportunities in this two-way approach to strategic HR planning. Alternative solutions to problems have to be generated. For example, if the low-cost strategy depends on hiring personnel at minimum wage, HR managers have to develop strategies to deal with rapid training and high turnover rates. This option will have to be compared with outsourcing, use of robots, or even increasing wages to reduce the costs of turnover. The HR manager is no longer the auditor, but a partner and problem solver. Linkages between the HR manager and other managers, both formal and informal, ensure that this partnership role is enacted. One HR manager describes her perspective on concurrent strategy formulation in Box 2.3.

BOX 2.3 A Concurrent Approach to HR Strategy

Bonnie Hathcock is the chief HR officer for Siemans Rolm Communications. She claims that a revolution in approaches to human resource management is needed for the challenges of the 21st century. "The 21st-century human resource imperative is to raise the company's human capital to sophisticated levels which produce competitive advantages for the enterprise," Hathcock asserts. This requires a shakedown for those in "personnel" who prefer to remain quietly on the sidelines administering employee requests.

The revolution begins with identifying the company's strategy and aligning HR work with strategic imperatives. Hathcock sees HR strategy as a planned response to corporate strategy. The HR role is to enhance the capabilities of the enterprise to execute its business strategies. Hathcock sees herself as the leader of the crusade to maximize human assets. Employees are not commodities to be treated as if they are expendable. The raison d'être for HR is to be the catalyst for human asset capability and commitment. Both dimensions are important: first, in building human commitment through culture management, and second, in building human asset capability through competency development. Hancock continues: "If the HR department is to achieve parity with other functions, then they must not just serve and support but must integrate fully with management in achieving business results."

Hathcock's efforts at Sieman's won her the Optimas Award for Human Resource Excellence in managing change in 1996.

Source: Adapted from B.C. Hathcock, "The New Breed Approach to 21st Century Human Resources," *Human Resource Management*, Summer, Vol. 35, No. 2 (1996), pp. 243–250.

Strategic Partnering

Human resource professionals recognize the need to play a more strategic role within the organization. Nearly nine out of ten Canadian HR executives surveyed in 2000 spoke of the need to operate more as a business partner.[21] HR managers defined their new role as one blending their HR technical skills with an in-depth understanding of the business and its goals. However, only two out of ten executives foresaw HR playing a strategic role.[22]

The reasons that executives give for not including HR in the strategic planning process are outlined in Box 2.4.

Why do executives ignore HR's contribution to strategy? Some argue that it is because management is not satisfied with HR services in general; that "people" issues belong only to HR, and HR can take care of any problems in executing the strategy.

These attitudes are changing, however, as organizations realize the impact that HRM strategy can have on organizational effectiveness and as HR managers develop the internal relationships to ensure that the strategy is effective. Nevertheless, only one-third of HR managers stated that they played a major role in strategic planning. Box 2.5 poses the question, Are you a strategic partner?

Formal mechanisms can ensure that HR is a partner in the planning process.

BOX 2.4 Why Is HR not a Strategic Partner?

- Top managers don't see a need. They don't see HR as a profession.
- HR personnel are seen as personnel experts, not experts in the business. HR is seen as economically illiterate.
- HR information is useful to HR but incompatible with business needs.
- Business managers have a short-term focus with an emphasis on current performance. Quarterly results are important, even though some investments in training and culture development won't pay off for years.
- HR professionals are unable to think strategically because they have an incomplete understanding of the business.
- Senior managers lack appreciation for the role that HR can play in enabling the organization to achieve its goals. HR is seen as an adversary, demanding unnecessary bureaucratic work in the managers' day-to-day jobs.
- Few functional managers see themselves as HR managers. They have functional responsibilities, but do not see that the principal role of management is to manage people.
- It is difficult to quantify the benefits or outcomes of HR programs. In the competition for organizational resources, why should HR be allocated any part of the resource pie?
- HR assets are not owned by the organization, and so any resource allocation to people programs is seen as a high-risk investment.
- HR initiatives almost always mean change, which can be resisted. Any program that requires different ways of treating or managing employees upsets the status quo and means learning new behaviours.[23]

BOX 2.5 Are You a Strategic Partner?

Do you understand the business? What financial indicators are important to the company? Who are your customers, and what is your competitive advantage? What major technological changes will affect your work?

Do you know what the corporate plan is? Can you quickly list the major initiatives of your organization?

Do you align HR programs, policies, and practices with organizational strategies and goals? How can HR position the organization to succeed? Are the people management processes focused and measured on deliverables and not functions? Does HR report on effectiveness or just efficiencies?

Are major organizational decisions made with your input?

Count the number of times you answered yes. The higher the number, the greater the likelihood that you are a strategic partner or have the ability to be one.

Ways to Become Involved in the Strategic Planning Process

Membership in the Executive Team

In order to involve HR in the strategic planning process, ensure that the person responsible for HRM is included as part of the executive team, occupying a position at the vice-presidential level. The president and CEO of Surrey Metro Savings Credit Union in British Columbia says that HR plays a critical role at the financial institution, and that is why it is important for the head of HR to be a vice-president on the senior management team. Most large organizations now position the most senior HR person at the executive vice-president level. More importantly, studies in the United Kingdom and Australia show that companies who included the HR director on the executive team experienced twice the growth in earnings per share compared to those who did not.[24]

Review/React Linkage

Another option is a review/react linkage, proposed by Cascio.[25] In this method, HR managers have the opportunity to review strategic plans before they are implemented. They can then approve or modify them.

However, this control or veto option is too passive and reactionary for significant input about a critical resource. Linkages have to be made at earlier stages. HR managers should be supplying information about employee capabilities, be part of the strategic planning committee, and be documenting implications of strategic thrusts.

Integrative Linkage

In a truly integrative linkage, as exhibited in some companies, the interaction between the members of the executive committee and the HR director are frequent, and the HR director is involved in strategic decisions, even when the HR implications are not readily apparent.[26] In some cases, the credibility of the HR department is so high that the CEO, vice-chair, and other top officials have all held the position of HR director as part of their career development.

Organizations are more responsive to integrative linkages when the environment is turbulent (increased competition, rapid technological change, and changing labour market demographics), resulting in difficulties recruiting the right kinds of people. Organizations with multiple divisions demanding different types of strategies, and therefore different HR practices for each division, also tend to elevate the role of HR. A culture or CEO with a strong belief in the asset value of employees will also result in more attempts at linking HR strategies with corporate strategies. The credibility of the HR director also influences the probability of a linkage. HR managers who were able to deliver information about labour supply, or critical personnel capabilities, in a quantifiable way were deemed more credible. Historically, HR professionals were asked to deliver operational outcomes, such as administrative efficiency and employee commitment. More recently, HR professionals have been asked to deliver strategic outcomes such as customer engagement and capacity for change. In the future, HR will be asked to deliver both. If HR directors are responsible for bottom-line results and are measured on them, they become more focused on delivering programs that make a difference. One organization tied 40% of the HR manager's compensation (pay at risk) to company performance.

Many effective linkages operate in organizations, and each of them possesses some of the characteristics of the traditional way of doing business, as well as the newer strategic model, outlined in Box 2.6.

To illustrate the alignment of HR programs with business strategy, Appendix A focuses on Porter's model and discuss two strategies: the low-cost provider strategy and the differentiation strategy. Although Porter recognized the importance of HRM, and even concedes that, in some firms, HRM holds the key to competitive advantage, he did not delineate any specific practices that can be aligned with business strategy. Appendix A attempts to fill this gap and provide one of the few "recipes" for using HR strategies to support a business strategy.

To illustrate how HR is aligned with strategies in real companies, Box 2.7 describes how United Parcel Service aligns its HR strategy with its low-cost-provider business goal, and Box 2.8 illustrates HR alignment with a differentiation strategy at Frost.

It seems feasible to design HR policies to match strategy, but what happens when an organization has more than one business and more than one business strategy? We attempt to answer that question in the next section.

BOX 2.6 Traditional versus Strategic HR

Factors	Traditional HR	Strategic HR
Responsibility for HR	Staff specialists	Line managers
Focus	Employee relations	Partnerships with internal and external customers
Role of HR	Transactional, change follower and respondent	Transformational, change leader and initiator
Initiatives	Slow reactive, fragmented	Fast, proactive, integrated
Time Horizon	Short term	Short, median, long (as necessary)
Control	Bureaucratic—roles, policies, procedures	Organic—flexible, whatever is needed to succeed
Job Design	Tight division of labour, independence, specialization	Broad, flexible, cross-training, teams
Key Investments	Capital, products	People, knowledge
Accountability	Cost centre	Investment centre

Source: From *Strategic Human Resource Management,* 1st edition by MELLO © 2002. Reprinted with permission of South-Western, a division of Thomson Learning: www.thomsonrights.com. Fax 800-730-2215.

BOX 2.7 Cost Reduction at United Parcel Service

United Parcel Service (UPS) employs 152 000 people to deliver parcels in an extremely competitive sector where "a package is a package." UPS profits by keeping costs low—a low-cost-provider strategy. How does it do this?

Its key is to manage labour costs. UPS starts by simplifying and standardizing the work to optimize efficiency. Early in the company's history, management used time and motion studies to measure the time each UPS driver spent each day on specific tasks. The engineers then changed some of these tasks to improve worker effectiveness, thus leading to work standards. For example, drivers were instructed how to place their keys on a key ring finger and step down out of the truck in standardized ways. As a result, workers were less tired at the end of each day. More than 1000 industrial engineers—experts in work efficiency—continue to monitor the work of workers engaged in repetitive tasks. The workers, who are unionized, earn about a dollar more than drivers at other companies and gain employment security if they perform at acceptable levels.

The cost-reduction strategy through work-process refinements enables UPS to gain a competitive advantage in a service sector—that of overnight delivery—that is relatively undifferentiated.

Source: Adapted from Schuller, R.S., and S.E. Jackson. 1987. "Linking Competitive Strategies with Human Resource Management Practices," *Academy of Management Executive*, Vol. 1, No. 3, pp. 207–213. Reprinted with permission.

BOX 2.8 Linking HR Strategy to Business Strategy at Frost

Frost, Inc. is a manufacturer of automobile parts with sales of over $20 million. The company was dependent on one product (overhead conveyor trolleys) in one sector (the automobile industry), and the president was concerned about the company's vulnerability in this cyclical industry. Attempts to design, build, and sell other products failed. The president set out to correct this problem, stating, "We had a single-purpose machine, and single-purpose people." He needed flexibility and a long-term orientation from his personnel.

To increase workers' identification with the long-term survival of the company, Frost gave each worker 10 shares of the closely held company. Employees were able to participate in a share purchase plan and a corporate profit-sharing plan. This move accomplished the goals of increasing employee commitment to the organization and promoting a long-term focus.

Next, the president set out to restructure the rest of the compensation package to improve innovation to achieve a differentiation strategy. A balance was needed between rewards for results (productivity) and rewards for process (manufacturing). Quarterly bonuses were given for productivity, but managers also were able to tap into a "celebration fund," which rewarded employees' significant innovations. Additional soft rewards of dinner with the president or weekend holidays for the employee and his or her spouse were used to reinforce innovative processes. Executive perks were eliminated to demonstrate the egalitarian nature of the innovative climate, and all employees had access to corporate information (except payroll) through terminals placed throughout the plant.

Frost paid employees to learn new skills, both through the company training programs and from outside vendors. Only those who had developed additional skills were eligible for advancement.

Source: Adapted from Schuller, R.S., and S.E. Jackson. 1987. "Linking Competitive Strategies with Human Resource Management Practices," *Academy of Management Executive*, Vol. 1, No. 3, pp. 207–213. Reprinted with permission.

HR Strategy by Division

Firms with more than one business strategy are likely to have more than one approach to HR strategy. The challenge is to treat employees across divisions in an equitable fashion while motivating different behaviours that align with the divisions' strategies or functions. For example, General Electric might adopt HR practices that support innovation in the research and development branch while adopting policies that support low costs in the manufacturing branch. But, to achieve equity, employees in both branches would have the same employee benefits.

Similarly, an employee could expect to be exposed to different HR practices within his or her career, even within one firm. Flexibility in behaviour and diverse skill sets will be required from most employees. The basic prescription is to design HR programs that support the business strategy since linking HRM strategy with business strategy can result in improved organizational performance.

Crises are often an opportunity to establish a linkage. If a company is experiencing high turnover and is unable to meet production quotas, or if a key executive departs and there is no groomed successor, many HR directors use this as an opportunity to promote the importance of HR strategic planning.

Changes in the environment overall can sometimes increase the attractiveness of HR strategy. Globalization, for example, forces managers to examine the cost–benefit of using national or international labour pools to attain desired cost and quality objectives. Either choice implicates strategic HR planning.

For all these reasons, most organizations have accepted the importance of including the HR director as part of the strategy formulation team. We offer guidelines to the development of an effective HR strategy in the next section.

Characteristics of an Effective HRM Strategy

The purpose of HR strategy is to capitalize on the distinctive competencies of the organization and add value through the effective use of human resources.[27]

It appears that effective HRM strategies include the following: external and internal fit, and a focus on results.

External and Internal Fit

Fit is an important consideration when designing HR programs. We look at two types of important fit: fitting HR strategy to organizational strategy (external fit), and linking the various HR programs to other functional areas and to each other (internal fit).

External Fit

HR programs must align with or fit the overall strategy of the organization. If the business strategy is to differentiate the organization from its competitors based on superior service, then selection and training programs should be developed to hire and train people in the skills and attitudes necessary to deliver superior service. Fit with other functional strategies is as important as fit with corporate strategies. HR senior management must be included in strategy discussions to be sure this happens.

Internal Fit

We look at two types of internal fit: a fit with other functional areas, such as marketing, and a fit among all HR programs. Fit with other functional areas is important. If the marketing department is developing an advertising plan that promises 24-hour access to customer service representatives but the HR plan does not include compensation differentials for shift work, the overall marketing strategy might fail.

As HR programs must fit with other functional areas, so too do they have to be consistent with each other. That is, training, selection, and appraisal must work together to support a strategy. If the training department decides to teach employees to use the Internet to handle customer service, the staffing department must hire people who either are computer literate or who have the kinds of intelligence that enable them to learn computer skills rapidly. This working together is commonly referred to as bundling HR practices.

Consistent cross-functional practices are critical to the achievement of an organization's goals. Imagine if the business strategy depended on exemplary customer service as its principal competitive advantage, but untrained employees were incapable of providing this level of service. It's clear, then, that the bundling of HR practices is necessary to ensure that the overall strategy is implemented consistently.

Focus on Results

The hard work of deciding on strategy is not its formulation but its implementation and the tracking of results. Many HR managers do not have the resources or skills to measure results to see if the goals have been achieved. Unless the strategy contains performance measures—that is, is results oriented—it will be difficult to know how successfully the strategy was implemented. Chapter 4 presents various methods for evaluating programs. As James Harrington says, "Measurements are key. If you cannot measure it, you cannot control it. If you cannot control it, then you cannot manage it."[28]

We've seen that an effective HRM strategy is aligned with organizational strategy, is integrated with other departmental and HR functional area goals, and is focused on results that can be measured. We've also seen that HR strategy must explicitly recognize the dynamics of the external environment (including the competition and labour markets) and work within a long-range focus of three to five years.

The final section in this chapter outlines the strategic HR planning model and sets the stage for the rest of the material in the book.

THE STRATEGIC HR PLANNING MODEL

The model we are using is based on generic corporate and business strategies linked with complex bundled HR policies and practices. Our perspective builds on earlier HR planning models (right numbers in the right places at the right times). Our search for a strategic HR planning model was triggered by practitioner needs for information. Most of the requests we receive from CEOs and executive vice-presidents of HR are of this nature: "Our organization is merging with another. How will this affect HR? What changes in our HR policies and practices do we need to make?" We have tried to provide answers for these managers.

Our model of strategic HR planning is presented in Figure 2.1. The numbers in parentheses refer to the chapters in which each of the topics is discussed.

This approach is different from classic approaches to HR planning but builds on the tools. Strategic HR planning complements the traditional

FIGURE 2.1 THE STRATEGIC HR PLANNING MODEL

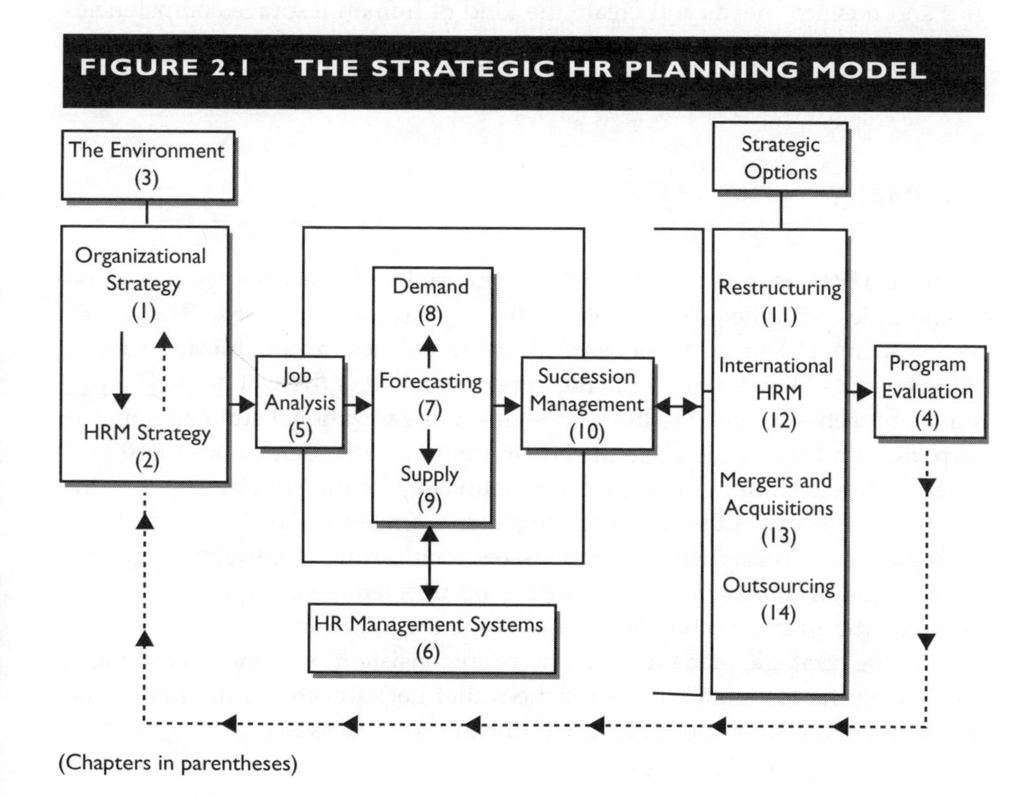

(Chapters in parentheses)

approach to HR planning (forecasting supply and demand) but adds more strategic choices.

The steps in the strategic model are the following:

1. Monitor, identify, and analyze external environmental factors influencing issues for the organization in order to develop strategies. Included in this are those factors that influence an organization's human resource capabilities. (Chapter 3)
2. Develop a tentative corporate or business strategy. (Chapter 1)
3. Assess the relative strengths and weaknesses of the organization's human resources, using forecasting and analysis techniques. Determine the KSAs of an organization and the capacity to learn and change. Identify the competitive advantages of the HR department. (Chapters 5 to 9)
4. Develop strategic plans for each division that are consistent with the overall strategic thrust and that ensure a fit with related components across functional areas. (Chapter 2, 10 to 14)
5. Identify HR policies and practices that will increase the likelihood of achieving the strategy and implement them. (Appendix to this chapter)
6. Measure results and modify plans as necessary. (Chapter 4)

Thus, at the most senior levels of the corporation, HR professionals move from a policing role to the role of strategic partner. They will understand strategies and business needs and create the kind of human resource competencies that build competitive advantage. Our approach not only serves as a strategic planning model, but also as the structure for the text.

Summary

Strategic HRM is a set of distinct but interrelated practices, policies, and philosophies with the goal of enabling the organization to achieve its strategy. By involving HR in discussions of strategic policies, an organization has a better chance of being effective in the implementation of these policies. The various approaches to linking HRM strategies to organizational strategies are the corporate strategy that leads to the HR strategy, the HR competencies that lead to the business strategy, and the interrelationship of the HR strategy and the corporate strategy, as the two work together seamlessly. Finally, the model of strategic HR planning we use emphasizes monitoring, identifying, and analyzing external environment factors; developing a tentative corporate strategy; assessing the strengths and weaknesses of the organization's human resources; developing strategic plans for each division consistent with the overall view; identifying the HR policies and practices that help to achieve the plans; and measuring the results and making modifications as necessary.

Key Terms

human capital, 23

strategic HRM, 22

Suggested Websites

www.shrm.org/research The Society for Human Resources Management Research Centre presents articles on strategic HR.

www.hrreporter.com/hr_strategies/ The *Canadian HR Reporter* website, with articles on strategic HRM.

www.human-resources.org/hr1-contents.htm A site of the Human Resources Learning Center (HRLC), which features innovative HR practices, including HR strategy.

Discussion Questions

1. Discuss the reasons that strategic HR planning is important. What value does it add? List the risks of trying a strategic HRM approach and the risks of not doing so.
2. Visit three large companies from three different sectors. Try a hospitality sector (hotels, fast food, etc.), a high-tech sector, and a manufacturing sector. Talk with a senior HR manager, and see if you can determine how such managers work with executives on strategy formulation and development. What is their role in the process?
3. The emphasis in this chapter was on private companies because much of the research in strategy has been done with for-profit organizations. But many people work for the public sector—that is, for nonprofit organizations. Does strategic HRM make any sense for these companies? Explain your answer, discussing organizational strategies for public companies.

Exercises

1. Using the Internet, find articles about the strategies of the Bay, Zellers, and Wal-Mart. Can you identify their business strategies? Talk to someone in the HR department of these companies or to a departmental store manager. Do their HR practices differ in any way? Then go to a retailer that competes on a differentiation strategy, such as Harry Rosen or Holt Renfrew. Determine the differences in their HRM practices.

2. When the employees of FCI Electronics Company heard that their plant would be closed, they did not apply for new jobs at other plants—they applied for a new company. The employees marketed themselves as a highly valuable workforce, with 26 engineers, 74 tool and die makers, 16 managers, 298 assembly-line workers, and 30 working in shipping. They figured that their hundreds of years in manufacturing, coupled with a perfect attendance record of eight years, would attract an employer to their small town of Clearfield in Pennsylvania. What type of HR strategy does this example illustrate? Do you think the group will be successful? Why or why not?

Case: A New Vision of HR

The HR department is typically organized by function. To ensure that HR policies and practices are aligned with the organization, a new vision of HR would be structured as follows.

Corporate HR

The key officer functions as a practice director, similar to what is found in consulting companies. This person plays several roles: influencing the CEO to design and implement an HR strategy removing barriers to changes suggested by two new departments, Services Inc. and Solutions Inc.; and developing another new department, the organizational capability consultants.

Services Inc.

The part of HR that is administrative, estimated to be 60% to 70% of HR work, is located in a separate unit called Services Inc. The administrative burden is reduced through call centres, use of the Internet and intranet. The types of HR work done in Services Inc. would be involved with compensation and benefits administration, training and education administration, staffing administration, and records management. There would be three levels of service: tier one is accessed through the computer or telephone, and deals with reports of changes in addresses—everything is processed without human intervention. Tier two directs HR requests for information not listed on tier one sites—such as a question about retirement eligibility or finding a course on innovation—to a call centre that can provide a quick response or explanation. Tier three consists of case workers—highly skilled professionals—who provide extensive and comprehensive assistance to complex issues such as employee relations or employee assistance.

Services Inc. is driven by cost reduction—it has to be the lowest cost and most efficient provider of service, which may be outsourced or dealt with in-house. It may be located in Information Services or anywhere that makes it part of an organization-wide effort to provide services through the centralization of technology and call centres.

Solutions Inc.

This branch of corporate HR consists of HR subject matter experts—all of whom possess professional credentials acquired through advanced study and extensive experience. Their role is to transform the organization through training and development, labour relations, compensation design, strategic staffing, and organizational development. They are responsible for creating solutions to organizational problems and for preparing the organization to achieve its strategic intents. These experts act like consultants to the organization and operate on a for-profit basis—that is, their efforts are measurable and must result in an increase in performance measures. The consultants are on the cutting edge of research and put innovative, state-of-the-art theories into practice.

Organization Capability Consultants

Operating as the third branch of corporate HR, the HR professionals in this unit are dispersed throughout the organization, providing guidance and assistance to operating units, with the goal of improving the effectiveness of the organization. If asked questions about changing benefits or dealing with a potential unionization threat, they hand out cards with the contact numbers for Services Inc. or Solutions Inc. They build organizational capabilities by aligning HR strategies, processes, and practices with the needs of the business. Their HR solutions should change existing processes to create "better-faster-cheaper" approaches.

Question

What are the advantages of this structure? Would managers and employees of an organization prefer this model to the traditional functional structure? Which structure do you think HR professionals would prefer and why?

References

Amit, R., and M. Belcourt. 1999. "Human Resources Processes as a Source of Competitive Advantage." *European Management Journal,* Vol. 17, No. 2 (April).

Anderson, W. 1997. "The Future of Human Resources: Forging Ahead or Falling Behind?" *Human Resources Management*, Vol. 36, No. 1 (Spring): 17–22.

Bratton, D. 2000. *Best Practices in HR Strategy*. Toronto: Carswell Publishers.

Brockbank, W. 2002. "Competencies for the New HR." Unpublished working paper, University of Michigan Business School.

Bamberger, P., and A. Feigenbaum. 1996. "The Role of Strategic Reference Points in Explaining the Nature and Consequences of Human Resources Strategy." *Academy of Management Review*, Vol. 21, No. 4 (October): 926–958.

Becker, B.E., and M.A. Huselid. 1999. "Overview: Strategic Human Resources Management in Five Leading Firms." *Human Resource Management*, Vol. 38, No. 4 (Winter): 287–301.

Belcourt, M., and S. Thornhill. 1999. "Growing from the Inside Out: Human Resource Practices for Growth Strategies." Proceedings of the Administrative Sciences Association of Canada.

Buller, P.F. 1996. "Successful Partnerships: HR and Strategic Planning at Eight Top Firms." *Organizational Dynamics*: 27–43.

Cascio, W. 1991. *Applied Psychology in Personnel Management*, 4th ed. Englewood Cliffs, N.J.: Prentice Hall.

Cheddie, M. 2001. "How to Become a Strategic Partner." *HR Focus*, Vol. 78, No. 8: 1, 13.

Collins, J. 2001. *Good to Great*. New York: Harper Business.

Cooke, R., and M. Armstrong. 1990. "The Search for Strategic HR." *Personnel Management* (December): 30–33.

Cowherd, D.M., and D.I. Levine. 1992. "Product Quality and Pay Equity Between Lower-Level Employees and Top Management: An Investigation of Distributive Justice Theory." *Administrative Science Quarterly*, Vol. 37: 302–320.

Harrington, J. 1991. *Business Process Improvement*. New York: McGraw-Hill.

Jackson, S.E., and R. S. Schuller. 1995. "Understanding Human Resource Management in the Context of Organizations and Their Environments." *Annual Review of Psychology*, Vol. 46: 237–264.

King, A.S. 1995. "Multi-Phase Progression of Organizational Ideology: Commitment." *Mid Atlantic Journal*, Vol. 31, No. 2: 143–160.

Lengnick-Hall, C., and M. Lengnick-Hall. 1990. *Interactive Human Resource Management and Strategic Planning*: New York: Quorum Books.

———. 1988. "Strategic Human Resources Management: A Review of the Literature and a Proposed Typology." *Academy of Management Review*, Vol. 13, No. 3: 454–470.

MacMillan, I.C. 1983. "Seizing Competitive Advantage." *Journal of Business Strategy*: 43–57.

Milkovich, G.T., and J.M. Newman. 1987. *Compensation*, 2nd ed. Dallas, Texas: BPI.

"The New HR Executive." Corporate Leadership Council, September 2000.

Rothwell, W.J., and H.C. Kazanas. 1988. *Strategic Human Resources Planning and Management*. Englewood Cliffs, N.J.: Prentice Hall.

Rollo, J.A. 2002. *Strategic Human Resources Management*. Cincinnati, Ohio: South Western Thompson Learning.

Schuller, R.S., and S.E. Jackson. 1989. "Determinants of Human Resources Management Priorities and Implications for Industrial Relations." *Journal of Management*, Vol. 15, No. 1: 89–99.

———. 1987. "Linking Competitive Strategies with Human Resource Management Practices." *Academy of*

Management Executive, Vol. 1, No. 3: 207–219.

Ulrich, D. 1991. "Using Human Resources for Competitive Advantage." In R.H. Kilman and I. Kilman, eds., *Making Organizations Competitive.* San Francisco: Jossey-Bass.

———. 1997. *Human Resource Champions: The Next Agenda for Adding Value and Delivering Results*. Boston: Harvard Business School Press.

Ulrich, D., M. Losey, and G. Lake, eds. 1997. *Tomorrow's HR Management.* New York: Wiley and Sons.

Weatherly, L. 2003. "Human Capital: The Elusive Asset." *Research Quarterly,* Society for Human Resources Management, www.shrm.org/research.

Wright, P.M., D.L. Smart, and G.C. McMahan. 1995. "Matches Between Human Resources and Strategy Among NCAA Basketball Teams." *Academy of Management Journal*, Vol. 38, No. 4: 1052–1074.

Zedeck, S., and W.F. Cascio. 1984. "Psychological Issues in Personnel Decisions." *Annual Review of Psychology,* Vol. 35: 461–518.

ENDNOTES

1. Rollo, 2002.
2. Jackson and Schuler, 1995.
3. "The New HR Executive," 2000.
4. Ulrich, 1997.
5. Weatherly. 2003.
6. Zedeck and Cascio, 1984.
7. Milkovich and Newman, 1987.
8. Wright et al., 1995.
9. Amit and Belcourt, 1999.
10. Becker and Huselid, 1999, p. 288.
11. Schuller and Jackson, 1989.
12. King, 1995.
13. Lengnick-Hall and Lengnick-Hall, 1990.
14. Lengnick-Hall and Lengnick-Hall, 1988.
15. MacMillan, 1983.
16. Anderson, 1997.
17. Lengnick-Hall and Lengnick-Hall, 1988.
18. Ibid.
19. Collins, 2001.
20. Bamberger and Feigenbaum, 1996.
21. Bratton, 2000.
22. Rothwell and Kazanas, 1988; Cheddie, 2001.

23. Ulrich et al., 1997.
24. www.accenture.com.
25. Cascio, 1991.
26. Buller, 1996.
27. Cooke and Armstrong, 1990.
28. Harrington, 1991, p. 28.
29. Brockbank, 2002.

APPENDIX
HR Alignment with Two Strategies

HR Alignment with the Low-Cost-Provider Strategy

A firm competing on cost leadership attempts to be the low-cost provider of a product or service within a marketplace. The product or service must be perceived by the consumer to be comparable to that offered by the competition and to have a price advantage. McDonald's uses this approach, as do Zellers and Timex.

Buyers are price sensitive, and businesses appeal to this price consciousness by providing products or services at prices lower than those of competitors. Survival is the ultimate goal, but organizations price low to gain market share (by underpricing competitors) or by earning a higher profit margin by selling at the going market rate. This strategy requires the company to balance the delivery of a product that still appeals to customers with not spending too much on gaining market share. McDonald's could deliver a cheaper hamburger, but would it have any taste? McDonald's could underprice its competitors, but it may risk its survival by going too low. The key is to manage costs down every year.

The adoption of a low-cost-provider strategy by a firm has immediate implications for HR strategy. Costs are an important element of this strategy, so labour costs are carefully controlled. Efficiency and controlling costs are paramount. The implications of a low-cost-provider strategy for five key components of HR are discussed below, but first we start with the job description of a typical employee working in a company that competes as a low-cost provider.

The Employee

To keep wages low, jobs have to be of limited scope so that the company can hire people with minimal skills at low wages. The job requires highly repetitive and predictable behaviours. There is little need for cooperative or interdependent behaviours among employees. The company directs its efforts at doing the same or more with less and capitalizing on economies of scale. For example, in 1987 Toyota produced about 3.5 million vehicles a year with 25 000 production workers, the same number of workers it employed in 1966 when it produced only 1 million vehicles. Toyota achieved what low-cost providers want—an increase in productivity and reduced output cost per employee. Doing more with fewer employees is the goal of most organizations with a low-cost-provider strategy.

Risk-taking on the part of the employee is not needed, but comfort with repetitive, unskilled work is necessary. Customers like those frequenting McDonald's are "trained" not to make idiosyncratic requests (such as a "medium-rare hamburger" or "hot mustard"), and so no unique response system is required. Employees are not expected to contribute ideas.

Another way to cut costs is to eliminate as many of the support or managerial layers as possible. The impact of cutting costs in this way is that employees may have to do more with less, make more decisions, and so on, which would require a more skilled employee. Alternatively, the jobs could be so tightly designed that little supervision is required, thus saving costs. Substituting technology for labour is another way to save costs.

Let us now look at six HR functions that will facilitate the personnel work at a low-cost-provider organization.

HR Planning

At the entry level, succession planning is minimal, ensuring only the feeder line to the next level. Outside labour markets are monitored to ensure that entry-level people are in adequate supply. The availability and use of fringe workers—those who are retired, temporarily unemployed, students, and so on—is part of the planning strategy, particularly if the employment market is offering better opportunities to the normal supply of low-skilled workers.

At the executive level, succession management assumes the same importance as in other organizations.

Selection

Recruitment is primarily at the entry, or lowest, level and is from the surrounding external labour market. Recruitment is by word of mouth, and application forms are available on-site, thus saving the costs of recruiting in newspapers. Most other positions are staffed internally through promotions from within. Thus, career paths are narrow.

Compensation

A low-cost-provider strategy includes lower wages and fringe benefits. Beyond the legal minimum pay requirements, firms with this strategy carefully monitor what their competitors are paying in the local labour market. These firms' strategy tends to be a lag strategy, where they attempt to pay wages slightly below industry norms.

One way of achieving these lower costs is to outsource production to sites with lower labour costs. In the United States, this means moving production from high-wage states, such as New York, to low-wage states, such as New Mexico. In Canada, wages are very similar across provinces, so firms analyze wage rates in countries such as India, which pay employees substantially less for similar productivity. Outsourcing has also meant moving the work from highly unionized plants, where workers make $20 or more an hour, to non-unionized smaller sites, where workers are paid slightly more than the minimum wage.

Cost reduction in wages can also be achieved through the use of part-time workers, who receive no fringe benefits. Canadian organizations pay around

30% in fringe benefits, so the savings gained by using part-time workers is substantial among large employers. Food franchises employ part-time workers almost exclusively to reduce labour costs.

Pay for performance, such as incentive compensation that is linked to productivity, rewards individual effort. Group rewards are based on explicit, results-oriented criteria and the meeting of short-term performance goals.

It is important to note that innovative compensation schemes may produce a competitive advantage. Programs designed to reduce labour costs, such as outsourcing or using part-time workers, can easily be imitated by competitors, and so may produce no long-term competitive advantage. However, an innovative compensation scheme that cannot be duplicated by rivals may provide a competitive advantage. For example, in an arrangement between the Great Atlantic and Pacific Tea Company (A&P) and the United Food and Commercial Workers (UFCW), workers took a 25% pay cut in exchange for cash bonuses. If the store's employees could keep labour costs at 10% of sales by working more efficiently or generating more store traffic, they would receive a cash bonus of 1% of store sales. This arrangement resulted in an 81% increase in operating profits. However, unions were opposed to the spread of this practice, and so A&P's rivals in the low-margin food business were unable to reduce their labour costs in the same way (Schuller and Jackson, 1987). Any incentives for performance would reward cost savings, or improvements in efficiency, as this example shows.

Training

Training is minimal, as few skills are required. Any training is based on increasing efficiency in the current job, or specialization for the current position. Such training is fast and inexpensive. McDonald's can train a new hamburger flipper or cashier in under an hour. There is little to no investment in the long-term development of the employee, nor in the acquisition of skills for jobs other than the current one.

The training staff is lean, with the organization relying on outside suppliers. However, most training takes place on the job in the form of direct instruction from or coaching by the supervisor. The jobs are so narrow in scope, so repetitive in nature, that little need for training exists.

Performance Evaluation

Short-term results, with explicit and standardized criteria, are used for evaluating an employee's performance. The feedback is immediate and specific. Individuals are held accountable only for their own behaviour or results, not for that of the team or the company (Ulrich, 1991). Only the supervisor provides input for the performance evaluation. Forms are kept to a minimum, and rating is done against check marks. Feedback, if based on a performance review, tends to be one-way, with little opportunity for the employee to debate the results or receive developmental feedback. Results are used for consideration for promotion.

Labour Relations

Low-cost providers try to prevent the formation of a union because they feel that unions drive up wages. Unions find low-cost providers, such as McDonald's, difficult to unionize because employees work shifts and part-time hours. Furthermore, employees quit often, and many low-cost providers absorb turnover rates of 300% annually as a cost of doing business. High turnover has the primary advantage of keeping compensation levels low.

Now that we have an idea of how HR programs align with a low-cost provider strategy, let us examine what these programs would be like under a differentiation strategy.

HR Alignment with the Differentiation Strategy

In most markets, buyer preferences are too diverse to be satisfied by one undifferentiated product. Firms providing features that appeal to a particular market segment are said to compete on a differentiation strategy. A firm competing on the basis of a differentiation strategy will offer something unique and valuable to its customers. Mercedes-Benz, Polo Ralph Lauren, Rolex, and Hewlett-Packard's scientific instruments divisions are firms that compete successfully by charging a price premium for uniqueness. The primary focus is on the new and different. Observation, experience, and market research will establish what buyers consider important, what has value, and what they will pay for these features. Then the firm can offer a product or service that commands a premium price, increase unit sales within this niche, and gain buyer loyalty among those who value these features. The extra price outweighs the extra costs of providing these features.

A firm can differentiate itself from its competitors in many ways:

- Having quality products
- Offering superior customer service
- Having a more convenient location
- Using proprietary technology
- Offering valuable features
- Demonstrating unique styling
- Having a brand-name reputation

These different features can be anything. Common examples show some firms competing on service (Four Seasons Hotels), on engineering design (BMW), on image (Polo Ralph Lauren), on reliability (Bell), on a full range of products or services (Procter & Gamble), on technological leadership (Corel), and on quality (Honda).

Most of the time, these competitive advantages are combined, such as by linking quality products with proprietary technology and superior customer service, thus providing the buyer with more value for the money. The key in this strategy is to provide the differentiation that is perceived to be of value to customers while keeping costs down. For example, a slice of lemon in a glass of ice water delivered to the table is an obvious way to differentiate the restaurant, but at low cost. After-dinner mints are less expensive than valet parking, but may be equally appreciated by diners.

A differentiation strategy calls for innovation and creativity among employees. HRM is affected in fundamentally different ways in organizations that want to use employees' brains rather than their limited (mainly manual) skills in the low-cost-provider strategy.

The starting point for aligning HR programming with a differentiation strategy is the employee.

The Employee

Organizations competing on a differentiation strategy require from their employees creative behaviour, a long-term focus, interdependent activity, and some risk taking, as well as an ability to work in an ambiguous and unpredictable environment. Their employees' skills need to be broad, and employees must be highly involved with the firm. Organizations encourage employees to make suggestions, through both informal and formal suggestion systems, for new and improved ways of doing their job. Employees at Corning Canada Inc., for example, submit their suggestions to their supervisors, who review them formally and give feedback directly to the employee. Contrast this with the traditional suggestion box, which many employees view as a recycling bin because of the lack of timely feedback.

To encourage innovative behaviour, 3M has an informal policy of allowing employees to "bootleg" about 15% of their time on their own projects. Job classifications are flexible.

HR Planning

In a company that has a differentiation strategy and that recognizes people are the key to competitive advantage, HR planning is taken very seriously. For example, at Sumitomo Metals in Japan, the business planning group reports to HR because the company understands that identifying what needs to be done is less difficult than planning how to do it.

Succession management is critical as employees would have to possess many attributes to move ahead in the organization. Thus, a strong emphasis on developing skills for the future is part of the promotion policy. Investments in career moves, training, and developmental experiences are substantial. Long-term job security and reciprocal loyalty are the norm.

Selection

Companies with a differentiation strategy need employees who have a broad range of skills and the ability to learn from others. An innovative atmosphere requires employees who are self-motivated and do not require a great deal of supervision. Employees are selected for their abilities to think creatively, to be flexible in work attitudes, and to be able to work in teams. However, selection for these characteristics is more difficult and usually involves team interviews and behaviourally based evidence of innovative performance. Employees would normally be recruited through reputation (word of mouth) or through graduate schools. Some testing for creative ability might be used.

Compensation

Compensation plans affect employee behaviour more directly than most HR practices. For example, Drucker describes a compensation scheme he implemented at General Electric (GE) in which pay for performance was based only on the previous year's results. As such, for 10 years, GE lost its capacity for innovation because investing in innovation affects expenses and decreases profits, so everyone postponed spending on innovation.

Compensation is carefully designed in firms that have a differentiation strategy. Pay rates may be slightly below average market rates but there are substantial opportunities to increase those base levels through incentive pay. Pay for performance is a large part of the compensation package and will be dependent on individual, group, and corporate results. These results are a combination of process and financial criteria and are set in advance, usually on a yearly basis.

There is more choice about the mix of components of compensation. Individuals may receive salary, bonus, or stock option incentives.

Internal equity is of greater concern than equity with the external market. Egalitarian pay structures are associated with greater product quality (Belcourt and Thornhill, 1999). Nonmonetary rewards also play a larger role in HR strategy in these types of firms. At Honda, the team that designs a unique transportation vehicle is awarded a trip to Japan.

Training

Training is part of the differentiation strategy, and companies with this strategy have a strong training team. The focus of training is on both skills and attitudes. Process skills, such as decision-making, the ability to work in teams, and creative thinking, are emphasized as much as skills needed for the current job.

The training itself is seen as an opportunity to generate new ideas and procedures. Indeed, customers and cross-functional teams might be included in the training program.

Developmental experiences are encouraged. The value of working in another division or another country is recognized and encouraged. Employees receive promotions or other job opportunities based, partially, on their willingness to undertake training and their track record in learning.

Performance Evaluation

In a company with a differentiation strategy, performance appraisal is not based on short-term results but instead on the long-term implications of behaviour. Processes that are deemed to lead to better results in the long term are rewarded. Thus, companies encourage and appraise attitudes such as empowerment, diversity sensitivity, and teamwork in an effort to build future bottom-line outcomes. Working beyond the job is encouraged, not punished. Failure is tolerated, although management tries to distinguish between bad luck and bad judgment or stupidity.

Evaluation tends to be based on a mixture of individual and group (and sometimes corporate) criteria. Thus, an individual might be evaluated on his or her ability to achieve results and to work as a member of the team, the group's performance might be measured against established quotas, and the company would be evaluated with regard to its overall financial performance.

Three-hundred-and-sixty-degree evaluations—that is, appraisals that include input from employees, functional experts, peers, and so on—are the norm. Organizations in the service sector are more likely to include customers as sources of input for performance appraisal.

Labour Relations

Any structure or process that reduces the capacity to be innovative and flexible is difficult to tolerate. Traditional unions, with rigid collective agreements, are encouraged to work collectively toward a new union–management relationship. The union–management relationship is characterized by shared information such as open books, shared decision-making about best approaches, and shared responsibility for solving problems as they arise.

References

Belcourt, M., and S. Thornhill. 1999. "Growing from the Inside Out: Human Resources Practices for Growth Strategies." Proceedings of the Administrative Sciences Association of Canada.

Schueller, R.S., and S.E. Jackson. 1987. "Linking Competitive Strategies with Human Resource Management Practices." *Academy of Management Executive*. Vol. 1, No. 3: 207–219.

Ulrich, D., 1991. "Using Human Resources for Competitive Advantage." In R.H. Kilman and I Kilman, eds., *Making Organizations Competitive*. San Francisco: Jossey-Bass.

3

ENVIRONMENTAL INFLUENCES ON HRM

Chapter Goals

To understand strategic HR planning, we must understand how HRM is affected by the environment in which it operates. Most HR managers actively scan their surroundings, looking at cultural changes or changes in laws and technologies that might affect the way that HR is practised. A good source is the daily news, where HR professionals can learn about such major legislative changes as Ontario's plan to eliminate mandatory retirement. HR planners want to track trends that influence the way in which employees can be managed. For example, the elimination of mandatory retirement affects the way performance appraisals will be conducted with long-term employees, benefit plans, pension contribution plans, health and safety accommodation—nearly everything! HR strategists need information about their environment in order to exploit the opportunities or cope with the threats.

After reading this chapter, you should be able to do the following:

1. Identify the sources that HR planners use to keep current with business and HR trends.
2. List several of the methods—including trend analysis, the Delphi technique, and impact analyses—used to predict future trends.
3. Discuss the challenges in scanning the environment.
4. Delineate the environmental factors, such as the economic climate, the labour force, the political and regulatory context, and the social and cultural climate, that influence the practice of HRM.
5. Describe the role of the stakeholder, and list several examples.
6. Understand how environmental scanning is practised.

We will look first at the sources and methods HR planners use to track these trends.

Environmental Scanning Sources and Methods

environmental scanning
systematic monitoring of trends affecting the organization

Managers have to develop strategies and keep a keen eye on what is happening in the world outside the organization. **Environmental scanning** is the systematic monitoring of the major factors influencing the organization. The goal of scanning the environment is to identify trends that might affect the formulation and implementation of both organizational and HR strategies.

"Environment" is a fuzzy term. It means anything outside organizational boundaries. Even talking about an environment suggests that the environment is different, and not part of the organization. But the organization and the environment are tightly integrated. Managers are influenced by the culture in which they operate—that is, they are not independent of the environment. A manager in Vancouver will treat her employees differently than a manager in New Delhi, and the employees in each city would have expectations about how managers should supervise. Rather than attempt a definition of the word "environment," we will simply list the methods used to scan the environment and the environmental factors that seem to influence HRM strategy formulation.

In the past, HR managers monitored changes that might affect their programs and policies by reading newspapers or trade publications. They would keep informed of issues regarding employment laws by subscribing to particular news services, and by being a member of the provincial HR associations. The scanning method was not perfect, because no one can accurately predict all the forces that will shape the future workplace and the workforce. However, some sources of information and scanning methods can help us do a better job. The next section describes the sources that HR professionals might use to monitor trends in the environment.

Sources of Information

When developing strategies and determining their likely impact on an organization, HR professionals rely on many sources of information. These include publications, professional associations, conferences, and professional consultants.

Publications

HR professionals actively scan Canadian newspapers, business publications, and HR magazines, journals, and newsletters. We are fortunate to have access not only to a wide range of Canadian sources of information but also to the extensive publication network originating in the United States. The authors' experiences suggest that Canadian HR trends lag behind U.S. trends by a year or two. For example, workplace violence and employee retention were hot issues in the United States three years before they became important in Canada. Thus, reading U.S. publications acts as an early warning signal for Canadian HR professionals. HR practitioners subscribe to many of the publications listed in Box 3.1.

Professional Associations

Canadian HR professionals and executives belong to a number of organizations that publish newsletters and updates on current events. Many of these organizations, such as the Human Resources Professionals Association of Ontario, have committees that actively scan the regulatory scene for upcoming changes. Some, like the Conference Board of Canada, conduct research with their members to track trends. Relevant associations are listed in Box 3.2.

Conferences and Seminars

Most professionals keep current and even ahead of emerging trends by attending conferences, seminars, and workshops in Canada and the United States. Most provincial HR associations hold annual conferences. The Human Resources Professionals Association of Ontario, for example, attracts over 1500 participants to its conference each February. Such events, including those sponsored by private organizations, are widely publicized in HR publications such as those listed in Box 3.1.

Professional Consultants

Organizations that have an active interest in understanding the influence of potential trends often hire consultants to research or interpret these trends for

BOX 3.1 Publications of Interest to HR Professionals

Canadian

Canadian Business
Canadian Compensation News
Canadian HR Reporter
Canadian Journal of Learning
The Globe and Mail Report on Business
HR Professional
Ivey Business Quarterly
The Training Report
Workplace today

U.S.

Business Week
Fortune
HR Focus
HR Magazine
HR News
People Management
Profit
Training
Work Week

Research Journals

Academy of Management Executive
Academy of Management Review
Benefits Canada
Business Horizons
Business Quarterly
California Management Review
Canadian Journal of Administrative Studies
Canadian Labour Law Reporter
Compensation
Compensation and Benefits Review
European Management Journal
Harvard Business Review
Human Resource Management
HR Research Quarterly
Journal of Applied Psychology
Journal of Business Ethics
Journal of Labor Research
Journal of Management
Journal of Staffing and Recruitment
Labor Studies Journal
Management Review
Occupational Outlook Quarterly
Organizational Behavior and Human Performance
Personnel
Personnel Journal
Personnel Psychology
Public Personnel Management
Training and Development Journal

them. The Hudson Institute is an example of a firm that specializes in this form of consulting. Most organizations have a person on staff, often the librarian, whose job is to bring information to the consultants' attention by actively scanning multiple sources.

Techniques for Scanning

HR professionals can use several methods to generate predictions about the future or extrapolate from current events to determine their impact on HR practices. These methods include trend analysis, the Delphi technique, and impact analysis.

BOX 3.2 Associations of Interest to HR Professionals

Administrative Sciences Association of Canada (HR division)
Canadian Association of Management Consultants
Canadian Council of Human Resource Associations—links to all provincial HR associations
Canadian Human Resource Planners
Canadian Industrial Relations Association
Canadian Payroll Association
Canadian Public Personnel Managers Association
Conference Board of Canada
Human Resource Planning Society
International Association for Human Resources Information Management Association
North American Human Resources Management Association
Ontario Society for Training and Development
Society for Human Resources Management
Society for Industrial and Organizational Psychology
World at Work

Note: The current websites for all these organizations can be found at www.hrm.nelson.com.

Trend Analysis

Trend analysis is a quantitative approach that attempts to forecast future personnel needs based on extrapolating information from historical changes in one or more organizational indices. A single index, such as sales, might be used. However, more complex modelling or multiple predictive techniques, used by professional planners, rely on a combination of several factors. These methods are described in Chapter 7.

trend analysis a forecasting method that extrapolates from historical organizational indices

Delphi Technique

The **Delphi technique** is a process in which the forecasts and judgments of a selected group of experts are solicited and summarized in an attempt to determine the future of employment. This method, too, is described in Chapter 7. However, Box 3.3 describes the Delphi Technique used by the Society for Human Resources Management.

Delphi technique a forecasting method in which expert opinions are solicited and summarized

Impact Analysis

Impact analysis, too, looks backward in order to look forward. Past trends are analyzed. A panel of experts then attempts to identify future probable events and study their effects on the extrapolated trend.[1] Unlike trend analysis, which is a objective statistical technique, impact analysis relies on subjective, but expert judgments.

Other methods for assessing the future include the nominal group technique, critical incident approach, scenarios, and questionnaires, and are all discussed in Chapter 7.

impact analysis a forecasting method in which past trends are analyzed by a panel of experts who then predict the probability of future events

BOX 3.3 The Experts Predict the Future of HRM

In 1997, experts in a variety of fields provided written responses to a series of questions developed by the Society for Human Resources Management. Leaders in HR were asked about business conditions and their implications for HRM. For example, one question was, "How will businesses utilize employee resources in the future?"

The experts agreed that the primary employment model would be one of self-employed individuals who form ad hoc services companies. A small number of core employees would remain part of the formal organization. The workforce would continue to become bipolar, with skilled workers having significant employment advantages over unskilled workers. Contingent workers would be treated better than they are now and would gain benefits. Security would be based on performance contracts in contrast to the present system of tenure or service years.

This study was repeated in 2002. The experts identified these top trends: increased use of technology to communicate with employees; rising health-care costs; increased vulnerability of intellectual property; greater demand for high-skilled workers than for low-skilled workers; change from manufacturing to information/service economy; increase in employment-related government regulations; focus on domestic safety and security; and ability to use technology to more closely monitor employees.

Sources: Adapted from M. Minehan, "SHRM: Futurist Task Force," *HR Magazine*, Vol. 43, No. 3 (1998): 77–84; D. Patel, "SHRM Workplace Forecast: A Strategic Outlook for 2002–2003," *SHRM*, July 2002.

An excellent evaluation of all these approaches can be found in Rothwell and Kazanas.[2] Readers are invited to experience a nominal group technique as part of a group exercise at the end of this chapter.

We have described rear-view-mirror ways of scanning the environment. If you examine studies or articles that are supposed to predict the future, you will see that they contain, for the most part, simple extensions of present trends. We assume that tomorrow will be much like yesterday, with minor variations. HR planners recognize that there are problems with these attempts to interpret the environment. At the time this text was written the hot issues in the United States were the following:

- Disengaged workers—Uncommitted employees who are underperforming in their jobs because they are not motivated or engaged at work are costing U.S. employers billions of dollars in lost productivity annually.
- Aging boomers—The generation born between 1946 and 1961 (the baby boomers) are moving through the organization like a goat through a snake. Now in their early fifties, the boomers will demand different benefits such as vision care. They also will lobby for more elder care, as they take care of their very elderly parents—the "old" old, who are over 85.
- Never married; childless couples—The proportion of those over 18 who have never married now represents one-quarter of the American population, and the number of childless couples is expected to reach 50% by 2010. This will affect benefits and work–family balance issues.

- Executive compensation—Employees and the U.S. public are concerned about the level of executive compensation. The average compensation level of executives rose about ten times faster than that of the average U.S. worker.
- Structure of the workforce—The use of contingent workers continues to grow, as do the disparities in wages and benefits between contingent workers and "permanent" employees. Contingent clerical workers earn about 10% less than full-time clerks while contingent blue-collar workers earn about 34% less than those working full time. It is expected that more legislation will be introduced in the United States to protect contingent workers.
- Labour shortages of highly qualified workers—The demand for employees with Master's degrees is expected to grow by 29%, contrasted with the 5% increase in demand for those who require only moderate on-the-job training. Quantity of the supply of educated labour is not the sole issue. American employers are concerned about the quality of the labour force, particularly its literacy level. A substantial portion of the workforce cannot write a letter explaining an error on a credit card or use a calculator to determine the difference between a sale price and a regular price.

Challenges in Environmental Scanning

There are problems in scanning the environment. These include our inability to accurately predict the future and to isolate what really is important to HR. The 21st century has arrived. Can we say what the world will look like in 2050? In 1900, could those working in HRM have predicted what it would look like in the year 2000? Not likely, because the field of HRM did not exist then. One hundred years ago, there were no payroll and benefits clerks. Even 20 years ago, it would have been difficult to forecast the flattening of organizations, downsizing, the impact of technology, outsourcing, telecommuting, and a range of other changes we now experience. Most HR strategists limit themselves to a two- to three-year time frame and extrapolate from current trends.

Isolating the Critical from the Insignificant

So much change is happening in so many arenas that scanners have trouble picking out the truly important events. As we enter the new millennium, we cannot determine which current issues are important enough to cause a shift in the way we practise HR. For example, which of these HR issues, taken from headlines in HR publications as this text is being written, are critical and which will prove insignificant: Increasing commitment among employees? Outsourcing of non-core functions? Workplace privacy?

The other difficulty is that few trends exist in isolation—no issue is an island. Take the issues of the difficulty of finding employees where labour shortages exist. There is a growing concern that universities will be unable to find enough professors to replace all those expected to retire within the next ten years. If this problem is addressed in isolation, two solutions might be to (1) increase the number of spaces for doctoral students who then graduate to become professors and/or (2) recruit professors from other countries. But other trends may influence the ability to find enough professors. The policy of mandatory retirement is being challenged through the courts, and in 2003 Ontario joined five other provinces in not making retirement mandatory at age 65. If the court challenges are successful in every province, some professors will not be forced to retire, so the shortages will not be as great as expected.

Just as there is a reaction for every action, for every trend there is a counter-trend, and counter-trends seem to develop in tandem with the trends. As globalization increases, so does "localization," and ethnic pride in customs and culture rises. This is not the same as thinking that the pendulum will always swing back. Trends are not cyclical in the sense that a trend appears and then disappears, returning the world to its original state. The current focus on work–life balance cannot be viewed just as a fad, with the resultant expectation that there will be another replacement fad within a few years. The concepts underlying work–family balance will be imbedded in our view of work, just as safety and labour laws are now permanently imbedded in the culture of work.

HR planners do not only react to current events. Sometimes they attempt to shape the issues that will affect their practice.

A Proactive Approach

Some HR managers do not like passively observing the game through their windows. They want to go outside and influence how the game is played. Thus, we find most professional associations have a group that lobbies for legislation that will favour the association membership. Most have public relations firms that try to shape the perception of the profession and its goals (thus influencing public opinion favourably toward regulations). For example, the Human Resources Professionals Association of Ontario attempted to influence the provincial government as it undertook a review of the Workplace Safety & Insurance Board policies.

Despite the challenges of environmental scanning, most HR strategists do monitor the environment and look for changes that may affect HR. We will now examine the major areas that these strategists typically scan.

Environmental Factors

Nearly everything, from birth rates to pollution levels, could be said to influence organizational and HR strategies. However, there are a number of factors that HR strategists monitor more closely because these factors seem more closely related to HRM. Following this tradition, we have included factors such as the economic climate, the labour force, the political and regulatory context, and issues related to technology, demographics, and social values and norms. For each factor we have provided some current examples of these forces, keeping in mind that such examples quickly lose their relevance.

Economic Climate

The economic indices that we are so familiar with from the media are also important to HR strategists. Let us look at a few examples of how these indices influence HR managers who are

- concerned with the unemployment rate because it affects their ability to recruit;
- worried about the value of the Canadian dollar because it affects the company's ability to sell products internationally, and thus affects employment levels;
- troubled by the amount of public debt because it affects business taxes, and, therefore, a company's ability to survive and grow; and
- anxious about interest rates because they affect how much a company is willing to borrow to grow its business and invest in employees.

Interestingly, sometimes HR acts as predictor of the economy. A drop in demand for contingent, temporary, and contract employees (as reported by search and placement firms) can predict an economic slowdown before these changes are reported by firms in their financial statements.

It could be argued that anything to do with the economy touches the management of human resources. However, it is impossible to deal with every economic indicator and change. We will provide two examples: the economic shift from hand work (manual production) to head work (the use of mental processes), and globalization.

From the Industrial Revolution to the Knowledge Revolution

The economy is shifting from one based on the production of goods to one in which services are delivered. One historic moment in this shift occurred when Wal-Mart became the largest corporation in America—the first service company to rise to number 1 among the Fortune 500 and pass General Motors (GM) and Exxon. The number of workers in the service sector increased from 40% of the workforce in 1945 to 75% in 1995.[3] These services may be "hard," such as the kinds of services a hair stylist offers, or "soft," such as the selling of information. The types of employees needed by the diminishing industrial sector are different from those needed by the service sector.

We are facing a paradox in this new century. On one hand, companies are downsizing and outsourcing. On the other, they are claiming that employees are a source of strategic advantage, and they are facing recruitment and retention problems with employees. Thus, for some types of jobs (low-skilled), the economic climate consists of part-time workers, contract workers, and those working for outsourcing organizations. For jobs requiring scientific and technological competencies there is high demand, and organizations must compete on compensation, culture, and benefits. Futurists say that the times of cost containment and downsizing are over; organizations will be focusing on innovation and exploring new growth opportunities. The kind of employees they will be looking for are multi-skilled, e-literate, entrepreneurial, and innovative.[4]

Globalization

Another trend to watch is increasing globalization. Globalization is the growth in flows of trade and financial capital across borders. Globalization affects sovereignty, prosperity, jobs, wages, and social legislation. McDonald's has a great deal of experience in globalization and when the company launches a restaurant in a new country, it works closely with all disciplines to "McDonaldize" a team, so that they know the business inside out. Eighteen to 24 months before the restaurant is opened, the company starts with HR. Some of the HR challenges it faced in other countries included the fact that part-time employment and multi-functional jobs did not exist.[5] HR managers will need to develop international competencies, as is discussed in Chapter 12.

The Labour Market

A labour market is the area from which an organization recruits its employees. Such an area may be metropolitan, regional, provincial, national, or international. The number of people available for work depends on factors such as the unemployment rate, geographic migration, graduation rates from educational institutions, and so on. However, labour markets in the 21st century will become international. Ford, GM, and Nestlé already employ more people outside their countries than within. Because of India's huge population of English-speaking software engineers, companies like Microsoft have employment centres in India. The labour market is changing, as highlighted in Box 3.4.

The labour market influences an organization's ability to implement strategy. An organization may decide to enter the high-tech field, only to discover itself unable to recruit enough electrical engineers to meet its personnel requirements, and so must abandon this particular strategy. This example is not hypothetical. A skills gap exists. Companies wishing to grow are facing problems in recruiting and retaining qualified scientists and technologists. There is a growing concern with the division of labour in Canada: the *shortage* of people with the right skills who can earn good money and expect benefits, and the *surplus* of people available to work in "McJobs." Human Resources Development Canada (HRDC), the government department concerned with employment issues, is addressing this concern through its National Skills agenda, which will encourage companies to increase their training budgets by one-third (to be in

BOX 3.4 Canadian Labour Market Facts

- Almost all labour market growth will be from immigrants.
- Visible minority populations are growing fast and will account for 20% of the Canadian population by 2016.
- The number of aboriginals in Canada grew by 22% since the last census in 1991, compared to a non-Aboriginal population growth of 2.4%. Aboriginals now make up 3.3% of the population.
- The participation rate of women grew by 13% since 1991, compared to that of men at 6%.
- The number of jobs requiring a university education grew by one-third over the last ten years; those requiring a community college diploma grew by 3.3% and those requiring a high school education decreased by 2%.

Source: www.12.statcan.ca/english/census01/release/index.cfm.

line with other countries), and by requiring that 65% of adult immigrants have post-secondary education.[6]

Political and Legislative Factors

Governments, both provincial and federal, can influence the business environment through political programs that result in changes to laws and regulations. For example, governments that wish to improve the climate for job creation emphasize tax cuts, legislate tax incentives to develop jobs, increase job-training opportunities, and create balanced labour legislation. Governments can spur economic growth by reducing the public debt, balancing the budget, and cutting taxes. Such measures encourage businesses to invest in that province (or Canada) and encourage consumers to spend, resulting in more jobs.

The employer–employee relationship is governed by a legal framework that includes common law (judicial precedents that do not derive from specific laws), constitutional law (e.g., the Charter of Rights and Freedoms, acts of federal and provincial parliaments), and contract law (e.g., collective agreements). You are probably familiar with some of these laws. For example, each province has employment standards that establish the maximum number of hours to be worked each day and human rights legislation that prohibits discrimination on the basis of sex, race, and so on. Additionally, governments often enact legislation that affects HR practices directly. For example, the Government of Quebec mandates that every organization must spend 2% of its payroll on employee training.

The actions organizations take have to be legal, and the law is relatively clear on what is and is not legal. A company may be competing on a low-cost strategy and be able to find people willing to work for $3 an hour. The employment standards legislation in each province, however, governs the minimum wage, and in no province is it as low as $3 an hour. Therefore, cost savings have to be achieved elsewhere in order to implement a low-cost strategy; it is not possible to do it through wages that fall below the legal requirements.

The decisions that are not governed by law are usually governed by morals or an ethical code. The concept of ethics is not as clear as laws are. Ethical and moral decisions and practices go beyond the law, from "you must" to "you should." An employer can require an employee to work overtime and not pay him or her overtime rates (as required by the law). How? The employer gives the employee the title of "manager" (a category exempted from overtime regulations), even when the employee has no managerial responsibilities. Legal? Maybe, but not ethical.

Ethical issues are sometimes raised and resolved by employees, and sometimes organizations have official policies on ethics. For example, most organizations have explicit guidelines on the kinds of "gifts" (kickbacks) that employees may accept from suppliers. But most HRM ethical decisions are much more complicated. Should a company produce goods in a country that employs child labour? Should an organization eliminate one unit (laying off the staff in the process) only to subcontract the work to an outside supplier that employs workers at one-half the compensation rates? Obviously, these ethical decisions affect strategy formulation and implementation.

Technological Factors

What is technology? Technology is the process by which inputs from an organization's environment are transformed into outputs. Technology includes tools, machinery, equipment, and software. Technology has already had a large impact on human resources and is predicted to continue to do so at an even faster pace—it took 75 years for telephones to reach an audience of 50 million people; 13 years for television and only 4 years for the World Wide Web to reach the same number.[7] Box 3.5 outlines the impact of technology.

Every HR function has the potential to become managed electronically. The trend started with payroll and benefits. Now software is used to manage training data and succession management information. On-line counselling for managers is available. Managers can complete performance appraisals interactively. By 2005, e-learning will be the single most used application on the web.[8] As the hardware becomes smaller and the software becomes smarter, we can expect most HR functions to be managed electronically.

There are related issues. The line is blurring between personal and professional lives as employees answer e-mail on vacation and use the phone to telecommute. Issues of privacy, the protection of intellectual property, and the safeguarding of company secrets are made more difficult because of the ease of transferring information by means of technology.

BOX 3.5 Impact of Technology on Organizations

- Requires changes in skills and work habits of employees—employees have to be provided with constant training and skills are no longer viable for decades.
- Elimination of some lower level positions and layers of management—routine tasks, normally done by those lowest in the organization hierarchy, are automated, and the surviving employees need more advanced skills. Fewer managers and fewer layers of management are needed.
- Less hierarchy, more collaboration—the adoption of technology decreases the need for management as a supervisory control technique. Power has shifted from management to technical workers, who hold the knowledge about system processes.
- Telecommuting options—telecommuting is estimated to be growing at 20% per year, allows employees to locate farther from their offices, and allows employers to choose office facilities farther from major cities.
- Electronic monitoring and employee privacy (one study estimated that 90% of employees have used their employer-provided computer for personal business on company time)—27% of employers monitor employee e-mail. If an employee uses his break to access sites related to personal health-care issues, which the employer monitors, has this employee's right to privacy been violated?

Demographic Factors

demographics the study of population statistics

Demographics, the study of population statistics, affects HR profoundly. The influence of women, the greying of the workforce, and the arrival of "Gen Xs" and "Gen Ys" all influence HR policies. The supply of workers, known as "baby boomers" (those born between 1945 and 1961), exceeds the demand for them in middle management and senior ranks. The combination of the surge of workers in their fifties and the flattening of organizations has created a cadre of plateaued workers. These boomers are approaching retirement. If a person starts working at 21, retires at 55, and dies at 89, this person will have spent 34 years at work and 34 years in retirement. Most boomers don't think the money will last that long and two-thirds of them expect to work during "retirement."

"Baby busters" (those born between 1963 and the 1970s) follow behind the boomers, who have created a bottleneck in the organization. There are far fewer baby busters, and they are very well educated and trained, so can command significant incomes.

Gen X employees (those born in the late '70s and the '80s) are now entering the workforce and have lived with technology all their lives. They have fewer expectations of organizations and perceive themselves as independent agents.

Members of Gen Y, those born between 1977 and 1997, are totally comfortable with technology and have a more global and tolerant outlook than people older than they are. They are not very interested in climbing a career ladder; indeed they start with the assumption that they will change jobs frequently.

Social and Cultural Factors

Society can express its intent through laws and regulations. However, society can also exert pressure on HR in less formal ways. Employees are shaped by the norms and values of the society in which they live. One issue that is receiving increasing public attention is the right to privacy. Does the employer have a moral (and legal) right to monitor employee activities through video surveillance cameras or reading e-mail? Dow Chemical Co. terminated 50 employees and disciplined another 200 because these employees sent or distributed offensive material using the company's e-mail system. Those who downloaded, saved, or distributed the material were disciplined or terminated; those who simply opened and deleted the material were not reprimanded.[9]

Another issue is the employee's attempt to balance a personal life with an ever more encompassing work life. Research on hours worked indicates that Canadians are spending more time at work. In 2001, the province of Ontario changed its employment standards to permit 60-hour work weeks, on a voluntary basis. Critics argue that the 60-hour work week will become an implicit part of job expectations.[10] Many employees face the challenges of trying to spend quality time with their families while vigorously pursuing a career. They are in a timing bind. People are generally most active in moving ahead in their careers between the ages of 25 and 45, exactly the same stage at which most people raise their children. Both roles are demanding. Both require long hours, during the same period (6 a.m. to 10 p.m.) The demographics of the aging workforce means that working adults will be stressed by the extra demands of caring for their elderly relatives, estimated to consume about 23 hours each month.[11] Organizations have responded to this issue by increasing workplace flexibility. Some options include flextime, part-time work, job sharing, telecommuting, elder care, and child care. The issue of employee well-being is also on the collective bargaining table, with unions asking for family support benefits such as subsidies for child and elder care, and access to wellness facilities. Although the unionized workforce is changing to include more women and older workers, many of the traditional union members, such as low-wage and hourly workers, factory and service workers, and outside workers, cannot take advantage of benefits such as flexible work hours, tele-work, or on-site gyms.

Violence in the workplace is also attracting attention. One study estimates that 5% of female employees in Canada and 4% of male employees reported being physically assaulted on the job.[12] Certain jobs, such as health-care providers and those in enforcement or inspection, are at higher risk, along with those handling money and working alone at night. Environmental factors influence the adoption and implementation of specific HRM strategies. The stakeholders are another major source of influence on HR strategy.

Stakeholders

When discussing HR strategy, the natural tendency is to think only about the organization under consideration and its managers and employees. However, there is a call for an expansion of these boundaries. Many groups have an influence on the organization's strategy. These groups can be referred to as the stakeholders.

Stakeholders are groups of people who have an interest in the projects, policies, or outcomes of an organization's decisions. Sometimes called constituent groups, they follow the actions of the organization and lobby to have their interests satisfied. These stakeholders affect strategy formulation. Employees want more wages and job security, suppliers want longer-term relationships, customers want faster service, and shareholders want more dividends and higher stock prices. Organizations will often adapt their strategies to accommodate powerful stakeholders such as unions or regulatory agencies or customers. Let us look at some of these stakeholders.

stakeholder groups of people who have vested interests in an organization's decisions

Shareholders

For private organizations, the primary stakeholder is the owner or those who hold shares: the **shareholders**. Public organizations are accountable to the taxpayer (the shareholder) through a complex system of departmental hierarchies and political webs. Most CEOs interviewed on television about some major change, such as a downsizing, will reply that their responsibility is not to the employee or the public but to the shareholder.

shareholders those who own shares of a company

Customers

A second stakeholder is the customer or client. Organizations have a moral duty to provide safe, hazard-free products. This appears relatively simple to do. However, if a provider knows that a product has an infinitesimal probability of being unsafe, the costs of withdrawing the product are often weighed against the costs of litigation. Car manufacturers make this kind of decision frequently. They will absorb the liability costs of an automobile that is unsafe under atypical conditions because these costs are less than the costs of redesign, remanufacture, or recall. Another example occurs when a powerful customer demands changes from its suppliers. Clients can influence the skill level of their suppliers. Wal-Mart will train their suppliers' employees in just-in-time order processing and deal (electronically) only with those suppliers who can provide this type of service. Suppliers are forced to change to match Wal-Mart's system and to train people in the system if they want Wal-Mart's business.

Suppliers

Suppliers can influence the skill level of their clients' employees. Polo Ralph Lauren Canada sends its own skilled staff to the Bay to help the department store merchandise the supplier's clothing, and in doing so raise the skill level of retail clerks in this chain of department stores.

Governments

The federal government gives extensive assistance with implementing employment equity programs in federally regulated corporations, thus encouraging sensitivity, training, and skill development not only in equity matters but also generally in management of change programs.

The Public

An increasingly important stakeholder is the community at large. This is evident when a company is the sole or largest employer in a small community. In this situation, the company would be influenced in its strategic decisions by the need to keep the community alive, the people employed, and the environment healthy in the long term. Another example occurs with the production and distribution of products such as alcohol, or with gambling casinos, which cause great hardship and upheaval to some individuals but result in programs and services that would not necessarily be affordable under normal taxation efforts.

The public expects very large organizations to be more socially responsible. Size matters, as can be seen by the research presented in Box 3.6.

Unions

The presence of unions in the environment will affect HRM strategy for firms entering new sectors with high unionization rates. The national unionization rate remains at 28%, but another 21% of the workforce would join a union if given the choice.[13] Employees who are currently unionized within an organization can influence strategy in two ways. One is a restrictive way, in which the collective agreement limits an organization's ability to make drastic changes in working methods or jobs to accommodate changes in strategic direction. A second way is that unions now play a larger role and are more cooperative than adversarial with regard to HR practices such as gain sharing, plant locations, selection procedures, and quality improvement. Savvy HR planners keep track

BOX 3.6 Size Matters

Larger organizations adopt more sophisticated HR practices partly because acceptable economies of scale are achieved when an organization has thousands of employees. Furthermore, large organizations are more visible and subject to pressures to engage in legitimate state-of-the-art HRM practices. Compared to small organizations, larger organizations are more likely to use sophisticated staffing and training practices and are more likely to include bonuses based on profit. Job security is higher at larger companies, but smaller companies listen more to their employees.

Source: B. McConnell, "Survey: Size, Age Make a Difference in HR Strategies," *Society for HR Management*, February 2002, pp. 6 and 9.

of the policies of key unions such as the Canadian Auto Workers (CAW) because they set the benchmark for hourly workers in Canada. Any innovative benefit will filter through the economy and affect other organizations' negotiations. The key issues for unions are job security, income security, working hours, and inflation protection.[14] Unionized employees receive higher wages and have better working conditions than their non-union counterparts.[15] One potential trend that is worth watching is the rise in the unionization of managers. According to Statistics Canada, 9% of managers are unionized, and the number has been slowly climbing.[16] Managers are interested in becoming part of unions in order to deal with their compensation and workload issues.

Employees

As indicated earlier, sometimes an organization's strategy is influenced by the kinds of competencies it already possesses. If employees are motivated, committed, and flexible, an organization might be more willing to grow rapidly through numerous product introductions. If the workforce is unusually multilingual, the possibility of growing through international markets becomes more attractive. Likewise, the strengths can reside in the HR department itself. If the HR department has excelled in its ability to grow rapidly by attracting, hiring, and orienting highly qualified candidates, corporate venturing or a joint venture becomes an attainable goal. If culture management is the HR department's strength, mergers and acquisitions can be considered as a strategic option.

Top Management

Much of the research on HR planning recognizes the powerful influence of the CEO on the organization's ability to attain its goals. The concept of the rational manager is well embedded in our business psyche. We assume that the head of an organization carefully analyzes the environment—looking at competitors' actions and technological changes—and then decides the best strategy to take advantage of opportunities and corporate strengths. But hearts may be as influential as heads. Managers are more than rational actors: they have personal values, ethics, attitudes toward risk, and ambition.[17]

Research has shown that different types of strategies require different types of managers and executives. Studies of these managerial elites have found that managers with certain personalities—for example, those with a tolerance for ambiguity—managed firms with a growth strategy more successfully than those with a harvest strategy.[18] Let's take just one of these managerial traits—attitude toward risk. From readings on corporate strategy, we know that managers who are risk avoiders will take the conservative, cautious approach with an eye on "guaranteed," short-term profits. Risk takers will be willing to sacrifice short-term gains to "gamble" on long-term bigger payoffs. But these studies fail to recognize that the entire employee pool must have the necessary skills and attributes to carry out the strategy.

The purpose of this section was to demonstrate that stakeholders can have a powerful influence on the choice of strategy. Before this, you learned about the methods HR strategists use to scan the environment and the areas they are concerned with. We turn now to an illustration of how this process works.

Environment Scanning: A Case Application

Scanning must have a purpose. It must not be the collection of information just to have reports gathering dust on executive bookshelves. The information must be analyzed for its impact on the organization, and particularly for its implications for the organization's HR strategy.

In Table 3.1, we describe how this might be done by imagining how an HR planner working for a large retailer in the Canadian market would use environmental information to determine how the HR practices in a retail environment could be affected.

Summary

HRM strategy is determined primarily by organizational strategy. However, there are environmental factors that shape HRM strategy, so HR managers and planners must continually monitor the environment. Typically, they scan by reading publications, retaining memberships in professional associations, attending conferences, or using professional scanners. A number of methods, such as trend and impact analyses and the Delphi technique, are used to identify future trends. The environmental factors that are monitored include the economic climate, the labour market, the political and regulatory climate, and social norms. Stakeholders such as shareholders, unions, customers, and executives contribute strongly to the formulation and implementation of strategy.

TABLE 3.1 TRENDS AND HR IMPLICATIONS	
TREND	**HR IMPLICATIONS**
Economic	
High unemployment rates	Low consumer spending, fewer staff needed
Global competition	Internationalization, possible domestic downsizing
Labour Market	
Outsourcing	Changing spending patterns
Aging workforce/consumers	More day clients, changing staff distribution
Flexible work arrangements	Less work clothing needed, more home office leisure clothes
Globalization	Outsourcing to low-wage countries Need for managers with global competencies
Regulatory	
Pay equity	Need to review systems, allow contingency funds
Workforce rights	More complex terminations; privacy issues
Part-time benefits legislation	Increased costs of part-time employees
Technological	
E-commerce	Increased need for employees with technological skills
Computerization of work	Increased telecommuting, nontraditional offices Need for results appraisals (not face-time judgments)
Social	
Workplace violence	Development of HR policies on safety; provision of secure environment
Retirement trends	Retiring of bulk of boomers, fighting for jobs
Work–family issues	Problems recruiting nontraditional shifts
Diversity	Workforce reflecting customer demographic
Stakeholders	
Union	Increasing move to nonadversarial arrangements
Public	Demands for excellent customer service, therefore need to train and upgrade sales skills
Customers	A few large customers control type of jobs and skills
Suppliers	Demand for seamless connections, need for employees
Top management	Move to recruit global executives

KEY TERMS

Delphi technique, 57
demographics, 65
environmental scanning, 54
impact analysis, 57
shareholder, 67
stakeholder, 67
trend analysis, 57

Suggested Websites

http://hrmanagement.ca This website is a virtual HR consultant for small and medium-sized businesses that do not have an HR professional on staff. The information is customized by province and grouped into categories such as recruitment, pay and benefits, employment standards, and terminations.

www.hrdc-drhc.gc.ca The website of Human Resources Development Canada is a good place to look for well-researched articles on trends in collective agreements, work–life balance, and other topics of interest to students and employers.

www.hrreporter.com The website of the *Canadian HR Reporter* magazine contains recent articles about HR trends, practices, changes in legislation, etc.

www.hc-sc.gc.ca/hppb/fitness/work A Health Canada website that offers trends in health and wellness.

www.jobquality.ca An excellent website of the Work Network of Canadian Policy Research Networks, which tracks trends in work issues, such as rewards, job rotation, health and safety, etc.

Discussion Questions

1. *Workforce* magazine has chronicled 80 events that have shaped HR (January 2002 issue, Vol. 81, No. 1, pages 26–56). These issues range from the creation of the Kelly Girl (first temp worker) to Cool Work (Ben and Jerry's credo that work should be fun). After you have read this article, identify an issue, and then describe why this issue was significant and what were the implications for HR policies and practices.
2. Current HR policies seem to be based on the assumption of a traditional career trajectory and a traditional life pattern of marriage, children, and retirement. What percentage of Canada's workforce fits the stereotype? What HR policies should be changed to adapt to the reality you discover in your research?
3. The events of September 11, 2001 ("9/11"), had the biggest impact on the aviation industry since World War Two. Assess the impact of 9/11 on employees in the aviation sector, and as an HR professional, outline what you would do to alleviate these impacts.

Exercises: The Nominal Group Technique

1. Form a group of four to six people. If you are working with a group of students, you will be discussing the future of the student role, or "job." If you are working with a group of people in the same occupation or job, your

group will be discussing the future of that occupation or job. Appoint a group leader.

2. Ask everyone to individually list the trends that may change, at some likely future time, the work methods or work outcomes for the "job" under consideration. Try a time span of three, five, or ten years. (Allow 15 minutes for this step.)
3. Each person then states the first item on his or her list and records this item on a flip chart or green board so that others can see it.
4. Each person, in turn, continues to state items until all are listed. If an item is mentioned more than once, the group leader asks for the number of people who listed this item. That number is recorded beside the item to give a rating of frequency.
5. Ask each person to discuss the relevance of his or her item to the job.
6. Ask each person to assign a rating from 1 to 10 to each item on the flip chart, 1 being the most important influence on the job and 10 being the least important. This is a rating of importance.
7. Analyze the results.
8. Use these results to prepare a group report on the future of the job.
9. Present this report to the class.

After the presentations, discuss the challenges of predicting the future in this manner. Should HR planners not scan the environment because of these problems? Is there a better way?

(Note that many of these steps can be done with group software, such as Lotus Notes.)

Case: Work–Life Family Balance

Magda Hyshka, manager of HR policies for the largest telecommunications company in Canada, TelPlus, had been asked by her director of HR to develop an innovative policy to address the work–family issues facing the company. As part of her research, Magda uncovered the following facts:

- Workers spend an average of 62 minutes a day (or ten days a year) commuting to and from work.
- Forty-six percent of workers reported moderate to high levels of stress in 1999, compared to 64% in 1989; one in five workers reported high levels of stress in 1991—this changed to one in three in 1999; 10% of the workforce was depressed in 1999; two out of five disability claims were due to depression or anxiety in 1999.
- Three-quarters of female employees felt that commitment to families is a barrier to career advancement; 41% report postponing pregnancy or not having a child at all.

- Twenty-seven percent of employees report moderate to high levels of stress from balancing work and family responsibilities, an increase of 75% in a decade.
- Technology enabled employees to work seven days a week and at any time during the day or night, and many felt that they were expected to be available (on-line) all the time.
- Since the events of September 11, 2001, many Canadians are rethinking their commitment to work, with 81% intending to spend more time on personal matters and less on the job.

Magda had also researched information from the United States, recognizing that Canada tends to lag behind the hot issues in the United States:

- The U.S. Bureau of Labor Statistics reported that work hours have been increasing steadily over the last decade. Twenty-five million Americans worked at least 49 hours per week, and 11 million Americans worked 59 hours a week.
- Forty-six percent of employees feel overworked and overwhelmed and lack the time to step back and reflect on their work; 61% say they would give up pay to spend more time with their families; 36% state that they would be willing to take a pay cut to have a shorter commute.
- Demographers predict that more than half the children born in the 1990s will be raised in a family home with both parents living with them; 62% of women with children under six are employed, and mothers with preschoolers make up the fastest-growing segment of the workforce. Forty-four percent of Americans between the ages of 45 and 55 have aging parents as well as children under 21.
- Paradoxically, the number of Americans living alone has surpassed the number of married couples with children.

Sources: Y.A. Laroche, *Fine Balance*. Ottawa: Canadian Centre for Management Development, 2000; D. Patel, *Workplace Visions*. Alexandria, Virginia: SHRM, Vol. 4, No. 2, 2002.

QUESTION

Continue the research started by Magda. Prepare a report summarizing your findings and recommending policies that will help your employees cope with work–family balance issues.

REFERENCES

Brown, D. 2001. "Following Nortel's Lead? Really?" *Canadian HR Reporter*, Vol. 15, No. 20 (November 19).

———. 2002. " Are You Prepared for the New Economy?" *Canadian HR Reporter*, Vol. 14, No. 3 (February 12): 1, 7.

———. 2002. "Ottawa Unveils National Training and Development Strategy." *Canadian HR Reporter*, Vol. 15, No. 5 (March 11): 3 and 6.

———. 2002. "CAW–Big Three Negotiations Set the Mark." *Canadian HR Reporter*, Vol. 15, No. 12 (June 17): 3 and 12.

Burack, E.H., and N.J. Mathys. 1987. *Human Resource Planning: A Pragmatic Approach to Manpower Staffing and Development*, 2nd ed. Lake Forest, Ill.: Brace-Park Press.

Currie, M.B., and D. Black. 2001. "E-merging Issues in the Electronic Workplace." *Ivey Business Journal*, Vol. 65, No. 3 (January/February): 18–29.

Duncan, L. 2002. "An Ounce of Prevention: Ending Workplace Violence." *Canadian Employment Safety and Health Guide*, Vol. 256 (January): 3.

Gupta, A., and V. Govindarajan. 1984. "Business Unit Strategy Managerial Characteristics, and Business Unit Effectiveness at Strategy Implementation." *Academy of Management Journal*, Vol. 27: 25–41.

Guth, W.D., and R. Tagiuri. 1965. "Personal Values and Corporate Strategy." *Harvard Business Review*, Vol. 43, No. 5 (September–October): 123–132.

Lawler, E.E., and S.A. Mohram. 1987. "Unions and the New Management." *Academy of Management Executives*, Vol. 26, No. 1: 293–300.

"Longer Work Weeks Unhealthy: Critics," *Canadian HR Reporter*, Vol. 14, No. 16 (September 24, 2001): p. 3.

Lowe, G. 1998. "The Future of Work." *Industrial Relations*, Vol. 53, No. 2 (Spring): 235–257.

Overman, S. 2002. "HR Is Partner in McDonaldizing Employees in New Countries." *HR News* (May): 7.

Patel, D. 2002–2003. *Workplace Forecast.* Alexandria, Virginia: SHRM.

Rothwell, W.J., and H.C. Kazanas. 1988. *Strategic Human Resources Planning and Management.* Englewood Cliffs, N.J.: Prentice Hall.

Tomlinson, A. 2002. "Trickle Down Effects of Retiring Boomers." *Canadian HR Reporter*, Vol. 15, No. 11 (June 3): 1 and 12.

www.statisticscanada.ca. Labour Force Survey 2000 Perspectives on Labour and Income.

Endnotes

1. Burack and Mathys, 1987.
2. Rothwell and Kazanas, 1988.
3. Lowe, 1998.
4. Brown, February 12, 2002.
5. Overman, 2002.
6. Brown, March 11, 2002.
7. Patel, 2002–03.
8. www.corporateleadershipcouncil.com, June 2002.
9. Currie and Black, 2001.

10. www.jobquality.ca or "Longer Work Weeks Unhealthy," 2001.
11. Tomlinson, 2002.
12. Duncan, 2002.
13. Brown, 2001.
14. Brown, June 17, 2002.
15. Lawler and Mohram, 1987.
16. www.statisticscanada.ca.
17. Guth and Tagiuri, 1965.
18. Gupta and Govindarajan, 1984.

4

EVALUATION OF HR PROGRAMS AND POLICIES

Chapter Goals

Aligning HRM programs and policies with organizational goals is the beginning of the strategic HR planning process. Assessing whether these policies and practices were effective is the end of one cycle in the planning process. HR professionals need to know how their programs and policies are doing.

After reading this chapter, you should be able to do the following:

1. Understand the importance of measuring the effectiveness of HRM activities.
2. Outline five aspects of HRM that can be evaluated using the 5C model for measuring effectiveness: compliance with laws and regulations, client satisfaction, culture management to influence employee attitudes, cost control of the labour component of the budget, and the contribution of HR programs.
3. Discuss methods of measurement, such as cost–benefit analysis, utility analysis, and auditing techniques.
4. Identify the challenges in measuring HR activities.

THE SCORECARD

Corporate scorekeeping allows organizations to make the adjustments necessary to reach their goals. The scorecard, with its measures of key indicators, focuses managers' and employees' attention on what is important to the organization. Focusing on desired results increases the ability to attain the results. Scorecard measures allow us to make judgments about the relative effectiveness of various policies and practices, just as baseball scores and records allow fans to track the success of sports teams.

The model of strategic HRM planning outlined in Chapter 1 called for the measurement of the success of the plan. The tracking of customer satisfaction or absenteeism rates not only measures progress, but also pinpoints weaknesses and identifies gaps. Just as organizations keep scorecards on their financial effectiveness, so too must the HR department track the effectiveness of its programs.

THE IMPORTANCE OF EVALUATING HRM

An article in *Fortune* magazine[1] called for the abolition of the HR function, arguing that HR managers are unable to describe their contribution to value except in trendy, unquantifiable, and "wanna-be" terms. The author also proposed that efficiencies could be increased by outsourcing legislated activities (such as payroll and equity) and returning "people" responsibilities to line managers. His exact words were "Blow up the HR department." Senior executives who read *Fortune* asked themselves, "Does HR make a difference?" Does it add value? Clearly, until HR managers can talk about the contribution and value of HR activities in the numbers language of business, the HR department and the HR profession will be vulnerable to destructive proposals such as the one in the *Fortune* article.

Increasingly, the HR department is being treated like other operational units—that is, it is subject to questions about its contribution to organizational performance. In the simplest terms, HRM must make a difference; if it doesn't, it will be abolished. Decision-makers within organizations view HR activities, such as training courses, as expenses. They view results as value. The deliverables, not the processes such as training, are what make a difference to the organization. Measurement of the HR function is critical for improving both the credibility and the effectiveness of HR. If you cannot measure contribution, you cannot manage it or improve it. What gets measured gets managed and improved.

Business is a numbers game. Some surveys have shown that HR practitioners, while familiar with some numbers (such as the number of people employed in the organization), can't always recite other key numbers (such as the sales volumes, market share, profit levels, and rates of return for their organization). When asked to assess their contribution, most HR professionals describe it in such terms as "number of training courses" or "new hires." They do not provide numbers for outcomes. They say things such as "One hundred and twenty people attended the training course," and rarely "The training courses resulted in a 15% improvement in customer satisfaction."

Resistance

Some HR managers resist measuring their work. They argue that HR activities cannot be measured, since outcomes such as employee attitudes or managerial productivity are impossible to calibrate meaningfully or precisely. They assert that they cannot control the labour market. But the finance department cannot control the inflation rate, and the marketing department has little control over product quality, and yet each of these departments measures its activities and is accountable for results. Measuring is expensive, but not as expensive as continuing an ineffective program.

Very few organizations measure the impact of HRM. About two-thirds of HR professionals in Fortune 500 companies measure HR productivity.[2] Interest in measuring HR is growing slowly, fuelled by

- business improvement efforts across organizations,
- attempts to position HR as a strategic partner, and
- the need for objective indicators of success to accompany the analysis of HR activities.

Deutsche Bank is a leader in the measurement—or metrics—of HR, because it reports human capital metrics in its annual report, as reported in Box 4.1. When introducing a new compensation scheme or training program, the proposer will have to be prepared to justify costs with predicted results, expressed in the numbers language of business. We will show you how to do this later in the chapter.

Rationale

Determining the quantitative impact of HR programs is so important that the Society for Human Resources Management, the largest HR association in the United States, has designated *HRM impact* as a top research priority and is funding research in this area.

There are seven compelling reasons for measuring HRM effectiveness:

1. Labour costs are most often a firm's largest controllable cost.
2. Managers recognize that employees make the difference between the success and failure of projects and organizations. Good performance can be rewarded objectively.

BOX 4.1 Human Capital Metrics

Deutsche Bank publishes indicators as part of its strategy to remain an attractive employer and maintain a balance of interest among employees, shareholders, customers, and society. In addition to numbers such as head counts, which are normally published in annual reports, Deutsche Bank provides the following information.

	2000	1999	1998
Employee commitment index	72	66	n/a
Absentee rate	2.3%	2.4%	2.7%
Employees leaving bank for a new job	7.8%	6.8%	5.7%
Expenses for training (in euros)	237.2	222.4	201.7
Employees purchasing shares	65%	65%	62%
Managers in Global Equity Plan	77%	79%	83%

Sources: www.db.com; and S. Gates, "How to Improve Human Capital Measurement," *IHRIM Journal*, Vol. 6, No. 6, November 2002, pp. 18–25.

3. Organizations have legal responsibilities to ensure that they are in compliance with laws governing the employer–employee relationship.
4. Evaluations are needed to determine which HR practices are effective because, at this point, managers and HR professionals cannot distinguish between a fad and a valid change program.[3] Professor Terry Wagar, of St. Mary's University, in Halifax, Nova Scotia, has studied fads and determined that many of the practices are not integrated with other HR systems, and that they are fragile and do not survive.[4] For example, take a current fad: emotional intelligence. There is little, if any, empirical evidence that emotional intelligence is correlated with either individual performance or organizational performance, according to Professor Victor Catano of St. Mary's University.[5] Professor Simon Taggar of Wilfrid Laurier University teaches students about validity by having them complete the emotional intelligence survey and feeding them randomly generated responses that are identical for every student. He then asks students to assess how valid their individual feedback is and how accurately the survey describes their personalities. Most feel that the feedback, with one or two exceptions, describes them well (although people who read horoscopes are left with the same impressions). He then asks the critical question: "Would you recommend this survey to your employer as a valid selection?" Most would, and then he reveals the procedure he has used to teach about validity.
5. Measuring and benchmarking HR activities will result in continuous improvements. Performance gaps can be identified and eliminated.
6. Audits will bring HR closer to the line functions of the organization.[6]
7. Data will be available to support resource allocations.[7]

The next section describes the areas in which HRM departments can be evaluated.

THE 5C MODEL OF HRM IMPACT

Executives, investors, customers, and HR professionals themselves make judgments in many ways about the effectiveness of the HR function. The numerous areas that are judged can be grouped into five clusters—the 5 Cs of evaluating HRM: compliance, client satisfaction, culture management, cost control, and contribution.[8]

COMPLIANCE

Senior management depends on HR expertise to ensure that organizational practices comply with the law. Many HR departments were started because of the need to record compliance with employment standards, such as hours worked and overtime payments. Legislation dealing with the employer–employee relationship is increasing. The areas of safety, health, employment equity, and industrial relations are all highly regulated. Indeed, some people estimate that 20% to 30% of the increase in the salaries of HR professionals is due to the need to trust someone with the responsibility for compliance.

Highly publicized cases of safety violations in which board members of industrial organizations have been fined hundreds of thousands of dollars or threatened with jail time serve as another wake-up call. Other public cases that have cost organizations not only the expense of fines but also loss in business have occurred because managers have been held responsible for the sexual harassment of their subordinates. HR can make a difference by ensuring that managers and employees comply with the law, thus saving the company legal costs, fines, and damaging publicity.

CLIENT SATISFACTION

Across Canada, many organizations are tracking their success by measuring customer satisfaction or soliciting input on client complaints and attitudes. These measures have been found to predict financial performance, on a lagged basis. This means that if employee morale drops, management can expect to see customer satisfaction levels drop in about six months.

Stakeholders are important. Stakeholders, who include external and internal clients, are those people who can influence or must interact with the HR department. External clients of HR are candidates for positions, suppliers of HR services such as technology, and government regulators. Internal clients include employees grouped by occupation, union leaders, and managers.

Managers are turning to client or stakeholder perceptions of the HR department for input about the effectiveness of HR performance. This approach stems from earlier efforts in total quality management and tries to reconcile the gaps between client expectations and levels of satisfaction. The bigger the gap, the less effective the HR department. This qualitative approach surveys stakeholders, such as managers and unions, about their perceptions of the effectiveness of the HR function. "Keeping the clients happy" has important political reverberations for the HRM department, as "clients" such as the CEO control the purse strings and have the authority to approve HR policies and programs.

ADVANTAGES OF MEASURING CLIENT SATISFACTION

The advantages of measuring client satisfaction with the HR department include the following:[9]

- Measuring client satisfaction reminds the HR department that it is indeed a "service" that must deal with the expectations of its clients. The clients, in turn, use assessment criteria that are important to them, such as response time and helping them to meet their goals.
- Surveying clients about their unmet needs increases the credibility of the HR function.
- Initiating and managing change by surveying stakeholders before, during, and after a change program increase the possibility that the HR department will understand the clients' perceptions, identify resistance to change and thereby overcome such resistance, and prove that the change program meets its goals.

METHODS OF MEASURING CLIENT SATISFACTION

Information can be gathered from clients in several ways.

INFORMAL FEEDBACK

Stakeholder perceptions can be obtained informally, as part of the feedback process, whenever the HR professional is undertaking an assignment or completing a routine task such as filling a position. People can simply be asked if they are satisfied with the service.

Informal feedback is of limited use, however, for several reasons. Line managers may be reluctant to give honest feedback face to face; an individual HR officer may not be able to see patterns in the feedback as there is no method for measuring the frequency of problems; and HR professionals have little incentive to report negative feedback to superiors in the organizational hierarchy. For these reasons, a more systematic method must be developed to identify gaps in the performance of the HR department.

SURVEYS

Surveys can be used to solicit feedback confidentially, anonymously, and from a larger number of stakeholders. One approach is to list the HR activities, such as selection, and ask specific questions about them, such as questions about satisfaction with the time it takes to fill a vacant position. Some questions that might be included in such a survey are

- To what degree do you find the HR department cooperative?
- How would you rate the quality of service given?
- To what degree are HR employees available to deal with problems?
- Do you have confidence in HR advice?
- How would you rate the effectiveness of HR solutions?
- What is your opinion on processing time?
- To what extent does HR understand the needs of your department?
- Overall, how satisfied are you with the HR department?

Another survey, developed by Ulrich,[10] asks managers to rate the quality of the various roles that HR plays in strategy formulation. Box 4.2 contains a sample of the questions used in this survey.

Managers could be asked to list the chief strengths and principal weakness of the HR department. Line managers could be asked questions about what the HR department has been doing particularly well or particularly poorly, what it should not be doing, how it could contribute more effectively, and so on.[11]

Critical Incident Method

In the critical incident method, clients are asked to describe a situation in which the HR department provided assistance that was particularly useful, the consequences of this help, and why it was seen as helpful. Similarly, they are asked to describe a situation in which the assistance was not at all useful, and why. Clients' responses help the HR department identify issues and services that affect unit effectiveness.

Problems with Measuring Client Satisfaction

Measuring client satisfaction is not without its weaknesses.

BOX 4.2 HR Role Assessment Survey

The following is a sample of the type of survey clients can expect.

Please rate your satisfaction with the HR department on the following items (1=low; 5=high):*

HR helps the organization accomplish business goals.

HR participates in the process of defining business strategies.

HR makes sure that HR strategies are aligned with business strategies.

HR is effective because it can measure how it helps make strategy happen.

HR is a business partner.

*The selected items measure the strategic role of HR.

Source: D. Ulrich, *Human Resource Champions.* Boston: Harvard Business School Press, 1996.

High Expectations of Clients

The goal of surveying clients is to identify gaps between their expectations and their satisfaction. If the clients in one business unit have extremely high expectations, their dissatisfaction scores will also be high, even though the level of HR service is constant across units. The temptation on the part of the HR department might be to promise or commit to less with regard to programs so as to appear to have performed better.

Conflicting Expectations

Another problem occurs when different stakeholders have competing or conflicting expectations. The employee group may desire extensive counselling (a nurturing role) from the HR department, while senior managers may be concerned about maximizing productivity per employee (an efficiency goal). One group will be dissatisfied because it is difficult for the HR department to be both nurturing and efficient.

Professional Affiliations

Furthermore, gaps between expectations and performance may occur because HR professionals are more closely tied to the norms and values of their profession than to the norms of managers or line operators.[12] For example, line managers may value how fast a job is filled, while the HR professional may value the creation of a valid selection test. In other words, the HR professional may be trying to do what is right in the profession ("validate the selection test"), rather than what managers consider important ("just hire someone fast").

Whatever the problems with the client satisfaction approach, the important message is that the viability of the HR function depends to a large extent on stakeholder perceptions of value and effectiveness. These must be measured and managed.

Culture Management

culture a set of important beliefs that members of a community share

attitudes perceptions or opinions about organizational characteristics

Highly effective organizations seek to influence employee attitudes through the development of an appropriate culture that will support optimum performance. (Remember that **culture** can be defined as the set of important beliefs that members of a community share—"the way we do things around here.") Executives carefully monitor cultural programs (such as that of empowerment) through attitude surveys of employees. The results of these surveys can then be linked to the objective results of the department.

The assumption underlying the culture management model is that HR practices can have a positive influence on employee attitudes, which in turn influence employee performance.

Attitudes, in an organizational context, can be defined as perceptions or opinions about organizational characteristics. Some examples include the attitudes expressed in these statements: "I think that management expects too much for the resources it gives me," or "I feel that I can talk to management about any problems I am experiencing." The most frequently measured attitudes in the organization are job satisfaction and commitment. Surveys of satisfaction and commitment measure attitudes toward supervisors, colleagues, pay, promotions, and the work itself. The research supports the proposition that attitude affects behaviour. Highly committed employees will make personal sacrifices for the job, perform beyond normal expectations, work selflessly, endure difficult times, and will not leave the organization for personal gain.[13] A landmark study of 800 Sears stores demonstrated that for every 5% improvement in employee attitudes, customer satisfaction increased by 1.3% and corporate revenue rose by 0.5%.[14]

Organizations should pay attention to employee attitudes and should attempt to manage the culture to improve individual and organizational performance.

Cost Control

Traditional organizations continue to see personnel as an expense. The labour component of the production process in service organizations, such as universities and government departments, is an organization's single largest expense. This cost represents up to 85% of the expenses in white-collar organizations. The costs of employees consists of pay and benefits, the cost of absenteeism, and the cost of turnover. HR practices can reduce labour costs by reducing the workforce while attempting to get the same volume of work done with fewer employees. One of the most frequently used ways to cut labour costs is to increase the use of technology. Technology to process benefits claims and pursue e-learning has replaced HR staff, resulting in cost savings of about 30%.[15]

HR departments can reduce expenses associated with employees in at least two other ways. The first is to increase the efficiencies of those working (i.e., achieve the same results at lower costs or faster speeds), and the second is to reduce the costs associated with behaviours such as absences or accidents that are, to some extent, under the control of the employee.

Increasing Efficiency

Efficiency is expressed in terms of the results achieved (outputs) in comparison to the resource inputs. Measures of efficiency include the following:

efficiency results achieved compared to resource inputs

- Time (e.g., average time to fill an opening, process a benefits claim)
- Volume (e.g., the number of people interviewed to fill a job, the number of requests processed per employee)
- Cost (e.g., cost per training hour or per test)

HR managers should measure these resource inputs and then attempt to improve the measurements—examples of which are listed in Box 4.3—over time or across units. The use of benchmarks is critical in comparing one organization's efficiency ratios against the best in the field. Data revealing a cost per hire of $500 or turnover rates of 15% are meaningless without relevant comparison

BOX 4.3 Examples of Efficiency Measures

Cost

Ratio of compensation expense to total operating expense
Benefit cost per employee covered
Ratio of benefits expense to total operating expense
Processing costs per benefit claim
Administration costs per benefit claim
Cost per training day
Cost per trainee per program

Volume

Number of training days
Number of interviews per selection
Ratio of filled positions to authorized positions
Percentage of employees with formal performance evaluations
Percentage of designated employees

Response Time

Time between requisition and filling of position
Time to process benefits
Time from identifying a training need to program implementation
Time to respond to requests by category

points. For example, a turnover rate of 15% among senior executives indicates a problem; a turnover rate of 15% in a fast-food restaurant is very low.

The ratios generated must be interpreted and analyzed by comparisons made over time, across departments, and against the benchmarks of best practices. These benchmarks allow the HR manager to make the following kinds of statements: "The cost per hire is $500, which is $50 less than last year and $60 less than another company. That shows we are doing a better job than we did last year and than other HR departments."

These efficiency measures must be managed with effectiveness in mind. Conceptually, it is possible to reduce training costs to zero, but the performance of employees would suffer in the long run. Therefore, most companies add a qualifier to the ratio when judging efficiency. For example, lowering the cost per trainee would be acceptable only if job performance remained the same or improved.

Cost of Employee Behaviour

The costs of absenteeism, turnover, and occupational injuries and illnesses can all be measured, benchmarked, and managed. Any introductory textbook in HRM will describe how to measure these factors and will provide prescriptions for reducing the costs related to them. To control the expenses associated with employees, organizations should carefully track and compare the rates of absenteeism, turnover, and occupational injuries and illnesses. Here are some figures to think about: the number of short-term absences has doubled from 2% of payroll in 1997 to 4.2% in 2000, with a direct cost of $3440 per employee.[16] The costs of turnover, which include termination, replacement, loss of revenue when the position is vacant, and the learning time for new employees to become productive, are estimated at between six and eighteen months of the employee's annual compensation. At Taco Bell, the stores with the lowest turnover yielded double the sales and 55% higher profits than stores with the highest turnover rates.[17] Box 4.4 provides an example of how a smoking cessation program for employees can result in cost savings.

In keeping with the trend to view employees as investments, and not just as expenses, the next section examines how organizations measure the return on this investment.

Contribution

Unless HR can demonstrate its impact on the bottom line, it will continue to be seen as "overhead," as a department that grabs resources while contributing nothing. Many executives feel that it is time for the HR department to identify and evaluate its contribution, as other departments are expected to do.

The thesis underlying the contribution model is that HRM practices shape the behaviour of employees within an organization, and thus help the organization achieve its goals. In other words, the effective management of people makes a difference to how well an organization functions. Research has shown that HR practices can affect organizational performance in measurable ways. Studies have established that sophisticated and integrated HRM practices have a positive effect on employee performance: they increase knowledge, skills, and

BOX 4.4 The Costs of Smoking

Decades of research have established that smoking is addictive, and that it is a health hazard. The costs to society of smoking include those associated with health care and income loss. The costs to organizations include those associated with absenteeism, medical care, morbidity and premature mortality, insurance, property damage and depreciation, maintenance, and passive smoking effects. It is estimated that about 35 minutes a day are lost to smoking, resulting in 18.2 lost days per year per employee. Smokers are absent three more days per year than nonsmokers. Furthermore, each smoker increases by about one-fifth the expenses incurred by nonsmokers (through involuntary smoke inhalation). If an employer were to forbid smoking for a year, the total cost saving per employee per year would, it is estimated, be around $3000 (U.S.). However, it may be illegal to prohibit smoking on company property. In a case involving Cominco Ltd. and the United Steelworkers of America, Locals 9705 and 480, the arbitrator ruled nicotine addiction is a disability similar to alcoholism or drug addiction and that Cominco's policy of no smoking on company property discriminates against heavily addicted smokers. Under section 13(1)(b) of British Columbia's Human Rights Code, discrimination in employment on the basis of physical or mental disability is prohibited. This case could set a precedent across the country.

Sources: Adapted from W.F. Cascio, *Costing Human Resources: The Financial Impact of Behaviour in Organizations*, 3rd ed., Kent Series in Human Resource Management. Boston: PWS Kent, 1991; and B. Delaney, "Smoking Breaks: How Frequent," *Canadian HR Reporter*, FAQ's www.canadianhrreporter.com, 2003.

abilities; improve motivation; reduce shirking; and increase retention of competent employees. These best practices have a direct and economically significant effect on a firm's financial performance.

How HR Contributes to Organizational Performance

Empirical studies have established some important findings:

- Organizations that used employee involvement practices (information sharing, rewards, skills training, etc.) reported a 66% higher return on sales, a 20% higher return on assets and investments, and a 13% higher return on equity.[18]
- Specific HR practices have been found to positively and significantly affect the financial performance of a company. For example, flexible work arrangements are associated with a 3.5% gain in market value, while 360-degree feedback systems negatively affect market value by 5%.[19]
- Fifteen percent of a firm's relative profit can be attributed to HR strategy.[20]
- HR systems can affect a firm's market valued by $15 000 to $45 000 per employee.[21]
- HR can affect the probability of survival of a new venture by as much as 22%.[22]
- HR can improve the knowledge, skills, and abilities of a firm's current and potential employees, increase their motivation, reduce shirking, and enhance retention of quality employees while encouraging nonperformers to leave the firm.[23]
- An increase in sophisticated HR practices of one standard deviation raises sales per employee by an average of $27 000 (U.S.) for one year, increases profits by $3814 (U.S.) per employee, and decreases turnover by 7%.[24] The advantages to employees of these high-performance firms may be higher wages and benefits and greater job security.
- Investments in HRM do pay off: proactive firms that plan for future labour needs and make investments in recruitment and selection for the job at the outset are rewarded with higher labour productivity. Firms that systematically develop their employees receive a productivity payoff.[25]

We will look now at two ways of measuring contribution: financial measures and measures of managerial perceptions of effectiveness.

Financial Measures

Survival

Private or for-profit organizations can measure a dramatic indicator of success: survival. This can be considered a zero-sum index. If the company survives—that is, does not go bankrupt or cease business—the organization is a success. Survival is the first measure of effectiveness, and the contributions of HRM practices should be judged against this life-or-death index. When researchers tracked the survival rates over five years of new organizations listed on the stock exchange, they found that HR practices were associated with this ultimate measure of a firm's performance.[26] This crude measure is not satisfying for most businesspeople, however, because it doesn't give relative measures of success. (Teachers who give a pass or fail, rather than an A, B, C, D, or F grade, leave the same sense of dissatisfaction among students.) Most employees desire a relative measure and will even ask, "How am I doing compared to the others?" at performance evaluation interviews. The most common measures of business success provide these points of comparison, which allow judgments to be made across divisions, companies, and even sectors. They are the bottom-line measures such as profits.

Profits or Return on Investments

All companies track sales, or revenues, return on investments **(ROI),** return on equity **(ROE),** expenses relative to sales, and other financial ratios. These indices measure the relative success of an organization in meeting its goals. Any HRM practice that contributes to these measurements would be endorsed by senior management. Measuring the impact of HRM investments in training or performance appraisal allows HR professionals to use the same language (e.g., basic costs, ROI) as other corporate units and provides a rational way of making decisions. Box 4.5 illustrates how this might work.

ROI return on investments

ROE return on equity

There are some limitations to financial analyses, however. They capture certain immediate aspects of performance, but they do not capture managerial perceptions of effectiveness.

Measures of Managerial Perceptions of Effectiveness

Sometimes financial measures are not available to researchers who are studying privately owned organizations, and sometimes financial measures are not appropriate for publicly owned companies. It is meaningless to talk about government departments in relation to profits, for example. Therefore, other measures have been sought. One method is to ask managers to assess their organization's performance relative to the performance of sector competitors.[27] Despite the biases that could be introduced into such a measure, these perceptions have been found to correlate positively with objective measures of a firm's performance.[28] The principal advantage of using a perceptual measure such as this one is the ability to compare profit-seeking firms with public organizations.

Templer and Cattaneo[29] argue that organizational effectiveness is not easily defined. Measures beyond survival and those discussed above may include the following: the achievement of one group's political objectives at the expense of a competing interest group, and the adaptation of an organization to its environment (which obviously contains an element of the survival measure).

The measure that supersedes all of these may be one of goal optimization.[30] Templer and Cattaneo combined these various perspectives to conclude that "an

BOX 4.5 Return on Investment Example

Safety Incentive Program: National Steel

National Steel was concerned about its safety record and was experiencing unacceptable accident frequency rates, accident severity rates, and total accident costs. A performance analysis indicated that the employees knew and understood safety guidelines and practices, so training was not the issue. The Central Safety committee felt that incentives were needed to motivate safe behaviour. The incentive plan was to offer each employee $75 cash (after taxes) for every six months without a medical treatment case. The committee established goals of reducing accident frequency from 60 to 20, and the disabling frequency rate from 18 to 0. They tracked the number of medical treatment cases, lost-time accidents, lost-time days, accident costs, hours worked, and incentive costs.

The costs over four years were as follows:

	Year 1 Before plan	Year 2 Before plan	Year 3 After plan	Year 4 After plan
Needs assessment costs	$1200	$1200	N/A	N/A
Plan administration/evaluation	$1600	$1600	N/A	N/A
Safety incentive pay-outs	$58 013	$80 730	N/A	N/A
Cost of accidents	$468 360	$578 128	$18 058	$19 343
Total costs accidents + prevention	$468 360	$578 128	$78 871	$102 873

ROI Calculation

The cost of the annual incentive payout (two-year average) plus annual administrative plan cost was $72 172. The benefits were calculated as an annual improvement of $431 372 (accident costs for year 1 and 2 totalled $1 046 488 for an average of $523 244 annually; accident costs for years 3 and 4 averaged $90 872, for an annual improvement of $431 372).

An interesting twist in this case is that managers were asked what contributed to these improvements, and they estimated that 80% was due to the incentive program and 20% to their renewed managerial attention. So the calculations of benefits were revised to indicate that 80% of the annual improvement ($345 898) was due to the incentive program.

$$\text{ROI of the safety incentive program} = \frac{\text{Net benefits}}{\text{Costs}} = \frac{\$345\ 898 - \$72\ 172}{\$72\ 172}$$

$$= 3.79 \times 100 = 379\%$$

Source: Adapted from *Human Resources Scorecard* by Phillips J., S. Stone, and P.P. Phillips, pp. 439–448, copyright © 2001, with permission of Elsevier Science.

effective organization is one in which the behaviour of employees contributes towards the attainment of organizational goals and enables the long-term adaptation of the organization to its environment"—that is, survival and effectiveness.

Which is the best measure of HRM performance? Managers will choose whichever of the 5C measures meets their needs for information. Some will require measurement of all the five Cs; others will focus on one important indicator, such as cost control. Some companies are moving toward a balanced approach. The **balanced scorecard** rests on the assumption that any successful business satisfies the requirements of investors (financial performance mea-

balanced scorecard a balanced set of measures to show contribution to organizational performance

sures), customers (market share, customer commitment, and retention), and employees (employee satisfaction and organization commitment).[31]

We have examined five areas in which HR practices and policies should be tracked. Now we turn to an examination of the various approaches to measuring the effectiveness of HR policies, practices, and programs.

Approaches to Measuring HRM Practices

This section outlines a number of quantitative and qualitative approaches to measuring the impact of HRM policies and practices. Typical ways of measuring HR activities include the following:

- Activity-based measures—the number of employees completing training; the number of employees hired
- Costing measures—the cost of the training program, the cost per hire
- Client satisfaction—the manager has a problem solved; the HR department changed an employee's benefits information quickly

Most of these methods use numbers, which can measure the impact of HRM in the language of business: costs, days lost, complaints, and so on. But the question has to be asked: Where is the added value? The next three approaches—cost–benefit analysis, utility analysis, and benchmarking—attempt to prove value.

Cost–Benefit Analysis

HRM activities, such as the process of selecting employees, cost money. Most organizations absorb the costs of these activities without conducting analyses to determine benefits. **Cost–benefit** analysis examines the relationship between the costs of a program and its benefits.

Costs included in these calculations are classified in several ways. **Direct costs** are those that are used to implement the program, such as the cost of selection tests or training materials. **Indirect costs** are those that an organization absorbs, such as the trainee's time away from work. Indirect costs are often unrecognized, and sometimes are not included in cost–benefit analyses. Box 4.6 contains an example of a cost–benefit analysis.

Most programs can be subjected to a cost–benefit analysis if hard data are available, or the value of a program can be estimated from soft measures such as supervisors' estimates of productivity.

cost–benefit analysis the relationship between the costs of a program and its benefits

direct costs the hard costs that can be measured by expenditures

indirect costs the soft costs whose value can be estimated but not measured easily by financial expenditures

Utility Analysis

Senior managers are often faced with decisions about the most effective programs. For example, to motivate employees, should HR managers implement

BOX 4.6 Measuring the Contribution of HRM Practices

A wholesale produce company hired, and then fired, seven ineffective sales representatives over a two-year period. The company calculated the costs of these actions.

Costs

Training	$493 738
Recruiting	$30 100
Management time to train and terminate	$25 830
Lower profits and higher waste due to poor performance	$1 612 000
Total costs	$2 161 668

The HR department interviewed line managers to develop a profile of the ideal sales representative and identified 12 critical success factors. Then the company's HR department developed a solution involving three types of training:

- Behaviour-based interview training for managers
- A training program for newly hired sales representatives to accelerate performance readiness or weed out those who didn't meet the standards
- Performance counselling training for managers so that they could learn to discuss performance problems and ensure that trainees accepted responsibility for their own learning and performance

The cost to implement these three programs was $15 400 (development and attendance costs).

The savings that resulted from this solution were then calculated.

Savings

Cost of the problem	$2 161 668
Cost of the solution	– $15 400
Total savings	$2 146 268

The cost–benefit ratio is as follows:

$$\frac{\$2\ 146\ 268}{\$15\ 400} = 139:1$$

Source: Adapted from D.M. Burrows, "Increase HR's Contributions to Profits," *HR Magazine*, September 1996, pp. 103–110. Reprinted with the permission of *HR Magazine*, published by the Society for Human Resource Management (www.shrm.org), Alexandra, VA.

a leadership training program or a pay-for-performance program for new supervisors? To hire the best candidate, should HR managers use peer interviews or the new selection test? HR managers would have much to gain if they were able to estimate if program A provided a greater return than program B. The training director, for example, could argue that grouping 100 managers in a classroom for training is more expensive and less effective than e-learning.

utility analysis a method of determining the gain or loss that results from different approaches

A tool that calculates, in dollar terms, the costs and probable outcomes of decisions would assist HR managers in making choices between programs. **Utility analysis** is such a tool. It is a method of determining the gain or loss to the organization that results from different courses of action. Faced with a decision, managers could use utility analysis to help them choose the strategy that produces the outcomes the organization is seeking.[32] This method measures the utilities (gains and losses) by using behavioural or cost accounting procedures. It seeks to quantify, in dollars, the value of improvements in HR activities, particularly selection. In utility analysis, which is an extension of cost–benefit analysis, the costs and benefits of alternative solutions to a problem are calculated and compared. The decision-maker then can use the quantitative data that result from utility analysis to choose the alternative with the highest net value. Box 4.7 provides an example of how utility analysis can be used to reach a decision.

Utility analyses have been used in various studies. Selection using assessment centres instead of first-level management assessment was found to have a utility, over four years, of about $12 000 (U.S.) in improved job performance per manager.[33] However, the computations involved are beyond the competencies of most managers. If you are interested in knowing more about this topic, see the book by Alan Saks of the University of Toronto (*Research, Measurement and Evaluation of Human Resources*) for a detailed treatment of decision-making using utility analysis.

Auditing and Benchmarking

A plan needs an audit. An **audit** measures progress against goals. If the goal of the HR function is to train 100 managers, at some point data need to be gathered to determine if that goal was achieved. Every other department is held accountable for its goals. Audits keep the HR department on track and are the primary tool to assess current performance to develop action plans and future goals.[34] Audits can be done annually or quarterly, but a consistent checking against the plan ensures no year-end surprises and allows managers to take corrective action. For example, if the goal is to achieve four out of five on an employee satisfaction scale, and an audit shows pockets of low satisfaction, the HR department can target those areas for remedial action before year end. The audit is not the last step in the cycle of plan, execute, and measure. The num-

audit a measurement method that assesses progress against plan

BOX 4.7 An Example of Utility Analysis

Utility analysis is statistically complex but can be illustrated by the following simple example.

An organization has a choice between two types of selection procedures (or can use neither). The utility of a selection procedure is the degree to which it results in a better quality of candidate than would have been selected if the selection procedure had not been implemented. Quality can be measured by tenure (Did the employee selected using the selection procedure remain with the organization at least one year?) or performance (Did the new employee rate above average in performance after one year?) or other objective outcomes (Did the employee sell more accounts or process more files?). The costs of using procedure one (an ability test), procedure two (peer interviews), or the usual selection method (or base rate) of managerial interviews are calculated. Then the benefits of the candidates chosen under each of the three methods are determined. If tests resulted in higher-performing candidates but cost more than the performance increase is worth, the tests have little utility. If peer reviews result in greater performance at no greater cost, peer reviews have great utility.

Source: M.L. Blum and J.C. Naylor, *Industrial Psychology: Its Theoretical and Social Foundations*, rev. ed. New York: Harper-Row, 1968.

bers used in auditing (number of dollars invested in training per employee) make sense only when compared to sector norms.

benchmarking an organized method for collecting data that can be used to improve organizational operations, through comparison with other operations

Benchmarking is an organized method for collecting data that can be used to improved organizational operations, through comparisons with other units or functions. It is a tool and can be used to accomplish the following:

- Stimulate an objective review of processes, practices, and systems
- Motivate employees to perform to a higher standard, by providing a common target for improvement
- Provide objective comparative data with best-in-class organizations
- Raise questions and stimulate discussions about better ways of operating.[35]

The process starts by targeting an area for improvement, such as university recruitment in the staffing function. Key measures are identified for comparison. In recruitment these might be cost per hire, quality of hire, processing times, and number of acceptances or rejections. The next step is to identify the best-practice organizations through publications, associations, experts, and awards ceremonies. There are four sources of benchmarking partners:

- Internal (e.g., compare university recruitment with high-tech recruitment)
- Competitive (compare exact functions)
- Sector (some conditions may differ for your organization)
- Best-in-breed organizations (whose products, culture, etc. may not be comparable). Except for competitors, many organizations are willing to share this information if there is an incentive for them, such as a copy of the report, access to your metrics, etc.

Benchmarking can be done by internal personnel or external consultants. Internal consultants have the advantage of knowing more about the organization and being trusted by the staff supplying the information. However, external auditors may be more objective, have greater numbers of outside references or benchmarks, and are more likely to convey bad news to management. Sometimes an independent body, such as the Conference Board of Canada, will act as the project manager for the benchmarking study so that confidentiality is not an issue in data collection. Obviously, the results obtained from audits can be compared with benchmarks obtained from previous years, with other organizational units, or even with other companies.

After the data have been collected and compared, the differences will be obvious. The best organization might have metrics such as a six-week processing time, while your organization processes in twelve weeks. Interviews during or after the data collection might reveal the reasons for the speed—perhaps the entire processing is done on the Internet. The goal then becomes to match the best target for each of the indices.

For instance, the training function can be examined as a percentage of payroll spent on training, training dollars spent per employee, profits per employee, training costs per hour, and so on. The results of these examinations can be compared to comparable figures for other organizations. As an example, in Canada, organizations spend about $800 per employee on training, and each employee receives about seven hours of training a year. These benchmark statistics can be used as guidelines. If statistics are available on the best-performing companies, organizations can attempt to match those figures. Read about how benchmarking helped the Bank of Montreal achieve its diversity objectives in Box 4.8.

Measuring the Worth of Employees

Many company presidents say, "Employees are our greatest assets," or, as the president of Dofasco said, "Our product is steel; our strength is people." What do they mean? There have been attempts to measure the worth of employees by counting them and then attempting to put a number value on their knowledge. Trying to assess the worth of intellectual capital or human capital in an organization is incredibly complex, and some methods are discussed in the appendix to this chapter. Our focus is not on measuring the worth of employees, however, but on measuring the effect of organizational practices and policies.

Readers interested in a fuller description of measuring HR effectiveness should consult *Research, Measurement and Evaluation of Human Resources*.[36] The choice of which measurement tool to use depends to a large extent on the organization's strategy and the stage of sophistication of its HR department. For

BOX 4.8 Metrics Drive Diversity

BMO Financial Group, which has 34 000 employees, included in its 1990 corporate strategic plan the goal of creating an equitable workforce. At that time, only 9% of female employees were executives, and 13% were in senior management, from a workforce that was 75% female. BMO has achieved remarkable success through the formation of its National Advisory Council on the Equitable Workplace, chaired by the CEO of BMO, and through other measures such as employee assistance programs, a comprehensive diversity index in the annual employee survey, goal setting, and monitoring. Here are the comparison rates of the percentages of females at senior levels:

Category	1990	2002
Vice-presidents	0%	30.8%
Executives	9	35
Senior management	13	42

PriceWaterhouseCoopers also uses metrics to measure the accomplishment of diversity goals. Three categories of metrics (communication, recruitment, and retention) assess progress toward goals. Within each category are subcategories such as "conversion of interns into hires" and "percentage increase of women partners." Meeting diversity targets is a component of executive bonuses.

Sources: Adapted from S. Black, "What Gets Measured Gets Done: Using Metrics to Support Diversity"; and S. Patten, "In 12 Years, BMO Women Execs Rise from 9 to 35%." Both in *Canadian HR Reporter*, December 16, 2002, pp. 13 and 17.

example, an HR department that continues to focus on administration in a support role to employees and managers will measure efficiencies. Reports from HR will include statements such as "Processed 1250 benefits questions; trained 10% more employees than last year." An HR department that is a business partner with line management will measure culture and employee productivity and will establish direct links with organizational performance.

The measurement of HR effectiveness is not easy. The next section outlines some of the difficulties faced by those attempting to track HR effectiveness.

CHALLENGES IN MEASURING THE IMPACT OF HRM

Measuring the effectiveness of HRM practices has been widely viewed as a progressive step in the development of HRM as a profession and the positioning of HR as a strategic partner at the boardroom table. But in fact, most organizations do not undertake this evaluation because the measurement of HRM activities is not easy and the problems in measurement are difficult to resolve. Let us look at some of the problems that arise when we attempt to measure the impact of HRM practices.

UNIVERSALITY OF BEST PRACTICES

No single best practice works in every situation. Some companies, such as banks, consist of many different companies, all with unique characteristics; in the case of banks these companies include insurance companies, discount brokerages, and venture capital firms,. The HRM policies and practices that affect performance in the bank may hinder performance in the venture capital arm. The environment and culture of the parts of the larger company are very different. For example, the routine transaction work of the bank lends itself to compensation systems based largely on base salaries, while the entrepreneurial, risk-taking nature of the venture capital firm cries out for incentive-based pay.

Furthermore, organizations and businesses may have different strategic goals. The goal of the financial sector is to maximize ROE, while the goal of the Department of Immigration may be to implement the government's immigration policy, which could include increasing the number of immigrants with certain skills. Within a single organization, the goals of one business unit may be to maximize market share (at the expense of profit), while another unit is attempting to maximize profit. These differences lead to the conclusion that the impact of HRM must be measured against unit goals, not against some generality such as growth or profits.

SEPARATION OF CAUSE AND EFFECT

The perennial problem in measuring the impact of HRM practices is separating cause and effect. For example, if a profitable company shares its profits with employees through bonuses, does the possibility of earning such a bonus make employees more productive and their companies more profitable?

Associated with the lack of confidence in the explanation of causal links between specific HRM practices and organizational performance is the observation that the culture of an organization may explain more than a specific HRM practice. The day-to-day norms of an organization may influence employee behaviour more than any specific practice. For example, if an organization is deeply committed to valuing employees, the day-to-day actions of all managers have more powerful effects than a stand-alone program such as 360-degree feedback.

Attitudes about Measuring the Impact of HRM

HR professionals may ask, What's in it for me? Measuring the impact of HRM is time-consuming and difficult and costs money, and, once done, the HR professionals may be blamed if the results aren't good.

However, researchers, and even managers, are arguing that these challenges should not be used as an excuse never to measure the effectiveness of HR practices. Without an objective estimation of the value of the HR role, the HR professional risks being marginalized at the strategy table.

Summary

This chapter attempts to close the loop in the strategic HR planning process by examining evaluation—when managers implement a plan, they need to know if the plan was successful. In addition, it is important to measure the impact of HRM, to prove the value of HR and to improve its performance. The 5C model for measuring HR effectiveness has five areas: compliance with laws and regulations, client satisfaction, culture management, cost control, and contribution. Methods to measure the impact of HRM include cost–benefit analysis, utility analysis, and audits. Benchmarking is a valuable tool that provides comparative data on key ideas and stimulates discussion about better ways to operate. There are challenges in measuring HR effectiveness, however: overall organization goals may not be applicable to all branches or subsidiary companies; it is difficult to relate cause and effect; and some HR professionals do not see the benefit in such measuring.

Key Terms

attitudes, 84
audit, 92
balanced scorecard, 90
benchmarking, 94

cost–benefit analysis, 91
culture, 84
direct costs, 91
efficiency, 85
indirect costs, 91
ROE, 89
ROI, 89
utility analysis, 92

Suggested Websites

www.physicianrecruiter.com/dept/ff/5981.htm An example of calculating the costs of recruiting physicians.

http://64.87.31.133/emerging/metrics.htm Articles on measuring the effectiveness of HR practices.

www.atkinson.yorku.ca/~hrresall The International Alliance for Human Resources Research posts articles on HR effectiveness, based on studies by Canadian university professors.

Discussion Questions

1. Refer back to the information contained in Box 4.1. Why did Deutsche Bank choose these performance indicators?
2. The president of your company has said, "I see no value in having an HR department. Let's get rid of it. We can outsource payroll and benefits. Anything else, like training, can be arranged by each manager." You, as the vice-president of HR, want to save the department (and your job!). Prepare a report, describing areas in which the HR department does (or can) make a difference to the company.
3. We all know that being able to prove that a program is effective is a good way to ensure continued funding. List the ways you might prove that a training program for supervisors is good for the organization. List some reasons why most HR managers would not want to measure the effectiveness of a training program.
4. A company wishes to increase the sales performance of its staff. It has been determined that for each $15 product sold, the company makes $5 in profit. Currently, employees, who are paid $20 an hour, sell an average of four products an hour. A consultant is persuading the company to purchase a four-hour training course. The consultant guarantees that sales capacity will increase by 25% and that the effect will last one year (50 weeks of selling time, assuming an eight-hour day). The cost of the course is $400 per employee. Should the company buy the training course for its ten sales representatives? Conduct a cost–benefit analysis to determine the answer.

Exercises

1. The Workforce Optimas Award for Vision is given to an HR department that has proactively dealt with an issue. GTE was the winner of this prestigious award in 2000 because it found a credible way to measure HR's contribution to the business. HR strategy at GTE had five targets to measure: managing talent, developing world-class leadership, customer service and integration, and HR capability. In groups, determine how you would measure the success of these targets. To start designing your research, ask these two questions: What are you trying to measure? How will the information be used?

   Source: C.M. Solomon, "Putting HR on the Scorecard," *Workforce*, Vol. 70, No. 3, March 2000, 94–98.

2. The host of *Workology*, a series broadcast on CBC Radio One, asked people on the street what they thought about HR. The HR stereotype of paper-pushing, picnic-planning policy-police is alive and well. Go to the *Workology* website (www.workology.cbc) to order the tape of the show aired on September 9, 2002, so you can hear how Monica Belcourt, coauthor of this textbook, responded to the challenges presented. How would you reply to the comments you hear from people on the street?

Case: Measuring HR Impact at Wells Fargo

The CEO of Wells Fargo declared, "The way I see it, when you take care of your employees, they take care of your customers, and your shareholders wind up winning." But could he prove it? Wells Fargo implemented an integrated group of HR practices and policies known as PACA (People As a Competitive Advantage). These practices included leadership training, 360-degree feedback and development process, competency-based interviewing, and communicating business plans and goals. Managers were held responsible for business planning and HR planning, selection, performance management, employee development, and communications. PACA was to affect three metrics: employee commitment, customer loyalty, and financial performance.

One hundred and twenty branches were chosen to be part of the research and were evenly divided between those with PACA and those without (the control group). Data would be collected over two blocked time intervals—one year prior to the implementation of PACA and one year after. The results were both expected and surprising. There were strong links between PACA usage and measures of employee commitment, satisfaction, and productivity. Strong correlations were also found between PACA usage and financial performance. For example, the use of PACA tools and practices increased revenue per FTE (full-time equivalent—i.e., number of full-time employees) by 5.1% or $10 511. Turnover was reduced by nearly 60% through the use of PACA. Overall, PACA improved ROE, ROA, and ER (the bank's efficiency ratio, which measures how much it costs the bank to generate one dollar of revenue). The surprising result was that there seemed to be no effect on various measures of customer satisfaction and loyalty. This finding contradicts earlier studies, which found a flow-through from employee measures to customer measures to financial measures.

Source: T.E. Lawson and R.L. Hepp, "Measure the Performance Impact of Human Resource Initiatives," *Human Resource Planning*, Vol. 24, No. 2, 2001, pp. 36–44. A. Kover, "Dick Kovacevich Does It His Way," *Fortune*, May 15, 2000, pp. 299–306.

QUESTION

As the CEO, would you accept these results (i.e., was it a well-designed study)? As the CEO, would you increase the HR budget to implement PACA (the entire package) in other branches? Defend your decision.

REFERENCES

Belcourt, M. 2001. "Measuring and Managing the HR Function: A Guide for Boards." *Ivey Business Journal* (January/February 2001): 35–39.

Brealey, R., and S. Meyers. 1991. *Principles of Corporate Finance*, 3rd ed. New York: McGraw-Hill.

Brown, D. 2001. "Short Term Absences Double in Three Years." *Canadian HR Reporter*, Vol. 13, No. 18 (October 15): 1.

Cascio, W.F., and R.A. Ramos. 1986. "Development and Application of a New Method for Assessing Job Performance in Behavioural/Economic Terms." *Journal of Applied Psychology*, 71: 20–28.

Catano, V.M. 2001. "Empirically Supported Interventions and HR Practice." *HRM Research Quarterly*, Vol. 5, No. 1 (Spring).

Caudron, S. 2001. "How HR Drives Profits." *Workforce*, Vol. 80, No. 12: 26–31.

Corporate Leadership Council. 2001. *The Evolution of HR Metrics*. May, Cat. No. CLC13LNPC.

Davidson, W.N. III, D.L. Worrell, and J.B. Fox. 1996. "Early Retirement Programs and Firm Performances." *Academy of Management Journal*, Vol. 39, No. 4 (August): 970–984.

Delaney, J.T., and M.A. Huselid. 1996. "The Impact of Human Resource Management Practices on the Perceptions of Organizational Performance." *Academy of Management Journal*, Vol. 39, No. 4: 949–969.

Dolan, S.L., and A. Belout. 1997. "Assessing Human Resource

Effectiveness: The Emergence of the Stakeholder Approach." *HRM Research Quarterly*, Vol. 1, No. 1 (Spring).

Fitz-enz, J. 2000. *The ROI of Human Capital*. New York: AMACOM.

Huselid, M.A. 1995. "The Impact of Human Resource Management Practices on Turnover, Productivity, and Corporate Financial Performance." *Academy of Management Journal*, Vol. 38: 635–672.

———. 1994. "Documenting HR's Effect on Company Performance." *HR Magazine*, Vol. 39, No. 1: 79–85.

Huselid, M.A., and B.E. Becker. 1996. "Methodological Issues in Cross-Sectional and Panel Estimates of the HR–Firm Performance Link." *Industrial Relations*, Vol. 20: 245–259.

———. 1995. "High Performance Work Systems and Organizational Performance." Academy of Management meeting, Vancouver.

Jones, G.R., and P.M. Wright. 1992. "An Economic Approach to Conceptualizing the Utility of Human Resource Management Practices." In K. Rowland and G. Ferris, eds., *Research in Personnel and Human Resources Management*, Vol. 10. Greenwich, Conn.: JAI Press.

Kiger, P.J. 2002. "Why Customer Satisfaction Starts with HR." *Workforce*, Vol. 81, No. 5: 26–32.

King, A.S., and T.R. Bishop. 1991. "Functional Requisites of Human Resources: Personnel Professionals' and Line Managers' Criteria for Effectiveness." *Public Personnel Management*, Vol. 20, No. 3 (Fall): 285–298.

Koch, M.J., and R. Gunther-McGrath. 1996. "Improving Labour Productivity: Human Resource Management Policies Do Matter." *Strategic Management Journal*, Vol. 17, No. 5 (May): 335–354.

Meyer, J.P, N.J. Allen, and C.A. Smith. 1993. "Commitment to Organizations and Occupations: Extent and Test of a Three Component Conceptualization." *Journal of Applied Psychology*, Vol. 78: 538–551.

Powell, T.C. 1992. "Organizational Alignment as Competitive Advantage." *Strategic Management Journal*, Vol. 13: 119–134.

Rothwell, W.J., and H.C. Kazanas. 1988. *Strategic Human Resources Planning and Management*. Englewood Cliffs, N.J.: Prentice Hall.

Saks, A.M. 1999. *Research, Measurement and Evaluation of Human Resources*. Toronto: ITP Nelson.

Steers, R.M. 1997. *Organizational Effectiveness: A Behavioral View*. Glenview, Ill.: Scott, Foresman.

Stewart, J. 1996. "Blow Up the HR Department." *Fortune* (January 15).

Templer, A., and R.J. Cattaneo. 1995. "A Model of Human Resource Management Effectiveness." *Canadian Journal of Administrative Studies*, Vol. 12, No. 1: 77–88.

Tsui, A.S. 1987. "Defining the Activities and Effectiveness of the Human Resource Department: A Multiple Constituent Approach." *Human Resource Management* (Spring): 35–70.

Tyler, K. 2001. "Evaluate Your Next Move." *HR Magazine*, Vol. 46, No. 11: 66–71.

Ulrich, D. 1996. *Human Resource Champions*. Boston: Harvard Business School Press.

———. 1997. "Measuring Human Resources: An Overview of Practice and a Prescription for Results." *Human Resource Management*, Vol. 36, No. 3 (Fall): 303–320.

Wagar, T. 2002. "Seemed Like a Good Idea, but... The Survival (and Death) of High Involvement Work Practices." *HRM Research Quarterly*, Vol. 6, No. 1 (Spring).

Welbourne, T.M., and A.O. Andrews. 1996. "Predicting the Performance of Initial Public Offerings: Should Human Resource Management Be an Equation?" *Academy of Management Journal*, Vol. 39, No. 4 (August): 891–919.

ENDNOTES

1. Stewart, 1996.
2. Corporate Leadership Council, 2001.
3. Dolan and Belout, 1997.
4. Wagar, 2002.
5. Catano, 2001.
6. Huselid, 1994.
7. Fitz-enz, 2000.
8. Belcourt, 2001.
9. Tsui, 1987; Dolan and Belout, 1997.
10. Ulrich, 1996.
11. Rothwell and Kazanas, 1988.
12. King and Bishop, 1991.
13. Meyer, Allen, and Smith, 1993.
14. Kiger, 2002.
15. Caudron, 2001.
16. Brown, 2001.
17. Fitz-ens, 2000.
18. Caudron, 2001.
19. www.watsonwyatt.com.
20. Huselid, 1995.
21. Davidson et al., 1996; Huselid and Becker, 1995, 1996.
22. Welbourne and Andrews, 1996.
23. Jones and Wright, 1992.
24. Huselid, 1995.
25. Koch and Gunter-McGrath, 1996.
26. Welbourne and Andrews, 1996.
27. Delaney and Huselid, 1996.
28. Powell, 1992.
29. Templer and Cattaneo, 1995.
30. Steers, 1997.

31. Ulrich, 1997.
32. Brealy and Meyers, 1991.
33. Cascio and Ramos, 1986.
34. Tyler, 2001.
35. Fitz-enz, 2000.
36. Saks, 1999.

APPENDIX
HR ACCOUNTING METHODS

THE HUMAN ASSET ACCOUNTING APPROACH

The *human asset accounting approach* attempts to use accounting principles, such as those used to calculate the historical costs or replacement costs of assets, to put a value on the worth of an organization's human assets. The models used in this approach measure the investment made in employees, treating them as capitalized resources, in economic terms.

- *Historical costs model:* The historical costs model of accounting measures the investment in employees (Cascio, 1991). The investment consists of the costs of acquisition, training, orientation, informal coaching, and experience and development. These costs are amortized over the expected working lives of individuals. Those expenses incurred on behalf of employees who left the company (the unamortized costs) are written off. This approach has the advantage of being relatively objective and consistent with the accounting treatment of other assets, thus allowing comparisons. Critics of this approach complain that this method is seriously flawed because the assets are not saleable, and, therefore, there is no independent check of valuation. They say that estimating costs of informal training and experience is too subjective a process. In addition, allowances have to be made for the changing value of the dollar. The main problem is that the process measures only costs and cannot distinguish between two employees: both may have cost the organization the same dollar amount in acquisition and training, but one may be an outstanding performer and the other a minimally effective worker.
- *Replacement costs model:* This model measures the cost of replacing an employee as an estimate of market value. The cost includes recruitment, selection, compensation, training, and orientation (Flamholtz et al., 1988). This model is unsatisfactory for several reasons. Although substituting replacement cost for historical cost provides an updated valuation, the actual opportunities to do these calculations are limited. Most organizations have limited turnover, particularly at senior levels, and so building a complex human asset formula into the accounting system would not be worthwhile. Furthermore, a badly managed HR department that incurred abnormal expenses in recruiting or selection might overestimate the cost of replacing an employee (Steffy and Maurer, 1988). A highly sophisticated system of staffing, orientation, and training would also generate high replacement costs, but the measure of the value added by exceptional employees would not be part of the accounting process.

- *Present value of future earnings model:* This model measures contributions, not costs. The organization tries to determine what an employee's future contribution is worth today by calculating future earnings, adjusted for the probability of an employee's death (Lev and Schwartz, 1971). Contribution is calculated by the compensation paid to an employee. Probability of death is estimated using mortality tables. The problem with this model is that it assigns a value to the average worker, rather than to an individual. No investment in individual employees—for example, in training—is taken into account, and yet this training investment should have a payoff in future contributions.

These three models of human asset accounting value employee service at gross book value (the original investment expenses), net book value (the original investment minus depreciation), and economic value (the anticipated financial return on the investment) (Cascio, 1991). These models, however, have not been accepted by HR professionals or by researchers for many reasons.

Limitations of Human Asset Accounting Models

As can be seen, the main problem with human asset accounting models is their failure to take into account employee effectiveness. They tend to measure only inputs, such as costs incurred in acquiring and training employees, and not outputs, such as employee productivity. Secondly, who is the best judge of employee worth—the employee, the manager, or the HR department? Another major problem is the cost and difficulty of obtaining these data. The most recent trend is to measure the intellectual capital—the brainpower—of employees in the hope of measuring actual and potential contributions.

Intellectual Capital Approach

The productivity of most organizations entering the 21st century is highly dependent on the intellectual capabilities of their employees. The software, communications, educational, and medical sectors, which provide 79% of all jobs, owe their success to the knowledge of their employees (Quinn et al., 1996). For example, the value of Microsoft was greater than that of General Motors, Ford, Boeing, Lockheed Martin, Deere, Caterpillar, USX, Weyerhauser, Union Pacific, Kodak, Sears, Marriott, Safeway, and Kellogg B combined! (Lermusiaux, 2002). Yet the real and only value of Microsoft is the knowledge of its employees.What is intellect and how is it measured?

Intellectual capital can be thought of as intellectual material (knowledge) that can be formalized, captured, and leveraged to produce a higher-valued asset (Stewart, 1994). Intellectual capital can be seen as employee brainpower, some of which is described in skills inventories and patent lists.

Quinn and his colleagues (1996) described and ranked the importance of this intellectual capital:

1. Cognitive knowledge (know what)
2. Advanced skills (know how)
3. System understanding and trained intuition (know why)
4. Self-motivated creativity (care why)

Employers pay premiums for smart workers. In the United States, men with postgraduate degrees earn incomes 130% higher than men who never finished high school (Quinn et al., 1996). The pay gap between men with these different levels of education has doubled since 1980. Companies like Scandia and Dow Chemical are struggling to identify, describe, and measure these intellectual assets in order to manage them. The chief financial officer for Northern Telecom states, "As a technology company, much of our ability to differentiate ourselves from our competitors depends on being able to market new product solutions more quickly than anyone else. For this, we rely on our intellectual capital" (Edwards, 1997).

Intellectual assets have characteristics highly distinct from other assets. First, intellectual assets grow with use. Anyone who has gone back to school or completed a training course realizes that the learning of new knowledge, and its application, lead to even greater knowledge and a motivation to acquire more. Intellectual capital can be shared and cannot be depleted. Sharing it results in increased feedback, acquisition of new knowledge, and modifications and adjustments to current knowledge. Some organizations, such as Accenture Inc., link via e-mail 82 000 employees in 360 offices in 76 countries, allowing the posting of problems on bulletin boards. They feel this taps dormant capabilities of employees and expands energy and solutions to problems. However, there are also disadvantages. One is exclusivity. If you own a capital asset such as a building, you can prevent competitors from using it. However, a highly knowledgeable employee can moonlight for other companies or leave to work for a competitor.

Issues in Measuring Intellectual Capital

Experts in this nascent field estimate that the intellectual assets of an organization are worth three to four times the tangible book value. A common approach is to claim that the intellectual capital of a firm is equal to the difference between a firm's capitalized stock value and its book value. It is still very difficult to put a dollar value on the brain resources of employees. The Canadian Imperial Bank of Commerce (CIBC) tries to do so by counting employee skills (e.g., the ability to manage a portfolio of clients), which can be used to build a competency inventory. But as skills change, the dynamics of measuring them become difficult. Furthermore, most of this asset is left idle: observers and employees alike guess that only 20% of the knowledge available in their companies is used (Edwards, 1997). You can see when a factory is producing at a reduced capacity; you cannot always determine if your knowledge workers are working at capacity.

Educational and medical institutions have measured intellectual capital for decades, relying on peer reviews (and publication records) for decisions about the worth of the faculty or professionals. Thus, first measures of intellectual capital include peer review, although in some cases, it may be done by colleagues working together on projects. Some organizations add another review level, that of customer or client evaluations of outputs (Quinn et al., 1996). Customers are asked to rank team participants on professional knowledge and specific project contributions, and on overall satisfaction with results. To supplement these human evaluations, some organizations add measures of efficiency and effectiveness, which normally are measured in business terms (e.g., costs, fulfilment time and accuracy, delivery times). Finally, some organizations track the intellectual assets created. CIBC charts the growth of intellectual capital by tracking the flow of knowledge among employees. The company counts, as indicators of intellectual capital, the number of new ideas generated, the number of new products created, and the percentage of income from new revenue streams.

The competitive advantage of intellectual capital is enormous. This asset cannot be traded or expropriated. Competitors fall farther behind because the top talent goes to organizations such as Microsoft to be part of a leading-edge organization.

Many researchers have tried and failed to come up with a single, limited criterion to measure the worth of an organization's human resources. Accountants cannot value intellectual capital because there is no market for it—it cannot be bought and sold, and so valued. After reviewing the literature, Scarpello and Theeke (1989) concluded that the search should be abandoned, despite its attraction for managers making internal management and external investment decisions.

References

Cascio, W.F. 1991. *Costing Human Resources: The Financial Impact of Behavior in Organizations*, 3rd ed. Kent Series in Human Resource Management. Boston: PWS Kent.

Edwards, S. 1997. "The Brain Gain." *CA Magazine* (April): 21–25.

Flamholtz, F.L.K., D.G. Searfoss, and R. Cof. 1988. "Developing Human Resource Accounting as a Decision Support System." *Accounting Horizon*, Vol. 2: 1–9.

Lermusiaux, Y. 2002. "Managing Human Capital in a Downturn." *Ivey Business Journal*, Vol. 66, No. 4 (March/April): 14–16.

Lev, B., and A. Schwartz. 1971. "On the Use of the Economic Concept of Human Capital in Financial Statements." *Accounting Review*, Vol. 46: 103–112.

Quinn, J.B., P. Anderson, and S. Finkelstein. 1996. "Leveraging Intellect." *Academy of Management Executive*, Vol. 10, No. 3.

Scarpello, V., and H.A. Theeke. 1989. "Human Resource Accounting: A Measured Critique." *Journal of Accounting Literature*, Vol. 8: 265–280.

Steffy, B.D., and S.D. Maurer. 1988. "Conceptualizing and Measuring the Economic Effectiveness of Human Resource Activities." *Academy of Management Review*, Vol. 13: 265–280.

Stewart, T.A. 1994. "Intellectual Capital." *Fortune* (October 3): 68–74.

Part 2

HR Planning

5

JOB ANALYSIS

CHAPTER GOALS

In this chapter, we will discuss the importance of job analysis, examine the process underlying a successful job analysis, and explore specific methods used by organizations to attain successful levels of performance.

After reading this chapter, you should be able to do the following:

1. Understand the central role played by job analysis in all HR activities, and especially in the effective conduct of HR planning.
2. Comprehend the two essential elements of any job: methods and time standards.
3. Explain common problems associated with the job analysis process.
4. Identify the five steps of the job analysis process.
5. Employ criteria to select job analysis methods that are best suited to the organizational jobs being examined.

6. Develop analytical questions that will permit an in-depth examination of the knowledge, skills, abilities, and other attributes required for successful evaluation of jobs.
7. Analyze the advantages and disadvantages of the most common methods of job analysis.

Introduction

job a grouping of related duties, tasks, and behaviours performed by one or more individuals, namely jobholders

positions refers to the number of individuals who are performing the duties, tasks, and behaviours required by a specific job

job analysis the analysis of subdivided work in the organization, both at the level of the individual job and for the entire flow of the production process

job description and **job specification** the written outcomes (documents) produced by the job analysis process. The job description emphasizes the duties or tasks to be carried out on the job. For job specifications, the emphasis is on identifying the competencies the jobholder must possess to be a successful performer in the specified job.

An organization's mission statement presents the guiding rationale for the activities of all sub-units and employees. As we move down the organizational hierarchy from the executive suites to the production floor, corporate and divisional strategic goals are subdivided and allocated to various units as their operational goals. To attain the strategic and operational goals, it is necessary to develop short-run production and operational budgets, as well as to specify the division of labour, commonly referred to as partitioning the work process into manageable units called jobs. A **job** can be defined as a grouping of related duties, tasks, and behaviours performed by one or more individuals, namely jobholders. Each job will have one or more **positions**—in other words, the number of individuals who are performing the duties required by that specific job. The analysis of subdivided work in the organization, both at the level of the individual job and for the entire flow of the production process, is referred to as **job analysis** and is the focus of this chapter. As HR planners, it is essential that we are knowledgeable about the nature of work and its overall contribution toward the attainment of the organization's mission. It is important for us to see how each individual job, when aggregated with others in a process referred to as departmentalization, contributes to the performance of essential organizational tasks without unnecessary duplication or redundancy. Furthermore, as HR planners, we are responsible for determining the demand for and supply of personnel in the organization. In order to do this we must have detailed knowledge about working conditions, employee qualifications, and the educational training and skill requirements of each job, as well as the nature of the organization's work process itself. For these reasons, knowledge of the job analysis process and methods of evaluating jobs are essential components in the formulation of the successful HR planning system.[1]

Job Analysis

Job analysis can be defined as an examination of the jobs in an organization with a view to documenting the knowledge, skills, and abilities (KSAs, e.g., experience) associated with successful performance of those jobs. The written outcomes of this process are referred to either as a **job description** or a **job specification**. The difference between the two documents centres on whether the emphasis is on the duties or tasks to be carried out on the job (i.e., the job description) or on the competencies or KSAs the jobholder must possess to be a successful performer in a specific job (i.e., the job specification). *KSAs* are defined as follows:

Knowledge: Knowledge is the body of information, usually of a factual or procedural nature, that allows an individual to perform a task successfully:

Skill: Skill is the individual's level of proficiency or competency in performing a specific task. Level of competency is typically expressed in numerical terms.

Ability: Ability is a more general, enduring trait or capability an individual possesses at the time when he or she first begins to perform a task.[2]

Other attributes: Other attributes include work experience.

HR practitioners refer to job analysis as the foundation for all HR activities, and there are extremely valid reasons for this assertion. Before we can meaningfully advertise jobs and recruit individuals to fill job vacancies identified by the HR planning process, to attract the desired applicants we must be able to specify the individual competencies that we are looking for. Once we have developed a pool of high-quality job applicants, the selection process will incorporate employment tests and interview questions based on the need to choose the individual who best meets the formal requirements for success identified by our job analysis process. The selection criteria that flow out of the job analysis process are also used in succession planning to appraise the organization's internal candidates for possible transfer or promotion to management or executive jobs. Once we have selected an individual to fill a job, he or she should be given a copy of the job description or specification for the job, which provides specific guidance on how to perform the job in accordance with the

BOX 5.1 Ensuring Job Descriptions Stay Relevant

Detailed written job descriptions can fail to maintain their relevance over time, as jobs change rapidly in today's dynamic global economy. Furthermore, if descriptions become outdated and do not reflect the changed realities of the contemporary job, they will be next to useless in facilitating the match between the individual's performance and career aspirations. Carla Joinson, a job analyst, recommends a minimalist approach to preparing job descriptions, reflecting a change in emphasis from detailed "skill-based" to shortened "role-based" documents. She suggests that shorter job descriptions, which are restricted to a few clearly written statements on the overall responsibilities and "roles" that will be performed by individuals holding specified jobs, are more much enduring and useful than the detailed and ponderous older descriptions. Detailed information on duties and tasks as contained in traditional job descriptions are not included in the new "minimalist job description." The advantage to this approach is that roles are more enduring than specific micro-level duties and tasks and will therefore provide better behavioural guidance over a sustained period of time, and are flexible enough to maintain their relevancy to jobholders.

Source: Adapted from C. Joinson, "Refocusing Job Descriptions, *HR Magazine*, Vol. 46, No. 1 (January 2001), pp. 66–72.

wishes of the organization. The performance appraisal process compares the individual's accomplishments over a predetermined period with the desired standards specified in the job description or specification. If the performance appraisal process reveals that the individual has deficiencies that can be rectified by training and development, specific programs or courses can be instigated to help the individual reach the desired standards. Furthermore, compensation systems in organizations typically use a classification process based on knowledge and skills, effort, responsibility, and working conditions, the four **compensable factors** of the job that are explicitly noted and formalized by the job analysis process.[3]

compensable factors knowledge and skills, effort, responsibility, and working conditions

Finally, successful career planning programs also draw heavily on the front-end requirement of a comprehensive job analysis. In planning future career moves, the individual and the organization note the employee's current KSAs and level of performance and compare these to the KSAs required in various target jobs for which the employee would like to apply. Once this information is provided by job analysis, the employee is informed of the explicit education and skills development that will be required prior to being considered for the target jobs. Job analysis, therefore, is not only a critical requirement for the proper implementation and operation of the HR planning process, as examined in this book, but is also an essential prerequisite for the success of virtually all other HR functions.[4]

Job analysis has a long history within the HR field. Efficiency expert Fred Taylor's **scientific management** studies were key contributions to the evolution of contemporary job analysis methods.[5] Taylor's industrial engineering approach was focused on reducing costs and improving the efficiency of the manufacturing worker. In particular, his analysis process concentrated on finding the "one best way" to do any job. This approach, still a central feature of present-day job analyses, examines two main aspects of each job in the organization: (1) the *methods employed* and (2) the *time measurement* for task completion.

scientific management examines two main aspects of each job in the organization: (1) the *methods employed* and (2) the *time measurement* for task completion

The first aspect is concerned with how the job incumbent performs the job—that is, with the minimum requirements for success in the job. These requirements include (a) the individual's knowledge of production techniques and processes (e.g., raw materials and other inputs, machinery, tools), cognitive (mental) abilities, mechanical abilities, (e.g., principles and spatial relationships), and psychomotor abilities, and (b) the working conditions in which the job is performed (e.g., whether the work is done by the individual alone or in conjunction with other members of a team).

The second aspect common to all job analyses is time measurement, or the cycle/production time required to produce the good or service to the performance standards of the organization. This time standard is completely dependent on the first aspect, which is concerned with the methods employed (or how the job is performed). Obviously, changing the process from individual to team-based production and modifying the number of raw material inputs or steps in the production process will substantially change the output or number of items that can be produced on a time basis per hour, shift, or day.

Problems Associated with Job Analysis

Having noted the importance of job analysis and its two constituent elements of methods and time, let's now turn to an examination of frequent problems associated with job analysis.

1. Job Analysis that Is Neither Updated Nor Reviewed

One has only to consider the topic of computer technology to recognize the impact that an extremely rapid rate of change has on how work is being performed. Job analyses must be reviewed on a regular basis by incumbents, supervisors, HR staff, and so on to ensure that the written job requirements reflect the reality of contemporary job performance. Recent changes in technology, materials, and processes must be incorporated into the amended job description or specification. Obsolete job descriptions not only fail to provide job incumbents with meaningful guidance as to their required duties and tasks, but also result in an HR planning process that is attempting to match individuals to jobs based on information that is no longer valid.

2. Job Description or Specification that Is Too Vague

If job analysis is to provide important information to allow us to select the individual who best meets job requirements, we must be specific as to what those exact requirements are. For example, organizations often specify that applicants must have a certain number of years' experience in a certain functional area instead of specifying the exact skills or competencies the applicant should have learned over that period. Without this specific information, experience or time spent on the job has little relevance for selection. Similarly, organizations may mistakenly include elements such as "dependability" as one of their job requirements without giving specific examples of what constitutes dependable behaviour (e.g., the individual arrives on time for meetings with all preparatory work properly completed). To be an effective component of HR planning, the job analysis process must produce detailed, specific behavioural examples of successful job performance for each job in the work process.

3. Contamination and Deficiency

Although brevity and clarity are definite virtues with respect to job analysis (a short, clear job description is of great use to both job incumbents and the HR staff), taken to an extreme these characteristics may cause problems during job analysis efforts. If our job description or specification fails to incorporate important aspects of the job that are required for success, this error of omission is referred to as **deficiency**. Conversely, if we include peripheral, unimportant aspects of a job in the formal job description, we run the risk of contaminating it by diverting attention from valid, important correlates of success. **Contamination** of our job analysis process may also lead to legal consequences if we use the information to select individuals based on factors not related to

deficiency an error of omission when a job description or specification fails to incorporate important aspects of the job required for success

contamination an error that occurs when unimportant or invalid behaviours or attributes are incorporated into a job description or specification

the job that are discriminatory under provincial or Canadian human rights legislation. For job analysis, therefore, we should try to be as brief and clear as possible but not at the expense of excluding any important behavioural or performance element of the job.

4. Time and Costs of Job Analysis

Some organizations are deterred from conducting job analyses due to the significant time and start-up costs perceived to be associated with the process. Typical costs include consulting fees for job analysts (if the organization does not have in-house HR staff with relevant qualifications); licensing fees associated with usage of copyrighted job analysis methods; the costs of lost production (or overtime) involved with interviewing and surveying job incumbents, managers, and so on; and the administrative costs involved with codifying, analyzing, drafting, revising, and disseminating the information that results from the process. However, many organizations that bemoan the large time and cost expenditures associated with job analysis do so only because they have not conducted a proper cost–benefit analysis with respect to this decision. For example, organizations should also consider the time and cost savings that result from the following: (1) better matching of individual skills to organizational requirements (e.g., reduced costs, and often lower absenteeism and turnover, associated with training and development),[6] (2) incorporation of the benefits of organizational learning with respect to product and process improvements, (3) reduced job ambiguity and wastage, (4) clarification of operating procedures and job relationships, (5) explicit definition of performance expectations for individuals and teams, and (6) facilitation of other HR programs. If organizations consider the full costs and benefits associated with entering into the job analysis process, the decision to proceed is invariably very clear!

The Process of Job Analysis

The process of job analysis involves following five steps to maximize the potential for success. We now examine each of the five steps in turn, noting the actions required at each stage.

1. Determine the Job or Process to Be Analyzed

Although the desired outcome of a job analysis is to have a comprehensive record of all organizational jobs and their associated duties, skill requirements, working conditions, and so on, reality dictates that organizations normally select certain well-defined jobs common throughout the industry that can be benchmarked externally—that is, the analysis commences with these well-known jobs first. Some of the factors that determine whether job analysis will be concurrent (all jobs analyzed at approximately the same time) or sequential (job analyses conducted in different stages over time) include (1) the degree to which the selected job is central or critical, (2) the availability of job analysts and other resources, and (3) the availability of external performance **benchmarks** for organizational jobs.

benchmark external comparators for organizational jobs and performance criteria

In the first instance, the more critical or central the job or process, the greater the tendency to analyze it and to defer examination of less central jobs or processes to a future time. The number and availability of job analysts, be they external consultants or internal HR specialists, are key factors influencing whether an organization is able to conduct concurrent job analysis or is forced to do it sequentially by stages.

Finally, the Canadian government's ***National Occupational Classification* (NOC)**, which contains standardized job descriptions on approximately 25 000 jobs, facilitates external benchmarking for the job analyst.[7] The NOC and its U.S. counterpart, the ***Dictionary of Occupational Titles* (DOT)**, provide information on the main duties and employment requirements of each classified job, along with a listing of other job classifications that are similar to the one being analyzed.[8] This information is invaluable as it facilitates comparison to similar jobs in other organizations with respect to required applicant specifications and performance standards for key duties and tasks.

***National Occupational Classification* (NOC)** the Canadian government database that contains standardized job descriptions on thousands of jobs

***Dictionary of Occupational Titles* (DOT)** the U.S. government's equivalent of the NOC

2. Determine Methods and Analyze the Job or Process

The second step in the job analysis process involves an appraisal of the most appropriate method(s) to use to study and record job-related behaviours. Selection criteria for job analysis methods include the following:

Cost: Cost includes licence fees for such things as copyrighted questionnaires, training, and administration.

Time: Time includes that spent on survey and interview training and assessment, data coding and analysis, and so on.

Flexibility of Methods: This criterion has to do with whether the method is appropriate for the particular circumstances (e.g., clerical service jobs as opposed to those in manufacturing).

Validity and Reliability: These criteria relate to whether the job analysis methods have been tested and found to be accurate measures of the job's essential elements and whether the results of these methods show a consistent pattern over repeated usage.

Acceptance: Some job analysis methods, such as direct observation and videotaping of work performance, may be considered intrusive by the workforce and, therefore, may be met with resistance.[9] Other methods, such as questionnaires and interviews, might be deemed more acceptable by the workers, who would then cooperate in providing information to the job analysts.[10]

The aforementioned selection criteria are used to evaluate the following common methods of job analysis.

Interviews

To gather information about a job, a job analyst may interview job incumbents, as well as co-workers, supervisors, suppliers, clients, and subordinates. This type of all-round analysis of a job is referred to as **360-degree evaluation**, as the job analyst has input from individuals who are in the job under evaluation and in other jobs that relate to it.

360-degree evaluation evaluation of attributes and performance dimensions of a job from "the full circle" around the job, i.e., feedback from subordinates, superiors, co-workers, clients, as well as the jobholder him/herself

Observation

Observation of a job can be either direct or indirect. In *direct observation*, analysts observe the production line for worker behaviours and the skills required for job success. Recording of the number and duration of individual behaviours is normally captured on a standardized recording sheet.[11] *Indirect observation* can incorporate a variety of means, such as a videotaped recording of the job being performed, for subsequent analysis by the analyst.

Questionnaires

Numerous standardized questionnaires are used for job analysis. Some of the more frequently used instruments include: (1) the *Position Description Questionnaire*,[12] (2) the *Functional Job Analysis*,[13] (3) the *Job Diagnostic Survey*,[14] (4) the *Dimensions of Executive Positions*,[15] and (5) the *Position Analysis Questionnaire*.[16] These survey instruments are normally completed by jobholders, their supervisors, and people who work in other jobs that are related to the specific job being investigated. The questionnaires vary substantially, but common elements are questions concerning the following:

a. Education, training, and skill requirements to be successful in the job
b. Responsibility or accountability (e.g., with regard to budgets, specific duties and tasks performed, number and type of people supervised, etc.)
c. Effort—that is, the cognitive and physical demands placed on the individual
d. Working conditions—for example, whether the work is done by an individual or team, the equipment or materials used, the job context or the environmental conditions of work (e.g., telephone line repairperson), the work shifts or hours of work, the potential health hazards, and so on

Journals and Diaries

This method of job analysis asks jobholders to maintain a written record of their job activities, and associated time expenditures, for a preset period that typically ranges from a complete work cycle or typical week to up to a month. Although the information can be useful in discovering actual time expenditures and activities—for example, it was a vital component of the Mintzberg (1973) research investigation into the nature of managerial work—there can be the

BOX 5.2 Rating Jobs Against New Values

Bayer Group AG, headquartered in Leverkusen, Germany, reorganized its three U.S. companies into one entity and in so doing revised their job analysis/evaluation processes. The new system was designed to meet the vision, culture, and goals of the unified company and to identify and measure competencies required for future organizational success. The existing Hay Guide Chart–Profile Method used previously was used as a starting point for the new system, although the language describing each work-value cluster was changed. Each of the following work-value clusters is matched to a numerical scale to enable Bayer to ensure internal equity through usage of point-based evaluation. Bayer's work-value dimensions are as follows:

1. *Improvement Opportunity:* "Describes the requirement for and assesses the ability to improve performance within the context of assigned roles and rate of change in the work environment."
2. *Contribution:* "Describes the requirement for and ability to achieve results that improve performance and define success."
3. *Capability:* "Describes the total of proficiencies and competencies required to support effectiveness and progress."

Each of these three work-value clusters also incorporates various sub-elements, such as the following components of the capability cluster:

a. *Expertise and Complexity:* "Measures the depth and breadth of specific technical and professional proficiencies and competencies required for expected individual and team performance."

b. *Leadership and Integration:* "Measures the ability to manage, coordinate, integrate, and provide leadership for diverse people, processes, and organizational resources to achieve common goals and objectives."

c. *Relationship-Building Skills:* "Measures the requirements for meeting internal and external customers' needs through effective listening, understanding, sensitivity, and analytical abilities. This capability also measures the requirements for proactive persuasiveness, organizational awareness, and collaborative influencing skills necessary to effect desired change and build effective, enduring relationships."

Source: Laabs, J. 1997. "Rating Jobs against New Values," *Workforce*, Vol. 76, No. 5 (May), pp. 38–49. Used with permission of ACC Communication/*Workforce*, Costa Mesa, CA.

problem of selective reporting and bias as the respondent is fully aware that his or her time and activities are being monitored.

Output and Production Analysis

Machine-generated output reports, as well as production reporting procedures, can obtain information about the job and its normal and peak levels of production. Although these techniques reveal little about the qualitative or process aspects of the job, they are useful in determining appropriate performance standards for output.

Current Job Descriptions and Specifications

In the quest for information about the job, a useful starting point, if a previous job analysis has been performed, is an examination of the existing job descriptions and specifications. Although the information contained in these documents is already dated, it is advantageous to see how the job in question has evolved and whether its component duties, tasks, and employee specifications, as well as the authority and status the job is accorded, have increased or diminished over time.

Despite Fred Taylor's best efforts, in fact there is no one best way to analyze a job, so most contemporary job analyses employ a combination of the aforementioned methods. This multi-method approach not only provides a more comprehensive examination of the job but also enables quantitative aspects (e.g., production reports, questionnaires, observation) as well as qualitative aspects (e.g., interviews, journals, observation) of each job to be recorded.[17]

3. Examine the Recorded Data on the Job or Process

Having selected the most appropriate methods to analyze the job, job analysts record the knowledge, skills, and abilities; job-related behaviours, duties, tasks, responsibilities; and working conditions of the job. The next step is to examine these data from a variety of perspectives to get a detailed profile of the current job. Some of the questions involved in the examination are as follows:

a. What is the purpose of this job? Why does it exist?
b. Where is the job physically performed? Are there compelling reasons why the job must be performed there?
c. What is the sequence of behaviours required for successful job performance? Are there ways to modify the methods and process to improve the job both qualitatively (e.g., worker and client satisfaction, worker motivation) and quantitatively (e.g., output)?
d. Who performs the job? What constitutes the employee specifications (e.g., education, training, skills, etc.) required for job success? Are these specifications optimal, or are they the minimum standards required for success on the job?
e. What are the means of performing the job? Are the materials, machines, group processes (if applicable), and operating procedures congruent with effective performance of the job?

After addressing all these issues, the job analysts start to form a clearer picture of the present job profile. This information is used to draft the job description or specification, which should be reviewed not only by the job incumbents but also by their supervisors. Reference is also made to the NOC, which provides an external comparison for the validity of the emerging job documentation. Any inconsistencies or discrepancies in the findings are examined by all the job analysts and are taken back to the jobholders and supervisors for further feedback and elaboration.

4. Define and Formalize New Methods and Performance Standards for the Job or Process

To this point in the process, the analysts have (a) examined existing descriptions and specifications for the job (if previous analyses have been conducted),

BOX 5.3 Job Descriptions at the Click of a Mouse

KnowledgePoint, an HR software company, has launched a fee-based Internet website that enables downloading of thousands of job descriptions. The website (www.jobdescription.com), entitled "Descriptions Now! Direct," contains job descriptions, which can be either automatically e-mailed to the user or downloaded by the client. The benefits of this service are not only speed and convenience, but also that you can customize the job descriptions, which are kept current by the site provider.

Source: Adapted from M. Frost, "Descriptions Now!" *HR Magazine*, Vol. 42, No. 8 (August 1997): p. 28.

(b) analyzed data on the job as it is presently performed by the jobholder(s), and (c) compared (a) and (b) to the job classification in the NOC and current practices in competitive firms. At this stage, the job analysts attempt to improve on current practices by recommending new methods and performance standards for the job. To do this, analysts must present the following questions to the incumbents and managers:

a. Would you recommend any changes to materials, machinery, behavioural sequencing, training, or procedures to improve performance on the job?
b. Are there any duties or tasks that should be added to or deleted from the job?
c. Would you recommend any changes in the specifications (e.g., knowledge, skills, or abilities) for individuals selected to perform this job?
d. What changes in working conditions would you recommend to improve performance on this job?
e. What is your rationale for these recommended changes?

Having gleaned the collective wisdom of all relevant parties regarding the performance of the job under examination, the HR specialists or job analysts write the new description or specification. This will incorporate improvements in how the job is performed (i.e., methods) as well as revisions to performance and output standards (i.e., time). These changes are formalized into written documents—either a job description or a job specification.

A job description is job-focused as it concentrates on the duties or tasks, responsibilities, and specific behaviours that are required to be a successful performer. These duties are listed in order of importance to the organization, with the most critical ones listed first. It is also common practice for job descriptions to indicate the amount or percentage of work time devoted to the performance of each job task. While this information is undoubtedly useful for the jobholder, it is important to remember that time-consuming tasks are not necessarily highly valuable or critical to the organization's success! Because of its emphasis on tasks, the job description is best employed for assessing individual performance.

Job specifications are person-focused as they detail the profile of the individuals who are best suited to perform the job. They concentrate on the knowledge, skills, abilities, experience, and physical capabilities required for job performance (e.g., the ability to clearly express ideas in oral communication) and are used by HR planners for recruitment and selection.

Both job descriptions and specifications contain the following information: (a) the job title, (b) the job code or classification number, (c) the compensation category, (d) the department or sub-unit, (e) the supervising job title (the title of the person to whom one reports), (f) the date of the approved description or specification, and (g) the name of the job analyst. This information facilitates quick access to the information by HR planners.

5. Maintain New Methods and Performance Standards for the Job or Process

It is one thing to have formal written documents specifying the duties, tasks, and KSAs required for job success, but it is quite another to ensure that these new methods and standards for performance are put into practice. There are four main methods to help ensure usage of the new techniques and to prevent relapses to the old, comfortable ways of performing on the job: (1) communication and training, (2) supervisory reinforcement, (3) employee feedback, and (4) reward systems.

BOX 5.4 Why Job Descriptions Are Not Used More

Despite the fact that job descriptions have a wide variety of uses in the organizational context—one study uncovered 132 uses for them—most managers use them infrequently and only for two or three purposes. Most often they are used for recruiting staff, designing the content of jobs, and occasionally for orientation processes. Dr. Philip Grant, an organizational researcher, investigated why job descriptions were fulfilling only a small part of their potential utility for organizations. He found that the most common reason provided by managers to explain the limited usage of job descriptions was that their organization did not unify or assemble all job descriptions into a well-organized, bound volume that was linked to the organizational chart and made available to all managers. Other reasons for their limited usage included the following:

1. Managers do not know how to use job descriptions or what to use them for.
2. Job descriptions are perceived to be lacking in sufficient detail and comprehensiveness.
3. Job descriptions are perceived to be inaccurate.
4. Managers are not motivated to use job descriptions.
5. Managers do not know what job descriptions are.
6. Job descriptions are not structured well.
7. The job is perceived to "escape definition," or it changes too often.

Source: Adapted from Grant, P. 1998. "Why Job Descriptions Are Not Used More," *Supervision*, Vol. 59, No. 4 (April), pp. 10–13. Reprinted by permission.

As soon as the job description or specification with its new methods and standards has received final approval, the affected jobholders must be given a copy of the revised job description or specification. The process of formally communicating the job changes must also provide sufficient time for questions and answers to ensure workers are clear on the new expectations for their job performance. Training and development programs may have to be instituted if there are significant changes in methods, materials, or the sequencing of behaviours required on the job.

After being formally notified of the changes, supervisors must spend considerable time ensuring that workers are, in fact, behaving in accordance with the new job procedures. (In a unionized environment, of course, the procedure for job reclassification will be specified under the terms of the collective agreement.) Coaching, modelling the desired behaviours, and reinforcing successful performance of the new methods are all effective techniques supervisors can employ to prevent relapses to the outdated, yet habitual, methods of performing the job.

Feedback is critical to the success of the job analysis process. We have already seen that all parties to the process must be consulted on an ongoing basis for their valuable input. Even after the written job analysis documents have been prepared, feedback is essential in ensuring the process has been successful. Employees must be given the freedom to express suggested improvements or concerns with respect to methods, performance standards, and so on if we expect them to become motivated and committed to their jobs. It is important to bear in mind that job analysis is a never-ending process of data gathering, coding, interpreting, and refining job methods and standards. Even if we "get it right" today, changes in technology, competitive practices, economic circumstances, and so on will ensure that we must change to reflect the realities of tomorrow. Besides, who is better able to provide valid feedback about the circumstances of the job than the actual jobholder?

A common downfall of work redesign and job analysis efforts is that although the job methods and standards have changed, the organizational reward system has not been altered, and it reinforces the undesirable old job behaviours.[18] Even if workers have been trained in the new methods of the job and have been provided with a written copy of their revised job description and with ample supervisory coaching, actual worker actions may be very different from formal requirements. For example, if the revised work process is team based, but the compensation system conflicts with job descriptions by being disproportionately weighted toward evaluation of individual performance, we can expect to see unplanned, dysfunctional behaviours and conduct from members of the team. In this instance, worker demeanour may be dysfunctional from the perspective of the organization or the team, but extremely functional and rewarding from the individual's point of view! The oft-repeated dictum "what gets measured gets done" comes to mind, and if workers are still rewarded for their individual actions and not for their contributions to team success, conflicting organizational systems will ensure we do not get the desired results from the job analysis process.

Specific Job Analysis Techniques

The final section of this chapter is devoted to an examination of specific job analysis techniques that are widespread in contemporary organizational usage. We will present five well-known and widely utilized techniques.

1. Critical Incidents Technique

critical incidents technique a qualitative process of job analysis that produces behavioural statements along a range from superior to ineffective performance for a specific job

The **critical incidents technique** is a qualitative process of job analysis that produces behavioural statements along a range from superior to ineffective performance for a specific job.[19] Several experts, normally trained jobholders with considerable experience in the job that is being examined, are asked to identify the key dimensions of their job. Subsequently they describe for the analyst, in writing or verbally, specific critical incidents that relate to success, as well as those that would lead to job failure. Once these critical incidents have been described, they are ranked with respect to their importance to success on the job. The behavioural statements are then used to provide specific guidance for HR planners in refining employee specifications for the job in question.

2. Behaviourally Anchored Rating Scales

Behaviourally Anchored Rating Scales (BARS) a job is divided into a number of key dimensions, and each dimension contains a range of statements of job behaviour "anchored" to a numerical scale

Behaviourally Anchored Rating Scales (BARS) are used by organizations for appraisal of employees' performance and for job analysis purposes. In essence, each job is examined and divided into a small number of key dimensions (e.g., customer relations). Next, behavioural statements are developed for each dimension on a continuum ranging from examples of superior performance to examples of unsuccessful performance. In this aspect, BARS is quite similar in its approach to the critical incidents technique. The next step involves anchoring the behavioural statements by assigning numerical values to them, with perhaps a value of 7 being allocated to a behavioural example of superior performance and a value of 1 to an example of an unsuccessful behaviour. This BARS analysis provides a qualitative and quantitative comparison of jobs based on the derived behavioural statements and numerical values generated by the process.[20]

3. Position Analysis Questionnaire

Position Analysis Questionnaire (PAQ)[22] a structured job analysis checklist that includes 194 items or job elements used to rate a job

The **Position Analysis Questionnaire (PAQ)**[21] is a structured job analysis checklist that includes 194 items or job elements that are used to rate a job. These job elements are incorporated into the following six dimensions:

1. *Information input:* How and where the worker obtains necessary information for job functioning
2. *Mental processes:* The types of planning, reasoning, and decision-making processes required by the job

3. *Work output:* The specific items produced by the worker and the tools he or she employs to produce them
4. *Relationships with other workers:* Important interpersonal contacts for the jobholder
5. *Job context and work satisfaction:* The physical and social working environments
6. *Other job characteristics:* Elements of the job that do not fall into the other five dimensions[23]

Although the job incumbent can complete the PAQ, typically a job analyst will interview the incumbent prior to directly observing his or her actions in fulfilling the performance requirements of the job. This enables the job analyst to score each of the 194 items on several five-point scales such as frequency of usage, importance to the specific job, and so on. The resultant quantitative score enables the comparison of jobs throughout the organization and for those jobs to be grouped according to similar scores on the six different dimensions.

4. Functional Job Analysis

Functional job analysis (FJA) was used to establish the U.S. government's DOT and had a strong formative influence on Canada's NOC.[24] The FJA employs a series of written task statements, each containing four essential elements: (1) a verb related to the task action being performed by the worker, (2) an object that refers to what is being acted on, (3) a description of equipment, tools, aids, and processes required for successful completion of the task, and (4) the outputs or results of task completion.[25] A compendium of various task statements covers all necessary tasks of the job and, although brevity and concise written statements are the norm, some analysts have devised as many as 100 statements for a job. The completed task statements are used to describe any job and contain three essential elements: (1) people (important interpersonal relationships on the job), (2) data (obtaining, using, and transforming data in aid of job performance), and (3) things (physical machinery, resources, and the environment). Each of these three dimensions is then rated on level of complexity and importance with respect to the job being analyzed. The result of the rating is a quantitative score that can be used to compare various jobs.

functional job analysis (FJA) analyses any job using three essential elements: (1) people (important interpersonal relationships on the job), (2) data (obtaining, using, and transforming data in aid of job performance), and (3) things (physical machinery, resources, and the environment). Each of these three dimensions is then rated by level of complexity and importance.

5. The Hay System

Edward Hay and Associates (HayGroup) has developed a system of job analysis that is used extensively for its consulting work in compensation and organizational analysis. The **Hay system** uses three key factors to analyze each job: (1) know-how (the specific knowledge and skills required to perform the job), (2) problem-solving (the decisions and problems that must be successfully handled on the job), and (3) accountability (the jobholder's responsibilities for critical task completion and for organizational resources, budgets, supervision

The **Hay system** uses three key factors to analyze each job: (1) know-how (the specific knowledge and skills required to perform the job), (2) problem-solving (the decisions and problems that must be successfully handled on the job), and (3) accountability (the jobholder's responsibilities for critical task completion and for organizational resources, budgets, supervision of people, etc.)

of people, etc.).[26] Points are assigned to each factor for (1) levels of knowledge (job depth) and (2) breadth of knowledge required to perform the job (job scope). The sum of the points assigned to the job locates it in an overall compensation scheme that provides higher remuneration to those jobholders whose jobs were rated higher by the job analysis.

Competency-Based Approaches

competency any knowledge, skill, trait, motive, attitude, value, or other personal characteristic that is essential to perform the job and that differentiates superior from solid performance

core competencies characteristics that every member of an organization, regardless of position, function, or level of responsibility with the organization, is expected to possess

role or specific competencies characteristics shared by different positions within an organization.[35] Only those members of an organization in these positions are expected to possess these competencies

Over the past decade, concerns have been expressed that in today's business environment, characterized by increased globalization, extremely turbulent environments, and fierce competition, traditional job analysis may be unable to keep up with the rapid rate of change faced by most organizations.[27] Furthermore, a great many organizations, even those that are highly profitable entities, have reduced their complement of full-time workers by "downsizing," thereby producing flatter organizational structures with fewer workers and greater reliance on self-managed teams in achieving desired organizational outcomes.[28] In this context, the increased desire for flexibility and cross-training of employees has led to a trend of examining **competency** modelling in order to identify general worker requirements associated with a broad range or category of jobs.[29] Although traditional job analysis is still firmly entrenched in most organizations, it is also true that most organizations have started to examine and institute competency-based practices into their work settings. Competency-based approaches have been used to develop successful professional performance for dentists, engineers, nurses, physicians, and police officers, etc.[30] Recent surveys have shown that approximately 75% to 80% of organizations have some sort of competency-driven applications currently in place.[31]

Competency advocates maintain that there are several differences in approach between more traditional job analysis methods and competency-based modelling. First, where traditional job analysis focuses on the KSAs required to perform specific jobs and examines the linkages among those jobs, competency models focus on individual-level competencies that are common to a broader occupational group or an entire level of jobs (e.g., executives, production workers, supervisory management). There is a deliberate focus on a much broader set of classifying variables than is typical for traditional job analysis.[32] Competencies are typically categorized as **core competencies** (characteristics that every member of an organization, regardless of position, function, or level of responsibility with the organization, is expected to possess) or **role or specific competencies** (characteristics shared by different positions within an organization.[33] Only those members of an organization in these positions are expected to possess these competencies). Second, some job analysts maintain that competency models are worker-focused, given their focus on identifying core competencies, whereas job analysis is much more focused on duties and tasks of work. In this regard, competency models include personality and value orientations (e.g., risk-taking) into the mix of what is required to "fit in" and succeed in the culture of a particular organization. Third, since much of the work in organizations is conducted by teams, it can be argued that team skills are much more relevant to today's organization than the classic interaction of individual job with well-defined boundaries. Management personnel recognize that workers know the limits of their jobs and could readily refuse to perform a task that fell beyond their written job description requirements. As such, managers seek to have increased flexibility and control over workers' behaviours. On the other hand, unions are justifiably concerned about management abuses of authority in the new "competencies" approach, which lack the important safeguards of written documentation and well-defined limits to arbitary displays of managerial power as are contained in traditional job descriptions and collective agreements.[34] Widespread problems with corruption, fraud, and executive mismanagement, as displayed by the corporate

BOX 5.5 Competency Models in Practice

Innovative organizations can utilize competency modelling in order to determine the behavioural requirements for employee success now and into the future. One organization, the American Institute of Certified Public Accountants, has developed a web-based competency assessment tool that enables accounting students and CPAs to compare their current knowledge and skill levels against those competencies that have been validated for success in a variety of jobs such as "staff accountant" or "CFO: chief financial officer." The competency models incorporate four different factors: (1) leadership qualities; (2) personal attributes; (3) functional specialties; and (4) broad business perspectives. By utilizing this convenient analytical tool, current and future accountants can get invaluable feedback about their progress toward personalized career goals. This information can also assist in developing and refocusing training and development priorities for accountants to ensure they have the knowledge and skills required for success in their desired positions.

Another area that has used competency models is the leisure or recreation business. Country, golf, and family clubs require managers who are able to successfully deal with a wide variety of complex issues on a day-to-day basis. The Club Managers Association of America conducted competency assessments during the 1990s but they wanted to see how or if the demands on managers would change in the new millennium. Industry experts and club managers identified and analyzed future changes that could be expected in the environment of clubs. The key finding of this competency analysis process was that in the future managers will have to be more effective in their time-management skills in order to be able to separate and sustain their personal and professional lives. Overall, eight competencies were identified (food and beverage management; club governance; building and facility management; human and professional resources; club accounting and finance; general management; marketing, sports, and recreation, management; and external and governmental interaction), which were reduced to three main categories: (1) accounting and finance, (2) human and professional resources, and (3) marketing. The findings will be used for future career planning, training, and development, and performance evaluation purposes for club managers across North America.

Sources: Adapted from K. Briggs, "Competencies—The Differential!" *Journal of Accountancy*, Vol. 194, No. 3 (September 2002), p. 79; and J. Perdue et al., "Competencies Required for Future Club Manager's Success," *Cornell Hotel and Restaurant Administration Quarterly*, Vol. 42, No. 1, (February 2001), pp. 60–65.

crashes of Nortel, Enron, and Worldcom, among others, show that unions, as the representatives of the organization's workforce, are well advised to tread carefully with respect to innovations in this area.

On the downside, competency approaches have been subjected to widespread criticisms as to their utility, including that they are so broad and ill-defined as to be of little practical use in guiding performance of job duties.[35] Another criticism is that competencies focus more on behaviours than results, and as such focus on how individuals are expected to perform and not their demonstrated achievements.[36] Furthermore, there has been a great deal of confusion among workers, HR practitioners, and academics as to what exactly is incorporated into effective competency models. There are a very wide range of definitions as to what exactly constitues a competency, and, as noted by Zemke, "the word 'competencies' today is a term that has no meaning apart from the particular definition agreed to by the person with whom one is speaking."[37] Secondly, it has been noted that competency modelling is far from being a novel or separate activity from job analysis, but is in fact merely an extension of job analysis that focuses on what is common across jobs and occupational groups and identifies the activities and worker characteristics that are core or critical on an organization-wide basis. Third, by focusing only on broad general competencies, it can easily be argued that a large portion of the activities required for an individual's successful performance in a job remains largely unexplained. Furthermore, it has been noted by a number of HR specialists that unlike job analysis, which is well understood by most HR practitioners and industrial/organizational psychologists, competency modelling is so ill-defined that they see absolutely no value in its approach and they expect it to die quickly![38] Only time will tell, so stay tuned!

BOX 5.6 Assessing Competencies and Skills in the Workplace

Research shows that managers and workers have different perceptions about the competencies and skills associated with various jobs in organizations. The main discrepancies between managers and workers exist in their different perceptions of "workplace autonomy" and "level of required skills." Workers report lower levels of autonomy in their jobs and higher levels of skills requirements for success than are reported by managers for the same jobs under analysis. Furthermore, it is suggested that workers do not see competency as a specific set of attributes, knowledge, skills, and abilities, but as the sum of their perceived experiences and meaning of work.

Sources: Adapted from F. Green, "Assessing Skills and Autonomy: The Job Holder versus the Line Manager," *Human Resource Management Journal*, Vol. 13, No. 1, pp. 63–74; and J. Sandberg, "Understanding Human Competence at Work: An Interpretative Approach," *Academy of Management Journal*, Vol. 43, No. 1 (February 2000), pp. 9–25.

Summary

In this chapter, we have examined a number of important aspects of the job analysis process in preparation for the next chapter's presentation on human resources management systems (HRMS). We have noted how an organization's work process is subdivided into meaningful units of work called jobs, and how the analysis of these jobs can take many forms, such as interviews, observation, and questionnaires. The investigation of jobs focuses on two specific aspects: namely, the methods employed to perform the job and the time standards for work completion. We examined a variety of traditional methods of job analysis (e.g., interviews, observation, questionnaires, journals and diaries, output and production analysis, etc.) including the recent trend of work analysis through competency-based approaches. Once job information has been collected and analyzed, it is stored in the HRMS or database to be used in the HR planning process. This stored job analysis information will be combined with personal information on the employees to try to make the best possible match between individual needs for fulfilling and rewarding work and the organization's requirements for specific work competencies.

Key Terms

Behaviourally Anchored Rating Scales (BARS), 124

benchmark, 117

compensable factors, 114

competency, 126

contamination, 115

core competencies, 126

critical incidents technique, 124

deficiency, 115

Dictionary of Occupational Titles (DOT), 117

functional job analysis, 125

Hay system, 125

job, 112

job analysis, 112

job description, 112

job specification, 112

National Occupational Classification (NOC), 117

position, 112

Position Analysis Questionnaire (PAQ), 124

role or specific competencies, 126

scientific management, 114

360-degree evaluation, 118

SUGGESTED WEBSITES

www.hr-guide.com A useful guide to Internet resources on HR.

www.worklogic.com/en/hrdc_noc.html Presents information on Canada's *National Occupational Classification.*

www.oalj.dol.gov/libdot.htm U.S. Department of Labor information on the *Dictionary of Occupational Titles.*

www.erieri.com Economic Research Institute's website on the *Dictionary of Occupational Titles.*

www2.hrnext.com Analysis from HR Next on job analysis procedures and processes.

www.jobdescription.com Knowledgepoint's website on job descriptions.

www.paq.com PAQ Services Inc. website presents the Position Analysis Questionnaire.

DISCUSSION QUESTIONS

1. One of the common reasons advanced for not conducting job analyses is the substantial cost that can be associated with such an undertaking. Present a more balanced perspective by identifying both the various benefits of conducting job analyses and the incremental costs that may occur if the process is not instigated.
2. In this chapter, it was stressed that effective job analysis incorporates qualitative and quantitative aspects, as well as a multi-method approach. Why is this additional complexity an important component of an effective job analysis intervention?
3. Jobs and the nature of work itself are dramatically changing in our information-based, global economy. How will the emerging patterns of work affect the nature of organizational participation, the nature of our jobs, and the process we employ to conduct job analyses in the future?

EXERCISE

Conduct a job analysis of the job you currently perform. Which methods will you utilize to conduct the analysis? Whom will you contact in order to obtain valid information about the duties, tasks, information, accountabilities, and KSAs required to perform your job? Complete the task by writing a new (or updated) job description for your job.

CASE: MADNESS AT MOOSEHEAD U

As a distinguished graduate of Moosehead University's HR program, you having been achieving considerable fortune and fame in your role as a consulting job analyst; your success is aptly reflected by your painfully fashionable clothes, the waterfront condo, the matching "his and hers" platinum Range Rovers, and of course your favourite possession, the isolated lakeside cottage in the Canadian Shield. Things are good! Well, things are good with *you* personally, but obviously there are problems that need to be addressed at your Alma Mater.

Just this morning you received a frantic phone call from Dr. Melinda Muckabout, the university's vice-president of Administration, seeking to engage your professional services. It seems that she has been receiving considerable pressure from her boss, Dr. Hamish Haberdashery (VP Academic) and the president, Dr. Carla Climber. They in turn have been receiving pointed directives for action from the funding arm of the Provincial Ministry for Universities. Specifically, they have been told bluntly by the deputy minister that if Moosehead doesn't take action within the next six months to implement "performance indicators" for university faculty members and professors, the university will be subjected to a severe funding cut. The politicians and civil servants are responding to ongoing pressure from students, parents, and other taxpayers for much greater emphasis on rewarding quality teaching, enhancing job performance, and obtaining accountability from all the provincial universities.

In your role as a job analyst, you will have your work cut out for you. Melinda let you know that for every five faculty members on campus there are probably at least six different opinions on the core elements of a faculty member's job. To quote her exact words: "It's complete madness here!" The only internal policy guide is a Senate document that specifies in very general terms that a full-time faculty member has three areas of duties and responsibility: (1) teaching, (2) research and scholarly activities, and (3) service. There are great variations within each of these three categories. Teaching workloads vary enormously among professors with respect to the number of different courses and topics taught; whether the courses are introductory or advanced, undergraduate, or graduate level; whether they are "live" or delivered by Internet; the number of students in the classes themselves; and the degree of teaching and marking support made available by the university. The second category, "research and scholarly activities" is so incredibly broad as to almost defy description. It includes not only research and publications in journals, books, and practitioner magazines, but also theatre performances; media interviews; art gallery presentations; lectures to professional groups, the public, and other bodies; and lending professional expertise to groups within and outside the university itself. There are also huge variations among faculty members with respect to the funding support they receive for research, course releases from teaching, and general computer and facility support for these "scholarly" activities. The final category, service, typically incorporates serving on various university committees and task forces at the department, faculty, or university-wide level, but it also incorporates service to community groups and outside agencies, activities that increase the prestige and visibility of the university.

Suddenly your decision to take the contract doesn't look so straightforward. Certainly this will be a much more difficult assignment than many you have taken in the private sector.

However, over and above your fond attachment to Moosehead University, you realize that the university officials are relying on you to come through for them as they will be hard-pressed to sustain one more budget cut on top of the past decade of slashed budgets and decreased financial support. The finished documents you produce will be used not only to annually assess the performance of faculty members on key explicit job dimensions, but also to generate quantitative scores for each faculty member on these dimensions that can be used for compensation and "merit" pay. Furthermore, the finished documents will be of a quasi-legal nature as they will guide and constrain decisions on faculty tenure and promotion, as well as the selection, training, developing, and career progression of Moosehead's faculty members. You certainly have your work cut out for you. It's time to get to it!

Source: K. McBey, *Madness at Moosehead U*, 2002.

Question

As the consulting job analyst to Moosehead University, prepare an intake evaluation report that contains your recommended steps and sequencing of activities to conduct this work analysis. List the various stakeholders you will consult, and indicate specific methods and techniques you will employ in successfully completing this contractual assignment.

References

Ashkenas, R., D. Ulrich, T. Jick, and S. Kerr. 1995. *The Boundaryless Organization.* San Francisco: Jossey-Bass.

Campbell, J., M. Dunnette, R. Arvey, and L. Hellervik. 1973. "The Development and Evaluation of Behaviorally Based Rating Scales." *Journal of Applied Psychology*, Vol. 57, No. 1 (February): 15–22.

Catano, V., S. Cronshaw, W. Wiesner, R. Hackett, and L. Methot. 2001. *Recruitment and Selection in Canada*, 2nd ed. Toronto: Nelson Thomson Learning.

Denton, J.C. 1975. *The Position Description Questionnaire*. Cleveland, Ohio: Psychological Business Research.

Employment and Immigration Canada. 1993. *National Occupational Classification*. Cat. No. MP 53-25-1-1993E. Ottawa: Minister of Supply and Services.

Fine, S. 1974. "Functional Job Analysis: An Approach to a Technology for

Manpower Planning." *Personnel Journal* (November): 813–818.

Fine, S., and W.W. Wiley. 1971. *An Introduction to Functional Job Analysis.* Kalamazoo, Mich.: Upjohn Institute for Employment Research.

Flanagan, J.C. 1954. "The Critical Incidents Technique." *Psychological Bulletin*, Vol. 51: 327–358.

Gael, S. 1988. *The Job Analysis Handbook for Business, Industry, and Government.* New York: John Wiley.

Gatewood, R.D., and H.S. Field. 1990. *Human Resources Selection,* 2nd ed. New York: Dryden Press.

Ghorpade, J.V. 1988. *Job Analysis: A Handbook for the Human Resource Director.* Englewood Cliffs, N.J.: Prentice Hall.

Godet, M. 1983. "Reducing the Blunders in Forecasting." *Futures*, Vol. 15, No. 3 (June): 181–192.

Grant, P. 1997. "Job Descriptions: What's Missing." *Industrial Management*, Vol. 39, No. 6 (December): 9–13.

Hackman, R., and G. Oldham. 1974. *The Job Diagnostic Survey: An Instrument for the Diagnosis of Jobs and the Evaluation of Job Redesign Projects.* Springfield, Ill.: National Technical Information Service.

———. 1975. "Development of the Job Diagnostic Survey." *Journal of Applied Psychology*, Vol. 60: 159–170.

Hayden, S. 1999. "Competency Based Management." *IHRIM Journal*, Vol. 3, No. 1: 16–18.

Hemphill, J.K. 1960. *Dimensions of Executive Positions.* Columbus, Ohio: Ohio State University.

Henderson, R. 1993. *Compensation Management*, 6th ed. Reston, Va.: Reston Publishing.

Hom, P.W., A.S. DeNisis, A.J. Kinicki, and B. Bannister. 1982. "Effectiveness of Performance Feedback from Behaviorally Anchored Rating Scales." *Journal of Applied Psychology*, Vol. 67, No. 5 (October): 568–576.

Intagliata, J., D. Ulrich, and N. Smallwood. 2000. "Leveraging Leadership Competencies to Produce Leadership Brand: Creating Distinctiveness by Focusing on Strategy and Results." *Human Resources Planning*, Vol. 23, No. 3: 12–23.

Jacobs, R., D. Kafry, and S. Zedeck. 1980. "Expectations of Behaviorally Anchored Rating Scales." *Personnel Psychology*, Vol. 33, No. 3 (Autumn): 595–640.

Jenkins, G.D. 1975. "Standardized Observations: An Approach to Measuring the Nature of Jobs." *Journal of Applied Psychology* (April): 171–181.

Kerr, S. 1975. "On the Folly of Rewarding A, While Hoping for B." *Academy of Management Journal* (December): 769–783.

Kingstrom, P., and A. Bass. 1981. "A Critical Analysis of Studies Comparing Behaviorally Anchored Rating Scales and Other Rating Formats." *Personnel Psychology*, Vol. 34, No. 2 (Summer): 263–289.

Levine, E.L. 1983. *Everything You Always Wanted to Know about Job Analysis.* Tampa, Fla.: Mariner Publishing.

Mahmoud, E. 1984. "Accuracy in Forecasting: A Survey." *Journal of Forecasting*, Vol. 3, No. 2 (April): 139–159.

McBey, K.J. 1996. "Exploring the Role of Individual Job Performance within a Multivariate Investigation into Part-time Turnover Processes." *Psychological Reports*, Vol. 78: 223–233.

McBey, K., and C. Hammah. 1990. "The Evolution of Managerial and Organizational Thought." In L. Allan, ed., *Introduction to Canadian Business.* Toronto: McGraw-Hill Ryerson.

McCormick, E.J. 1976. "Job and Task Analysis." In M.C. Dunnette, ed., *Handbook of Industrial and Organizational Psychology.* New York: Rand McNally.

McCormick, E.J., P.R. Jeanneret, and R.C. Meecham. 1972. "A Study of Job Characteristics and Job Dimensions as Based on the PAQ." *Journal of Applied Psychology*, Vol. 56, No. 4 (August): 347–368.

Mintzberg, H. 1973. *The Nature of Managerial Work.* New York: Harper and Row.

Prien, E., and W.W. Ronan. 1971. "Job Analysis: A Review of Research Findings." *Personnel Psychology*, Vol. 24: 371–396.

Reynolds, R., and M. Brannick. 2001. "Is Job Analysis Doing the Job? Extending Job Analysis with Cognitive Task Analysis." *Society for Industrial and Organizational Psychology*, July.

Risher, H.W. 1989. "Job Evaluation: Validity and Reliability." *Compensation and Benefits Review*, Vol. 21, No. 1 (January): 32–33.

Sanchez, J. 1994. "From Documentation to Innovation: Reshaping Job Analysis to Meet Emerging Business Needs." *Human Resource Management Review*, Vol. 4, No. 1: 51–74.

Schippmann, J., R. Ash, M. Battista, et al. 2000. "The Practice of Competency Modeling." *Personnel Psychology*, Vol. 53, No. 3 (Autumn): 703–737.

Schuler, R.S., and J.W. Walker. 1990. "Human Resources Strategy: Focusing on Issues and Actions." *Organizational Dynamics:* 5–19.

United States Department of Labor. 1994. *Handbook for Analyzing Jobs.* Washington, D.C.: U.S. Government Printing Office.

Walker, J.W. 1980. *Human Resource Planning.* New York: McGraw-Hill.

———. 1994. "Integrating the Human Resource Function with the Business." *Human Resource Planning*, Vol. 17, No. 2: 59–77.

ENDNOTES

1. Walker, 1994; Schuler and Walker, 1990.
2. Gatewood and Field, 1990.
3. Risher, 1989.
4. Walker, 1980.
5. McBey and Hammah, 1990.
6. McBey, 1996.
7. Employment and Immigration Canada, 1993.
8. United States Department of Labor, 1994.
9. Jenkins, 1975.

10. Gael, 1988; Ghorpade, 1988; Prien and Ronan, 1971.
11. Jenkins, 1975.
12. Denton, 1975.
13. Fine and Wiley, 1971; Fine, 1974.
14. Hackman and Oldham, 1974; 1975.
15. Hemphill, 1960.
16. McCormick et al., 1972.
17. Schuler and Walker, 1990; Godet, 1983; Mahmoud, 1984.
18. Kerr, 1975.
19. Flanagan, 1954; Ghorpade, 1988.
20. Campbell et al., 1973; Hom et al., 1982; Jacobs et al., 1980; Kingstrom and Bass, 1981.
21. McCormick et al., 1972.
22. Fine and Wiley, 1971; Fine, 1974.
23. McCormick, 1976.
24. Fine, 1974; Levine, 1983.
25. Henderson, 1993.
26. Reynolds and Brannick, 2001; Sanchez, 1994.
27. Ashkenas et al., 1995.
28. Hayden, 1999.
29. Catano et al., 2001.
30. Schippmann et al., 2000.
31. Ibid.
32. Catano et al., 2001, p. 176.
33. Sanchez, 1994.
34. Intagliata et al., 2000.
35. Cited in Schippmann et al., 2000, p. 706.
36. Schippmann et. al., 2000, p. 731.
37. Fine and Wiley, 1971; Fine, 1974.
38. Hemphill, 1960.

6

HR MANAGEMENT SYSTEMS

CHAPTER GOALS

To become effective HR planners, it is essential that we have current, relevant information readily available for our planning purposes. Specifically, to correctly calculate personnel demand and supply levels, we must have access to information on the numbers, availability, skill qualification levels, performance evaluation results, career development plans, succession or replacement scenarios, training needs, and so on of our entire workforce. It is to these elements of information, among many others, that we devote this chapter on **Human Resources Management Systems** (**HRMS**), also known as **Human Resources Information Systems** (**HRIS**). The HRMS constitutes the integrated database system that is essential to permit high-quality, informed HR planning decisions to be made.

Human Resources Management Systems (HRMS)/Human Resources Information Systems (HRIS) the integrated database system that is essential to permit high-quality, informed HR planning decisions to be made

After reading this chapter, you should be able to do the following:

1. Understand the critical importance of the HRMS to the HR planning process.

2. Appreciate the increasing complexity associated with the normal three-stage evolution of HRMS.
3. Use selection and design criteria that will allow you to evaluate various HRMS as to their degree of fit with specific organizational configurations.
4. Evaluate specific data elements, which are inputs to the HRMS, and evaluate their utility based on selection criteria.
5. Comprehend the necessity for operating restrictions and safeguards on the access and usage of data contained in the HRMS.
6. Discuss the importance of various reports that can be developed as output formats from the HRMS, and evaluate their relative utility to a specific organization.

In Chapter 5, we noted that the job analysis process identifies the employee specifications (KSAs) required to successfully perform the duties and tasks of the various jobs in an organization. This information is typically stored on a computer database to enable matching comparisons to be conducted between the organizational requirements, as identified by the job analysis process, and the current state of employee competencies. The degree of congruence between the two is the key factor in instigating HR programs such as training and development, work redesign, re-evaluation of compensation (e.g., pay for performance, skill-based pay, merit pay) and other terms of employment, as well as various staffing initiatives (e.g., recruiting, layoffs, hiring freezes, attrition).

The information contained in the HRMS is critical to effective HR planning, so it is essential that it be accurate, up to date, relevant, and of high quality, and in sufficient quantity to make effective decisions. HRMS data are

BOX 6.1 The Myths and Realities of HR Technology Usage

Despite the widespread availability of comprehensive, integrative HRMS from vendors such as Peoplesoft and SAP, it is clear that many organizations are still using HR technology primarily for documentation and office administration purposes. A 2002 study of 135 U.S. organizations conducted by *Canadian HR Reporter* and Watson Wyatt found that 62% of responding organizations were using many home-grown systems to support their HR functions in lieu of employing an integrated client-server HRMS (21% of organizations). The top reported uses for the HR technology were for conducting office and HR administration, HR transactions, and file and document handling. However, fewer than a quarter of the responding organizations used their HR technology for employee self-service functions, training and development, conducting skills inventories, or career planning. Furthermore, other studies have shown that the key contributions that can be made by using an HRMS/HRIS for analyzing HR issues arising from mergers and acquisitions are frequently overlooked.

Sources: Adapted from *On the Charts, Canadian HR Reporter*: Guide to HR Technology supplement, March 10, 2003, p. G3; and "Mergers and Acquisitions—The Neglected HRIS Challenge," *HR Focus*, Vol. 79, No. 9 (September 2002), pp. 6–7.

used to make policy decisions that affect a variety of different areas including the following: (1) legal compliance, (2) absenteeism and turnover reports, (3) the organization's demographic composition, (4) performance appraisal rating history, (5) succession and replacement plans, (6) compensation reviews, (7) assessment of training and development needs, (8) career counselling and planning, (9) matching of individual and organizational needs, (10) work redesign and restructuring planning, and (11) assessment centre and potential ratings.[1]

At the outset of HRMS development, the various systems available on the market tended to be extremely expensive, highly structured, and designed to meet the needs of large multinational corporations. However, over the last decade a great deal of effort has been expended by HRMS vendors in developing systems that are more flexible and less expensive to implement and operate. As a result, much of the recent growth in HRMS has been linked to medium and small enterprises, who have welcomed the easier-to-use systems, which facilitate skill tracking, succession planning, and the "self-service" capability available to their employees.[2]

Three Stages of HRMS Development

Having noted the requirement to match the needs of both the individual employee and the organization, we now turn to a discussion of the organizational evolution of HRMS. Generally, we can classify an organization as being in one of three stages of development with respect to its HRMS. The three stages are discussed below.[3]

1. Basic Personnel System

A number of Canadian companies are still operating at stage one with a **basic personnel system**. This bare-bones approach to an HRMS incorporates databases that often mix written records on file with other data elements stored on a computer database. The data maintained by this type of system focus on the following areas: (1) employee records (e.g., individual profile, personal information sheet, application form, orientation acknowledgment, employment agreement or contract); (2) payroll (wage or salary, attendance and vacation entries, and pension and benefit data); (3) staffing (job descriptions for executive and key organizational jobs only); and (4) basic data required for compliance with pertinent labour legislation.[4] This information is used almost exclusively by HR staff in stand-alone applications. The focus is on correct record-keeping of the organization's personnel activities, so the system is oriented toward the past. Because of this situation, the basic personnel system is reactive in nature and of limited use for HR policy decision-making and strategic HR planning.

basic personnel system a bare-bones HRMS approach incorporating databases that may mix written records on file with other data elements stored on a computer database

2. Augmented HR System

augmented HR system occurs when the organization decides to commit the resources to become more proactive with respect to HR policy decisions

Movement to the second stage, an **augmented HR system**, occurs when the organization decides to commit the resources to become more proactive with respect to HR policy decisions. A stage-two setup requires the HRMS to move beyond the basic record-keeping function of a stage-one system. In stage two, the HRMS becomes entirely computer based, and the data elements in stage one typically are augmented by a variety of information determined by a needs analysis. Given the increasing memory and data-processing capabilities of present-day computers, there are almost limitless possibilities for data inclusion. As we shall see later in this chapter, the organization must give priority to the addition of data that are of greatest relevance to its operations. If, for example, absenteeism and turnover have been noted as problems, the augmented HR system can track individual absences or separations by a variety of combinations of worker classification, geographical location, authority level, and so on. This enables HR planners to identify more readily developing problem areas or trends and thereby be proactive in developing or modifying personnel policies to effectively deal with such problems.

3. Comprehensive and Interactive HRMS

comprehensive and interactive HRMS an HRMS configuration that enables the HR planning staff to run "what if" scenarios to determine the best future policy alternatives given a range of possible outcomes

relational databases enable the user to customize the HR data to be investigated, thereby offering a wide variety of searches and analyses to be conducted

Relatively few companies have evolved to the stage-three setup of a **comprehensive and interactive HRMS.**[5] This type of HRMS configuration enables the HR planning staff to run future "what-if" scenarios to determine the best future policy alternatives given a range of possible outcomes.[6] As well, **relational databases** enable the user to customize the HR data to be investigated, thereby offering a wide variety of searches and analyses to be conducted. A typical example would be the use of such a system to develop a candidate list for attendance at an assessment centre and for future management-development programs. In such an instance, the computer search could select candidates who had (1) performance appraisal ratings of "above average" or higher over the past five years, (2) successfully completed a graduate degree (preferably an MBA), and (3) a minimum of five years' seniority in the organization. The program coordinator of management development could then review the list produced by the database search, using input from senior managers and executives, to decide whom to include or exclude from the list. Although the list would undoubtedly be modified through the review by HR staff and managers, using the HRMS would save considerable time and expense in developing a comprehensive list of management trainees. This list would then form the basis for comment and review.

Although a comprehensive and interactive HRMS is the goal of many organizational HR planning systems, especially because of its orientation toward analysis of future scenarios and decision-making options, it is not necessarily optimal for all organizations. Only very large multinational and gov-

BOX 6.2 How Canadian Organizations Use Their HRMS

A study of 378 Canadian organizations conducted by *Canadian HR Reporter* found that 48% of the organizations had a computer-based HRMS. However it is clear from the findings that these organizations are a long way from obtaining the maximum benefit from their systems as many capabilities are not being fully exploited. The HRMS were primarily used for

- Basic employee data
- Company costs
- Company work location
- Employee job grades and job history
- Payroll
- Employee compensation
- Benefits information
- Employee absences
- Employee terminations

The least used HRMS features included important HR activities such as

- Career planning
- Succession planning
- Occupational health and safety
- Labour relations
- Job postings
- Hiring requisitions
- Employee job competencies

Source: Adapted from Pearson, George. 2001. "HRMS Does Make a Difference," *Canadian HR Reporter*, Guide to HR Technology supplement, October 22, G1 & G4. Adapted by permission of Carswell, a division of Thomson Canada Limited.

ernmental organizations, particularly those operating in the transportation, communications, and utilities industries, tend to use complex, integrated statistical systems for their HRMS and forecasting procedures.[7] Furthermore, it is reported that many firms, despite having the financial resources to afford sophisticated systems, had, in fact, reverted to relatively simple systems because of their ease of use and environmental stability. Therefore, although there is support for the three-stage evolution of an HRMS, a contrasting view is that many organizations opt for simplicity or concurrently use sophisticated *and* primitive forecasting techniques.[8] A variety of factors have to be weighed to determine the right system configuration for each organization. We now turn to an analysis of a few of these factors.

Selection and Design Criteria for HRMS

1. System Security and Access Control

Given that the HRMS contains sensitive personal information about the workforce, as well as planning scenarios for such things as replacement and succession, it is vital that proper attention be given to controlling access to this

personal identification numbers (PINs) alphanumerical combinations that are used to restrict access to authorized users

information.[9] This is especially important in those organizations that are devolving or decentralizing HR functions to the operational line managers. Access should be granted only on a "need-to-know" basis, with passwords, **personal identification numbers (PINs)**, and codes serving as entry barriers prohibiting unauthorized access to other data elements that are not required by the legitimate work requirements of a particular jobholder. Some HRMS also offer data encryption options to ensure that confidential data cannot be viewed or altered by non-authorized personnel. Second, access requirements should be reviewed on a regular basis to determine if continued access to the specific data elements is still valid; if not, the job incumbent should be denied entry to the confidential database. A third element with respect to access concerns the individual employee's right to examine his or her personal record to ensure that it is accurate and contains only job-related information. This right of access is upheld by the Canadian Privacy Act to prevent discriminatory material or information that is not related to the job from entering into selection and employment decisions, which are regulated by federal and provincial human rights legislation.

2. User Friendliness of the HRMS

HRMS software varies substantially with respect to the training time and ease of use for HR staff. Systems that build on common HR terminology and are designed to run in conjunction with other widespread computer operating systems (e.g., Microsoft Windows and MS DOS, UNIX), will require less preparatory training of staff than would very specialized HRMS applications. Second, HRMS vary substantially as to the degree to which they can be customized to meet user requirements. Users should consider explicitly the degree to which the selected system will allow customization of HR forms and reports to meet actual operating requirements. The wise purchaser will note that many HRMS are not con-

BOX 6.3 Tips for Data Security

The financial and legal implications of poor data security can be enormous. Fraud, loss of proprietary information, sabotage, and breach of personal, privileged information all can result from improperly secured data. The journal *Workforce* presented some helpful advice on ways to enhance data security. As the biggest security threat is normally from inside the organization—that is, from current members of the workforce—it is essential that the organization train and educate workers on data handling, storage, and usage considerations, and have explicit, well-communicated security policies in place. Procedures to enhance security of data include the usage of PINs and passwords; the usage of encryption devices or software when sending sensitive e-mail; providing regular, ongoing education and reinforcement of clearly defined organizational policies; and turning off systems when they are not in use.

Source: Adapted from S. Greengard, "How Secure Is Your Data?" *Workforce*, Vol. 77, No. 5 (May 1998), pp. 52–60.

figured to enable end-user modification of the HRMS. Therefore, the formats are as delivered by the vendor's assessment of your needs, which may be very different from your actual requirements now and especially in the future.[10]

3. Flexibility and Interface with Other Organizational Systems

When purchasing HRMS software, the organization must consider the linkage between existing computer hardware and the proposed software system, as well as staff computer literacy with the various systems.[11] It is important to ensure that there is a smooth interface between hardware and software, thereby minimizing the errors or "bugs" occurring as a result of the joint operation of the two.[12] In addition to close scrutiny of operational requirements and programming sequences, smart purchasers will ask for demonstrations and a trial period of operating the HRMS to ensure successful and problem-free operation of the system before a purchase commitment is made.

4. Appropriateness for Meeting Organizational Needs

Some companies make the mistake of purchasing HRMS software because of beneficial features in one specific area (e.g., compensation). Vendors naturally are delighted to expound on all the nifty features of their particular HRMS system. The wise purchaser will take time to identify and rank the organization's HR goals for the HRMS. Doing so will lead to search behaviour that is focused on the "must haves" and will lessen the purchaser's distraction by peripheral options that are only "nice to have."[13]

With respect to the vendor, it is important to research the wide variety of HRMS software vendors offering products. A comprehensive and comparative analysis, such as that provided by HRMS Directions Inc.,[14] can facilitate intelligent comparison of vendors. One must consider not only the price (annual licensing fee), but also a variety of factors, such as (1) the number of years the software company has been in existence (incorporated); (2) whether the vendor specializes in HRMS or they are only a peripheral sideline for its other information system activities; (3) post-purchase service support packages; (4) the number of clients in Canada, and the degree of Canadian content; (5) the number of actual installations in Canada (which can be dramatically different from the number of clients!) and, of course; (6) the vendor's reputation for reliability in the industry.[15]

5. System Costs and Service Support

With respect to HRMS implementation costs, organizational purchasers sometimes forget to factor in the training expense of converting HR and other staff users to operating the new system. Furthermore, some purchasers take a very myopic approach to cost analysis because they consider only the annual licensing fee for the HRMS (which can vary from several hundred dollars to several hundred thousand dollars per year, depending on the size and complexity of the HRMS). However, in addition to this annual licensing fee, one has to consider the ongoing costs of providing assistance, technical support, and upgrades to the newly established system. Vendors vary widely as to the post-purchase support they offer to clients, and the supplemental costs to clients for these services typically run in the range of 15 to 25% of annual licensing fees.[16] For this money, you might receive a combination of user training, use of a toll-free telephone help line, e-mail help through the Internet, installation of HRMS upgrades, newsletters, and so on. The wise customer shops carefully to get the specific vendor support required and does not pay extra for superfluous assistance that can be provided by in-house organizational resources.

management information system (MIS) or **decision support system (DSS)** personnel trained in computer and information technology who operate and provide support to management and the decision-making infrastructure of the organization

Speaking of organizational staff, the HR and **management information system (MIS)** or **decision support system (DSS)** staff must be involved in developing the HRMS decision criteria and selecting the final system because these people will be the primary source of on-site expertise and assistance once the system is running successfully. It is absolutely essential that the selected HRMS build on this staff's knowledge of computer operating systems and software so that the system can be improved as time goes on. Programming development for HRMS uses a wide variety of languages, depending on the particular system purchased. Some systems use C, PASCAL, or ORACLE, as well as more traditional programming languages such as COBOL and BASIC. Ensure the HRMS purchased either can use a variety of different programming languages or, at the bare minimum, operates those developmental procedures that are established and well known by your HR and MIS/DSS staff.

BOX 6.4 Employing the HRMS Strategically

It is clear that many organizations are failing to take advantage of the wide range of capabilities offered by their HRMS. If more attention was devoted to conducting "what-if" analyses, and to utilizing health and safety, training, employee performance, and absenteeism data, considerable improvement in HR policy implementation, with an associated reduction in unnecessary expenditures, could be achieved. In order to employ the HRMS more strategically, organizations may have to conduct supplemental employee training that combines vendor training programs with other HRMS training obtained from external third parties. Vendors typically offer training at their own locations and based upon their own standardized programs and schedules, which may not be suitable for your organization's needs. Courses should be developed to reflect the realities of employee availability, work patterns, and production schedules of the using organization. Furthermore, by means of conducting "train the trainer" programs, the number of employees who have to take external training courses might be significantly reduced. Finally, remember to develop criteria to evaluate HRMS training to assess whether the courses worked well in meeting the stated training aims.

Sources: Adapted from F. Jossi, "Get the Most out of HRIS Training," *HR Magazine*, Vol. 46, No. 3 (March 2001), pp. 121–128; and G. Safran, "Getting the I out of Your HRIS," *Canadian HR Reporter*, February 26, 2001.

BOX 6.5 The New HRIS: Good Deal or $6-Million Paperweight?

The successful implementation of a new HRIS depends on consideration of technological, people, and process issues. With regard to technology, it is important that the HRIS dovetails with the organization's current and future requirements for technology. The biggest issues concern people, including the requirement for top management support for the system, consideration of ways to get end-users to use system features, and ensuring that in-house systems/DSS (decision support system) personnel have the proper skills to implement and support the HRIS. With respect to process, there is a requirement for either a customized HRIS to fit existing processes or modifications to existing organizational processes to conform to the off-the-shelf HRIS configuration.

Source: Adapted from B. Roberts, "The New HRIS: Good Deal or $6-Million Paperweight?" *HR Magazine*, Vol. 43, No. 2 (February 1998), pp. 40–46.

6. HRMS Future Expansion

Given the considerable time expenditures and costs associated with implementing an HRMS, paying the ongoing annual licence and service-support fees, training the organizational staff, and, of course, the critical informational outputs of the HRMS, it is hoped that our selected system, like a new car, will stand us in good stead well into the future. Accordingly, we must buy now with an eye to probable future requirements for our HRMS.[17]

Currently, over 75 integrated and specialist HRMS are available to the Canadian business organization.[18] **Integrated systems** are those that offer a variety of HR record and decision-making functions, whereas **specialist programs** are tailored to servicing customer needs in one or two narrowly defined areas (e.g., compensation—that is, payroll plus benefits). The individual components contained in a basic integrated system differ substantially among vendors. Typically, we see record-keeping, payroll and compensation, time and attendance tracking protocols, and elements for job analysis information, as well as for performance appraisal, contained in the basic package. Irrespective of the integrated system obtained, it is wise to inquire about vendor options or modules, which can be added to the current HRMS to expand its capability at a future date. As we move from the augmented to a more comprehensive and interactive HRMS, we must always consider not only current organizational requirements, but also future needs. Notwithstanding the benefits of any one HR component, if the HRMS system cannot provide modular add-ons to the existing database, it will probably be of limited value in meeting your future organizational needs.

integrated systems
systems that offer a variety of HR record and decision-making functions

specialist programs
programs tailored to servicing customer needs in one or two narrowly defined areas (e.g., compensation)

Typical modules that can be added to an HRMS include the following: (1) performance appraisal; (2) employment equity; (3) replacement, succession, and career planning; (4) accounts receivable (e.g., for employee pay advances); (5) accounts payable (e.g., for training program costs); (6) pension administration; (7) job applicant and résumé tracking; (8) occupational health and safety;

(9) job analysis and evaluation; (10) compensation (payroll and benefits); (11) staff scheduling (attendance and time, including flextime program options); (12) training and development; (13) severance and termination; (14) adherence to legislation; (15) labour relations (e.g., discipline and grievances); (16) multinational staffing planner; and (17) accounting and billing.[19] The degree to which various vendors have developed these modules and their associated costs, as well as your in-house capability to develop local procedures, must all be considered with respect to future use of the HRMS. Finally, as we have noted earlier, a stage-three comprehensive and interactive HRMS should be able to conduct HR research by offering a relational database with a variety of flexible search options and capabilities. These should include methods of portraying research results, including graphic protocols such as scatter plots, bar charts, graphs, and so on; the ability to run mathematical and statistical procedures, such as multiple regressions and linear programming; and the ability to create succession charts and vacancy models used in HR forecasting.

Criteria for Data Inclusion in the HRMS

There are countless elements of data that could be entered into an organization's HRMS. The key aspect with respect to data inclusion is not how much data are collected and stored, but how useful the data will be for HR staff and organizational decision-makers.[20] In particular, we should remember the old computer programmer's maxim—"**GIGO**": if you put Garbage In, invariably you will get Garbage Out! Paying attention to the specific data requirements of your organization will help minimize the time-consuming and expensive labour costs associated with the entry and updating of personal data into the HRMS. Before the data fields are established for the HRMS, it is important to conduct a needs analysis that explicitly identifies why the data are required and provides a justification for their collection and updating (e.g., justification related to legalities, accounting and compensation, career development, and job assignment). Furthermore, the needs analysis will estimate the frequency of access for each element of data (per day, week, or month), identify the jobholders who will be permitted to have access to and use of the data, estimate the memory storage requirements, develop the data access safeguards, and so on.

GIGO if you put Garbage Into your HRMS, invariably you will get Garbage Out!

Databases that contain substantial personal and confidential data—for example, Canada Customs and Revenue Agency's taxation data and Statistics Canada's census data—require very extensive user safeguards to restrict access to information and prevent its use for reasons other than those explicitly stated in the HRMS objective statements. As mentioned earlier in the text, data encryption, passwords, personnel security clearances, and so on are vital elements linked to the appropriate employment of personal, privileged information.

BOX 6.6 HRMS Facilitates Strategic HR Planning

With the increasing importance of knowledge capital in today's global economy, the HRMS is an important factor in facilitating effective strategic planning and decision-making. Many companies, such as Fluor Daniel Inc. and National Semiconductor Corporation, utilize the information technology of the HRMS for services such as on-line résumé scanning for recruitment, interview question databases based on job requirements, e-mail, and corporate intranets. Furthermore, the existence of the HRMS enables administrative elements of HR to be centralized, while concurrently enabling HR field personnel to concentrate on the provision of services to line management and employees, such as training and development interventions.

Source: Adapted from G. James, "IT Helps HR Become Strategic," *Datamation*, Vol. 43, No. 4 (April 1997), pp. 110–114.

Given the legal penalties and adverse public relations outcomes that may arise if we fail to comply with Canadian and provincial human rights acts, control of data collection and data access is absolutely critical. Although we can legitimately include in our HRMS entries age, marital status, and employee dependants for medical and health-care benefit purposes, if this data from the HRMS is used inappropriately—for example, for selection purposes where decisions based on marital status and age are considered discriminatory—the organization would be in contravention of federal and provincial human rights legislation and would be legally liable to provide redress to the individual.

Notwithstanding the above, some data elements are common to most organizational HRMS databases. It is to these core data elements that we now turn our attention.

Core HRMS Data Entries[21]

1. Identification and Personal Record

The following are some common elements of the identification and personal record:

- Surname, first and middle names, previous names
- Address (including postal code), telephone numbers (residence, office, and mobile), e-mail address
- Next of kin (including address and telephone number)
- Gender
- Date of birth

- Marital status, dependants
- Nationality, work permit number
- Designated group membership or race (for employment equity purposes)
- Social insurance number, health card number, employee number, union membership

2. Work History

Work histories often include the following elements:

- Date of hire
- Employment status (full-time, part-time, contract, etc.)
- Current job title, manning number, authority level or classification, location of employee (department or division)
- Length of time in current job
- Previous job titles in the organization and dates of service for each
- Work history prior to joining the company (including employers, positions held, dates of service, etc.)

3. Career and Competencies

Most HRMS databases typically include the following types of data on career and competencies:

- Employee's desired future positions, target positions recommended by employee's supervisors
- Individual performance-appraisal data; assessment centre and appraisal test results; and ratings regarding potential, promotability, and readiness for movement
- Specific skills and competencies, licences
- Certificates, diplomas, and degrees, each listed with the granting educational institution, date of completion, and field of study (major)
- Recent training activities
- Hobbies and interests
- Community and volunteer activities
- Professional or trade association memberships
- Geographical location preferences
- Foreign-language competencies
- Honours and awards, publications

4. Accounting and Compensation Data

Accounting and compensation data usually include the following types of information:

- Gross compensation (salary, hourly wage)
- Compensation band and location on the salary range
- Hours/shifts worked per week
- Overtime and bonuses
- Merit or incentive plan membership
- Date of the last salary or wage change
- History of compensation changes: amounts and dates, planned date and amount of next change
- Vacation taken or banked
- Benefit package selected
- Life insurance
- Medical and dental coverage
- Deductions (e.g., pension plan contributions, parking, union dues, income tax, unemployment insurance)
- Leaves of absence

BOX 6.7 Time and Costs Associated with HRMS Implementation

A study by *Canadian HR Reporter* discovered that only 97 of 181 Canadian organizations surveyed had any idea of the costs associated with their HRMS implementation. Of those that had tracked the information, costs varied enormously, from a low of $1000 to a high of $12 million. The report subdivided organizations into four categories: (1) fewer than 500 Canadian employees; (2) 501 to 2000 Canadian employees; (3) 2001 to 5000 Canadian employees; and (4) more than 5000 Canadian employees. The associated median costs of implementation for these four categories were (1) $10 000, (2) $90 000, (3) $300 000, and (4) $2 million.

Using these aforementioned four categories of organizations, the report investigated the time associated with implementing HRMS in Canadian organizations. There are three steps in the sequence of implementing the HRMS: (1) needs analysis to selection of an HRMS; (2) selection of the HRMS system to "go live"; and (3) go live to a stable operational state.

The investigation found that the total implementation time increased along with the size of the organization (measured by number of Canadian employees). The associated implementation time for the aforementioned four categories of Canadian organizations were (1) more than a year (16.7 months), (2) 22.9 months, (3) 27.6 months, and (4) almost three years (35.4 months).

Source: Adapted from Johnston, John. 2001. "What Does It Take to Put in an HRMS," *Canadian HR Reporter*, Guide to HR Technology supplement, October 22, 2001, G3. Adapted by permisson of Carswell, a division of Thomson Canada Limited.

skill and management inventories contain information on each employee on matters such as compensation and benefits, education and training, performance history, jobs held, and target jobs. Management inventories contain supplemental information on budget and staff supervisory accountabilities, management training received, etc.

intranet an organization's internal Internet, which facilitates the link between employees and the information they require to perform their jobs effectively

Once all this data are transferred from the **skill and management inventories**[22] into the HRMS, a wide variety of reports and output formats can be produced and analyzed, including the following:[23]

- Employee rosters
- Actual versus authorized staffing
- Analyses of gender, age, designated group membership, seniority, salaries, pay equity, full- and part-time distributions
- Performance appraisals
- Position tenure and movement, blockages
- Vacant positions
- New hires and cohort analysis
- Attrition through voluntary turnover and termination
- Absenteeism
- Job transfers and reassignments
- Job reclassifications
- Succession short lists

BOX 6.8 HR Intranets

Organizations have been establishing **intranets** to facilitate the linkage between their employees and the information they require to perform their jobs effectively. In an era typified by reductions in the number of HR staff as well as in mid-level managers, along with an associated increase in the number of self-managed teams, a user-friendly, cost-effective, and efficient internal e-business is a desired state of affairs for many organizations. Some of the many possible uses of these HR intranets are for (1) e-learning, (2) expense reporting, (3) conducting employee surveys, (4) updating personnel records, (5) selection and staffing, (6) enrolling in and administering benefit plans, and (7) employee discussion groups.

However, it is clear that many of the current intranets are fraught with problems that are precluding their effective use by employees. For example, organizations often have a variety of intranets presented in different formats that are confusing and not internally linked. Similarly, employees may have difficulty in determining exactly who is responsible for each intranet, leading to frustration and a perceived lack of accountability by the organization. Frequently, employees shun the intranets because the information on them does not get updated, the sites lack effective search engines, and the information is not presented in an easy-to-use format. As a result, many so-called "intra-messes" have been shunned by employees who nevertheless are competent computer users and frequent browsers of websites on the external Internet.

Sources: Adapted from S. Chu, "Intranets Become 'Intramess'," *The Globe and Mail*, March 7, 2002, p. B17; and R. Brillinger, "Getting Your HR Intranet Right," *Canadian HR Reporter*, Vol. 14 (August 13, 2001): 7–9.

FIGURE 6.1 SAMPLE SKILLS INVENTORY

Malachi Marine Adventures

NAME: ____________________ CURRENT DATE: ____________________

CURRENT POSITION: ____________________ DATE OF HIRE: ____________________

EMPLOYEE NUMBER: ____________________ DEPARTMENT: ____________________

Education and Training Qualifications:
Please list licences, certificates, diplomas, degrees, and other training qualifications, along with the year of graduation and the relevant training institution.

Honours, Awards, and Professional Memberships/Responsibilities:

Previous Work Experience: (Malachi Marine and other work experience):
Please provide the job title and code, key responsibilities, dates held, location, and company name (list chronologically, most recent job first).

Hobbies and Interests, Community and Volunteer Activities:

Career Plans:

(continued on next page)

Performance Summary (strengths, development needs):
____
____
____
____
____

Current Performance Rating, Present Job (scale 1 to 7): _____

Date of Commencement of Present Job: ______________

Promotability Readiness Code: ______
(a = now, b = 1 year, c = 2 years, d = review/not yet determined)
Potential Rating Code: _______
(++ = promotable 2 levels, + = promotable 1 level, ~ = suited current level, ? = review/not yet determined. Include date and name of assessor/s.)

Targeted Positions:
____
____
____
____
____

Development Plan:
____
____
____
____
____

General Commentary:
____
____
____
____
____

Signature: ______________________________ Date: _______________

Review and Approval: ______________________ Date: _______________

CONFIDENTIAL (when completed)

BOX 6.9 HRMS Facilitates Strategic HR Planning

With an increasingly competitive global marketplace, organizations are turning their attention to strengthening the links between individual performance and organizational profitability. To tighten up organizational work processes, HR systems should be implemented with the following guidelines in mind:

- Integrate re-engineering and system implementation efforts.
- Get senior leadership involved early and often.
- Involve employees in the effort.
- Be sure the system's design supports the organization's business strategy.
- Consider an organizational readiness assessment.

Source: Adapted from N. Horney and I. Ruddle, "All Systems Go?" *Bank Marketing*, Vol. 30, No. 1 (January 1998), pp. 20–26.

Summary

The HRMS is an essential element of a properly functioning HR planning process. In this chapter we have presented information relating to the normal three-stage evolution of the HRMS—a basic personnel system, an augmented HR system, and a comprehensive and interactive system—along with the associated changes in capability that are linked to each step in the process. The selection and design criteria are security and control of access, user friendliness, flexibility and ability to be used with other systems in the organization, degree of appropriateness for the organization's needs, the costs for the system and support, and need for future expansion. The HRMS must be selected based on explicit, previously established operating requirements and organizational goals. Skills and management inventories provide input to the HRMS, and identifying the specific rationale for including each type of data are required to prevent unfocused, costly, and time-wasting database management. Given that the HRMS uses sensitive personal information, various options for operating restrictions and safeguards ensure that access to and use of data are restricted to approved users engaged in operations required by the organization. Finally, a wide variety of output formats and reports can be generated by the HRMS, which are of use not only to the HR planning staff but also to line managers and individual workers.

In the next chapter, we turn to a presentation of the HR forecasting process, which integrates information about the job, as revealed by means of the job analysis process, with personal and organizational data elements contained in the HRMS database.

Key Terms

augmented HR system, 140
basic personnel system, 139
comprehensive and interactive HRMS, 140
decision support system (DSS), 144
GIGO, 146
Human Resources Information Systems (HRIS), 137
Human Resources Management System (HRMS), 137
integrated systems, 145
intranet, 150
management information system (MIS), 144
personal identification numbers (PINs), 142
relational databases, 140
skill and management inventories, 150
specialist programs, 145

Suggested Websites

www.adp.ca HRMS vendor ADP's website.

www.canpay.com Website for Canpay HR software.

www.ceridian.ca Ceridian's corporate website.

www.hrtech.com HRMS vendor HR Technologies' website.

www.hrsoft.com HRMS vendor HRsoft's website.

www.hrware.com HRMS vendor Hrware's website.

www.oracle.com/ca HRMS vendor Oracle's website.

www.peoplesoft.com HRMS vendor PeopleSoft's website.

www.sap.com HRMS vendor SAP's website.

Discussion Questions

1. An HRMS is essential for conducting effective HR planning. Define HRMS, and identify various data elements that act as inputs to the system. Discuss the various output formats that could be of use to HR planning staff.
2. The HRMS contains a wide variety of personal and sensitive data that necessitate security, privacy, and usage policies to be set by the organization. What are some of the safeguards, operating restrictions, and policies that should be developed for users of an HRMS?

Exercise

Identify the criteria that should be used when selecting an HRMS for your organization. Rank these criteria for system selection. Are they a universal set of criteria that apply to all organizations? Describe the selection procedures for the selection and implementation committees for the chosen HRMS. Who would serve on these committees?

Case: HRMS at Canada Bread Limited

Canada Bread, one of the 14 operating companies of Maple Leaf Foods, employed approximately 6000 workers in 2002, a dramatic increase in personnel from 1998, when the company employed only 3000 people. During the same period, sales increased from $500 milllion to more than $1 billion. Furthermore, three separate businesses were amalgamated to form Canada Bread, and each of them had their own procedures and ways of handling HR information, the majority of which utilized manual records, with the exception of payroll issues. This consolidation and the rapid level of corporate growth prompted a search for an HRMS that could interface with the new payroll system Canada Bread already had in place. The search for the HRMS was done by an HRIS selection committee made up of HR leaders from Maple Leaf's 14 companies, as there was a need for uniformity and commonality of systems to support Maple Leaf's global reach and operations. They were looking for an HRMS that would operate on a client/server basis on Maple Leaf's nation-wide computer network, meaning that the centralized, up-to-date data could be accessed from any of Canada Bread's 125 operational sites.

The decision to adopt an HRMS from HRWare was based not only on price but also on the fact that the database was compatible with Microsoft's software programs. Initially the IT (information technology) staff were not as fully engaged in the system as they could have been, and, even in 2002, a number of functions (e.g., succession planning and labour administration modules) were not yet implemented. Nevertheless, applicant and employee head-count tracking, organizational demographics, work analysis, and compensation (salary, bonus, and benefits) administration were in place and operational. And as the HR staff and employees became more competent with the system, they learned to demand more information from the system by drawing more substantially on its capabilities to provide them with current information for decision-making purposes. Vince Fornella, Canada Bread's HR manager, noted that the HRMS implementation did not result in a downsizing of the HR department; instead the focus and function of staff changed, leading them to become much more efficient and strategic in their approach to HR issues as there was much less "paper-pushing" involved in their day-to-day work. A key challenge, however, was to ensure that the system was properly maintained and that regular data input kept information current.

Source: Adapted from Moralis, M. 2001. "Canada Bread Gets a Rise through Software," *Canadian HR Reporter*, Guide to HR Technology supplement, October 22, G1 & G7. Adapted by permisson of Carswell, a division of Thomson Learning.

Question

Prepare a report assessing Canada Bread's implementation of its HRMS. What elements would you change or do differently? Prepare recommendations that will move Canada Bread from its current state of having a basic operational HRMS to a system that is fully functional throughout the organization.

References

Adams, L. 1992. "Securing Your HRIS in a Microcomputer Environment." *Human Resource Management* (Fall): 56–61.

Anthony, W. 1977. "Get to Know Your Employees: The Human Resource Information System." *Personnel Journal* (April): 179–186.

Bassett, G.A. 1973. "Elements of Manpower Forecasting and Scheduling." *Human Resources Management* (Fall): 35–43.

Bechet, T.P., and J.W. Walker. 1993. "Aligning Staffing with Business Strategy." *Human Resource Planning*, Vol. 16, No. 2: 1–16.

Berry, W. 1993. "HRIS Can Improve Performance, Empower and Motivate 'Knowledge Workers.'" *Employment Relations Today* (Autumn): 297–303.

Braderich, R., and J. Bourdreau. 1991. "The Evolution of Computer Use in Human Resource Management: Interviews with Ten Leaders." *Human Resource Management*, Vol. 30, No. 4: 485–508.

Brillinger, R. 2001. "Getting Your HR Intranet Right." *Canadian HR Reporter*, Vol. 14, No. 14: 7–9.

Brooker, R. 1992. "What Hardware Means to the HRIS." *Personnel Journal* (May): 122–138.

Burack, E.H., and N.J. Mathys. 1996. *Human Resource Planning: A Pragmatic Approach to Manpower Staffing and Development*, 3rd ed. Northbrook, Ill.: Brace Park.

Chu, S. 2002. "Intranets Become 'Intramess'." *The Globe and Mail*, March 7, B17.

Diers, C. 1992. "Common Mistakes in Implementing an HRIS." *Employment Relations Today* (Autumn): 265–271.

Fiorito, J., T.H. Stones, and C.R. Greer. 1985. "Factors Affecting Choice of Human Resource Forecasting Techniques." *Human Resource Planning*, Vol. 8, No. 1: 1–17.

Grabosky, P., and D. Rosenbloom. 1975. "Racial and Ethnic Integration in the Federal Service." *Social Science Quarterly*, Vol. 56, No. 1 (June): 71–84.

HRMS Directions Inc. 1995. *HR Matrix*. Mississauga, Ont.: HRMS Directions.

———. 1997. "Harness the Power of HRMS: The Wild Ride, but Worth It." *Workforce* 76, No. 6 (June): 28–33.

Greiner, L. 1988. *Power and Organizational Development: Mobilizing Power to Implement Change*, rev. ed. Reading, Mass.: Addison-Wesley.

Johnson, B., G. Moorhead, and R. Griffin. 1983. "Human Resource Information Systems and Job Design." *Human Resource Planning*, Vol. 6, No. 1 (March): 35–40.

Johnston, J. 2001. "What Does It Take to Put in an HRMS." *Canadian HR Reporter*, Guide to HR Technology, October 22: G3.

Kaumeyer, R.H. 1979. *Planning and Using Skills Inventory Systems.* New York: Van Nostrand Reinhold.

Kossek, E.E., W. Young, and D. Gash. 1994. "Waiting for Innovation in the Human Resources Department: Godot Implements a Human Resource Information System." *Human Resource Management*, Vol. 33, No. 1: 135–159.

Martin, R. 1967. "Skills Inventories." *Personnel Journal* (January): 28–83.

Mason, D. 1994. "Scenario-Based Planning: Decision Model for the Learning Organization." *Planning Review*: 6–11.

Mathys, N., and H. La Van. 1984. "Issues in Purchasing and Implementing HRIS Software." *HR Magazine*, Vol. 29, No. 8 (August): 91–97.

McBeath, G. 1992. *The Handbook of Human Resource Planning: Practical Manpower Analysis Techniques for HR Professionals.* Oxford: Blackwell.

O'Connell, S. 1994. "Planning and Setting Up a New HRIS." *HR Magazine* (February): 36–39.

Pearson, G. 2001. "HRMS *Does* Make a Difference." *Canadian HR Reporter*, Guide to HR Technology Supplement, October 22: G1.

Raphael, T. 2002. "HRMS Gets Easier, Better for Smaller Companies." *Workforce*, Vol. 81, No. 2: 46–49.

Seamans, L. 1978. "What's Lacking in Most Skills Inventories." *Personnel Journal* (March).

Stone, T., and J. Fiorito. 1986. "A Perceived Uncertainty Model of Human Resource Forecasting Technique Use." *Academy of Management Review*, Vol. 11, No. 3: 635–642.

Walker, J.W. 1980. *Human Resource Planning.* New York: McGraw-Hill.

———. 1989. "Human Resource Roles for the '90s." *Human Resource Planning*, Vol. 12, No. 1: 55–61.

Endnotes

1. Bechet and Walker, 1993.
2. Raphael, 2002.
3. Adapted from Braderich and Bourdreau, 1991; Burack and Mathys, 1996; Greiner, 1988; Stone and Fiorito, 1986; Walker, 1989.
4. Bassett, 1973.
5. Burack and Mathys, 1996.
6. Mason, 1994.
7. Stone and Fiorito, 1986.

8. Stone and Fiorito, 1986; Fiorito et al., 1985.
9. Adams, 1992.
10. Mathys and La Van, 1984.
11. Ibid.
12. Brooker, 1992.
13. Diers, 1992.
14. HRMS Directions Inc., 1995; 1997.
15. Ibid.
16. Ibid.
17. O'Connell, 1994.
18. HRMS Directions Inc., 1995; 1997.
19. Anthony, 1977; Berry, 1993; Braderich and Bourdreau, 1991; Johnson et al., 1983; Kossek et al., 1994.
20. Anthony, 1977; Diers, 1992; McBeath, 1992.
21. Adapted from McBeath, 1992; Anthony, 1977; Burack and Mathys, 1996.
22. Grabosky and Rosenbloom, 1975; Kaumeyer, 1979; Martin, 1967; Seamans, 1978.
23. Adapted from McBeath, 1992; Walker, 1980.

7

THE HR FORECASTING PROCESS

CHAPTER GOALS

HR forecasting, which constitutes the heart of the HR planning process, can be defined as ascertaining the net requirement for personnel by determining the demand for and supply of human resources now and in the future. After determining the demand for and supply of workers, the organization's HR staff develop specific programs to reconcile the differences between the requirement for labour in various employment categories and its availability, both internally and in the organization's environment. Programs in such areas as training and development, career planning, recruitment and selection, managerial appraisal, and so on are all stimulated by means of the HR forecasting process.

HR forecasting
constitutes the heart of the HR planning process, and can be defined as ascertaining the net requirement for personnel by determining the demand for and supply of human resources now and in the future

After reading this chapter, you should be able to do the following:

1. Identify the three different categories of HR forecasting activity and their relationship to the HR planning process.
2. Understand the considerable advantages that accrue to organizations from instituting effective HR forecasting procedures.

3. Discuss the rationale for giving special attention to specialist, technical, and executive personnel groups in the HR forecasting process.
4. Comprehend the impact of environmental and organizational variables on the accuracy and time period or horizon of estimates derived from future estimates of HR demand and supply.
5. Identify the various stages in the process of determining net HR requirements.
6. Understand the policy and program implications of an HR deficit or an HR surplus.

Forecasting Activity Categories

transaction-based forecasting forecasting that focuses on tracking internal change instituted by the organization's managers

event-based forecasting forecasting concerned with changes in the external environment

process-based forecasting forecasting not focused on a specific internal organizational event but on the flow or sequencing of several work activities

Forecasting activity can be subdivided into three categories: (1) **transaction-based forecasting**, (2) **event-based forecasting**, and (3) **process-based forecasting.**[1] Transaction-based analyses focus on tracking internal change instituted by the organization's managers, while event-based forecasting is concerned with change in the external environment. Process-based forecasting is not focused on a specific internal organizational event but on the flow or sequencing of several work activities (e.g., the warehousing shipping process). All three categories are important if we are to have a comprehensive method for ascertaining our HR requirements.

Forecasting is only an approximation of possible future states and is an activity that strongly favours quantitative and easily codified techniques. As such, it is important that an explicit effort be made to obtain and incorporate qualitative data into our analyses.[2] Furthermore, not only are more successful HR forecasting processes those that use both qualitative and quantitative data, but a number of studies have clearly shown that accuracy of prediction

BOX 7.1 HR Forecasting in a Global Economy

Organizations that operate globally face additional challenges to their effective and efficient use of human resources. For starters, differences in time zones and the vast geographic dispersion of operational units and workforces can present a problem. Technology can help companies through use of the Internet and organizational intranets, as well as e-mail and video-conferencing systems. Global HR planning managers should encourage employee collaboration through (1) maximizing use of technology such as e-mail, (2) explicitly scheduling work to take advantage of time zone differences that can be used to the company's advantage (e.g., preparation of a contract by employees in an advanced time zone, which can then be sent to a client firm that is in a time zone several hours behind that of the preparing unit), and (3) elimination of redundant costs through centralizing data in the HRMS.

Source: Adapted from C. Solomon, "Sharing Information Across Borders and Time Zones," *Workforce*, Vol. 3, No. 2 (March 1998), pp. 12–18.

BOX 7.2 Successful Workforce Planning

Given the plethora of organizational CEOs who state that "people are our greatest asset," it could be assumed that human resources and workforce planning activities would be among the best-developed functions in organizations and regularly receive top priority with respect to funding and other resource allocations. In reality, many organizations devote insufficient time and resources to HR planning activities, which have three main factors associated with their success. Specifically, HR planning should be (1) strategic and forward-looking, (2) comprehensive and encompass all employee groups and management functions, and (3) tailored to the specific culture and attributes of the organization to which it is being applied. Furthermore, by being proactive and avoiding the "feast or famine" swings in personnel numbers associated with reactive workforce staffing, HR planning can dramatically cut labour costs, increase productivity, reduce the number of "surprises," and rectify problems before they grow more complex and costly. In order to achieve these ends, workforce planning should give priority to forecasting and assessment, recruitment and selection, leadership development, and succession planning programs.

Sources: Adapted from J. Sullivan, "Workforce Planning: Why to Start Now," *Workforce*, Vol. 81, No. 12 (November 2002), pp. 46–50; and J. Woodard, "Three Factors of Successful Work Force Planning," *The Journal of Government Financial Management*, Vol. 50, No. 3 (Fall 2001), pp. 36–38.

improves significantly when we use a variety of forecasting techniques.[3] Effective forecasting also hinges on obtaining a fine balance between global and local control of the process. A study of multinational corporations operating in Ireland showed that most of the firms that were analyzed adopted a local approach to forecasting, with the (global) headquarters maintaining a vigilant yet loose monitoring of financial costs and other performance criteria.[4]

Benefits of HR Forecasting

A great number of important benefits accrue to organizations that take the time to institute effective HR forecasting processes, and the forecasting techniques employed do not have to be sophisticated to be of value to the firm.[5] A few of the more important advantages of HR forecasting are discussed below.

1. Reduces HR Costs

Effective HR forecasting focuses on a comparison between the organization's current stock of workforce KSAs (e.g., experience) and the numbers, skill competencies, and so on desired in the workforce of the future. This inherent comparison facilitates a proactive, sequential approach to developing internal workers and is concurrent with activities focused on obtaining the best external recruits from competitors, universities, and training programs.[6] In this manner, organizations can reduce their HR costs as they take a long-run planning approach to HR issues. This means that organizations will be less likely to have to react in a costly last-minute crisis mode to unexpected developments in the internal or external labour markets.

2. Increases Organizational Flexibility

An oft-cited advantage of HR forecasting is that its proactive process increases the number of viable policy options available to the organization, thereby enhancing flexibility.[7] With regard to labour supply considerations, forecasting processes develop program options that can determine whether it is more advantageous and cost effective to retrain current members of the workforce to fill anticipated job openings or fill these openings with external recruits who are already in possession of the required competencies and skills. Given that HR forecasting is predicated on trends, assumptions, scenarios, and various planning time horizons, the process itself encourages the development of a wide range of possible policy options and programs from which the HR staff can select. Furthermore, each of the various HR programming options are ranked, subjected to cost–benefit analyses, and allocated organizational resources after being carefully examined as part of the HR forecasting process.

3. Ensures a Close Linkage to the Macro Business Forecasting Process

A serious problem develops in some organizations when the personnel planning process becomes divorced and disconnected from the overall business goals of the organization.[8] The implementation of an HR forecasting process helps to eliminate the possibility that personnel policies will veer away from the overall operating and production policies of the organization. First, HR forecasting, although an ongoing process, takes its lead from specific production, market share, profitability, and operational objectives set by the organization's top management. These objectives have been established through proactive internal and environmental scans of market and competitor strengths, weaknesses, opportunities, threats, resources, and policy actions.[9] Once these have been established, specific HR forecasting analyses are set in motion to determine the feasibility of the proposed operational objectives with respect to time, cost, resource allocation, and other criteria of program success. The HR analyses are subsequently sent back to top management, and they either confirm the viability of the original business objectives or indicate that changes (e.g., the allocation of additional resources) need to be made to enable the objectives to be met.

The business forecasting process, therefore, establishes overall organizational objectives, which are input into the HR forecasting process.[10] The HR staff analyze whether the explicit objectives, with their associated specific performance parameters, can be met with the organization's current HR policies

BOX 7.3 Why HR System Implementation Efforts Fail

1. The organization's top management has not communicated the need to implement new technology or new systems.
2. People resist change efforts because they are not asked to help develop new business strategies, solutions, and plans.
3. Organizations underestimate the time, energy, budget, and planning required to successfully implement new technology.
4. Different groups within an organization either cannot agree on what a system needs to do or overburden it with too many requirements.

Source: Adapted from N. Horney and I. Ruddle, "Why HR System Implementation Efforts Fail," *Bank Marketing*, Vol. 30, No. 1 (January 1998), p. 24.

and programs or whether specific changes have to be instituted, with their associated costs, to achieve the objectives. These analyses and the subsequent feedback of the HR forecast summaries to senior management help to ensure that the top decision-makers in the organization (1) are aware of key HR issues and constraints that might affect organizational plans for success and (2) ensure the HR objectives are closely aligned with the organization's operational business objectives.[11]

4. Ensures That Organizational Requirements Take Precedence over Issues of Resource Constraint and Scarcity

As we present each step of the HR forecasting process in sequence throughout this book, it will quickly become evident that the first step in the process is the calculation of organizational requirements, or **demand** for human resources. Determining the source of personnel—that is, the availability or **supply** of workers—is done only once the process of evaluating personnel requirements for current and future time horizons has been finalized. This sequence is not accidental, and it reinforces the fact that attainment of desired organizational goals and objectives must take priority over all issues concerning resource scarcity and other implementation issues.

human resources demand the organization's projected requirement for human resources

human resources supply the source of workers to meet demand requirements, obtained either internally (current members of the organization's workforce) or from external agencies

Key Personnel Analyses Conducted by HR Forecasters

Although the forecasting process for personnel in an organization is conducted to determine the number of employees and the skill competencies required by sub-units, as well as the entire organization, a number of personnel categories typically are given greater-than-average attention in the forecasting process. These categories are discussed below.[12]

1. Specialist/Technical/Professional Personnel

Workers holding trade qualifications that are in high demand or that require lengthy preparatory training for attainment of skill competency constitute a key area of focus for HR forecasting. In our increasingly global economy, these workers will be in high demand by competitive firms both in Canada and abroad, which means we will have to give special attention to programs to induce these workers to join our organization. Furthermore, we must give attention to benchmarking compensation schemes to meet or lead industry standards so as to attract and retain people who perform well in these categories. With respect to supply issues, a longer lead time is often required to recruit technicians and professionals because of the need for a more comprehensive and larger geographic search for this specialist talent pool.

2. Employment Equity-Designated Group Membership

designated groups identifiable groups deemed to need special attention; in the case of Canadian HR these are people of aboriginal descent, women, people with disabilities, and members of visible minorities

Provincial and federal governments in Canada have enacted employment-equity legislation and guidelines in response to public pressure for employment practices that reflect the rapidly changing face of Canadian society. In particular, four main **designated groups** require special attention with respect to their degree of use or equitable employment in organizations: (1) people of aboriginal descent, (2) women, (3) people with disabilities, and (4) members of visible minorities. Particular attention must be paid to monitoring members of these designated groups with respect to the opportunities they receive for employment, promotion, training, and so on as compared to those received by the dominant population of the organization.[13] Furthermore, the composition of the organizational workforce should reflect the underlying characteristics of the society in which it is embedded, so the supply issue, as it relates to proportional representation of designated groups in the organization, is a key area for HR forecasting.

3. Managerial and Executive Personnel

To be successful, any organization must ensure that its executives and managers possess the skills required for success in their specific environmental niche. Executives (CEO, president, vice-presidents, etc.) interact with key environmental stakeholder groups on behalf of the organization and are responsible for setting the goals for the organization's future direction. Managers, acting as the supervisory layer of authority between executives and the operating shop-floor level, are responsible for coaching, directing, training and developing, and controlling worker behaviours to achieve the goals established by the executive group. Although there is no shortage of managers and executives who can function effectively in relatively benign, predictable, environmental situations, researchers believe that organizational leaders who are able to transform organizational culture and anticipate external change, and who possess the dynamic personal attributes necessary to unify the organization, are very rare indeed in most public and private-sector organizational settings.[14] For this reason, not only must greater attention be paid to identifying leadership talent within the organization, but assessment centres or appraisals also must be conducted to match the "right person to the right job at the right time."[15] The organization's survival and future success depend directly on succession and replacement planning!

4. Recruits

As was the case with succession and replacement planning, recruiting trainees is extremely important to the success of the organization's overall HR policies. When determining whether to obtain trainees from the internal workforce or externally, a wide variety of factors must be considered. For example, selecting current employees to attend training courses leading to promotion rewards loyalty and past performance and simultaneously diminishes the need for the organizational socialization of newcomers from outside. However, current employees may be very comfortable with the status quo and existing methods of organizational operation, and therefore may not be well suited for employment on novel, creative work processes that differ substantially from established practices. Furthermore, new entrants can bring the organization insights into how competitors structure and operate their business and may, as well, bring with them the latest trends and practices taught in universities and specialist training agencies. The relative balance of internal to external personnel to be selected for training courses is a key factor in the HR forecasting and programming operations of many organizations.

BOX 7.4 Profitable Personnel

Critics have applied the sarcastic label "big hat, no cattle" to HR managers whom they believe have little effect on the performance of the organization. The United Kingdom's University of Sheffield Effectiveness Program disputes this assertion because its research discovered that not only was "people management" critical to business performance, but it far outstripped the emphasis on quality, technology, competitive strategy, or research and development in its influence on the organization's bottom-line performance. Although research findings with respect to the relationship between individual satisfaction and job performance have been mixed, the Sheffield research found that at the macro level, satisfaction of the work group across a wide range of areas—for example, developing skills, creativity, and recognition processes—was critical to organizational productivity.

Source: Adapted from M. West and M. Patterson, "Profitable Personnel," *People Management*, Vol. 4, No. 1 (January 1998), pp. 28–31.

The goal of HR forecasting is to obtain sufficient numbers of trained personnel who will be able perform successfully in jobs when those jobs need to be filled. To do this, the *forecasting process* has five stages:[16]

1. Identify organizational goals, objectives, and plans.
2. Determine overall demand requirements for personnel.
3. Assess in-house skills and other internal supply characteristics.
4. Determine the net demand requirements that must be met from external, environmental supply sources.
5. Develop HR plans and programs to ensure that the right people are in the right place.

Before turning to aspects concerned with determining personnel demand, we will examine the effects of environmental uncertainty and of planning time horizons on HR forecasting.

Environmental and Organizational Factors Affecting HR Forecasting

The HR forecasting process is extremely complex, requiring specific numerical and skill competency targets for personnel to be met despite operating in circumstances of high uncertainty.[17] This uncertainty arises from both external environmental factors and from inside the organization itself. Given this uncertainty and the natural rate of change resulting from operating in a turbulent, global economy, the key factor for HR forecasters is to incorporate flexibility into the program responses associated with demand and supply forecasts.[18]

BOX 7.5 Selected Factors Affecting the HR Forecasting Process

Internal/Organizational	External/Environmental
Corporate mission statement, strategic goals	Economic situation
Operational goals, production budgets	Labour markets and unions
HR policies (e.g., compensation, succession)	Governmental laws and regulations
Organizational structure, restructuring, mergers, etc.	Industry and product life cycles
Worker KSAs/competencies and expectations	Technological changes
HRMS level of development	Competitor labour usage
Organizational culture, workforce climate and satisfaction, and internal communications	Global market for skilled labour
Job analysis: workforce coverage, current data	Demographic changes

When considering the following discussion of environmental and organizational factors, it is important to remember that these factors may affect the forecasting of demand, supply, or both of these key planning variables.

HR Forecasting Time Horizons

As we have discussed earlier in the text, environmental and organizational factors increase uncertainty for HR forecasters and necessitate flexibility in the programs they devise to balance personnel demand and supply. The key point to consider from an analysis of environmental and organizational factors is that uncertainty decreases our confidence in our ability to predict the future accurately and hence reduces the HR forecasting time horizon.[19] Large organizations with substantial resources and sizeable numbers of well-trained personnel who also perform well may be better able to weather the storms of future change in environmental, economic, technological, and competitive market factors. If this is the case, they will be able to extend their HR forecasting process further into the future with greater confidence in the accuracy of their predictions. Irrespective of their situation with regard to environmental and internal factors, organizational forecasters use several different time horizons for forecasting. Although there are variations among organizations with respect to how they define their specific time parameters, the typical HR forecasting time horizons are as follows:[20]

1. *Current forecast:* The current forecast is the one being used to meet the immediate operational needs of the organization. The associated time frame is up to the end of the current operating cycle, or a maximum of one year into the future.
2. *Short-run forecast:* The short-run forecast extends forward from the current forecast and states the HR requirements for the next one- to two-year period beyond the current operational requirements.
3. *Medium-run forecast:* Most organizations define the medium-run forecast as the one that identifies requirements for two to five years into the future.
4. *Long-run forecast:* Due to uncertainty and the significant number and types of changes that can affect the organization's operations, the long-run forecast is by necessity extremely flexible and is a statement of probable requirements given a set of current assumptions. The typical long-run forecast extends five or more years ahead of the current operational period.

The outcome of forecasts derived from these four time horizons leads to predictions and projections. A **prediction** is a single numerical estimate of HR requirements associated with a specific time horizon and set of assumptions, whereas a **projection** incorporates several HR estimates based on a variety of assumptions.[21] The forecasting term **envelope** is synonymous with projection, as one can easily visualize the four corners of an envelope, with each corner

prediction a single numerical estimate of HR requirements associated with a specific time horizon and set of assumptions

projection incorporates several HR estimates based on a variety of assumptions

envelope an analogy in which one can easily visualize the corners of an envelope containing the upper and lower limits or "bounds" of the various HR projections extending into the future

containing a specific prediction; for example, corner 1 contains an optimistic sales assumption (time 1), corner 2 contains a pessimistic sales assumption (time 1), corner 3 contains an optimistic sales assumption (time 2), and corner 4 contains a pessimistic sales assumption (time 2). The four corner predictions serve to anchor the envelope, which may also contain a number of other specific predictions (e.g., the most likely assumption, which may be to maintain the current sales level). The use of a combination of predictions and projections provides the necessary forecasting flexibility required to cope with the uncertainty and change associated with the environmental and organizational factors described previously.

scenario a proposed sequence of events with its own set of assumptions and associated program details

contingency plans plans to be implemented when severe, unanticipated changes to organizational or environmental factors completely negate the usefulness of the existing HR forecasting predictions or projections

HR forecasters therefore devise a set of alternative **scenarios**, each with its own set of assumptions and program details associated with HR functions such as training and development, staffing (advertisement, recruiting, and selection), and succession or replacement planning.[22] Naturally, organizations must also conduct **contingency planning** to have HR policy responses ready if substantive unanticipated changes occur. Contingency plans are brought into action when such severe changes to organizational or environmental factors completely negate the usefulness of the existing HR forecasting predictions or projections (e.g., a substantial drop in consumer demand occurs due to adverse public relations, as was seen in the Classic Coke and Tylenol cases).

Determining Net HR Requirements

Thus far we have discussed the importance of HR forecasting, key personnel groups targeted for special attention, environmental and organizational factors influencing supply and demand of personnel, and forecasting time horizons. The final part of this chapter addresses the process of determining net HR requirements. The next two chapters will be devoted to an examination of specific methods used to calculate HR demand (Chapter 8) and supply (Chapter 9), but, for now, we will lay the foundation for these chapters by examining the overall process.

1. Determine HR Demand

As we previously mentioned briefly, it is essential that we calculate our requirement or demand for personnel in terms of numbers and obligatory skill competencies before we consider how we will meet those requirements (i.e., what supply or source of personnel to use). In determining demand, a variety of factors have to be considered. First, each organizational sub-unit has to submit its net personnel requirement to the corporate forecasting unit, based on future needs for labour required to meet the agreed-on corporate and sub-unit

BOX 7.6 HR Forecasting for the Canadian Federal Public Service Workforce

The Research Directorate of the Canadian Public Service Commission uses two sophisticated forecasting models for analyzing the federal public service, specifically, ithink and PERSIM software packages. These models can be used to conduct HR forecasting with respect to overall and departmental staffing levels, gross flows (out- and in-flows) of personnel with their associated rates of movement through the organization, for developing career paths, and for conducting detailed demographic analyses of the Canadian federal public service.

The ithink Model

Ithink was developed by High Performance Systems Inc. in the United States in 1985. It enables the user to build dynamic models for simulation and scenario testing. Based on traditional historical rates of personnel movement (e.g., promotions, retirements, recruitments, and turnover), the model enables the different scenarios to be tested and it notes the overall aggregate effect on the system of the various assumptions and personnel movement estimates. Specifically, ithink conceives of the federal public service workforce as "stocks" (i.e., populations—e.g., all employees in a particular department or region, or all employees in a specific occupational group, an employment equity group, etc.) and "flows" (inflows into a stock include promotions, transfers, external hires, while outflows incorporate retirement and turnover [voluntary and involuntary]). The assumptions regarding rates of personnel movement are derived from outside the model, typically by historical trends or by user-developed scenarios. Ithink traces movement thoughout the system based on "*pull*" assumptions where outflow patterns (see above) are used to forecast the needed inflow personnel requirements; however, "*push*" models could also be readily developed.

The PERSIM Model

PERSIM (Personnel Simulation Model) was developed in Canada by Statistics Canada, and in many ways it operates very similarly to the ithink model, as it uses historical patterns of personnel movement, as well as user-driven scenarios, to forecast HR movement and requirements. Its strength lies in its ability to also conduct micro-simulations that can develop career paths for every individual in an organization based on its operating assumptions and historical data. This differs from the ithink model in that PERSIM is not limited to looking at aggregated groups of individuals or overall movement of personnel. PERSIM is therefore extremely useful not only for determining career paths, but also for ascertaining future staffing levels, in- and out-flows of personnel, and overall demographic composition of the Canadian federal public service.

Source: *Demographic Analysis of the Federal Public Service Workforce: The ithink, and PERSIM Forecasting and Succession Planning Models.* www.tbs-sct.gc.ca/hr-rh/psds-dfps/dafps_f_model1_e.asp. Treasury Board of Canada, 2002. Reproduced with the permission of the Minister of Public Works and Government Services Canada, 2003.

objectives (e.g., market share, production levels, size or expansion, etc). It is critical to note that this HR demand figure must incorporate the individuals needed to maintain or replace the current personnel who retire, die, are fired or otherwise terminated, or take long-term leave (e.g., for reasons such as disability, training courses, etc.), as well as the replacements for individuals who are promoted or transferred out of the department. All these elements must be included in the calculation of departmental or sub-unit HR demand. These sub-unit labour demands are then aggregated and used as the starting point for the HR demand forecasts.

Next, planned future changes in organizational design or in restructuring (e.g., expansion of certain departments, downsizing of mid-level management, planned redundancy, and elimination of specific jobs), with their associated increases or decreases in staffing levels, must be incorporated into the equation to revise the aggregated net departmental demand requirements. Furthermore, forecasters have to consider how to replace nonproductive paid time (e.g., vacation and sick days) either by increasing demand for full- or part-time personnel (i.e., slack resources[23]) or perhaps by using overtime with the existing set of current employees to prevent loss of productive capacity and required level of service to organizational clients. Finally, consideration of all these issues leads us to the *net HR demand,* broken down into the forecasting time horizons mentioned previously and containing (1) the number of employees required by each sub-unit and by the organization in total and (2) the employee skill sets, competencies, or specifications required for each of the positions. Finally, we conduct a cost estimate (HR budget) for the net HR demand figure as a reality check to determine whether our forecasts are realistic, given financial resource considerations. Often, at this stage, sub-units are asked to rank their HR demand, identifying jobs that are most critical to the achievement of their departmental objectives.[24]

2. Ascertain HR Supply

internal supply refers to current members of the organizational workforce who can be retrained, promoted, transferred, etc., to fill anticipated future HR requirements

external supply potential employees who are currently undergoing training (e.g., university students) or are working for competitors, or who are members of unions or professional associations, or currently are in a transitional stage, between jobs or unemployed

skills inventory personal database record on each employee

Step one produced an estimate of personnel requirements or demand. Step two examines exactly how we plan to fill the anticipated future requirements for personnel. In essence, there are two supply options: (1) **internal supply,** which refers to current members of the organizational workforce who can be retrained, promoted, transferred, etc., to fill anticipated future HR requirements, and (2) **external supply,** which refers to potential employees who are currently undergoing training (e.g., university students) or working for competitors, or who are members of unions or professional associations, or currently are in a transitional stage, between jobs or unemployed. Typically, most organizations use a mix of both internal and external supply, rewarding loyal employees who perform well with promotion and advancement possibilities and recruiting outside individuals who possess competencies not held by the present workforce.

With respect to internal supply, the ability to meet HR demand hinges on the size of the current workforce and especially its level of or ability to perform certain jobs. The number and the KSAs of the workforce are analyzed using the HRMS (as described in Chapter 6), which contains a *personal record* or **skills inventory** of each member of the workforce. Included in the inventory (see Figure 6.1) are items such as employee name, seniority, classification, part- or full-time work status, work history and record of jobs held in the organization, education, training, skill competencies, history of performance appraisals, and future jobs desired by or recommended for the individual, as well as hobbies and interests that may be useful for organizational planning.[25] For example, a computer search of the HRMS database could enable us to quickly determine the numbers, names, and employment status of, and performance records for, all employees who have successfully completed a graduate degree in statistics. If the search procedure fails to find a sufficient number of employees with the necessary KSAs to meet HR demand, the policy options would be either to identify and retrain employees with related KSAs who perform well or to turn to external sources for personnel.

Although some organizations hire recruits externally only when their internal searches and job posting or bidding process fail to identify sufficient numbers of high-quality internal candidates,[26] there are several other reasons why many organizations use external labour to meet their HR demand. First, and most obviously, if it is necessary to expand our operations without increasing labour efficiency or implementing labour-saving technology, we might have to increase the size of the workforce by hiring externally. Second, internal employees are socialized and may be comfortable in their modus operandi, whereas external applicants can introduce to the organization competitive insights and highly creative novel operational techniques recently learned in external institutions. Third, an internal candidate may be considerably more expensive (due to collective agreement provisions relating compensation to seniority) than an individual who is recruited from outside the organization. Finally, if organizational objectives require a shift in operating techniques, culture, and past practices, hiring external candidates is often desirable for shaking up the organization!

Irrespective of the reasons why organizations seek external recruits, the key factor in determining whether the organization will be effective in meeting HR requirements from external supply sources is an analysis of how HR policies are perceived by individuals who are potential employees. By benchmarking competitor practices with respect to compensation, it is possible to examine staffing and compensation policies to make them more attractive to high-quality applicants. An organization's ability to attract the "cream of the crop" will be substantially enhanced if the organization is perceived as being the industry leader with respect to compensation, rather than just meeting or lagging behind (following) its competitors. As well, recruiting policies must be fine-tuned to ensure communication is established with the appropriate labour markets. For example, it might be possible to fill many production jobs from local labour market sources, but specialized technicians and professionals may require external recruiting, which is national, if not international, in scope. In this case, additional resources, time, and effort may be required if we are expected to fully meet the numerical and KSA requirements specified by our HR demand process. Finally, obtaining external applicants requires not only identifying where these individuals live and work, but also ascertaining the most appropriate media to use to contact and attract them. These media may include job fairs, open houses, and career days, as well as advertising in industry and professional association journals, publications, newspapers, and websites read by potential external applicants who are trained in the skills needed.

BOX 7.7 Categorizing Forecasting Models

Forecasting models can be categorized in three ways: (1) time series models, (2) cause and effect models, and (3) judgmental models. Time series models use past data in order to extrapolate and extend trends into the future. These models are simple to use and are typically confined to short-term forecasting. An example of a time series model is trend forecasting. Cause and effect models assume that an ongoing relationship exists between one or more causal or "independent" variables that produce change in the target or "dependent" variable. An example is the significant negative relationship existing between market rate of interest (cost of capital) and the demand for construction workers. Cause and effect models are used for short-, medium-, and long-term HR forecasting; the best known example is regression, as discussed in Chapter 8. Finally, judgmental models are used for new ventures, situations where past data do not exist or are unreliable, or when the forecasting period extends into the distant future. They rely on the subjective judgments of experts to derive the forecasts; one widely used example is the Delphi technique.

Source: Adapted from Jain, C. 2002. "Benchmarking Forecasting Models," *The Journal of Business Forecasting Methods and Systems*, Vol. 21, No. 3 (Fall), pp. 18–20. Reprinted with permission.

3. Determine Net HR Requirements

The third step in the process involves the determination of net HR requirements. From steps one and two above, the following equations are derived:

HR demand = external supply + internal supply

HR demand – internal supply = external supply

Personnel who can fill organizational HR demand requirements must be found from either the current internal workforce supply or from external environmental sources. As explained above, if we are unable to meet the numerical and KSA demands for personnel from internal sources, either because of the qualification or performance deficiencies of current workers or because of an explicit organizational decision to recruit new blood, the residual supply not met through current employees must come from outside:

external supply requirements = replacement + change supply components

replacement supply = hiring to replace all normal losses

(Normal losses are those that result from retirements, terminations, voluntary turnover, promotions, transfers, and leaves, and these losses must be replaced to keep the workforce size at the current level.)

change supply = hiring to increase (or decrease) the overall staffing level

Recall from our earlier discussion of HR demand that future personnel requirements must not only replace the current workforce employees (in terms of numbers and skill competencies), but also reflect desired future changes to staffing levels. Therefore, the first element in deriving our external supply calculation is to meet our replacement needs—that is, to maintain operations at the current level by hiring new employees to replace workers who have left due to firing, transfers, retirements, promotions, leaves, and so on. Next, if we are to increase or decrease our staffing levels, based on organizational and sub-unit objectives, we have to consider the change component that moves the overall size of the workforce to its new future level. This process can be represented by the following equation:

external supply = current workforce size x (replacement % per year + change % per year)

Using the example of an organization with a current workforce size of 1000 workers, an annual historical replacement/loss rate of 11%, and a desired future growth rate of 7%, the net external supply requirement is that 180 individuals be hired per year:

external supply = 1000 (.11 + .07) = 110 + 70 = 180

Of the new hires, 110 people are allocated strictly to replacement of departing workers, and the other 70 individuals constitute the change requirement for new growth.

Another organization with a workforce of 450, which has a historical annual replacement/loss rate of 8% and a corporate downsizing policy that will reduce overall staffing levels by 9.5%, has the following supply requirement:

external supply = 450 (.08 + [-.095]) = 36 - 43 = -7

(In the equation above, note that the figure 43 was rounded up from 42.75.) In this case, the annual replacement/loss rate is insufficient on its own to reduce the size of the organization's workforce to the desired lower staffing level. The result is *a net* ***HR surplus***, and the organization must not only institute a freeze on external hiring but also further reduce the current internal workforce complement by seven positions to meet the mandated downsizing policy!

HR surplus occurs when the internal workforce supply exceeds the organization's requirement or demand for personnel

In many cases, the existence of a collective agreement between the management and the union representing the employees may result in the organization not being able to specify which workers are to be terminated due to seniority and layoff articles in the agreement.

4. Institute HR Programs: HR Deficit and HR Surplus

When a forecast of HR demand is reconciled with the current workforce supply of personnel (i.e., HR internal supply), the result is the net HR requirement, which will be either a deficit or a surplus (unless we are exceedingly lucky and achieve parity with an exact balance of the two!).

HR deficit = HR demand > HR internal supply

HR deficit occurs when demand for HR exceeds the current personnel resources available in the organization's workforce (HR internal supply)

Simply stated, an **HR deficit** means that forecasted HR demand requirements cannot be satisfied solely by use of the current internal workforce supply of employees. Therefore, policy options focus on external supply considerations of recruitment, selection, and compensation schemes to attract new employees. It might be possible to hire part-time employees, full-time employees, or a combination of both in an attempt to address the deficit. Similarly, it might be possible to recall any workers (depending on their KSAs and training) who were laid off because of past lower levels of HR demand. Also, retired employees might be enticed back to work on at least a part-time basis by means of attractive, flexible work schedules. The use of temporary workers also can help the organization meet a short-run HR deficit, although in the long run, further attention to providing promotion and transfer opportunities for internal workers by means of training and development programs usually proves more advantageous.

HR surplus = HR demand < HR internal supply

An HR surplus occurs when the internal workforce supply exceeds the organization's requirement or demand for personnel. In this instance, a number of policy options can be considered. Employees might be laid off to reduce the excess labour supply to a level equal to the demand requirements. Alternatively, employers might terminate employees if certain jobs are considered redundant and the skill sets associated with these jobs will not be required in the future. **Job sharing** occurs when two or more employees perform the duties of one full-time position, each sharing the work activities on a part-time basis. This policy option is gaining strength in Canadian industry as it allows the company to retain valued employees, albeit with reduced hours and lower income levels, with the hope of reinstating them to full-time status once HR demand levels increase at some time in the future.

job sharing occurs when two or more employees perform the duties of one full-time position, each sharing the work activities on a part-time basis

Other programs for addressing an HR surplus include reducing the number of hours, shifts, or days worked by each worker so that all workers can be retained, while reducing overall work hours to the level required by operational demand imperatives. Secondments or leaves occur when the organization lends some of its excess workforce to community groups or permits those surplus workers to take educational leave or training away from the operational workplace. **Attrition** is the process of reducing an HR surplus by allowing the size of the workforce to decline naturally due to the normal pattern of losses associated with retirements, deaths, voluntary turnover, and so on. This decrease of internal supply over time can be accentuated by a **hiring freeze**, which is a prohibition on all external recruiting activities. Early retirement packages attempt to induce surplus workers to leave the organization when granted severance benefits and outplacement assistance. Finally, if internal supply exceeds HR demand for specific positions, organizational retraining and development, and assistance with the expenses associated with

attrition the process of reducing an HR surplus by allowing the size of the workforce to decline naturally because of the normal pattern of losses associated with retirements, deaths, voluntary turnover, etc.

hiring freeze a prohibition on all external recruiting activities

moving to a better labour market (geographic mobility), as well as transfer and demotion, can also be considered as possible policy options for the organization's affected personnel.[27]

Summary

This chapter has examined a wide variety of aspects associated with HR forecasting. The advantages of instituting effective forecasting procedures include reducing the costs of HR, increasing the flexibility of the organization, ensuring a close link to the process of business forecasting, and ensuring that the requirements of the organization take precedence over other specific issues. Some groups—executives or specialist/technical personnel, for example—attract special attention in the HR demand and supply reconciliation process. Both environmental and organizational factors have a tremendous impact on various forecasting procedures, and many of these factors have to be addressed explicitly in HR forecasting procedures. The various stages associated with the HR forecasting process are: determining the demand, ascertaining the supply, determining net HR requirements (formulae were supplied), and instituting the program. Finally, we discussed the policy implications of reconciling HR demand and supply, ending up with either an HR deficit or surplus, and the various programs that may have to be instituted by organizations to address these varying situations; these programs include job sharing, attrition, and a hiring freeze.

The next two chapters are devoted to an examination of specific techniques used by organizations to calculate HR demand and supply. Chapter 8 presents specific techniques employed by organizations to derive HR demand forecasts.

Key Terms

attrition, 174
contingency plans, 168
designated groups, 164
envelope, 167
external supply, 170
event-based forecasting, 160
hiring freeze, 174
HR deficit, 174
HR forecasting, 159
HR surplus, 173
human resources demand, 163
human resources supply, 163
internal supply, 170
job sharing, 174
prediction, 167
process-based forecasting, 160

projection, 167

scenario, 168

skills inventory, 170

transaction-based forecasting, 160

Suggested Websites

www.statcan.ca Statistics Canada website.

www.hrdc-drhc.gc.ca Human Resources Development Canada (HRDC) website.

www.bls.gov U.S. Government's Bureau of Labour Statistics website.

Discussion Questions

1. Over the past decade, there have been dramatic employment shifts in many industries because of product life cycles and technological change, as well as general changes in demand for workers with specific KSAs—for example, in computer and systems engineering. Select a particular industry and conduct a literature review and Internet search for business and labour employment statistics related to its operations (access the Internet websites for industry associations and Statistics Canada). Based on this historical review and your knowledge of current business trends, forecast possible employment shifts for the specific industry you have selected. How would you use this information as an HR planner?
2. A wide range of HR programming options is available to address either an HR deficit or an HR surplus. However, these programs have widely divergent consequences for the workforce, service to clients, and the local labour market, as well as for the organization's financial bottom line. Identify specific criteria to evaluate and differentiate the effectiveness of the various HR program options.

Exercise

Conduct a comprehensive analysis of the various stakeholders involved in an organization with which you are familiar. From this analysis, ascertain the key uncertainties that would be associated with the HR forecasting process for this organization. Based on the material in this chapter and your own knowledge, how would you address these environmental and organizational uncertainties in your modifications to the HR forecasting process?

CASE: Sun Microsystems

Sun Microsystems has experienced extremely rapid growth as the company has evolved from an entrepreneurial operation to a major player in the computer systems industry. As a result, there is a strong need to forecast and identify managerial and executive talent both within and outside of the corporation. Ken Alvares, vice-president of human resources, is well aware of the need to "grow" high-potential employees into these key managerial appointments.

Sun has a total of 600 directors, which is the entry-level executive job, and these individuals report to 110 vice-presidents, who in turn report to the president and the 11 executives who sit on Sun's senior management team. Alvares pays close attention to the profile and performance of each of these individuals: "We watch the directors closely, but give more attention to the VPs. We look at each person's particular profile and tailor individual coaching to their needs." Because of this policy, the forecasting and developing of senior managerial and executive talent at Sun takes on a very personalized approach, one that seems to be working, at least to date.

Alvares says he has a good idea who would fill a job if something happened to a specific person, but he is still unsatisfied with Sun's system. "When you look at our bench strength, I don't get the feeling that we've got ourselves covered. I worry about developing people to step up to the next level. In some cases, I have one guy who can fill 10 jobs. If I have to use him, then I'll have to do some scrambling."

Source: "Heirs Unapparent: Sun Microsystems," *HR Magazine* (1999), Society for Human Resource Management. Reprinted with the permission of *HR Magazine*, published by the Society for Human Resource Management (www.shrm.org), Alexandria, VA.

Question

Prepare a report analyzing Sun Microsystem's forecasting program for managerial and executive talent. What additions, modifications, or changes would you make to this program?

References

Atwater, D.M. 1995. "Workforce Forecasting." *Human Resource Planning*, Vol. 18, No. 4: 50–53.

Bechet, T.P., and J.W. Walker. 1993. "Aligning Staffing with Business Strategy." *Human Resource Planning*, Vol. 16, No. 2: 1–16.

Beck, B.M. 1991. "Forecasting Environmental Change." *Journal of Forecasting*, Vol. 10, No. 1: 3–19.

Bucalo, J. 1974. "The Assessment Center: A More Specified Approach." *Human Resource Management* (Fall): 2–12.

Burack, E. 1995. *Creative Human Resource Planning and Applications: A Strategic Approach.* Englewood Cliffs, N.J.: Prentice Hall.

Burack, E.J., and N.J. Mathys. 1996. *Human Resource Planning: A Pragmatic Approach to Manpower Staffing and Development,* 3rd ed. Northbrook, Ill.: Brace Park.

Butinsky, C.F., and O. Harari. 1983. "Models vs. Reality: An Analysis of 12 Human Resource Planning Systems." *Human Resource Planning,* Vol. 6, No. 1: 11–20.

Connolly, S. 1975. "Job Posting." *Personnel Journal* (May): 295–299.

Fulmer, W. 1990. "Human Resource Management: The Right Hand of Strategy Implementation." *Human Resource Planning,* Vol. 12, No. 4: 1–11.

Godet, M. 1983. "Reducing the Blunders in Forecasting." *Futures,* Vol. 15, No. 3 (June): 181–192.

Grabosky, P., and D. Rosenbloom. 1975. "Racial and Ethnic Integration in the Federal Service." *Social Science Quarterly,* Vol. 56, No. 1 (June): 71–84.

Hogan, A. 1987. "Combining Forecasts: Some Managerial Experiences with Extrapolation." *Socio-Economic Planning Sciences,* Vol. 2, No. 3: 205–211.

Kaumeyer, R.H. 1982. *Planning and Using at Total Personnel System.* New York: Van Nostrand Reinhold.

Mahmoud, E. 1984. "Accuracy in Forecasting: A Survey." *Journal of Forecasting,* Vol. 3, No. 2 (April): 139–159.

Martin, R. 1967. "Skills Inventories." *Personnel Journal* (January): 28–83.

Mason, D.H. 1994. "Scenario-Based Planning: Decision Model for the Learning Organization." *Planning Review:* 6–11.

McEnery, J., and M. Lifter. 1987. "Demands for Change: Interfacing Environmental Pressures and the Personnel Process." *Public Personnel Management,* Vol. 16, No. 1 (Spring): 61–87.

McLaughlin, G. 1975. "A Professional Supply and Demand Analysis." *Educational Record,* Vol. 56, No. 3 (Summer): 196–200.

Meehan, R., and B.S. Ahmed. 1990. "Forecasting Human Resources Requirements: A Demand Model." *Human Resource Planning,* Vol. 13, No. 4: 297–307.

Monks, K. 1996. "Global or Local? HRM in the Multinational Company: The Irish Experience." *International Journal of Human Resource Management,* Vol. 7, No. 3 (September): 721–735.

Schuler, R.S. 1989. "Scanning the Environment: Planning for Human Resource Management and Organizational Change." *Human Resource Planning,* Vol. 12, No. 4.

Schuler, R.S., and J.W. Walker. 1990. "Human Resources Strategy: Focusing on Issues and Actions." *Organizational Dynamics* (Summer): 4–19.

Seamans, L. 1978. "What's Lacking in Most Skills Inventories." *Personnel Journal* (March).

Stone, T., and J. Fiorito. 1986. "A Perceived Uncertainty Model of Human Resource Forecasting Technique Use." *Academy of Management Review,* Vol. 11, No. 3: 635–642.

Thompson, J. 1967. *Organizations in Action.* New York: McGraw-Hill.

Treasury Board of Canada Secretariat. 2002. *Demographic Analysis of the Federal Public Service Workforce: The ithink, and PERSIM Forecasting and Succession Planning Models,* http://www.tbs-sct.gc.ca/hr_connexions.

Walker, J.W. 1980. *Human Resource Planning.* New York: McGraw-Hill.

Zaleznik, A. 1977. "Managers and Leaders: Are They Different?" *Harvard Business Review,* Vol. 55, No. 3 (May): 67–78.

ENDNOTES

1. Atwater, 1995.
2. Godet, 1983.
3. Hogan, 1987; Mahmoud, 1984.
4. Monks, 1996.
5. Stone and Fiorito, 1986; Meehan and Ahmed, 1990.
6. Walker, 1980.
7. Beck, 1991; Schuler, 1989.
8. Fulmer, 1990.
9. McEnery and Lifter, 1987.
10. Fulmer, 1990.
11. Schuler and Walker, 1990.
12. Adapted from Burack and Mathys, 1996.
13. Grabosky and Rosenbloom, 1975.
14. Zaleznik, 1977.
15. Bucalo, 1974.
16. Adapted from Schuler and Walker, 1990.
17. Beck, 1991.
18. McEnery and Lifter, 1987; Schuler, 1989.
19. Beck, 1991; Butinsky and Harari, 1983.
20. Adapted from Bechet and Walker, 1993; Walker, 1980.
21. Burack and Mathys, 1996.
22. Mason, 1994.
23. Thompson, 1967.
24. Burack, 1995.
25. Martin, 1967; Kaumeyer, 1982; Seamans, 1978.
26. Connolly, 1975.
27. McLaughlin, 1975.

8

HR DEMAND

CHAPTER GOALS

This chapter is devoted to a presentation and examination of various real-world techniques used by organizations to forecast their HR demand. As we progress through the chapter, you will note that the techniques presented vary according to their forecasting time horizon and that these techniques tend to be either qualitative or quantitative. Successful organizations combine statistically driven quantitative forecasts with more qualitative expert processes to achieve the most comprehensive demand forecasts possible.[1] As well, organizations must consider demand for personnel not only for the current operational period, but also well into the future to ensure the right numbers of workers with the requisite skills and competencies are ready and available to work when the organization requires them.

After reading this chapter, you should be able to do the following:

1. Understand the importance of demand forecasting in the HR planning process.
2. Recognize the linkages between the HR plan, labour demand forecasting techniques, and the subsequent supply stage.

3. Compare and contrast the advantages and disadvantages of various demand forecasting techniques: index/trend analysis, expert forecasts, the Delphi technique, the nominal group technique, HR budgets (staffing or manning tables), envelope/scenario forecasting, and regression analysis.

Index/Trend Analysis

trend analysis the historical relationship between an operational index and the number of employees required by the organization (demand for labour)

Examining the relationship over time between an operational business index, such as level of sales, and the demand for labour (as reflected by the number of employees in the workforce) is a relatively straightforward quantitative demand forecasting technique commonly employed by many organizations (see Table 8.1).[2] This technique, also known as **trend analysis**, reveals the historical relationship between the operational index and the number of employees required by the organization (demand for labour).[3] Although sales level is probably the most common index used by organizations, other operational indices include (1) the number of units produced, (2) the number of clients serviced, and (3) the production (i.e., direct labour) hours. Similarly, although the relationship between the operational index and workforce size (number of employees) can be calculated for the entire organization, as well as for the department or operational sub-unit, some organizations use trend analysis to ascertain demand requirements for (1) direct labour and (2) indirect labour (e.g., HR staff).

There are five steps to conducting an effective index/trend analysis.

1. Select the Appropriate Business/Operational Index

The HR forecaster must select a readily available business index, such as sales level, that is (a) known to have a direct influence on the organizational demand for labour, and (b) subjected to future forecasting as a result of the normal business planning process.

2. Track the Business Index over Time

Once the index has been selected, it is necessary to go back in time for at least the four or five most recent years, but preferably for a decade or more, to record the quantitative or numerical levels of the index over time.

3. Track the Workforce Size over Time

Record the historical figures of the total number of employees, or, alternatively, the amount of direct and indirect labour (see above) for exactly the same period used for the business index in step 2.

BOX 8.1 Index/Trend Analysis

Puslinch Pottery

Year	Sales ($ Thousands)	Number of Employees	Index (Sales [$ Thousands] per Employee)
2002	$2800	155	18.06
2003	3050	171	17.83
2004	3195	166	19.25
2005	3300	177	18.64
2006	3500[a]	188[b]	18.64[c]
2007	3600[a]	193[b]	18.64[c]
2008	3850[a]	207[b]	18.64[c]

a Time now is the year 2005. We are forecasting labour demand for 2006, 2007, and 2008, and therefore sales figures for those years are future estimates.

b Employee numbers are historical, except for the figures for 2006, 2007, and 2008, which are our future HR demand forecasts.

c The index used to calculate future demand (number of employees) can be the most recent figure, or an average of the up-to-date period (e.g., the past four years, for which the average is 18.44). In this trend analysis, the most recent index (18.64) for the year 2005 was used for forecasting.

4. Calculate the Average Ratio of the Business Index to the Workforce Size

In this step, a ratio of the number of employees required for each thousand dollars of sales (e.g., for each pottery item produced) is obtained by dividing each year's number of employees by the level of sales (e.g., the number of pieces of pottery produced). This **employee requirement ratio** is calculated for each year over the period of analysis so an average ratio describing the relationship between the two variables over time can be determined.

employee requirement ratio the relationship between the operational index and the demand for labour

5. Calculate the Forecasted Demand for Labour

Multiply the annual forecast for the business index times the average employee requirement ratio for each future year to arrive at forecasted annual demand for labour. For example, obtain future sales forecast figures for the next five years. For each of the years, multiply the level of sales by the average employee requirement ratio to obtain the forecasted numerical demand for labour for each future year.

Although employment of index/trend analysis is widespread due to its ease of use, it is important to remember that the analysis incorporates only the relationship between a single business variable and demand for labour (workforce size). By design, any single-variable relationship provides a simplistic forecast for demand. For more comprehensive analyses that reflect a variety of factors affecting business operations, such as interest rates, level of unemployment, consumer disposable income, and so on, the quantitative techniques normally employed are multivariate regression or other similar modelling/ programming models.[4] Although these sophisticated, multiple-predictor techniques require detailed knowledge of statistics and systems programming, we will present an example of simple regression later in the chapter.

Expert Forecasts

Direct managerial input is the most commonly used method for determining workforce requirements.[5] Using experts to arrive at a numerical estimate of future labour demand is considered to be a qualitative process for determining future labour requirements because it is a detailed process of stating assumptions, considering potential organizational and environmental changes, and deriving a rationale to support the numerical estimate.

A wide variety of individuals may be considered experts for their knowledge of organizational operations, competitive HR practices, international trends in the labour markets, etc.[6] First and foremost, the organization's own line managers, who each have detailed knowledge of workload, responsibilities, and overall task responsibilities for his or her own department, are in possession of important insights into how future demand for labour should or might change in their own areas of responsibility. Second, the organization's HR and business planning staffs certainly have critical information that can enable them to provide wise guidance in forecasting future levels of labour demand. For example, the planning staff may use econometric and strategic models to predict the future level of sales of or demand for the organization's goods and services, as well as provide important insights into future economic indicators affecting labour demand such as interest rates, change in gross national product, level of consumer disposable income, savings, and so on. The HR staff, whether they are HR generalists or a team of HR planning specialists, are able to draw up a detailed set of assumptions with respect to industry, local, and international labour market trends that have an impact on how the organization organizes and employs its own workforce. Third, business consultants, financial analysts, university researchers, union staff members, industry spokespersons, and others possess detailed knowledge of specific industries or types of organizational activity and are able to give rich, detailed, and largely impartial judgments on future labour demand because of their external perspective relative to the organization. Finally, but not exclusively, federal, provincial, and local governmental staff and officials are important individuals to consult because they possess knowledge of future environmental changes in labour and business legislation that can dramatically change labour demand not only for a specific organization, but also for the industry in general. For example, pending legislation to ban the use of certain materials in product manufacturing might cause a substantial drop in demand for these products and hence an associated reduction in demand for employees who are involved in their manufacture.

Governmental ministries and departments, most specifically those devoted to labour, human resources, and economic development, and, of course, the highly regarded Statistics Canada, can all provide expert information for our labour demand forecasting process. Irrespective of which experts we select, a number of options are available for obtaining labour demand estimates and assumptions from those concerned. Interviews, questionnaires (conducted in person or by mail or e-mail), and telephone conference calls are some of these options, but other techniques can be employed to maximize the benefit of each expert's contributions in specific circumstances. We now turn our attention to two of these methods of facilitating high-quality labour demand forecasts—namely, the Delphi technique and the nominal group technique.

Delphi Technique

The **Delphi technique**, which was named after the Greek oracle at Delphi, was developed by N.C. Dalkey and his associates at the Rand Corporation in 1950 and is an especially useful qualitative method for deriving detailed assumptions on long-run HR demand.[7] This forecasting technique is "a carefully designed program of sequential, individual interrogations (usually conducted through questionnaires) interspersed with information feedback on the opinions expressed by the other participants in previous rounds."[8] A key feature of this demand forecasting technique is that once a group of experts is selected, the experts do not meet face to face.[9] Instead, a project coordinator canvasses them individually for their input and forecasts by means of a progressively more focused series of questionnaires. The advantage of the Delphi technique is that it avoids many of the problems associated with face-to-face groups, namely, reluctance by individual experts to participate due to (1) shyness, (2) perceived lower status or authority, (3) perceived communication deficiencies, (4) issues of individual dominance and groupthink (i.e., group conformity pressures [Janis 1972]), and so on.[10] Because the Delphi technique does not employ face-to-face meetings, it can serve as a great equalizer and can elicit valid feedback from all expert members. It is also advantageous that the Delphi technique can effectively utilize experts who are drawn from widely dispersed geographical areas.[11]

Delphi technique
"a carefully designed program of sequential, individual interrogations (usually conducted through questionnaires) interspersed with information feedback on the opinions expressed by the other participants in previous rounds"

There are disadvantages associated with the Delphi technique, as indeed there are with all forecasting techniques. In particular, because of the series of questionnaires administered to derive a forecast, the time and costs incurred

BOX 8.2 The Delphi Technique in Action

The Delphi technique is used in a wide variety of applications for HR forecasting. One was at an agricultural research organization, which started by deriving nine organizational core competencies from interviews and internal organizational documentation. The experts were identified by the organization, which asked them to respond to set of questionnaires based on the Delphi technique. The questionnaires investigated (1) the importance of human competencies in the future, (2) the capacity of the organization's current human resources, and (3) ranking the nine organizational core competencies in order of priority. HR policy interventions were developed from the resulting information.

A three-round Delphi procedure was used to identify the basic competencies of research chefs, who develop new products, create new recipes, and conduct food testing. Thirty-three expert chefs were involved in the Delphi undertaking, and they were asked questions concerning (1) factors differentiating successful from less successful research chefs, (2) knowledge and skills required by successful research chefs, and (3) how tasks differ for a research chef from ordinary chefs. The experts identified 19 basic competencies that a successful research chef should possess.

Finally, subsequent to the September 11, 2001, terrorist attacks on the United States, the Delphi technique was used by the government and insurance and risk managers to estimate the possibility of future losses due to terrorism, and the likely types of terrorist acts various organizations might experience. Experts used the Delphi technique to analyze databases on landmarks, tourist attractions, "vital points," and property assessment data to come up with their forecasts.

Sources: Adapted from T. Guimaraes et al., "Forecasting Core Competencies in an R&D Environment," *R&D Management*, Vol. 31, No. 3 (July 2001), pp. 249–255; K. Birdir and T. Pearson, "Research Chefs' Competencies: A Delphi Approach," *International Journal of Contemporary Hospitality Management*, Vol. 12, No. 3 (2000), pp. 205–209; and B. Coffin, "Forecasting Terrorism Losses," *Risk Management*, Vol. 49, No. 11 (November 2000), pp. 8–9.

when using the Delphi technique can be higher than those incurred when using alternative forecasting methods. Another deficiency is that since the results cannot be validated statistically, the process is greatly dependent on the individual knowledge and commitment of each of the contributing experts.[12] Furthermore, if the experts are drawn from one specific field, it may be that their common professional training will guide them along a single line of inquiry rather than pursuing more innovative and creative courses of action. Finally, if insufficient attention has been paid to developing criteria for the identification and selection of experts, the personnel selected to derive the demand forecasts may lack sufficient expertise or information to contribute meaningfully to the process.[13]

There are six steps associated with using the Delphi technique for HR demand forecasting.

1. Define and Refine the Issue or Question

During this stage, a project coordinator is assigned, and he or she works with the HR staff to determine the specific personnel category or activity that will be the focus of the Delphi technique. It is essential that the group targeted for HR forecasting be well defined so that relevant, focused, and detailed feedback based on a minimum of assumptions (redundant assumptions are associated with loss of the experts' time) can be derived.

2. Identify the Experts, Terms, and Time Horizon

The project coordinator, normally in conjunction with the HR staff, identifies and selects a team of individuals who are deemed to be experts with respect to the specific personnel grouping that requires a forecast. Next, given that in many cases the group of experts will include individuals who are not members of the organization, it is important to set the context and to be explicit with definitions. For example, the team of experts must be absolutely clear as to which jobs constitute "production workers" if those experts are being asked to derive a demand forecast for this category. Similarly, the exact time horizon(s) must be specified for the personnel category being analyzed.

3. Orient the Experts

In addition to identifying the relevant time horizon(s) and clarifying which personnel groups are of interest, the orientation process for experts includes an overview of the demand forecasting decision process (which is very similar to the structural framework in which you are now engaged!). The experts are told either that there will be a predetermined number of questionnaire iterations or that the sequence will continue until a majority opinion exists among the experts.

4. Issue the First-Round Questionnaire

The project coordinator sends each expert the questionnaire in person, by mail, or by e-mail and includes a time frame for completing and returning it. Typically, this first questionnaire is focused on defining both the explicit assumptions made by each of the experts and the background rationale supporting his or her own particular demand estimate.

5. Issue the First-Round Questionnaire Summary and the Second Round of Questionnaires

Following the completion of the first questionnaire, the project coordinator sends the second and subsequent rounds of questionnaires to the experts with a written summary of the findings from the first round. The aim of the subsequent questionnaires is to focus the experts' initial assumptions and estimates by providing summarized feedback from all members of the group. Points of commonality and conflict are identified in the summary, as is the need to clarify specific assumptions identified by the responses to the previous round.

6. Continue Issuing Questionnaires

The project coordinator continues to issue questionnaires until either all the predetermined questionnaire stages have been completed and summarized or the group reaches a clear majority decision. In either case, the majority or nth-round summary makes up the experts' future demand estimate for the HR category under analysis.

Nominal Group Technique

nominal group technique (NGT) long-run forecasting technique utilizing expert assessments

Although the **nominal group technique (NGT)** is also a long-run, qualitative demand forecasting method, it differs from the Delphi technique in several important respects. First, unlike in the Delphi technique, the group does, in fact, meet face to face and interact, but only after individual written, preparatory work has been done and all the demand estimates (idea generation) have been publicly tabled, or written on a flip chart, without discussion.[14] Second, each demand estimate is considered to be the property of the entire group and to be impersonal in nature, which minimizes the potential for dominance, personal attacks, and defensive behaviour in support of estimates presented in the group forum.[15] Finally, the expert forecast is determined by a secret vote of all group members on their choice of the tabled demand forecasts. The estimate receiving the highest ranking or rating during the voting process is deemed to be the group's forecast.[16]

BOX 8.3 Assessing the Utility of the Nominal Group Technique

Studies have shown that nominal group technique (NGT) is especially effective for brainstorming sessions to ensure all participants have an equal voice in the sessions, and when a problem or issue stems from several widely diverse causes. Furthermore, studies have shown that NGT provides highly reliable and valid qualitative data that is ranked by importance and is superior to that derived from focus group sessions. Nominal group sessions investigating teaching performance competencies on 13 dimensions (technical knowledge, planning and organizing, managing interaction, commitment to teaching objectives, proactive orientation, student development orientation, class presentation ability, impact on the class, adaptability and flexibility, personal motivation, listening skills, oral communication skills, and presentation skills) were dramatically superior to information obtained from focus groups. The study predicted that nominal group technique will replace focus groups as the qualitative research method of choice and will reduce the need for the administration of surveys.

Sources: Adapted from B. Andersen and T. Fagerhaug, "The Nominal Group Technique," *Quality Progress*, Vol. 22, No. 2 (February 2000), pp. 144–145; and B. Langford et al., "Nominal Grouping Sessions vs. Focus Groups," *Qualitative Market Research*, Vol. 5, No. 1 (2002), pp. 58–70.

There are seven steps associated with implementing the nominal group technique.

1. Define and Refine the Issue or Question and the Relevant Time Horizon

This step is similar to the first step of the Delphi technique. The HR forecasting staff or coordinator is responsible for identifying the specific personnel category or activity that will be the focus for the nominal group technique. The more refined the problem definition is, the more likely it is that relevant, focused, detailed feedback will be derived with a minimum of redundant assumptions. Second, it is essential that the time horizon(s) of interest for the demand estimate be clearly specified. Overall, the issue is often phrased as a question: "What will ABC Corporation's demand for production workers be in the year 2008 (or in five years from the present)? Please provide your demand estimate and the explicit assumptions and rationale supporting your forecast."

2. Select the Experts

In the second step, the coordinator or HR forecasting staff selects the individuals who have expert knowledge of the specific personnel group being analyzed. Experts are then contacted to confirm their participation in the process and to schedule the time for the face-to-face meeting.

3. Issue the HR Demand Statement to the Experts

During the third step, the coordinator for the nominal group process sends each of the experts a concise statement of the HR demand they are being asked to address. As stated in the first step, the issue is normally framed as a question that the experts are being asked to answer, and an accompanying sheet of terms, definitions, and assumptions may accompany the question or issue statement.

4. Apply Expert Knowledge, State Assumptions, and Prepare an Estimate

Having received the issue or question posed by the coordinator on behalf of the organization, each expert now considers his or her specific knowledge of the particular personnel group that is the subject of the demand estimate. In particular, experts will undoubtedly have personal insights or insider information not available to other members of the group and should explicitly state the various assumptions that arise from this information, as well as the numerical estimate of demand. In this way, once the nominal group meets face to face, the supporting rationale for what may be widely divergent demand estimates quickly becomes apparent to the group as a whole.

5. Meet Face to Face

Having prepared their individual assumptions and a numerical estimate of demand, the experts then meet face to face. The first item of business will be a brief presentation of each expert's demand estimate with the associated supporting assumptions. Individual interaction and discussion are strictly forbidden so as not to stifle creativity. The coordinator will arrange for individual introductions and ice-breakers to facilitate group interaction only after all estimates have been tabled. He or she will also specify the process for the nominal group's subsequent actions.

6. Discuss the Demand Estimates and Assumptions

After each expert has presented his or her demand estimate, the process shifts to detailed analyses and group discussion of the estimates and their assumptions. To minimize individual defensiveness and personal ownership of estimates, group members are asked to focus on ascertaining supportive information for estimate assumptions and to avoid attacks on the soundness of any specific estimate. The question, answer, and discussion session continues until all pertinent information affecting the HR demand estimates has been presented to the satisfaction of the experts in attendance, or at least to the point where all positions and assumptions are clear to group members.

7. Vote Secretly to Determine the Expert Demand Assessment

A secret vote is taken, and the estimate drawing the highest ranking or number of votes from the experts is selected to be the group's HR demand estimate solution to the question posed in the first step.

HR budgets quantitative, operational or short-run demand estimates that contain the number and types of personnel (i.e., personnel classes, such as bank clerks, loans officers, and branch managers) required by the organization as a whole and for each sub-unit, division, or department

HR Budgets: Staffing or Manning Table

HR budgets are quantitative, operational, or short-run, demand estimates that contain the number and types of personnel (i.e., personnel classes, such as bank clerks, loans officers, and branch managers) required by the organization as a whole and for each sub-unit, division, or department (see Table 8.1).[17] These HR budgets are prepared by the HR staff in conjunction with line managers and take into consideration information from historical company staffing trends, competitor staffing practices, industry and professional associations, and Statistics Canada.

The HR budget process produces what is referred to as a **staffing** or **manning table**, which contains information related to a specific set of operational assumptions or levels of activity (e.g., maintain the current organization structure, increase the sales level by 5% over last year's level). The staffing or manning table presents the total HR demand requirement, as well as the number of personnel required, by level (e.g., vice-presidents) and function (e.g., marketing personnel).

staffing or **manning table**
total HR demand requirement for operational or short-run time periods

In this way, HR planners can determine short-run future demand requirements for sub-units and the organization as a whole. This enables budgeting processes to incorporate changes in compensation costs linked to the level of future personnel demand.

Envelope/Scenario Forecasting

Previously, we noted that an HR budget is focused on deriving short-run operational HR demand and a staffing or manning table for each organizational department, as well as for the entire organization, assuming a specific future

TABLE 8.1 STAFFING TABLE AND HR BUDGET

ENNOTVILLE EATERIES

Staff Demand Requirements	**Sales ($ Millions)**			
Administrative Positions	**$1–10**	**>$10–25**	**>$25–50**	**>$50–75**
President	1	1	1	1
Vice-presidents	1	1	2	3
Marketing managers	1	1	2	2
Sales staff	4	7	10	18
HR staff	2	4	5	7
Treasurer	1	1	1	2
Financial staff	3	5	7	9
Clerical and general staff	5	8	12	14
Production Positions				
Executive chef	1	1	1	1
Chef	2	4	5	6
Cook	8	15	25	35
Haggis helper	10	20	30	40
Saucier	1	3	5	6

outcome (e.g., a constant level of sales). This constitutes a *prediction* or single estimate of future HR demand. If, however, we wish to conduct much more comprehensive future planning of operational and short-run HR demand, we should instigate ***envelope/scenario forecasting***. Simply put, envelope/scenario forecasts are projections, or multiple-predictor estimates, of future demand for personnel predicated on a variety of differing assumptions about how future organizational events will unfold.[18]

envelope/scenario forecasts projections, or multiple-predictor estimates, of future demand for personnel predicated on a variety of differing assumptions about how future organizational events will unfold

Scenario forecasting is based on the premise that since we have no certain knowledge of the future course of events, we would be well served by developing several plausible sets of outcomes. Based on certain assumptions, experts search for causality by linking cause and effect events together. Scenarios are developed by having brainstorming sessions with line managers and human resource managers, who formulate the group's combined expert view of the workforce five years or more in the future, and then work back in time to identify key change points. The group members then try to make sense of the various future states by further developing and discussing the linkages and courses of action that will lead from the present to the proposed future scenarios.[19] Figure 8.1 illustrates envelope/scenario forecasting.

This flexible demand forecasting process is much more useful for incorporating the effects of uncertainty and change into our strategic HR planning process than is consideration of the single assumption of an HR budget. Each of the scenarios or predicted future states contains its own set of assumptions, resulting in an entirely different estimate presented in *a single staffing or manning table for each specific course of action*. In this way, an organization's HR staff

FIGURE 8.1 ENVELOPE/SCENARIO FORECASTING

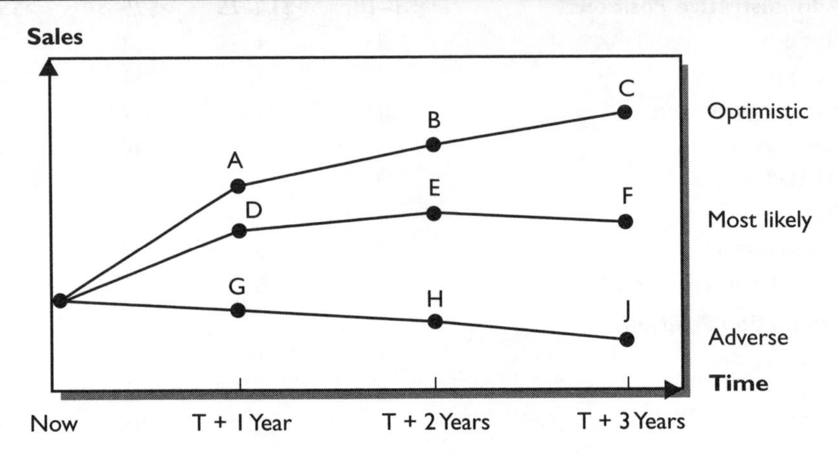

Note that A=Staffing table A; B=Staffing table B, etc.

are able to develop, with the associated staffing tables, future scenarios that are optimistic (e.g., sales levels will increase by 10% to 15%), realistic or most likely (e.g., sales levels will increase by 5% to 10%), or pessimistic (e.g., sales levels will remain constant or increase by less than 5%). Furthermore, as we consider the optimistic, realistic or most likely, and pessimistic scenarios extended into the future, the impact of the time horizon (e.g., year 1, year 2, year 3, year 4, and year 5) forms the shape of a letter envelope. The optimistic and pessimistic scenarios, and their associated staffing tables, constitute the four corners of the envelope from the initial time period to the final time period being forecasted. Other scenarios are plotted as midpoints on the envelope. By means of this comprehensive, explicit set of staffing tables, which reflect a wide variety of future organizational circumstances, the scenario/envelope technique allows us to have ready access to flexible, preplanned demand estimates when circumstances rapidly change.

BOX 8.4 Meeting HR Demand Requirements Through E-Recruiting

Utilizing information systems technology to meet HR demand requirements is not only cost and time efficient compared to placing ads in journals or hiring recruiting firms, but it allows applicants to submit résumés from the comfort of their own homes. Organizations such as Hewlett-Packard, Dell Computer, and Cisco Systems conduct e-recruiting by placing job postings on-line (company or third-party Internet career websites), and utilize tracking systems that sort résumés and candidates by conducting content-based analyses of the applicants' résumés. However, e-recruiting should not be regarded as a stand-alone tool, as it should be incorporated into an integrated HR system that also uses behavioural and skills assessments, job analysis, performance management, and training tools to enhance individual and team productivity and satisfaction. These integrated systems increase the demand for effective decision-making and communication skills and highlight the fact that fast and efficient data collection is insufficient without fast and efficient decisions resulting from the process!

With online recruiting sites often being the first point of contact between the potential applicant and the organization, it is critical that the technological processes associated with e-recruiting do not frustrate and deter applicants, especially the "best and brightest" who are well versed in leading-edge technology. Cumbersome application forms with poor instructions, accompanied by lengthy and marginally relevant on-line test and assessment instruments, can discourage applicants, as can the fact that having completed the online process, many people do not even receive a thank-you message acknowledging the receipt of their application! This can leave applicants feeling that the company is cold, impersonal, not trustworthy, and perhaps even manipulative in its relations with employees, perceptions that can prove extremely detrimental to any firm!

Sources: Adapted from E. Goodridge, "Online Recruiters Feel the Pinch," *InformationWeek*, No. 837 (May 14, 2001), pp. 83–84; B. Cullen, "E-Recruiting Is Driving HR Systems Integration," *Strategic Finance*, Vol. 83, No. 1 (July 2001), pp. 22–26; and I. Kotlyar and L. Karakowsky, "If Recruitment Means Building Trust, Where Does Technology Fit In?" *Canadian HR Reporter* (October 7, 2002), p. 21.

Regression Analysis

regression analysis presupposes that a linear relationship exists between one or more independent (causal) variables, which are predicted to affect the dependent (target) variable—in our instance, future HR demand for personnel (i.e., the number of personnel)

The final demand forecasting technique to be discussed in this chapter is **regression analysis**.[20] Regression analysis is a very effective quantitative forecasting technique for short-, medium- and long-range time horizons and can be easily updated and changed.[21] This section presupposes that readers possess a basic knowledge of statistical techniques as instruction in statistics is not the focus of this book. The section will enable HR practitioners to understand the essence of what regression can do for them[22] but will not get involved in the mathematical derivation of the regression equation from first principles. Individuals who would like more information about such statistical methods should refer to any one of a number of high-quality statistical textbooks. Regression is such a powerful technique for forecasting demand, however, that we will present a brief and simple explanation of the underlying rationale and basic principles behind its use in HR planning.

Simply put, regression analysis presupposes that a *linear relationship* exists between one or more *independent (causal) variables*, which are predicted to affect the *dependent (target) variable*—in our instance, future HR demand for personnel (i.e., the number of personnel required). Based on logic similar to that used in trend analysis, regression projects into the future based on the past historical relationship between the independent and dependent variables. *Linearity* refers to the observed relationship between the independent and dependent variables. For example, if a per-unit increase or decrease in the level of sales, and the market rate of interest, result in a concurrent associated change in HR demand (the dependent variable), then the assumption of linearity might be met and regression analysis could be used for our demand forecasting. If, however, the relationship between the independent and dependent variables was random or nonlinear, the use of regression to forecast future demand would not be valid. If there are several causal or independent variables, such as the market interest rate (i.e., the cost of capital), the unemployment rate, the organization's sales level, and so on, then the analysis is referred to as a *multivariate regression analysis*. Because of the complexity of the calculations, such multiple regressions are inevitably carried out by statistical software programs such as SPSS (Statistical Program for the Social Sciences) or the SAS Programming Language. For our purposes, we will present an example of what is referred to as *simple regression:* a prediction model based on the impact on HR demand (the dependent variable) of a single causal independent variable.

Simple Regression Prediction Model

The simple regression prediction model is as follows:

$$Y = A + BX$$

Y = the *dependent variable* (HR demand/number of personnel required)

A = constant (intercept)

B = the slope of the linear relationship between X and Y

X = the *independent/causal variable* (e.g., level of sales, production output)

where

$$B = \frac{\Sigma XY - N(\bar{X})(\bar{Y})}{\Sigma(X^2) - N(\bar{X})^2}$$

$$A = -Y - B\bar{X}$$

In other words, the predicted value for HR demand (Y) will be a function of a constant starting point (A) (i.e., the value of Y when X = 0) plus the interaction between the value of the causal/independent variable (X) multiplied by a slope factor (B). Let's turn to a specific example to make sense of it all!

Regression Exercise

As HR planning manager for Keele Kontainers Ltd., a dynamic, fast-growing company located in Wawanesa, Manitoba, you have an important task to fulfil. To continue the company's history of successful growth, you need to forecast the number of marketing personnel required for $8 million and $10 million of sales activity. You have the following historical information available to guide your regression analysis and HR demand forecast:

X Sales Level ($ Millions)	Y Number of Marketing Personnel
2.0	20
3.5	32
4.5	42
6.0	55
7.0	66

Note that the above information represents five sets of observations for both the independent (X) and dependent (Y) variables: set 1 (2.0; 20), set 2 (3.5; 32), set 3 (4.5; 42), and so on. Record that N = *the number of sets of observations*, in this instance, five.

There are five steps to conducting the regression analysis:

1. *Calculate XY, X^2, average X ($\bar{X}$), and average Y ($\bar{Y}$):* We can do this by extending the two columns shown above to a four-column set. XY is simply the result of multiplying each observation set's X level by the associated Y level, and X^2 is determined by multiplying the X value by itself:

X Sales Level ($ Millions)	Y Number of Marketing Personnel	XY	X^2
2.0	20	40	4.00
3.5	32	112	12.25
4.5	42	189	20.25
6.0	55	330	36.00
7.0	66	462	49.00
23.0	215	1133	121.50

Average X or $\bar{X} = 23/5 = 4.6$

Average Y or $\bar{Y} = 215/5 = 43.0$

Recall N = 5, and Y = A + BX

2. *Calculate the value of B (slope of the linear relationship between X and Y):*

$$B = \frac{\Sigma XY - N(\bar{X})(\bar{Y})}{\Sigma(X^2) - N(\bar{X})^2}$$

Plug in the values calculated in step 1; therefore

$$B = \frac{1133 - (5)(4.6)(43)}{121.5 - (5)(4.6)^2}$$

$$B = \frac{1133 - 989}{121.5 - 105.8} = 9.17$$

3. *Calculate A (constant or intercept):* Recall that

$$Y = A + BX$$

Then

$$A = \bar{Y} - B\bar{X}$$

Plug in the values calculated in step 1; therefore

$$A = 43 - (9.17)(4.6) = 0.82$$

4. *Determine the regression prediction equation:* We know that the general prediction model for regression is

$$Y = A + BX$$

For our specific problem, we have calculated A and B, so we insert these values into the equation, which will be used to calculate our HR demand (Y) as follows:

$$Y = 0.82 + (9.17)(X)$$

What does this mean? For our comparison between the level of sales (the independent/causal variable represented by X) and the predicted HR demand for marketing personnel (the dependent variable represented by Y), even when level of sales is at a zero level (i.e., less than $1 million of sales), the A value (the constant/intercept) shows that we have one marketing person (0.82 of a person rounds to 1.0). Furthermore, the prediction model shows that for every one unit ($1 million) increase in the level of sales (the independent variable X), there is a predicted increase of 9.17 marketing staff (Y) associated with that change.

5. *Calculate predicted HR demand (Y) by inserting values for X:* To predict our HR demand for marketing personnel at $8 million and $10 million of sales, as has been asked of us, we simply plug these levels into the values of X as follows:

For $8 million of sales (X = 8)

$$Y = A + BX = 0.82 + (9.17)(8) = 74.18$$

or 74 marketing staff are required

For $10 million of sales (X = 10)

$$Y = A + BX = 0.82 + (9.17)(10) = 92.52$$

or 93 marketing staff are required

As we can see, regression models can be extremely valuable tools for the HR planner. In our calculation of the simple regression problem above, we used five years or sets of observed historical data for our organization with respect to matching levels of sales and their relationship to levels of marketing personnel (HR demand). Most recent sales levels of $7 million of sales were associated with a marketing staff size of 66 personnel. We wish to predict into the future what our personnel requirements for $8 million and $10 million of sales will be. Our calculations of the regression equation noted that for every $1-million increase in sales, our marketing staff increased by approximately 9 (9.17) personnel, indicating the linear relationship between the two variables. Furthermore, we now know that for $8 million and $10 million of sales, we require 74 and 93 marketing staff respectively. This valuable forecasting technique enables us to plan and execute recruitment, selection, training, and development programs in a planned, proactive fashion to ensure the trained marketing staff are on hand exactly when required by the organization.

SUMMARY

In this chapter we examined various techniques that are used by organizations to forecast future requirements for HR demand. We noted that index/trend analysis examines the historical relationship between workforce size and a measure of operational efficiency, such as sales, to determine the ratio between the two measures for forecasting purposes. Expert forecasts revealed that there are a number of individuals, not necessarily just those who are HR staff, who have valid information on organizational policies, procedures, and planned future changes. This information can have a dramatic impact on deriving accurate forecasts of numbers and types of employees required for the organization's workforce of the future.

With respect to experts, we saw that the Delphi technique and the nominal group technique can be used effectively to obtain demand estimates from individuals while minimizing the time wastage and interpersonal dominance that often occurs in group settings. The HR budget process produces staffing or manning tables that are concerned with short-run operational time horizons in planning HR demand. Specifically, the staffing table presents a prediction of the number of personnel required by authority or functional level, given a specific set of assumptions regarding the future organizational activity. Plotting a wide variety of possible future scenarios produces what is referred to as envelope forecasting of HR demand, in which each corner of the envelope has its own specific staffing table.

Finally, we demonstrated the tremendous usefulness of the regression analysis technique in determining future workforce requirements. Our example of simple regression revealed how this statistical technique can enable us to be proactive with respect to determining future HR requirements and planning and programming to fulfil those requirements.

We have examined specific techniques associated with the first element of HR forecasting—that is, the calculation of demand or requirement for personnel. In Chapter 9, we look at specific methods used to ascertain personnel supply. The sources of labour supply will derive from either the current organization (internal workforce) or from the external environment.

KEY TERMS

Delphi technique, 185
employee requirement ratio, 183
envelope/scenario forecasts, 192
HR budgets, 190
nominal group technique, 188
regression analysis, 194
staffing or manning table, 191
trend analysis, 182

SUGGESTED WEBSITES

www.jobsetc.ca/jobs Provides information on Canadian HR demand, work and labour trends.

www.osha.gov Provides information on standardized U.S. industrial classification job codes.

www.hrmanagement.gc.ca HR resources for business presented by the Canadian government.

DISCUSSION QUESTIONS

1. The Delphi technique and the nominal group technique are often used to facilitate creative and innovative solutions to HR demand issues. List the conditions associated with successful employment of each of these two demand forecasting techniques.
2. Index or trend analysis can be a very effective method for determining HR demand. Identify a wide variety of relevant indices that can be used for this demand forecasting technique in different organizational contexts, including public nonprofit organizations, as well as in diverse industrial settings in the private sector.

EXERCISE

As HR forecasting manager for the Downsview University Dating Service, you have been faced with a tremendous increase in customer demand over the company's five years of operations. As a result, you are using regression analysis to ascertain future requirements for staff to handle customer inquiries. In particular, you need to forecast the number of customer service representatives required for 5000 and for 7000 dating contracts. The following information will help guide your regression analysis:

X Dating Contracts (Thousands)	Y Customer Service Representatives	XY	X^2
1.5	9		
2.0	14		
3.0	21		
3.8	25		
4.2	27		

Case: Recruiting with Bells and Whistles

In February of 2000, Alcatel, a telecommunications corporation, launched The Talent Network, which utilized its 3000 employees as recruiters by offering cash rewards as high as $8000 for individual employees who delivered top-notch new recruits. Over the first six months the program netted 160 employee referrals, accounting for approximately 35 to 40% of the personnel hired during that time, and the percentage of employee referrals continued to rise steadily. The company also tracks and contacts its "alumni"—former employees who have left for positions in other companies—in an attempt to let them know about the positive events and opportunities that exist in Alcatel. They don't hide their attempts to lure their ex-employees back to the company. Alcatel employs a "holistic" approach to recruiting, using all available tools including newspaper ads, on-site career fairs, and web-based career sites, in an attempt to attract scarce skilled labour.

High-tech firms such as Nortel and Lumenon use stock options, signing bonuses, profit-sharing, free trips, and finder's fees, among a wide variety of other incentives, and such media as mobile billboards, club advertising, and recruiting booths at conferences and rock concerts, in order to attract new recruits. Retention is encouraged by means of rewarding staff with barbecues, "time-outs" at the go-kart track, cruises, white-water rafting adventures, golf outings, beer festivals, and treats ranging from jackets and T-shirts to hockey tickets and $10 000 cash incentives.

"Quite frankly, I couldn't care less if they come in wearing their pyjamas," said an organizational recruiter. "Those days are gone forever where people coming in had to wear a navy blue suit, white shirt and red striped tie. They can come in with a paper bag over their heads and the eye holes cut out. If they have the skills we're looking for, that's what we're interested in."

Source: Adapted from The Ottawa Citizen Online. 2000. High Tech Supplement: "The HR Crisis," October 17. Reprinted with permission.

Question

Prepare a report discussing the benefits and limitations of using the techniques described to fulfil organization demand for labour. Consider the impact of environmental factors such as competitor response to such actions.

References

Bechet, T.P., and J.W. Walker. 1993. "Aligning Staffing with Business Strategy." *Human Resource Planning*, Vol. 16, No. 2: 1–16.

Bramwell, L., and E. Hykawy. 1999. "The Delphi Technique: A Possible Tool for Predicting Future Events in Nursing Education." *Canadian Journal of Nursing Research*, Vol. 30, No. 4: 47–58.

Burack, E.H., and N.J. Mathys. 1996. *Human Resource Planning: A Pragmatic Approach to Manpower Staffing and Development*, 3rd ed. Northbrook, Ill.: Brace Park.

Cascio, W.F. 1991. *Applied Psychology in Personnel Management*, 4th ed. Englewood Cliffs, N.J.: Prentice Hall.

Delbecq, A.L., A.H. Van de Ven, and D.H. Gustafson. 1975. *Group Techniques for Program Planning*. Glenview, Ill.: Scott Foresman.

Drui, A.B. 1963. "The Use of Regression Equations to Predict Manpower Requirements." *Management Science* Vol. 9, No. 4 (July): 669–677.

Fusgeld, A.R., and R.N. Foster. 1971. "The Delphi Technique: Survey and Comment." *Business Horizons* (June).

Gatewood, R.D., and E.J. Gatewood. 1983. "The Use of Expert Data in Human Resource Planning: Guidelines from Strategic Forecasting." *Human Resource Planning*, Vol. 6, No. 2 (June): 83–94.

Georgoff, D.M., and R.G. Murdick. 1986. "Manager's Guide to Forecasting." *Harvard Business Review*, Vol. 64, No. 1.

Green, T.B. 1975. "An Empirical Analysis of Nominal and Interacting Groups." *Academy of Management Journal* (March): 63–73.

Hampton, D.R., C.E. Summer, and R.A. Webber. 1987. *Organizational Behavior and the Practice of Management*, 5th ed. Glenview, Ill.: Scott Foresman.

Hughes, C. 1995. "Four Steps for Accurate Call-Center Staffing." *HR Magazine* (April): 87–89.

Janis, I.L. 1972. *Victims of Groupthink*. Boston: Houghton Mifflin.

Luthans, F. 1992. *Organizational Behavior*, 6th ed. New York: McGraw-Hill.

Mason, D.H. 1994. "Scenario-Based Planning: Decision Model for the Learning Organization." *Planning Review*: 6–11.

McBeath, G. 1992. *The Handbook of Human Resource Planning: Practical Manpower Analysis Techniques for HR Professionals*. Oxford: Blackwell.

McLaughlin, G. 1975. "A Professional Supply and Demand Analysis." *Educational Record* Vol. 56, No. 3 (Summer): 196–200.

Meehan, R., and B.S. Ahmed. 1990. "Forecasting Human Resources Requirements: A Demand Model." *Human Resource Planning*, Vol. 13, No. 4: 297–307.

Milkovich, G., A. Annoni, and T. Mahoney. 1972. "The Use of Delphi Procedures in Manpower Forecasting." *Management Science*, Vol. 19, No. 4 (December): 381–388.

Milkovich, G.T., and T.A. Mahoney. 1978. "Human Resource Planning Models: A Perspective." *Human Resource Planning*, Vol. 1, No. 1.

Rohrbaugh, J. 1981. "Improving the Quality of Group Judgement: Social Judgement Analysis and the Nominal Group Technique." *Organizational Behavior and Human Performance* (October): 272–288.

Schuler, R.S., and J.W. Walker. 1990. "Human Resources Strategy: Focusing on Issues and Actions." *Organizational Dynamics* (Summer): 5–19.

Tullar, W. 1991. "Theory Development in Human Resource Management." *Human Resource Management Review*, Vol. 1, No. 4 (Winter): 317–323.

Van de Ven, A.H. 1974. *Group Decision-Making Effectiveness*. Kent, Ohio: Kent State University Center for Business and Economic Research Press.

Van der Heijden, K. 2000. "Scenarios and Forecasting: Two Perspectives." *Technological Forecasting and Social Change*, Vol. 65: 31–36.

Ward, D. 1996. "Workforce Demand Forecasting Techniques." *Human Resource Planning* Vol. 19, No. 1: 54–55.

ENDNOTES

1. Schuler and Walker, 1990.
2. Cascio, 1991; Ward, 1996.
3. McLaughlin, 1975. Example adapted from Hughes, 1995, and Cascio, 1991.
4. Meehan and Ahmed, 1990.
5. Ward, 1996.
6. Gatewood and Gatewood, 1983.
7. Luthans, 1992.
8. Helmer, 1970, cited in Bramwell and Hykawy, 1999.
9. Fusgeld and Foster, 1971.
10. Hampton et al., 1987; Milkovich et al., 1972; Milkovich and Mahoney, 1978.
11. Bramwell and Hykawy, 1999.
12. Meehan and Ahmed, 1990.
13. Bramwell and Hykawy, 1999.
14. Van de Ven, 1974.
15. Rohrbaugh, 1981.
16. Delbecq et al., 1975; Green, 1975.
17. McBeath, 1992.
18. Mason, 1994; Bechet and Walker, 1993; Burack and Mathys, 1996.
19. Van der Heijden, 2000; Ward, 1996, p. 55.
20. Drui, 1963.
21. Georgoff and Murdick, 1986; Meehan and Ahmed, 1990.
22. Tullar, 1991.

9

ASCERTAINING HR SUPPLY

Chapter Goals

In the preceding chapter, we examined a variety of methods that are used in the process of forecasting HR demand. Many of these procedures (e.g,. the Delphi technique, the nominal group technique, index/trend analysis) can also be used to determine personnel supply.

After reading this chapter, you should be able to do the following:

1. Understand the relationship between demand and supply forecasting techniques in the HR planning process.
2. Recognize the importance of the HRMS in implementing effective supply forecasting procedures.
3. Comprehend the critical relationship between supply forecasting and succession planning.
4. Discuss and evaluate the advantages and disadvantages of the following specific methods of determining external and internal supply of an organization's personnel:

a. Skills and management inventories
b. Succession/replacement analysis
c. Markov models
d. Linear programming
e. Movement analysis
f. Vacancy/renewal models

When considering the issue of supplying personnel to meet organizational demand, one aspect of the analysis is quite simple. Our personnel must be obtained from a source that is either *internal* (current employees) or *external* (individuals currently not employed by the organization) or, more commonly, some combination of these. Many organizations give preference to internal supply because selecting these individuals for training and development, and subsequent promotion, enables the organization to reinforce employee loyalty and performance. Other reasons for giving preferential consideration to your own workforce to fill job openings include the following: (1) your employees are already socialized to the norms, rules, and procedures of your organization, (2) employee motivation and commitment to the organization may increase when you reinforce their past loyalty and performance, and (3) you possess knowledge (e.g., HRMS files) on their performance and KSAs (e.g., work history and experience). We now turn our attention to this latter point concerning organizational databases on current workforce members—namely, skills and management inventories.

Skills and Management Inventories

A good first step in the supply analysis is an examination of the number and capabilities of our current employees. Individual records on the HRMS database are called inventories, of which there are two types, skills inventories and management inventories.[1] A **skills inventory** is an individualized personnel record held on each employee except those currently in management or professional positions. Typically, a skills inventory contains information for each individual on the following areas: (1) personal information (e.g., name, employee number, job classification and compensation band, emergency notification, and telephone number); (2) education, training, and skill competencies (e.g., certificates, licences, and diplomas or degrees completed, including the area of specialization, dates of attendance, and names of the institutions attended); (3) work history (e.g., date of hire, seniority, current job and supervisor, and previous jobs held in the organization and the dates associated with them); (4) performance appraisals (i.e., a numerical score of the employee's history of performance in jobs in the organization); (5) career information (e.g., future jobs desired by employee and those recommended by supervisors); and (6) hobbies and interests (including community and volunteer associations).[2] This skills inventory record is entered into the HRMS database and can be

skills inventory an individualized personnel record held on each employee except those currently in management or professional positions

searched when we are looking for people with the skills and competencies required by a specific job. For this reason, skills inventories must be kept current, and employees should be given frequent opportunities to update or correct their personal entries; otherwise, an employee may not be considered for a job that he or she could fill successfully.

Management inventories can be considered to be enhanced skills inventories because they contain all the above information and the following: (1) a history of management or professional jobs held, (2) a record of management or professional training courses and their dates of completion, (3) key accountabilities for the current job (i.e., organizational resources, including the size of the budget controlled, the number of subordinates, important organizational outcomes for which the incumbent is primarily responsible), (4) assessment centre and appraisal data, and (5) professional and industry association memberships. Only when an organization has a properly functioning HRMS, complete with the skills and management inventories described above, is it really able to assess correctly the numbers and competency levels of its current workforce. In this way, HR planners can determine the organization's workforce strengths and weaknesses and plan training and development courses accordingly, while noting which job openings must be filled from external sources because current employees lack the skill competencies required.

management inventory
an individualized personnel record for managerial, professional or technical personnel that includes all elements in the skills inventory with the addition of information on specialized duties, responsibilities, and accountabilities

Succession/Replacement Analysis

Succession planning is critical to effective organizational functioning.[3] With demographic trends predicting even greater shortages in the market supply of skilled labour, organizational succession planning is assuming much greater importance than in past periods. It is absolutely essential that organizations create systems that meaningfully reward managers for developing and retaining their employees. If organizational performance management and compensation systems do not differentially evaluate and reinforce managers on the basis on their succcess in training and developing and in retaining their subordinates, it is very likely that these critical tasks will not be performed.[4] Furthermore, the highly dynamic and changing global business environment is forcing HR managers to expand their succession planning beyond the traditional identification of a shortlist of replacements for specific jobs. Increasingly, the focus is on identifying and developing the broad skills and behaviours (i.e., competencies) that will be required by the organization to accomplish its competitive strategy.[5]

There are two aspects to succession planning: (1) *long-term succession,* which is a process of training and work experience to enable individuals to assume higher-level job appointments in the future; and (2) *short-term emergency replacement* of individuals who have quit, been terminated because of performance problems, have died, and so on. Succession planning can help the organization be more effective in filling vacant positions.

There are several reasons why succession planning is critical for effective HR planning:[6]

1. Succession planning enables an organization to respond appropriately and stay on track when inevitable and unpredictable changes occur. It provides for continuity and future direction even in the turmoil of change.
2. It helps develop people as they prepare for new experiences and jobs, and this development can also help improve their performance in current positions.
3. When succession planning takes into account employees' performance and promotes them for it, employees are positively motivated.
4. It supports new organizational structures and flexibility by explicitly providing backups to various positions, thereby reducing organizational dependency on any one employee.
5. It saves time and money by having plans already in place to enable smooth internal employee movement and continuity, and therefore external hiring is an exception to the process.

It should come as no great surprise that the skills and management inventories described in the previous section are extremely useful information for succession and replacement planning. Furthermore, they are important for matching an individual's qualifications to the requirements of a specific job in the organization (e.g., those needed by the HR planning manager) and for identifying possible successors for specific positions. The key requirement for succession and replacement planning to function effectively is that supervisors, in conjunction with the HR staff, must develop *succession/replacement charts and tables* for key executive, managerial, and professional jobs in the organization (see Tables 9.1 and 9.2). The information that fuels this process is derived not

BOX 9.1 Take Steps to Keep Business All in the Family

A study by Deloitte & Touche states that the majority of Canada's family businesses are facing a leadership crisis due to a lack of succession planning. John Bowey, a Deloitte & Touche partner, says that family businesses in Canada account for 4.7 million full-time jobs, 1.3 million part-time jobs, and $1.3 trillion in annual sales. Furthermore, customers often prefer these businesses because of the personal contact and perceived high standards of credibility and quality. However, a full 75% of family business owners believe that the future success of their business depends wholly on them, reflecting a failure to develop future leaders and a neglect of the succession and replacement planning process. Almost half (44%) of these same business owners doubt their businesses will survive once they bow out of the operations. To cast a further dire light on the situation, 27% of the family business owners plan to retire within five years, a further 29% in six to ten years, and 22% in eleven to fifteen years.

Source: Adapted from Harvey, I. 1997. "Take Steps to Keep Business All in the Family." *Toronto Sun*, January 19, p. 27. Reprinted with permission.

only from current managerial assessments of subordinates, but also from information contained in the inventories concerning education, training, and skills, as well as historical records of each potential successor's performance appraisals. Obviously, given the large amount of personal information used and the sensitive nature of the information, succession planning documents are highly confidential. Access to the succession/replacement charts and tables, and to their supporting documentation, must be strictly controlled and limited on a "need-to-know" basis to such people as the CEO, vice-president of HR, HR planning staff, and divisional executives. Access by the latter should be restricted solely to their own area of responsibility.[7] Although a manager should naturally consider his or her current subordinates in the process of developing succession plans, the skills and management inventories are important to ensure that other employees who have been transferred, seconded to other divisions, or are working in areas different from those for which they received functional training will not be overlooked. In fact, such employees will be identified by the search capabilities of the HRMS.

The first type of document used in succession planning is referred to as a succession/replacement chart. As you will notice from Figure 9.1, it closely resembles a typical organizational chart in that it represents the organizational hierarchy and the key jobs with their inherent reporting relationships.

FIGURE 9.1 SUCCESSION/REPLACEMENT CHART

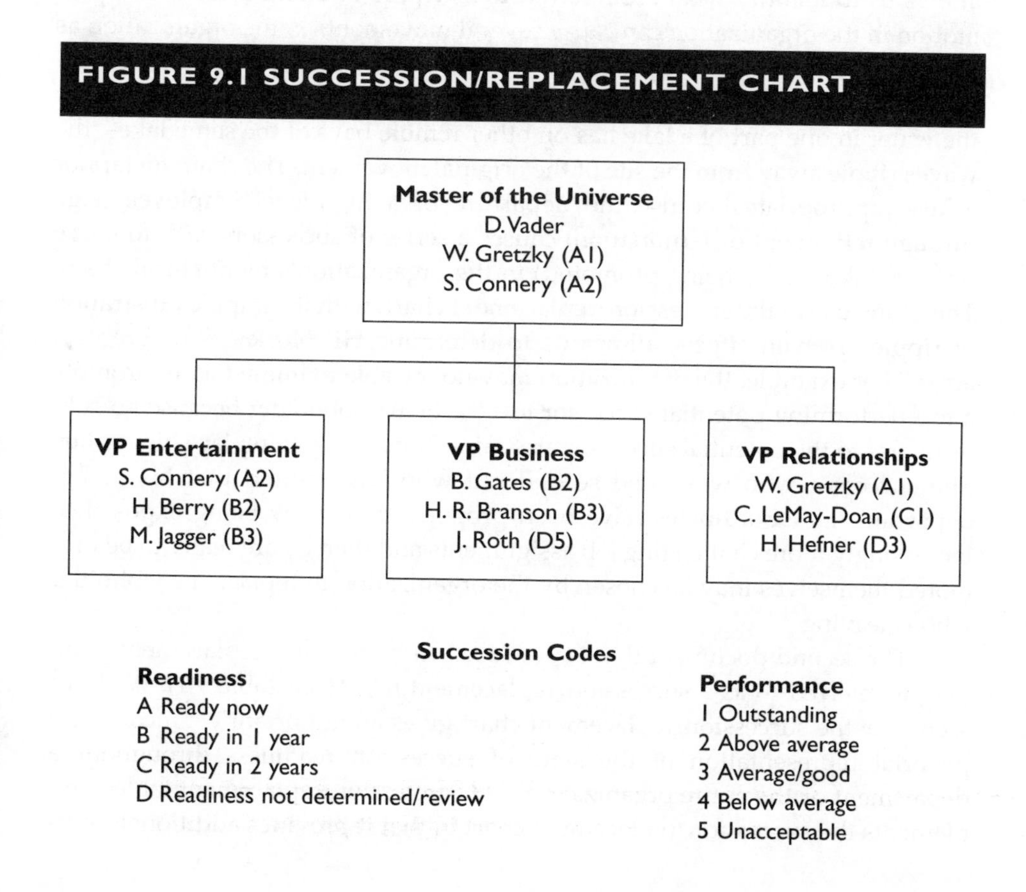

However, on closer inspection, the succession/replacement chart provides more detailed information on each job, specifically, the name of the current job incumbent and a short list (determined by managers in conjunction with the HR staff) of the top internal candidates who might replace the incumbent if he or she left the job.

An important aspect of the succession/replacement chart is the **succession readiness code**, which is listed next to the names of all employees. This code contains two elements of information essential for succession planning: (1) the employee's level of performance in the current job (e.g., represented by a value on a five-point scale ranging from 1 to 5, where 1 = outstanding and 5 = unacceptable) and (2) the employee's readiness for movement or promotion (e.g., A = ready now, B = probably ready within one year, C = needs development [i.e., probably ready in two years], D = not suitable for this job). By including the two elements of the succession code next to the name of each employee on the succession chart (e.g., Mary Bloggins B2), we are able to get an accurate, although admittedly incomplete, picture of the state of succession readiness for each department and for the entire organization.

succession readiness codes codes listed next to the names of all potential successors; contain two elements of information essential for succession planning: (1) the employee's level of performance in the current job and (2) the employee's readiness for movement or promotion

Although we will have to refer back to specific inventories, performance appraisal records, and assessment centre reports to get further information on potential successors, the key benefit of a succession/replacement chart is that it allows us to identify what are referred to as **ripple** or **chain effects**: one promotion in the organization can cause several movements in the organization as a series of subordinates are promoted to fill the sequential openings.[8] The term ripple effect is used because it is similar to the effect that a fish jumping out of the water in one part of a lake has on other remote bays of the same lake—the waves ripple away from the site of the original movement. The chain metaphor is also appropriate because the departure of a high-level employee (e.g., through retirement or termination) causes a series of successors each to move up one link (i.e., by being promoted) in the organization's hierarchical chain. Therefore, use of the succession/replacement chart, with its graphic illustration of ripple or chain effects, allows us to determine HR blockages or problem areas.[9] For example, the organization may not be able to immediately promote a top-performing potential successor to a particular jobholder because no subordinates to the potential successor are trained and ready to replace him or her. The successor who was rated second but who has ensured that his or her departmental subordinates have been properly trained by being exposed to increasingly more challenging job assignments and thereby are ready to be promoted themselves may be chosen by the organization to replace the jobholder who is leaving.

ripple or **chain effects** the effect caused when one promotion or transfer in the organization causes several other personnel movements in the organization as a series of subordinates are promoted to fill the sequential openings

The second document that is produced for succession/replacement planning is referred to as a succession/replacement table (see Table 9.1). We have seen how the succession/replacement chart gives an important yet incomplete pictorial representation of the state of succession readiness throughout a department or the entire organization. The succession/replacement table complements the succession/replacement chart in that it provides additional infor-

BOX 9.2 Car Dealers Steer Clear of Succession

According to a survey by Coopers & Lybrand and DesRosiers Automotive Consultants Inc., a great many of Canada's more than 3400 new car retailers and dealerships have a looming succession problem. The study found that more than 80% of dealers plan to retire or be semi-retired within ten years. Yet almost half of the dealers who responded to the survey did not have a succession plan, including a full third of those older than 55 years of age. Approximately 70% of dealers would like to keep their dealerships within their families, but less than half (44%) think that will actually happen. Dealers are facing this succession problem because of their short-run orientation on selling cars today, without considering the costs and implications of not planning for the future.

Source: Adapted from Keenan, G. 1998. "Car Dealers Steer Clear of Succession," *The Globe and Mail* (June 16), p. B14. Reprinted with permission from *The Globe and Mail.*

mation on each specific job, the incumbent jobholder, and all potential internal successors.

A succession/replacement table is prepared for each key job in the organization. In considering a replacement for the HR planning manager, for example, although the succession/replacement chart provides us with the top two or three candidates and their succession codes, all it may indicate is that promoting any of these individuals could be problematic for a variety of reasons (e.g., because of their performance or lack of training). By turning to the succession/replacement table, we get a list of *all* potential internal successors, not just the shortlist or top three individuals, as well as a very detailed information code for each candidate. Typically, a series of alphanumerical code combinations will provide us with important information not presented on the succession/replacement chart because of space limitations. Succession/

TABLE 9.1 SUCCESSION/REPLACEMENT TABLE

KEITH KILTMAKERS
CHIEF EXECUTIVE OFFICER (POSITION A11)

Incumbent	Employee Number	Current Appointment and Tenure[a]	Expected Date of Movement
Robert James	060422	CEO	06 April 2008
Potential Successors			**Succession Codes**
June Catharine	070121	VP Operations (A21)/61	H, F
Roderick Alexander	010753	VP Legal (B24)/52	S, D
Kenneth James	010956	VP HR (D19)/48	B, F, D
Donald Martin	290959	VP Systems (C24)/16	Y, D

[a] The tenure of the current appointment is listed in number of months' duration.

replacement table codes summarize information on personal career and training preferences, long-run historical data on performance appraisal, family and geographical posting preferences, and so on, all of which may affect movement or promotion and are not included on the succession/replacement chart.

The succession/replacement tables and charts are very useful tools for HR planners who are analyzing the state of the current workforce. Once we have used these two instruments of succession/replacement analysis, other details concerning specific job blockages or problems with our current internal workforce and the resultant requirement to process new hires from external sources become much clearer.[10] We may find that a perceived shortage of labour is the result of specific personnel policies concerning how we use our workforce and is not due to any shortage in the actual number of workers.[11] Chapter 10 contains further detailed information on succession planning.

MARKOV MODELS

Markov model a model that produces a series of matrices that detail the various patterns of movement to and from the various jobs in the organization

Markov models are the most popular technique used for contemporary supply-side HR planning applications.[12] These models are widely used in both educational and personnel planning processes.[13] Furthermore, they have been found to be more accurate than regression models when used in HR planning systems.[14] **Markov models**, also referred to as *probabilistic* (using probabilities of various movement options) or *stochastic models*,[15] determine the pattern of employee movement throughout an organization's system of jobs.[16] Markov analysis produces a series of matrices that detail the various patterns of movement to and from the wide variety of jobs in the organization. When considering employee movement patterns in the organization, an employee has five possible options: (1) remaining in the current job, (2) promotion to a higher classified job, (3) a lateral transfer to a job with a similar classification level, (4) exit from the job (e.g., termination, layoff, voluntary leaving by the employee), and (5) demotion (which is relatively rare).[17] Probabilistic or Markov models do not examine individual employees but instead examine overall rates of movement between various job levels, and this movement between jobs is based on historical movement patterns.[18] It is normally assumed, for calculation purposes, that the pattern of employee movement is relatively stable over time. If this is not the case, then adjustments have to be made to the historical data to allow them to be used for HR planning in the present day. However, it is important to note that Markov techniques depend on stable transition probabilities, so dynamic and unstable environmental scenarios may preclude the effective usage of Markov models.[19]

There are three main steps to using a Markov model for HR planning purposes.[20] First, we must collect historical data on mobility rates between jobs in the organization. Second, based on this data we develop matrices to forecast future personnel movement between jobs. Third, we use the forecasts of the

BOX 9.3 Using Markov Models to Forecast Ocean Deck Officers

An interesting application of Markov models concerns its usage by the Taiwanese Ministry of Communications to develop a five-year moving average of the "transitional probabilities" that the supply of ocean deck officers available to be employed on ships based in Taiwan would be able to meet forecast demand. The key forecasting issue was that the demand for deck officers was rising annually and exceeded supply, due to expansion in the local economy that resulted in an increased number of ships operating from Taiwan. The forecasting issue was of critical importance for several reasons. First, Taiwan is a significant maritime power as two local carriers—the Evergreen and Yang Ming shipping companies—rank among the 20 biggest shipping companies in the world. Second, since Taiwan is a maritime nation, the shipping industry is a key contributor to the success of the local economy.

The Markov model was derived from historical information about the current number of shipping officers in the four hierarchical levels (masters, chief officers, ship officers, and deck officers), the seniority time at each level, as well as the supply of new shipping officers who have obtained their certificates of proficiency. Demand information was obtained from the five-year plot of the grand total of ships that operated domestically as well as ships that used Taiwan as their flag of convenience.

The resulting findings, which reconciled demand with supply, came up with a number of important conclusions. Not only did the study confirm that demand exceeded supply for shipping officers, the forecasts predicted this situation would worsen in the future, leading to a 64% shortage in positions just three years into the future. Second, the worst imbalance in supply was for the lower ranking positions, specifically deck officers and shipping officers. Concurrent research determined that graduates from the marine university in Taiwan perceived military service in the navy as offering the most prestigious and desirable jobs following graduation and that they would prefer not to work on a commercial vessel. Policy recommendations that derived from the study included (1) having the government establish ocean internships to support the shipping industry; (2) encouraging increased support for martime colleges and universities to expand training programs for their ships' officers; (3) aggressively encouraging crew members to seek opportunities to train for their officer certificates; and (4) helping alleviate supply shortages by conducting overseas recruiting.

Source: Adapted from Lin, C., S. Wang, and C. Chiang. 2001. "Manpower Supply and Demand of Ocean Deck Officers in Taiwan," *Maritime Policy & Management*, Vol. 28, No. 1, pp. 91–102. Reprinted with permission of Taylor and Francis, Ltd. http://www.tandf.co.uk.

model to analyze our HR policies and programs and instigate the necessary adaptive measures.[21]

By using employee movement data from the past five years or so, we are able to calculate *transitional probabilities*, or the likelihood that an individual in a specific job will exhibit one of the five aforementioned movement behaviours, normally one year into the future. By multiplying the total number of employees or positions in a particular job (e.g., 18 managers) by the associated probabilities for each of the five possible movement scenarios, the HR planner derives numerical data on employee flow patterns throughout the organization, and between various job levels (see Table 9.2).

The sequences of movements between various job states are referred to as *Markov chains*.[22] Detailed examination of the Markov model enables us to determine the number of external recruits required at various levels of the

TABLE 9.2 MARKOV MODEL

OTTERMERE OUTBOUND ADVENTURES

		Year 2007[b]			
		Chief Outfitter	Outfitter	Guide	Exit
Year 2006[a]	Chief Outfitter (n=4)	3 (.75)	—	—	1 (.25)
	Outfitter (n=12)	1 (.08)[c]	9 (.75)[a]	—	2 (.17)[c]
	Guide (n=16)	—	3 (.19)	9 (.56)	4 (.25)
	Supply=32	*4*	*12*	*9*	*7*

[a] The current year is shown on the vertical axis.

[b] The future year is shown on the horizontal axis.

[c] The probabilities of movement (percentages) are expressed horizontally and sum to 1 (100%).

organizational hierarchy to fill openings caused by turnover, termination, promotion, and so on. Furthermore, we earlier made reference to blockages or problems in succession planning, and these problems become readily apparent when we use this supply model based on historical trends of movement probability. The Markov model enables us to determine the specific number of replacements or successors required for any job family annually, as well as for specified future planning periods (based on normal attrition assumptions), and this can help us to be more proactive in our external recruitment programs. Additionally, we can calculate the chain of movement from an entry-level job all the way to the CEO appointment, along with forecast times of arrival, stay, and departure, in conjunction with breaks in career progression along the way. In fact, White refers to the length of a vacancy chain as its *multiplier effect,* and his study of U.S. churches showed that for any one retiring minister, a chain of movement for five subsequent ministers was created.[23] The length of an average chain is approximately three.[24] Apart from its obvious appeal for the career planning of individuals who have upward aspirations in the organization,[25] we can use the derived information to plan when training and development courses, job rotations, and so on should be conducted for a specific group of employees, based on predicted time to move from their current jobs to target jobs several levels higher in the organization's hierarchy.[26] Therefore, the use of a Markov model has great value for determining (1) the

BOX 9.4 Managing the Firm's Internal Labour Market: Lessons from the Field

Professors at Simon Fraser University's Faculty of Business Administration have uncovered four lessons in properly using internal labour markets to supply the organization's staffing requirements based on their study of a large manufacturing firm. The lessons are these:

1. Managers should recognize that there are often *multiple internal labour markets* typically operating in one firm.
2. Managers should conceptualize their staffing task as managing a system of human resource *flows*.
3. Managers need to develop an appreciation for the *temporal* and *situational contexts* within which staffing decisions are made.
4. Staffing decisions themselves can be appropriately viewed as garbage-can models in which *multiple issues* and *multiple criteria* are typically invoked in matching individuals and jobs.

Source: Adapted from L. Pinfield and V. Bushe, "Managing the Firm's Internal Labour Market: Lessons from the Field," Burnaby, B.C.: Faculty of Business Administration, Simon Fraser University. Paper presented at the Western Academy of Management Annual Meeting, Spokane (April 1992).

number of personnel who move annually, and over specified time periods, between various job levels; (2) the number of external hires that are required by the organization, and where the specific jobs are needed; (3) the movement patterns and expected duration in specified jobs associated with patterns of career progression for employees in the organization (i.e., career paths);[27] and (4) the number and percentage of all starters at a particular job level who will successfully attain a future target job level by a specified time period.[28] All this information provides us with important insights in calculating the most appropriate balance between training and promoting internal employees on the one hand, and external recruiting on the other. All in all, the Markov model is a very useful tool for analyzing HR supply.

Linear Programming

Linear programming is a mathematical procedure commonly used for project analysis in engineering and business applications. It has utility for HR planners because it allows us to determine the future supply of personnel based on achieving the best staffing outcome while minimizing constraints such as labour costs.[29] Furthermore, conditions such as desired staffing ratios (e.g., the internal/external mix of employees) can be programmed into the equation for determining HR supply. The optimum or best supply-mix solution is provided by the model, and the best conditions obviously vary among organizations.[30] Some companies may seek to minimize turnover or total labour costs, while others may seek to achieve an optimum level of staffing with respect to designated groups (e.g., visible minorities, women, Aboriginal people, people with

linear programming a complex mathematical procedure commonly used for project analysis in engineering and business applications; it can determine an optimum or best-supply mix solution to minimize costs or other constraints

disabilities) in all job levels throughout the organization.[31] By providing the level of personnel supply that is best with respect to explicitly defined constraints or criteria, linear programming enables us to calculate "what if" scenarios by changing or relaxing various model assumptions in order to determine the impact these changes will have on final numerical requirements for supply, both internal and external. To use linear programming, our assumptions must be similar to those used in regression analysis (discussed in Chapter 8), namely, that the mathematical model must contain variables that have *linear relationships* among the various constituent elements. If this situation does not hold, we have to employ nonlinear or quadratic programming techniques to determine supply requirements. As linear programming is a relatively complex mathematical procedure normally performed on a computer, a detailed presentation on this technique is beyond the scope of this book. For further information, see the References section.

Movement Analysis

movement analysis a technique used to analyze personnel supply, specifically the chain or ripple effect that promotions or job losses have on the movements of other personnel in an organization

Movement analysis is a technique used to analyze personnel supply, specifically the chain or ripple effect that promotions or job losses have on the movements of other personnel in an organization.[32] Specifically, we are able to identify the total number of vacant or open positions in the organization or department, as well as the total number of personnel movements that are caused by replacing and filling these vacant positions. The total number of personnel movements is always greater than or equal to the number of vacant positions to be filled. If we rely solely on external personnel, the number of vacant positions to be filled is exactly equal to the number of new hires obtained by the organization, as there are no internal promotions of current employees to replace the losses. Conversely, if we rely heavily on current employees (i.e., internal supply) to fill position openings, the total number of personnel movements will be greatly in excess of the number of open positions because any one opening (e.g., due to a promotion or termination) will result in a whole chain of subordinates sequentially moving up one authority level to fill the gaps.[33] Movement analysis enables the HR planner to select the desired mix or percentage of internal and external supply for those positions requiring replacements, ranging from a promote-from-within policy to the other extreme of replacing losses entirely through hiring personnel from outside the organization.

Movement analysis can be performed for the organization as a whole, although analysts normally find it more useful to conduct separate analyses for each department, division, or functional area.[34] The normal planning time horizon is one year, and we start by identifying the number of personnel in each authority or compensation band level at the start of the forecasting period. Next, we consider changes in the level of staffing for the department—that is, whether we are going to increase the number of jobs in some or all authority levels or downsize to reduce the total number of employees in the department. Having increased or decreased the personnel requirement from that which was forecast at the start of the period, we now turn to calculating the losses requiring replacement for each authority level of the department. We are interested only in losses (e.g., because of promotions, transfers out of the department, voluntary turnover, termination) that need to be *replaced*; therefore, it is important that we not "double-count" positions that have already been incorporated into the staffing changes column! Changes in staffing level are added to personnel losses requiring replacement to give us the total number of positions requiring replacement. At this stage, having determined the total number of positions to be filled, the actual number of personnel movements, as briefly described previously, can vary widely, depending on our organization or department's desired policy concerning the supply mix of internal and external replacements. To demonstrate, we now turn to a practical example of a movement analysis.

Movement Analysis Exercise

As HR forecasting manager of Keele Kontainers Ltd., your focus of interest is the organization's finance department. You wish to determine (a) the total number of positions requiring replacements over the next one-year period, and, equally important, (b) the impact these openings will have on the current employees' movements throughout the department. Keele Kontainers has a policy of "promote from within" for all authority levels above the basic entry level (level 9), which obviously must be filled externally with new recruits. The finance department does not have any personnel in authority levels 1 to 3 inclusive (i.e., president, senior vice-president, vice-president); the senior appointment is a level 4 (senior manager) position. Based on historical trends and information provided by the strategic planning cell, you know the following:

1. A 5% staffing (position) increase for each of authority levels 6 to 9 inclusive will be required to meet additional financial processing activity in the department; one additional senior manager (level 4) will be required, as management wants one senior manager to handle financial forecasting while one senior manager is responsible for financial claims (i.e., current operations); six additional managers (level 5) will be required to supervise the financial analysts and clerks (i.e., the increases in levels 6 to 9 mentioned above) added over the course of the year.
2. Historical annual loss rates include the following:
    a. Retirements (requiring replacements): two positions for level 5, 15% of current positions for levels 6 to 9 inclusive

    b. Turnover = resignations (voluntary) + terminations (involuntary):
    Levels 5 and 6 = 10% of positions at start of period
    Level 7 = 15% of positions at start of period

Level 8 = 20% of positions at start of period
Level 9 = 25% of positions at start of period

Note: The loss rates can be grouped into one column or broken into individual components (e.g., terminations, retirements).

3. The number of personnel/positions at the start of the year are as follows:

   Level 4 (senior manager) = 1
   Level 5 (manager) = 6
   Level 6 (senior analyst) = 20
   Level 7 (analyst) = 32
   Level 8 (clerk) = 40
   Level 9 (clerical assistant) = 50

In calculating our movement analysis, we construct two separate tables: the first determines the total number of positions to be filled, while the second identifies the internal and external personnel movements required to fill the open positions identified. When conducting a movement analysis, there are two basic rules to follow:

1. Work from the top down: Start at the highest authority or hierarchy level in the organization, since normal personnel movement in organizations is upward as people are promoted to replace higher level losses.
2. Calculate the movement figures for one authority or compensation level at a time.

Let's construct a movement analysis table, shown in Table 9.3, and use historical information to calculate position replacement requirements or positions to be filled.

By using historical information, we are able to determine that the finance department, with 149 positions at the start of the year, requires 68 positions to be filled over the year. These positions are needed because of a planned staffing increase of 15 positions and because 53 individuals are required to replace personnel losses (i.e., losses due to retirements, resignations, and terminations). The calculations to arrive at these numbers are straightforward. For example, the increased staffing requirement for level 7 is determined by multiplying the original number of positions at that level by the percentage increase (i.e., 32 × 0.05 = 1.6 positions), and since we don't normally hire fractions of people, the requirement is for two new positions! Similarly, total personnel losses for level 8 consist of fourteen positions, which is the sum of six retirements (i.e., 40 starting positions times 15%) plus eight turnover losses (i.e., 40 starting positions times 20%).

Starting with the "Positions to Be Filled" column from Table 9.3, we construct a second table, Table 9.4, that reveals the employee movement at all levels of the finance department caused by promotions to fill the identified vacancies.

What does this all mean? Overall, to fill the 68 positions that require replacements over the next year, a total of 167 movements will occur in the finance department due to the ripple or chain effect on promotions. In Table 9.3,

TABLE 9.3 NUMBER OF POSITIONS TO BE FILLED

Authority Level	Number of Positions at Start of Period	Staffing Changes		Personnel Losses		Positions to Be Filled
4	1	1	+	0	=	1
5	6	6		3		9
6	20	1		5		6
7	32	2		10		12
8	40	2		14		16
9	50	3		21		24
	149	15		53		68

Sources: Adapted from E.H. Burack and N.J. Mathys, *Human Resource Planning: A Pragmatic Approach to Manpower Staffing and Development*, 3rd ed. Northbrook, Ill.: Brace Park, 1996; D. Bartholomew, *Stochastic Models for the Social Sciences*, New York: Wiley, 1982; E. Burack and J. Walker, *Manpower Planning and Programming*, Boston: Allyn & Bacon, 1972; R. Grinold and K. Marshall, *Manpower Planning Models*, New York: Elsevor North-Holland, 1977; R. Niehaus, "Models for Human Resource Decisions," *Human Resources Planning*, Vol. 11, No. 2 (1988), pp. 95–107; J. Walker, *Human Resources Planning*, New York: McGraw-Hill, 1980; and H. White, *Chains of Opportunity: System Models of Mobility in Organizations*, Cambridge, Mass.: Harvard University Press, 1970.

TABLE 9.4 PERSONNEL MOVEMENT

Positions to Be Filled		Total Ripple or Chain Movement						Personnel Movement				
1		–		–		–		–		–		1
9	+	1		–		–		–		–	=	10
6	+	1	+	9		–		–		–	=	16
12	+	1	+	9	+	6		–		–	=	28
16	+	1	+	9	+	6	+	12		–	=	44
24	+	1	+	9	+	6	+	12	+	16	=	68
68		5		36		18		24		16	=	167

Sources: Adapted from E.H. Burack and N.J. Mathys, *Human Resource Planning: A Pragmatic Approach to Manpower Staffing and Development*, 3rd ed. Northbrook, Ill.: Brace Park, 1966; D. Bartholomew, *Stochastic Models for the Social Sciences*, New York: Wiley, 1982; E. Burack and J. Walker, *Manpower Planning and Programming*, Boston: Allyn & Bacon, 1972; R. Grinold and K. Marshall, *Manpower Planning Models*, New York: Elsevor North-Holland, 1977; R. Niehaus, "Models for Human Resource Decisions," *Human Resources Planning*, Vol. 11, No. 2 (1988), pp. 95–107; J. Walker, *Human Resources Planning*, New York: McGraw-Hill, 1980; and H. White, *Chains of Opportunity: System Models of Mobility in Organizations*, Cambridge, Mass.: Harvard University Press, 1970.

note that for level 5, although we start off with having to find replacements for nine open positions, we also have to promote one individual from level 5 to fill the requirement for an additional senior manager at level 4. Therefore, the total number of individual movements at level 5 is ten, although only nine open positions had to be filled at that level. Similarly, at level 6, in addition to having to fill six open positions, we also have to promote nine individuals to fill the openings one level higher at level 5, and one individual must be promoted to replace the level 5 individual who was promoted to level 4. Although there were only six open positions at level 6, the ripple or chain effect of sequential movement means that 16 individuals had to move to fill the organizational job openings. Furthermore, our assumption that we promote from within means that all 68 new hires originate from outside (i.e., from an external supply) at the entry level of clerical assistant (level 9). All other vacancies are filled by upward movement of current employees. Additionally, 99 promotions occur for current employees (i.e., internal supply) as is reflected in the ripple or chain effect matrix (i.e., 99 promotions = 5 + 36 + 18 + 24 + 16). In other words, movement analysis has allowed us to identify that for this year's need to fill 68 position vacancies, a total of 167 individual moves will be required because of extensive promotion from within. If we were to balance external and internal supply, the only adjustment would be that fewer individuals would be promoted from within the organization. This would lead to a decrease in the individual moves to a number closer to the number of open positions to be filled.

Vacancy Model

vacancy, renewal, or **sequencing model** analyzes flows of personnel throughout the organization by examining inputs and outputs at each hierarchical or compensation level

The **vacancy model**, sometimes referred to as a **renewal** or **sequencing model**, analyzes flows of personnel throughout the organization by examining inputs and outputs at each hierarchical or compensation level.[35] Vacancy models have been found to have more predictive capacity than Markov models over short- and long-term periods (of three, five, and ten years),[36] although the common time frame for this model is one year into the future. It is important that we always calculate our personnel supply requirements one level at a time in a "top-down" fashion, beginning at the highest relevant authority level, because the normal direction of personnel movement in the organization is from the bottom to the top. In other words, vacancies at the top are often filled by promoting individuals from lower organizational levels. The underlying rationale behind the vacancy model is simple. Our need for personnel must be met either by external recruiting or by internal promotions of current employees or by some combination of the two. More specifically, the supply needs of each salary level are determined by staffing changes—the number of personnel who are promoted away from the level—and personnel losses (e.g., retirements, departures, terminations).

Organizational policy will determine the extent to which these openings will be filled by internal and external supply. Personnel losses are normally based on historical trends with respect to the percentage of personnel at each level who normally exit from that level annually, while growth estimates are based on the normal business forecasting process. Overall, vacancies in the organization lead to a sequence of internal promotions from lower levels as the open positions are filled by the replacement personnel. The model identifies the specific number of external and internal personnel required at each level and for the organization as a whole. We now turn to an illustrative example of the vacancy model.

Vacancy Model Exercise

Steeles Sinsational Snacks Ltd. offers high-quality, low-cost snacks and meals to budget-conscious students at Moosehead University. Based on the following information, calculate the company's vacancy model for next year's HR supply forecast.

1. Staffing changes: None (i.e., stable size)
2. Personnel losses during the year:

Level 1 (president)	= 100% (compulsory retirement)
Level 2 (vice-presidents)	= 15%
Level 3 (managers)	= 17%
Level 4 (team leaders)	= 20%
Level 5 (associates)	= 25%
Level 6 (trainees)	= 50%

3. Personnel replacement policy (% external supply : % internal supply)

	% external hiring	% internal promotion
Level 1	0	100
Level 2	10	90
Level 3	20	80
Level 4	30	70
Level 5	55	45
Level 6	100	0

Remember that the key to successful completion of the model is to start your calculations at the top of the organization and work down one level at a time. So let's start our analysis at level 1, the position of the president:

Level	No. of personnel at start of year	Annual losses	Promotions to level	Level outflows	External hiring
1	1	1	1	1	0

The president of Steeles will be retiring this year, so there will be an annual loss of one person. The company's personnel replacement policy states that for the president's job (level 1), all (100% of) loss replacements will come from internal promotions, in this case, from level 2 below. Therefore, there is one promotion to level 1 (from level 2) with no external hires, and annual losses are exactly equal to outflow at that level. Now consider the situation for level 2:

Level	No. of personnel at start of year	Annual losses	Promotions to level	Level outflows	External hiring
1	1	1	1	1	0
2	6	1	2	2	0

Having completed level 1, we now calculate the personnel flows one level lower in the organization's authority or compensation system. For level 2, the annual losses are one, consisting of the number of personnel at that level at the start of the year multiplied by the historical loss rate (i.e., 6 x 0.15 = 0.9, rounded to one person). Next, it is crucial to note that the outflows from level 2 are not the same as losses because we must take losses due to termination, retirement, and so on of one person and add to that the one individual who was promoted to level 1 to replace the retiring president. Therefore, our total personnel outflows from level 2 are two people. Total outflows from any organizational level are equal to losses at that level plus promotions to higher levels.

Now we refer to the company's personnel replacement policy, which dictates that we are required to replace the two personnel who left level 2 by 10% external hires and 90% internal promotions. Naturally, we do not deal in fractions of people, so 2 x 0.9 = 1.8, which is rounded to two persons. Both replace-

BOX 9.5 Developing Effective Employee Retention Policies

Although most organizations tend to devote considerable time and resources to the process of *attracting* new workers, a great many fall short by not placing enough emphasis on *retaining* the high-quality personnel they currently employ. In order to rectify this situation, studies note the importance of making retention policies a top corporate priority. Several studies have clearly shown that managers at all levels should be held responsible for the retention of their personnel, and managerial performance evaluation should incorporate specific measurable goals in this matter. Greater importance should be placed on identifying high-performing and high-potential employees, as well as their associated values, interests, needs, etc., before they leave to work for your competitors. Organizations should conduct a demographic analysis and compensation reviews by using their HRMS. These analyses will enable HR planners to identify potential gaps in the personnel ranks and develop policies to ensure sufficient well-trained, high-quality employees are on hand over the medium and long term. Other retention policy recommendations include (a) forming a "retention task force" to include HR personnel, line unit managers, as well as senior executives; (b) reinforcing employee loyalty and performance by "promoting from within" wherever possible; (c) measuring turnover on an ongoing basis at corporate, division, and local levels, utilizing multiple measures; (d) holding line managers responsible for retention; and (e) reviewing and addressing compensation and working condition issues before they become issues for dissatisfaction that prompt employees to leave the organization.

Sources: Adapted from M. Young, "The Case of the Missing CEO," *Canadian HR Reporter*, February 14, 2000: 117–120; and M. Abrams, "Employee Retention and Turnover: Holding Managers Accountable," *Trustee*, Vol. 55, No. 3 (March 2002), pp. T1–T4.

ments are promoted from level 3, and we do not hire any individuals externally for the level 2 losses. The analysis continues in a like manner until all organizational levels have been completed. The finished vacancy model is as follows:

Level	No. of personnel at start of year	Annual losses	Promotions to level	Level outflows	External hiring
1	1	1	1	1	0
2	6	1	2	2	0
3	18	3	4	5	1
4	45	9	9	13	4
5	88	22	14	31	17
6	156	78	0	92	92
	314	114	30	144	114

In this instance, our vacancy model meets the specified requirement of a stable workforce size (i.e., no growth) as annual personnel losses of 114 are exactly replaced by 114 new hires from outside the organization. Furthermore, we know that in addition to the 114 annual losses (from a stable organizational workforce of 314), there are 144 total personnel movements, consisting of 114 new hires from external supply sources and 30 internal promotions across all levels. If instead of a no-growth scenario we predict a staffing increase or decrease, the above table is merely revised with the growth percentages (e.g., 5% at level 3, 8% at level 5) multiplied by the original number of personnel in each level to arrive at a column containing the revised (increased or decreased) number of personnel. This adjusted number of personnel is then used as the base point for calculating losses, promotions, and other flows from and to each authority level in the organization. Given the vacancy model information, it is possible to calculate the promotion rate (sometimes called the "upward mobility rate") for each authority level in the organization. For example, the promotion rate for level 4 is 8.8%, which is obtained by dividing 4 (the four people who were promoted to level 3) by 45 (the total number of personnel who are in level 4). As we can see, the vacancy model is a very useful tool for ascertaining specific personnel supply requirements for internal promotions of current employees, as well as for specifying the exact number of external new hires required at each level of the organization.

HR Supply and Retention Programs

Any presentation on HR supply would be incomplete without a discussion of the need for organizations to monitor and control levels of absenteeism and employee turnover ("labour wastage," in British parlance). It may be helpful to

BOX 9.6 Taking Proactive Steps to Address Canada's Skills Shortage

Widespread attention has been given to the growing shortage of skilled workers in Canada's economy. Apart from insufficient numbers of qualified personnel graduating from Canada's training infrastructure, an ever-increasing global economic reach has led to strong recruiting drives from organizations based in the United States, Europe, and elsewhere to "poach" skilled Canadian workers, further exacerbating an already significant skills shortage. The Canadian Human Resources Technology Board, made up of government personnel and practitioners, has drafted an action plan to address this problem based on several main strategies: (1) enact a Canada-wide coordinated approach to skills training; (2) market careers to students emphasizing skilled trades facing extreme personnel shortages; (3) enhance career awareness by working with educational institutions to promote the benefits of skilled trades occupations; and (4) reduce barriers to recognizing prior learning and foreign skilled-trade qualifications, thereby better utilizing the potential of Canada's current labour force.

Sources: Adapted from D. Brown, "Give Us Your Poor, Your Hungry—Your High-tech Workers," *Canadian HR Reporter*, September 25, 2002; and *Canadian HR Reporter*, "HR Technology Board Tackles Skills Shortage," February 20, 2003.

think metaphorically of the organization's supply of employees as the level of water in a bathtub. Even with the water taps fully open and water pouring into the tub, if the drain plug is not in place, inevitably we will soon be looking at an empty tub! Organizationally, even if we are highly successful in *recruiting* a large number of high-quality applicants (a situation that is increasingly rare for most organizations, given demographic and competitive factors), if we are unable to *retain* experienced, high-performing employees, we face dire consequences, not only in the short run in failing to achieve desired organizational goals, but perhaps even more critically in an inadequate HR supply and lost opportunities for future succession. Apart from normal levels of retirement and voluntary turnover, high levels of involuntary turnover normally signify a mismatch between the individual and the organization.[37] Attention should be paid to selection procedures to ensure that proper skills and competencies are possessed by the individual, as well as to orientation and training and development in ensuring that personnel are provided with clear guidance with regard to their employment and desired performance levels.

With labour shortages projected for the next decade, and unemployment rates remaining at low levels, retention programs are no longer an option for most North American companies; they are fast turning into a key requirement for organizational survival.[38] The costs of replacing workers can be staggering. Apart from "hard" costs (e.g., advertisements, headhunter and recruiting fees, interview training and travel costs, administration expenses, cost of lost production, bonuses or increased salaries to act as inducements to join, etc.), there are also the "softer" elements (such as lost business and customer contacts, decreased quantity or quality of work due to training and "learning curve" gaps, orientation and training time, decline in team morale and productivity, and increased turnover due to the "follow-me" effect) to consider. It is esti-

BOX 9.7 Want to Solve Your HR Supply Problems? Try Some R-E-S-P-E-C-T in the Workplace!

Given the widespread greed, fraud, and corruption scandals involving corporate executives and the propensity of many senior managers to terminate large numbers of employees' jobs even when their business units are operating in a highly profitable fashion, it should come as no surprise that worker loyalty and trust in organizations and executives are at an all-time low. The layoffs, plant closings, mergers and acquisitions, and downsizings of the 1990s, all conducted for the benefit of executives and shareholders and to the detriment of the organization's employees, have largely destroyed the bonds of trust and loyalty workers may have felt previously for their senior managers or toward the organization itself. However, in an era when many other organizations are having tremendous problems attracting high-quality applicants, SaskTel, Saskatchewan's Crown-owned telephone company, with a history of unwavering consideration and respect toward its employees, is still viewed as "the employer of choice" for workers in the Canadian prairie province. Since its formation in 1908, SaskTel has never laid off an employee, and the company is swamped with job applications from university and college graduates, allowing it to pick and choose only "the best and brightest." Furthermore, the company's employees have rewarded their employer with high levels of performance that have enabled the firm to outperform and fend off several out-of-province competitors in the long-distance market, in which SaskTel holds a 90% market share, the top performance level in Canada.

Too many executives just don't seem to get it: employees have learned to mistrust them because of lack of congruence between their espoused statements and subsequent self-serving actions. Faced with this organizational mismanagement, workers remain in their companies only for as long as unfavourable market or external family or personal conditions prevent them from leaving. Many of today's executives have a long way to go to try to re-establish relationships based on trust and respect, and to close the gap between them and the workers in the organization. Studies show that, in order to achieve this end, there is an overwhelming need for multidirectional open communcations, and for transparency and equity in workplace policies and compensation matters through clearly written, well-disseminated policies that minimize executive favouritism and subjectivity in the assignment of rewards and work assignments. Furthermore, simply "throwing money at employees," however well intentioned, rarely solves the problem as workers leave companies for many reasons apart from compensation, most notably a lack of trust, respect, and challenge in the workplace. Recommended actions to heal the wounded relationships executives have created with their workers include (a) clearly linking professional development training with career planning and compensation; (b) ensuring a direct connection between demonstrated individual performance and compensation received; (c) implementing HR policies that enhance the personal and family lives of employees (e.g., flextime, telecommuting, employee wellness programs, promotion of employee volunteer activities in the community, etc.); (d) enhancing upward as well as downward communication in the firm, by means of e-mail bulletins, meetings with management to discuss proposed changes and to respond to questions and concerns from the employees, and confidential suggestion boxes; and (e) employee recognition, incentive, and retention programs that reinforce and celebrate the successes of all members of the workforce.

Sources: Adapted from S. McGovern, "Earning the Trust of Employees Is a Major Factor in Staff Retention," *Montreal Gazette*, February 26, 2001; "No Layoffs, Plenty of Loyalty," *Maclean's*, November 5, 2001, p. 51; and T. Sothern, "Retaining Employee Talent," *CA Magazine*, Vol. 135, No. 3 (April 2002), pp. 39–44.

mated that the cost of replacing a trained work ranges from 70 to 200% of the departing person's annual salary![39] Successful retention programs not only consider the organization's desire to "fill the job slots," but also explicitly attempt to address the needs of its workforce. Organizations that demonstrate flexibility and a genuine effort to assist their employees are perceived to be more attractive places to work. Retention can be greatly facilitated by offering effective communication programs, facilitating an enjoyable and collegial work atmosphere, designing *meaningful jobs,* formulating and administering performance and compensation systems that identify and differentially reward better performers—based on clearly communicated criteria—and offering more flexible and attractive work arrangements (e.g., flextime, telecommuting, cafeteria-style benefits plans). The need is clear as is the fact that our employees—or "human capital"—are our key competitive advantage, self-renewing resources that clearly differentiate between organizational success or failure.[40] The onus is on organizational and HR managers to deliver!

Summary

This chapter presented six models or techniques used by organizations to determine future HR supply requirements. Skills and management inventories contain information that allows a detailed analysis of the current workforce to determine whether we can meet the demand for personnel replacement from current employees in the organization. Succession/replacement analysis expands on the inventories approach by using succession/replacement charts and tables to identify specific replacements for key organizational jobs and to examine whether problem areas or blockages would occur if specified individuals were to be promoted or transferred. The Markov model uses historical patterns of individual movement between jobs in the organization and attaches transitional probabilities for promotion, transfer, and remaining in the particular job for an annual or specified future period. In this way, we are able to derive exact numbers of open positions throughout the organization and can track career progression and the time required for individuals to reach specified target jobs. Linear programming uses mathematical equations to determine the optimal or best mix of personnel supply given specified constraints, such as minimizing labour cost or achieving a desired mix of diverse employee group memberships. Movement analysis enables us to identify not only the location and number of open positions that must be filled by the organization, but also the total number of individuals who will be moved to fill these openings. The vacancy model provides specific information on total personnel flows into and out of each authority or compensation level, as well as for the organization as a whole. Accordingly, we are able to calculate the exact numbers of internal promotions and external recruits that will be required by the organization.

Finally, we concluded our discussion of HR supply by pointing out the need for organizations to develop retention programs to control absenteeism and turnover.

Key Terms

linear programming, 213
management inventory, 205
Markov model, 210
movement analysis, 214
ripple or chain effects, 208
skills inventory, 204
succession readiness code, 208
vacancy, renewal, or sequencing model, 218

Suggested Websites

www.hr.com Useful source of information on HR supply, jobs, etc.

www.hrdc.gc.ca Work, career, and self-assessment tools for workers.

www.cipd.co.uk Website for the Chartered Institute of Personnel and Development, the U.K.'s HR professional association.

Discussion Questions

1. A Markov model provides important information to the HR supply analyst with respect to movement or flows of personnel through various jobs in the organization. Discuss how this supply-forecasting technique could also provide useful information to rank-and-file members (i.e., non-HR staff) of the organization's workforce.
2. Movement analysis analyzes the ripple effects or workforce movements resulting from various supply policy options selected by the organization. Discuss the varying implications of using internal sources of labour (i.e., the current workforce) rather than external sources of labour (i.e., recruits) for the supply needs of an organization. What are the advantages, disadvantages, costs, and benefits associated with the different options?

Exercise

Dave's Dumpsters offers a low-cost disposal system for the high-quality campus food served at Moosehead University, as well as for many other institutions of higher learning. The company has retained your services on a lucrative contract to calculate the vacancy model for next year's HR forecast, based on the following assumptions:

A. Workforce complement at beginning of period (i.e., before staffing changes):

   Salary level 1 = 1
   Salary level 2 = 4
   Salary level 3 = 18
   Salary level 4 = 40
   Salary level 5 = 75
   Salary level 6 = 136

B. Organizational growth: 5% increase in each salary level with the exception of salary level 1 (CEO), which remains at one position.

C. HR losses during year:

   Salary level 1 = 100%
   Salary level 2 = 20%
   Salary level 3 = 22%
   Salary level 4 = 25%
   Salary level 5 = 30%
   Salary level 6 = 50%

D. HR supply policy:

	Outside %	Inside %
Salary level 1	0	100
Salary level 2	10	90
Salary level 3	20	80
Salary level 4	30	70
Salary level 5	50	50
Salary level 6	100	0

Case: Ontario's Faculty Shortage Crisis

According to Dr. Deborah Flynn, the former president of the Ontario Confederation of University Faculty Associations (OCUFA), in 2002 Ontario universities were facing a dire shortage in the supply of professorial talent and needed to hire 15 300 new faculty by the year 2010 in order to keep pace with enrolment growth and retiring faculty members, and to reduce Ontario's student to faculty ratio to the Canadian national average. Citing a variety of studies, including one conducted by PricewaterhouseCoopers, she noted that there were already 2000 fewer professors in the Ontario university system than there were just 10 years previously, a figure representing over 15% of the total faculty complement.

This shortage will increase substantially when the baby boomer faculty retire in just a few years' time. More than one-third of all Ontario faculty members were currently between 55 and 64 years of age, and they will be retiring over the next few years just as universities are facing a substantial increase in enrolments because of the demographic increase in the "echo" generation students (18 to 24 years of age) entering university. In total, this represents 5500 additional professors who have to be hired.

Further adding to the problem was the impact of secondary school reform ("the double cohort"), which saw as many as 33 500 additional students seeking access to universities over the next two years. As well, changing workforce requirements and the need for "lifelong learning" to secure and retain meaningful employment in a knowledge-based economy had led students to demand university courses that could be taken over an extended period of time (i.e., they never really leave university) in order to keep their knowledge and skills relevant in an extremely dynamic environment.

Compounding the problem was the fact that university administrators had been addressing their budgetary problems (and associated reductions in provincial government funding) by reducing the number of full-time faculty members and relying on part-time course directors. These individuals often had part-time jobs at several educational institutions or alternatively work full-time in other jobs and lectured on the side, but they were not full-time employees of the universities. Furthermore, the relatively low pay scales offered to university faculty, as compared to people with equivalent qualifications in private industry or in other public institutions, further diminished the available pool of potential faculty members. Readers may be surprised to note that fewer than 40% of all people holding earned doctorates in Canada are employed in universities (COU, 2000). Furthermore, OCUFA commissioned the HayGroup to conduct a compensation analysis of skills, qualifications, and jobs that were equivalent to university professors in the public and private sectors. They found that salaries favoured employment outside of universities, as the average salary of university professors was $78 001, whereas comparable jobs in the public sector paid $84 100, and salaries were a full one-third higher in the private sector at $103 900 (all figures 1998–99). The competition for available faculty was not just from the local public and private sectors. All provinces across Canada were also facing faculty shortages, as was the case worldwide, with the situations being especially acute in the United States and the United Kingdom.

The consequences of this situation were that university students, who had seen their average tuition fees rise by 60% over the previous five years, were now facing a reduced number of course options, crowded classrooms, reductions in services and contacts with professors, and a decreased quality of education. For the faculty members, the time and quality of their research and teaching was affected as faculty workloads skyrocketed to handle the increased number of students and the decreased number of faculty colleagues to deal with these issues. The result was often a migration of faculty member to other institutions and employment opportunities in Canada or abroad, further exacerbating an already bad situation.

Source: Ontario Confederation of University Faculty Associations (OCUFA), 2001. "Less Isn't More: Ontario's Faculty Shortage Crisis," *OCUFA Research Reports*, Vol. 1, No. 4 (January), pp. 1–18.

Reprinted with permission. The report cites numerous other reports by the Association of Universities and Colleges of Canada (AUCC), Statistics Canada, Council of Ontario Universities, and PriceWaterhouseCoopers (1999).

Question

Conduct a detailed analysis of causes of the supply deficit among Ontario's university faculty. What were the causal factors? How could this situation have been prevented? Finally, specify the steps that should be taken by the various stakeholder groups to rectify this supply crisis.

References

Bartholomew, D. 1996. *Mobility Measurement Revisited in the Statistical Approach to Social Measurement*. San Diego: Academic Press.

Bartholomew, D.J. 1973. *Stochastic Models for the Social Sciences*. London: Wiley.

———. 1982. *Stochastic Models for the Social Sciences*, 3rd ed. New York: John Wiley.

Bechet, T.P., and W.R. Maki. 1987. "Modeling and Forecasting: Focusing on People as a Strategic Resource." *Human Resource Planning*, Vol. 10, No. 4: 209–217.

Blakely, R. 1970. "Markov Models and Manpower Planning." *Industrial Management Review* (Winter): 39–46.

Burack, E.H., and N.J. Mathys. 1996. *Human Resource Planning: A Pragmatic Approach to Manpower Staffing and Development*, 3rd ed. Northbrook, Ill.: Brace Park.

Cooke, R. 1995. "Succession Planning." *Credit Union Management* (October): 27–28.

Foot, D., and R. Venne. 1990. "Population, Pyramids, and Promotional Prospects." *Canadian Public Policy*, Vol. 16, No. 4 (December): 387–398.

Glen, J.J. 1977. "Length of Service Distributions in Markov Manpower Models." *Operational Research Quarterly*, Vol. 28, No. 4: 975–982.

Gridley, J. 1986. "Who Will Be Where When? Forecast the Easy Way." *Personnel Journal*, Vol. 65, No. 5 (May): 50–58.

Guinn, S. 2000. "Succession Planning Without Job Titles." *Career Development International*, Vol. 5, No. 7: 390–394.

Heneman, H.G., and M.G. Sandiver. 1977. "Markov Analysis in Human Resource Administration: Applications and Limitations." *Academy of Management Review* (October): 535–542.

Kaumeyer, R.H. 1979. *Planning and Using Skills Inventory Systems*. New York: Van Nostrand Reinhold.

Kohl, N. 2000. "HR Managers Losing the Retention Game." *Pro2Net*, November 7: 2.

Konda, S., and S. Stewman. 1980. "An Opportunity Labor Demand Model and Markovian Labor Supply Models: Comparative Tests in an Organization." *American Sociological Review*, Vol. 45, No. 2 (April): 276–301.

Law, H. 1977. "A Projection Model and a Rational Policy for the Supply and Demand of Human Resources from an Educational Institution." *Applied Mathematical Modeling*, Vol. 1, No. 5 (June): 269–275.

Lewin, D., and J. Keith. 1976. "Managerial Responses to Perceived Labor Shortages: The Case of Police." *Criminology*, Vol. 14, No. 1 (May): 65–92.

Lofgren, E., S. Nyce, et al. 2002. "Will You Be Stranded by a Worker Shortage?" *Electric Perspectives*, Vol. 27, No. 3: 22–29.

Martin, R. 1967. "Skills Inventories." *Personnel Journal* (January): 28–83.

McBey, K., and L. Karakowsky. 2000. "Examining Sources of Influence on Employee Turnover in the Part-time Work Context." *Leadership and Organization Development Journal*, Vol. 21, No. 3: 136–144.

Meehan, R., and B.S. Ahmed. 1990. "Forecasting Human Resources Requirements: A Demand Model." *Human Resource Planning*, Vol. 13, No. 4: 297–307.

Monks, K. 1996. "Global or Local? HRM in the Multinational Company: The Irish Experience." *International Journal of Human Resource Management*, Vol. 7, No. 3 (September): 721–735.

Nielsen, G.L., and A.R. Young. 1973. "Manpower Planning: A Markov Chain Application." *Public Personnel Management* (March): 133–143.

Patz, A.L. 1970. "Linear Programming Applied to Manpower Management." *Industrial Management Review*, Vol. 11, No. 2 (Winter): 131–38.

Rothwell, W. 2002. "Putting Success into Your Succession Planning." *Journal of Business Strategy*, Vol. 23, No. 3: 32–37.

Rowland, K., and M. Sovereign. 1969. "Markov Chain Analysis of Internal Manpower Supply." *Industrial Relations* (October): 88–99.

Sandefur, G. 1981. "Organizational Boundaries and Upward Job Shifts." *Social Science Research*, Vol. 10, No. 1 (March): 67–82.

Seamans, L. 1978. "What's Lacking in Most Skills Inventories." *Personnel Journal* (March).

Stone, T., and J. Fiorito. 1986. "A Perceived Uncertainty Model of Human Resource Forecasting Technique Use." *Academy of Management Review*, Vol. 11, No. 3: 635–642.

Tuma, N. 1976. "Rewards, Resources, and the Rate of Mobility: A Nonstationary Multivariate Stochastic Model." *American Sociological Review*, Vol. 41, No. 2 (April): 338–360.

Vassiliou, P.C. 1976. "A Markov Chain Model for Wastage in Manpower Systems." *Operational Research Quarterly*, Vol. 27, No. 1: 57–70.

Venezia, I., and Z. Shapira. 1978. "The Effects of Type of Forecasting Model and Aggregation Procedure on the Accuracy of Managerial Manpower Predictions." *Behavioral Science*, Vol. 23, No. 3 (May): 187–194.

Walker, J.W. 1980. *Human Resource Planning*. New York: McGraw-Hill.

Weigel, H., and S. Wilcox. 1993. "The Army's Personnel Decision Support System." *Decision Support Systems*, Vol. 9, No. 3 (April): 281–306.

White, H. 1970a. *Chains of Opportunity: System Models of Mobility in Organizations*. Cambridge, Mass.: Harvard University Press.

———. 1970b. "Matching Vacancies and Mobility." *Journal of Political Economy*, Vol. 78, No. 1 (January): 97–105.

Zeffane, R., and G. Mayo. 1995. "Human Resource Planning for Rightsizing: A Suggested Operational Model." *American Business Review*, Vol. 13, No. 2 (June): 6–17.

Endnotes

1. Martin, 1967; Kaumeyer, 1979.
2. Martin, 1967; Seamans, 1978.
3. Cooke, 1995.
4. Rothwell, 2002.
5. Guinn, 2000.
6. Adapted from Cooke, 1995.
7. Cooke, 1995.
8. White, 1970b.
9. Foot and Venne, 1990.
10. Ibid.
11. Lewin and Keith, 1976.
12. Bechet and Maki, 1987; Konda and Stewman, 1980; Weigel and Wilcox, 1993.
13. Bartholomew, 1973; Law, 1977.
14. Venezia and Shapira, 1978.
15. Meehan and Ahmed, 1990.
16. Heneman and Sandiver, 1977; Vassiliou, 1976.
17. Bechet and Maki, 1987.
18. Blakely, 1970.
19. Stone and Fiorito, 1986.
20. Zeffane and Mayo, 1995.
21. Ibid.
22. Neilsen and Young, 1973.
23. White, 1970a.
24. Stone and Fiorito, 1986.
25. Gridley, 1986.
26. Sandefur, 1981; Bartholomew, 1996.
27. Tuma, 1976.
28. Rowland and Sovereign, 1969; Glen, 1977.
29. Weigel and Wilcox, 1993.
30. Patz, 1970.
31. Walker, 1980.
32. Bartholomew, 1982; 1996; Burack and Mathys, 1996; White, 1970a; b.
33. White, 1970a; b.
34. Monks, 1996.
35. White, 1970a; b; Bartholomew, 1982; 1996.
36. Konda and Stewman, 1980.
37. McBey and Karakowsky, 2000.
38. Kohl, 2000.
39. Ibid.
40. Lofgren et al., 2002.

10

SUCCESSION MANAGEMENT

CHAPTER GOALS

The City of Richmond, British Columbia, was rated as one of the top five employers in Canada in a Mediacorp survey and was one of only three municipalities that made it to the list to achieve this distinction. Three developmental programs helped them achieve this rating. One was a job shadow program in which an employee from one division would follow an employee in another division for a day (unofficially known as groundhog day). The benefits were two-fold: employees saw it as a meaningful opportunity to learn more about the organization and, secondly, those being shadowed felt honoured that their jobs interested others. Related to this was another program in which the City of Richmond staff experts assisted other smaller municipalities that did not have the resources to hire specialized expertise. The City of Richmond paid the salaries; the municipalities covered expenses such as travel. Secondment onto teams working on special assignments was another key developmental tool. Employees who were deemed to be creative were seconded from their regular jobs and asked to deal with problems such as, "How do you dig a ditch without digging a ditch?" For example, the pipe buyer was seconded to HR for a year to develop a succession plan.[1] These methods developed employees and prepared them for future jobs within the corporation.

After reading this chapter, you should be able to do the following:

1. Understand why succession management is important.
2. Trace the evolution of succession management from its roots in replacement planning, comparing the two models with respect to focus, time, and talent pools.
3. List the steps in the succession management process.
4. Compare and contrast the job-based and competency-based approaches to aligning future needs with strategic objectives.
5. Discuss the four approaches to the identification of managerial talent.
6. Describe several ways to identify high-potential employees.
7. Evaluate the advantages and disadvantages of the five management development methods: promotions, job rotations, special assignments, formal training, and mentoring and coaching.
8. Recognize the difficulties in measuring the success of a management succession plan.
9. Be familiar with the employee's role in the succession management process.
10. Describe the limitations of succession management, and propose some possible solutions to these limitations.

Importance of Succession Management

succession management the process of ensuring that pools of skilled employees are trained and available to meet the strategic objectives of the organization

Executives of any organization must develop the next generation of leaders, just as sports teams need to develop the next generation of players. **Succession management** refers to the process of ensuring that pools of skilled employees are trained and available to meet the strategic objectives of the organization. Succession management consists of a process of identifying employees who have the potential to assume key positions in the organization and preparing them for these positions. The identification of talent is always paired with ongoing programs to develop that talent. Succession management ensures continuity in leadership and, like any rookie program, develops the next generation of players.

As Peter Drucker says, the ultimate test of good management is succession management, ensuring that there is a replacement for the CEO.[2] Organizations must prepare for expected and unexpected turnover, for key players do die, retire, or quit. The story about the fiery young entrepreneur who builds a hugely successful business only to see it fail in the hands of his untrained children has been repeated thousands of times. Succession management is the great failing of entrepreneurs. Many Canadian dynasties (Eaton's, Woodward's, McCain's) have failed because their heirs were incapable of managing the business. See Box 10.1 for a discussion of the problems facing family firms.

Goldman Sachs Group Inc. is an extremely successful investment bank because its president spends much of his day not doing deals as might be expected but dealing with issues of succession, staffing, and compensation. Getting the right people in place was the key element in ensuring that the company passed successfully to a new generation of partners. The founding partners of Goldman Sachs realized profits of $75 million (U.S.) when they sold the company because the president got the people part right. Contrast the Goldman Sachs case to that of Gordon Capital, a company that has been humbled significantly because it suffered from "founder's mentality," never nurturing the next generation of leaders. Its executives were working 16-hour days because there were no skilled replacements to relieve them. The firm never realized its potential.

Succession management is needed even when retirements and company sellouts are predictable. The baby boomers who currently hold most of the leadership positions are retiring (see Box 10.2). Twenty percent of top management positions and 25% of middle management positions will become vacant in 2005 and will accelerate beyond that.[3] An organization that can weather this type of management change will survive.

BOX 10.1 Family Firms Fail

Family-owned businesses represent a significant part of the economy in Canada, generating $1.3 *trillion* in revenues, and employing 4.7 million full-time employees and 1.3 million part-time employees. Yet only 40% of these family firms have a business plan, and less than 25% have a long-term strategic plan. Four out of five owners will retire in the next 15 years; 70% say that they have not selected a successor; and 66% indicate that they have no process for succession management. Nearly half of these owners believe that the business will not survive without them, which could result in an economic disaster for Canada. They are right. Research has established that hereditary owners have a poor track record: businesses handed to sons and daughters fail 50% of the time. There is no such thing as the "lucky sperm club"—the factors that drive entrepreneurs to succeed cannot be passed down. As A. Mac Cuddy, the bitter founder of Cuddy International, a multimillion-dollar poultry producer whose company was torn apart in a family feud among his five sons, said, "You can hire better than you can sire."

Two of Canada's largest family-owned businesses, Thomson Corporation and Magna International, are handling succession management well. Ken Thomson's family owns 70% of Thomson Corp., a $30-billion giant founded by Roy Thomson, father of Ken. David Thomson, Ken's son, has been groomed since birth to take over the company and did so in 2002. Investors have not reacted negatively because Thomson Corp. has always used independent professional management that remains intact. Belinda Stronach had been groomed for 16 years in managerial and philanthropic positions and in 2001, she took over as CEO of Magna International. Since then, Magna has outperformed the competition.

Sources: "Leadership Crisis," *CMA Management*, Vol. 73, No. 5 (June 1999), pp. 25–27; M. McClearn, "A New Era," *Canadian Business*, Vol. 75, No. 5 (March 18, 2002), p. 24; T. Watson, "The Rich 100—Succession: Family Circus," *Canadian Business*, Vol. 74, No. 24 (December 31, 2000), pp. 104–110.

BOX 10.2 Early Retirement and the Impending Labour Shortage

One in three Canadians is 50 or older. While retirement has been welcomed by both unions and workers as the start of a new life, data from statistics Canada suggest that one impact will be a shortage of experienced workers. Organizations predict that one-third to one-half of their management and professional employees will be eligible to retire in the next few years. Workers are retiring earlier, from an average of 65 in the late 1970s to 61 in the late 1990s. Over the same period, the employment rate for those 55 to 64 has declined.

Early retirement produces many benefits, including creating job opportunities for those entering the labour force. Younger workers are often less expensive than those they replace, because they are employed at the low end of scales, including vacation entitlements and pay levels. However, because of the impending labour shortages, there have been over 60 federally sponsored pilot projects to test ideas about how to keep these older workers in the labour force, including phased retirement.

Sources: D. Brown, "Impending Labour Shortages Put Focus on Older Workers," *Canadian HR Reporter* (August 12, 2002), pp. 1 and 11; R. Stuart and C. Graham, "Early Retirement on the Bargaining Table," *Canadian HR Reporter* (January 27, 2003), pp. 12–13.

At a minimum, firms need to plan for replacements, and personnel planning was the first step in the march toward sophisticated models of succession management. Some reasons for succession management are listed in Box 10.3. The next section traces this evolution.

BOX 10.3 Reasons for Succession Management

1. Provide increased opportunities for high-potential workers.
2. Identify replacement needs as a means of targeting necessary training, employee education, and employee development.
3. Increase the talent pool of promotable employees.
4. Contribute to implementing the organization's strategic business plans.
5. Help individuals realize their career plans within the organization.
6. Tap the potential for intellectual capital in the organization.
7. Encourage the advancement of diverse groups.
8. Improve employee's ability to respond to changing environmental demands.
9. Improve employee morale.
10. Cope with the effects of voluntary separation programs.
11. Decide which workers can be terminated without damage to the organization.
12. Cope with the effects of downsizing.
13. Reduce headcount to essential workers only.

Source: Portions of this material in *Effective Succession Planning*. http://www.amanet.org.

Evolution of Succession Management

Replacement planning can be defined as the process of finding replacement employees for key managerial positions: if the CEO dies, who will be prepared to take over that position? Is there a replacement for the vice-president of marketing if she suddenly quits to take another job? The events of September 11, 2001, tragically presented a worst-case scenario. Bond trading firm Cantor Fitzgerald lost 700 of its 1000 World Trade Center staff, including most of its executives. The Fire Department of New York lost 343 employees, including most of its supervisors.

replacement planning the process of finding replacement employees for key managerial positions

Formal and methodical replacement planning has existed for over 30 years. This section examines how replacement planning has evolved into succession management by

- broadening the focus,
- expanding the time horizon,
- creating a talent pool of replacements, and
- improving the evaluation system.

Broader Focus

The focus of replacement planning was the job, and having a replacement ready to fill that job if the incumbent died or quit. This concept referred mainly to the succession and replacement charts for the high-level or key positions in the organization. Each key position was represented by a box on the chart, with the name and possible retirement or departure date of the incumbent in the box. Below the box were the names of two or three potential successors, with codes next to their names. These would be, for example, codes such as "PN" for "promotable now" or "RD" for "ready with development."

In short, replacement planning consisted of a periodically updated table of employees who might be nominated if a need arose. This type of planning focused on the high-potential candidates (replacement track stars), all ready to step into vacant positions, and in doing so set off a chain effect throughout the organization. This model assumed that people have single careers within one organization. Thus, replacements were replicas of the current jobholders.

This planning depended on a stable future, where the KSAs of future managers looked pretty much like those of the current managers. Jobs of the next five to ten years were assumed to be identical to the existing jobs. Organizational structures (i.e., how the organization was set up along divisional lines, product lines, or functional lines) were unchanging, and few new competitors were seen on the horizon. Obviously, this type of scenario just doesn't exist for most companies.

In replacement planning, the starting point was the job, whereas in succession management, the starting point is the strategy of the organization.

Employees are selected based on long-term goals, and the developmental plans for employees are aligned with strategic plans, not position replacements.

A case might best illustrate how succession management aligns with strategy. Traditionally, the goal of a large utility like Ontario Hydro was to provide safe, reliable energy. Its core competencies were reliability of distribution, measurement of consumption, and the maintenance of its power plant. However, deregulation and a more competitive environment forced Ontario Hydro to compete on price and services. Sales and marketing were the new competencies needed. The strategy changed from providing energy to marketing energy. Thus, in the long run, Ontario Hydro must identify or develop managers who have not only sales and marketing abilities, but also the ability to change a production culture to one of marketing.[4]

Time Horizon

The traditional planning approach was concerned with immediate and short-term replacements. Who is our backup for the vice-president we are planning to promote in six to twelve months? A strategic focus of under one year is a "business as usual" perception, which, if repeated, will not be true over a ten-year period. This short time perspective does not allow for the intake or career management of those with different skills in growth areas.

Succession management looks at a longer term (after ensuring that immediate replacements are in place) and focuses on a future of two years or more. Obviously, this is harder to do, and so rather than identify one replacement, succession managers identify talent pools.

Talent Pools

Traditional models of HR planning looked at succession as the passing of the baton to the next capable runner. Managers would identify their top performers, who would be groomed for success. Sometimes two or three successors would be identified, and they would be in a race to the finish line of executive promotion. This practice may have worked when organizations consisted of dozens of levels, each manager having many assistant managers. Currently, organizations have found that their designated backup personnel fill only 30% of the open positions for which they were slotted.[5] Flatter organizations with fewer "apprentices" can no longer rely on this approach.

As employees cannot trust organizations to provide lifetime job security, so too, organizations cannot rely on single individuals or a small group of employees for their succession plans. Organizations are trying to identify and develop as many employees as possible to ensure employee departures and changing needs will not leave them harmed, and also to avoid the "crown prince" syndrome.

The organization needs a pool of talent and must develop many employees with flexible job skills and competencies. A "pool" is a good description of the next generation of talented leadership because the term implies fluidity and responsiveness to the impact of forces. The talent pool is considered a corporate resource and is not the property of individual organizational units. This evolution from personnel planning to succession management has led to a model of generating pools of leadership talent within an organizational context of global competition, environmental turbulence, de-layered organizations, and new technologies.

Furthermore, a succession management approach should not depend only on internal candidates, but should also track external candidates. Rather than rely on inbred internal managers, the new generation of succession managers tracks high performers in the external market, thus ensuring that new skills and ideas flow into the organization. Large companies such as IBM and AT&T have recruited over half their executives from outside the organization to obtain the skills that these megacompanies were unable both to predict they would need and to develop internally. Box 10.4 compares the advantages and disadvantages of internal and external candidates.

Rating System

Traditional planning relied on the identification of the replacement people by a single rater. Previously, only the boss of the high-potential employee supplied information about that employee, and the information on which succession plans were based could be both out of date and unreliable. The gathering and

BOX 10.4 Internal Versus External

Advantages of Internal Candidates

- Organizations have more and better information about internal candidates.
- Organizations that offer career development and opportunities to internal candidates increase commitment and retention among their employees.
- Internally developed leaders preserve corporate culture.
- Internal candidates can hit the road running, because they know the organization, its people, and its processes. The other employees know the internal candidate, and there is less internal disruption, waiting to see who the new executive is and what changes he or she will make. Internally chosen executives do not replace those who report to them as often as external candidates do; externally chosen candidates often get rid of the "old guard."
- Recruitment and selection costs are lower. For example, the replacement cost of a CEO is estimated to be $750 000, including the use of a search firm and lost opportunities getting the external candidate up to speed.

Advantages of External Candidates

- The external candidate may have better skills to lead the organization through a major transformation or change in strategy.
- The external candidate brings new knowledge and skills to the organization and prevents the organization from becoming inbred and stale.

recording of these judgments may have been seen as a personnel function, which incorporated little understanding of the real needs of the organization. Thus, managers may not have bought into the process.

In a succession management approach, several raters give current evaluations on an employee's performance. The increasing use of 360-degree feedback mechanisms sheds light on various aspects of any candidate's style and performance. Box 10.5 compares replacement planning and succession management.

Succession Management Process

The succession management process links replacement planning and management development. Until recently, in some organizations, succession planners worked with one database, management trainers with another. Now, both databases are integrated, with succession managers working in strategic planning committees, performance management groups, and organizational learning and training functions.

The succession management process is simple to understand but difficult to implement. The process involves five steps, each of which we will now consider in some detail.

1. Align Succession Management Plans with Strategy

Management development has to be linked to business plans and strategies. If the business plan focuses on global markets, then managers have to be trained to manage global businesses. How does this translate into everyday skills? To build global talent, an organization could start by asking these questions: What

BOX 10.5 Comparison of Replacement Planning with Succession Management

Factors	Planning	Management
Environment	Stable	Dynamic
Focus	Jobs	Strategy
Time frame	6–12 months	2+ years
Selection criteria	Job experience	Competencies
Appraiser	Immediate manager	360-degree feedback
Selection pool	Internal	Internal and external
Successors	Slated individuals	Talent pools
Development	Limited	Flexible, multiple

are the specialized skills and perspectives necessary to compete globally? How many managers possess these skills? What percentage of employees could represent the firm to the world? How many could have an extended dinner with key international customers?[6]

The strategic connection is important, so organizations must start with the business plan. Coupled with environmental scanning, managers try to predict where the organization will be in three to five to ten years.

2. Identify the Skills and Competencies Needed to Meet Strategic Objectives

From the strategic plan, managers can then develop a list of the employee skills and competencies needed. There are at least two approaches to identifying the characteristics of successful managers: the job-based and the competency-based approaches.

Job-Based Approach

The first impulse is to start with the job. We know that employees have jobs with duties and responsibilities (discussed under "Job Analysis" in Chapter 4). The job-based approach suggests that employees who have significant experience as managers and have acquired job skills such as motivating, delegating, marketing, or managing finances, will make successful managers. Additionally, organizations such as Procter & Gamble insist that their leaders understand the marketing of brand names.

Others suggest that this job-based approach to successors is not adequate because jobs change rapidly. Furthermore, the increase in knowledge work has led many organizations to search for a different approach to employee development, particularly for those employees at the managerial level. Therefore, many organizations are turning to a competency-based approach in which the capabilities of individuals are the primary focus.[7]

Competency-Based Approach

Competencies are the capabilities that lead to success. **Competencies** are groups of related behaviours that are needed for successful performance.[8] They are measurable attributes that differentiate successful employees from those who are not. These competencies are a collection of observable behaviours and can be "hard" or "soft." Hard competencies might be the ability to build new technologies. Soft competencies might be the ability to retain top talent. Given an uncertain future in which skill needs change rapidly, succession management should focus on the development of competencies.

competencies groups of related behaviours that are needed for successful performance

Consulting firms are the perfect example of companies in which the skills and capabilities of individuals drive the business, and business opportunities drive the development of new capabilities. Thus a list of skills (rather than jobs or positions) forms the basis for succession management. Rather than moving *up* a career ladder, individuals move *through* a certification process, developing increasingly complex capabilities along the way. There may be several skill acquisition paths, rather than one sure path to the top.

A good place to start preparing a list of competencies is to look at what experts have said about the competencies of successful managers. Many lists are available that outline the kinds of generic skills and competencies managers should possess. Box 10.6 presents a list of these characteristics.

The skills managers need to possess are endless, and each "expert" develops a preferred list. These lists could be used as a starting point and then be customized to identify and develop managers in any organization. By emphasizing competencies rather than job skills, individuals will be more flexible in adapting to changing organizational needs. (Skills and competencies are terms that are often used interchangeably. However, skills are narrower and refer more specifically to skills for one job; competencies are broader and can be applied to many jobs at many levels. For example, proficiency in PowerPoint and installing Windows are skills; the ability to think creatively and work in teams are competencies.) Catano and his colleagues provide a full discussion of competencies in their text *Recruitment and Selection in Canada*, 2nd edition (2001). In the chapter devoted to competencies, they distinguish between several types of competencies:

> *Core competencies—characteristics, such as thinking skills, that every member of the organization is expected to possess.*
>
> *Role or specific competencies—characteristics, such as business knowledge, shared by different positions within an organization.*
>
> *Unique or distinctive competencies—characteristics, such as expertise in media relations, that apply only to specific positions within an organization.*[9]

BOX 10.6 Managerial Competencies

General mobility skills and knowledge: These competencies facilitate re-employment and include effectiveness in group process, communication skills, and flexibility and adaptation.

General managerial core competencies: These competencies were identified by studying successful managers and include "being able to build a cohesive team" and "being able to persuade employees to accept much needed organizational changes."

Detailed, job-specific competencies: Job-specific competencies vary by function, but in HR would include "the ability to implement a change program" and to "identify the best selection tool to identify high-potential candidates." These abilities would vary by level, with a junior manager mastering the ability to identify performance gaps in a subordinate and a senior manager being able to initiate change programs to improve performance.

Source: Adapted from E.H. Burach, W. Hochwarter, and N.J. Mathys, "The New Management Development Paradigm," *Human Resource Planning*, Vol. 20, No. 1 (2000), pp. 14–21.

3. Identify High-Potential Employees

Once we know what competencies are needed, we can turn to the identification of employees who might ultimately acquire these sets. Regularly scheduled discussions about succession force the leaders of the organization to think about the future of the business and the kinds of employee skills needed to facilitate the chosen strategy. By concerning themselves with the future directions of the organization, executives focus on the managers who will guide that future. The performance appraisal process becomes meaningful and not just another personnel form to complete. Executives come to "own" the succession and development plans because they are integral to the success of the organization.

Organizations use several approaches to identify managerial talent,[10] including the following:

1. *Temporary replacements:* At the most primitive level, most individual managers will have identified a designated backup and potential successor. This is done in case the manager is away from the office for extended periods (e.g., vacations, training). A manager who fails to pick a successor may never be promoted as no replacements would be ready to succeed him or her.
2. *Replacement charts:* At the next level, some organizations prepare replacement charts with predicted departure dates of the incumbents, along with a shortlist of possible successors. This is usually done around performance appraisal time, using the performance evaluation data. Typically, a handful of senior executives targets a diverse list of employees for growth and creates annual development plans. These executives stay in touch with each individual assigned to them and become responsible for the development of the leadership competencies of those individuals. The list identifies those candidates who are ready now, those who will be ready in three to five years, and the long shots. These approaches tend to replicate current strengths (and weaknesses) and are not necessarily future oriented, nor are they strategically aligned with the needs of the business. This stair-step approach is too rigid during times when organizational structures are changing rapidly and employee loyalty is weak.
3. *Strategic replacement:* A more advanced succession management program exists in an organization that is less inclined simply to replicate existing incumbents but instead identifies the leadership competencies it needs, based on organizational plans. The organization then tries to support and train these managers from within. The identification of high-potential people moves beyond the evaluations conducted by one or two managers. The Public Service Commission of Canada, for example, uses a formal assessment centre to identify those public servants who will become the future executives in the federal public service. Wary of evaluations done by only one individual with one perspective on employee performance, many organizations are moving to a 360-degree evaluation. For many employees, such an evaluation is the first time they have received feedback on how

others perceive them. Some employees likened the experience to holding up a mirror, others to a breath of fresh air.[11] Employees who had undergone 360-degree feedback reported that they felt their peers often knew better than their managers how to improve the employees' performance.

All these systems favour the selection of internal candidates. As such, these systems have a motivating impact on employee performance. However, they are limited in their ability to introduce new ways of thinking and working and may not suit the strategic direction of the organization. In the next approach, the managers more actively scan the environment to identify and retain top talent.

4. *Talent management culture:* Many organizations, whose CEOs lie awake at nights worrying about their ability to find and keep top talent, have adopted a talent management culture.[12] The winners in the war for talent have developed a talent mindset—that is, they believe that talent matters and it must be developed not only at the top level, but at all levels. Managers are committed to define and model an employee value proposition that answers the question "Why would a talented person want to work here?" The employee "brand" is managed as much as the company brand. See Box 10.7 for a discussion of brand positioning to attract and retain employees. Managers actively scan the environment (e.g., for the actions of their competitors or the actions of the world's best industry leaders in other areas with overlapping functions, such as finance or logistics) looking for external talent. They have developed both internal and external lists of high-potential candidates.

Recruitment is opportunistic—that is, when a top candidate is found, that person is hired regardless of whether there is a vacancy. As David Guptil, vice-

BOX 10.7 Building the Brand: An Employee Value Proposition

Some companies develop an employee value proposition (EVP) that will help attract and retain employees. They base this EVP on concepts that they have learned in customer attraction and retention. An EVP is a brand positioning aimed at employees so that the company will be seen as an employer worth working for, and all company messages sent to the labour market are compelling and consistent. The external brand of Southwest Airlines is "Freedom to Fly," and their employee brand is "Freedom begins with me"—freedom to learn, to be financially secure. Key candidates seem to be attracted to companies that pose one of four brand positions:

- A "winning" company, which is characterized by growth and development
- A "big risk, big reward" company, which offers great potential for advancement and compensation
- A "save the world" organization, which is attractive to those wanting a mission
- A "lifestyle" company, where employees want flexibility and a good relationship with the boss

Source: S. Cliffe, "Winning the War for Talent," *Harvard Business Review*, Vol. 76, No. 5 (September/October, 1998), pp. 18–19; S. Hood, "The PR of HR," *HR Professional* (February/March 2001), pp. 17–21.

president of HR Lafarge Canada, a large supplier of construction materials, states,

> *What keeps me awake at night is my very thin bench strength.... We are resisting that temptation to scale back on strategic recruiting. And when I say strategic recruiting, what I mean is that you don't wait for a vacancy and the predicted retirees. I and our senior managers are always on the lookout for talent that may be available. If I find a very talented person ... my freedom is to go out and hire that person whether we have a vacancy or not.*[13]

The process of continually searching for talent is correlated with success. A McKinsey study found that nearly one-third of HR directors at top-performing companies constantly search for talented executives, compared to less than 10% at average-performing companies.[14] These talent management companies analyze turnover statistics and always include in their reports the reasons for the voluntary turnover. Managers, not HR, have the responsibility for identifying and cultivating talent.

Finally, some companies operate with all four approaches, using replacement planning for highly predictable jobs such as accounting, and talent management to deal with rapid changes in strategic needs.

Assessing employees to identify high-potential candidates must be done both fairly and accurately: fairly so that employees buy into the process and feel that the search for talent is an equitable procedure, and accurately so that the selection process is both reliable and valid. Organizations typically use the direct supervisor's informal judgments and formal evaluations such as performance appraisals and assessment centres. (More information can be found in the performance evaluation chapter of any introductory HRM text.) Box 10.8 contains a brief description of common assessment methods. Usually about 10% of employees are identified as high potential. Syncrude Canada Ltd., an oil producer, with headquarters in Fort McMurray, Alberta, has identified about 8% of its 3600 employees as high potential.[15]

4. Provide Developmental Opportunities and Experiences

Before we discuss the methods used to develop managers, we should first consider two issues:

Are leaders born or made?

Should organizations produce their own managerial talent or buy it on the open market?

Born or made? Many great leaders have had no formal management training. Shouldn't we just select leaders with the inherent qualities of leaders and not try to teach leadership skills to those with no talent?

Peter Drucker, considered by many to be the founder of management as a discipline, is credited with saying, "Most managers are made, not born. There

BOX 10.8 Techniques for Assessing Employee Potential

Performance appraisals: Managers identify high-potential employees through performance appraisal systems. Raters, who may include the supervisor, colleagues, customers, and subordinates of an employee, evaluate the employee against some predeveloped standards. The goal is to identify and communicate the employee's performance strengths and weaknesses. The information is then used for developmental purposes, so that gaps in performance can be closed. High-potential employees are tracked in this way using a standardized organizational assessment tool. Managers are forced to identify high-potential employees through performance appraisal systems and may be rewarded for developing employees.

Assessment centres: Assessment centres involve a process by which candidates are evaluated as they participate in a series of exercises that closely resemble the situations faced on the job. Simulations include negotiating a merger, handling the press, managing interdepartmental conflicts, or making a decision without all the facts. Trained and experienced managers observe the candidates' behaviour during this process and provide an evaluation of their competence and potential. The newest form of assessment centres is the Acceleration Centre, in which the first stop is a website where candidates can learn everything about the fictitious company they will manage for a day. All testing, correspondence, and decisions are completed online, enabling the assessors to compare candidates more objectively.

HRMS: Large amounts of information about employees' KSAs can be stored in databanks and used to identify employees with needed skills. Employee files can document their experiences, skills, abilities, and performance evaluations. Employees' interests and career objectives may also be recorded. Basic matching to identify high-potential candidates is simplified with an effective HRMS. A useful feature of HRMS is their ability to construct scenarios. Planners can create "what-if?" models to determine the effect of employee movements.

has to be systematic work on the supply, the development, and the skills of tomorrow's management. It cannot be left to chance."[16]

Buy or make? Organizations invest many dollars and other resources to develop managers, but perhaps experienced, trained managers could simply be hired from other organizations.

Some organizations do prefer to pick up their needed executive talent by buying it on the open market. For example, Elliot Whale, president and CEO of Dylex Ltd., had been president of Toys R Us (Canada) Ltd. and director of player personnel for the Toronto Blue Jays baseball club before he moved to Dylex. Selecting outsiders allows companies to bring in fresh perspectives, people who can lead the organization through a transformation. By bringing in an outsider, the board of directors sends a strong message to employees and shareholders that the old way of doing things is going to change.[17] Other organizations feel strongly that they want to indoctrinate and train their own leaders, who then have a deep commitment to the organizational vision.

There are no easy answers to these questions. Organizations may find outstanding leaders by chance, or they may commit to the development process. Some may choose to hire from the outside to obtain fresh approaches; others will commit significant time and money to train their own managers.

However, most large organizations have a policy of promotion from within. There are many advantages to this: the organization has accurate records of employees' past performance, and employees understand and are committed to organizational objectives, know the ropes, and know how to get things done. Most large organizations have formal management development programs to ensure a ready supply of "promotables." Let us look at some of the methods such organizations use.

Management Development Methods

In the succession management process, the focus in management development is on the development of competencies, not just on job preparation. Because the goal is to develop many skills that may be needed in an uncertain future (in contrast to simply replicating the skills of the present incumbents), management is much more open to various approaches to develop the talent pool. More traditional approaches might have relied on a senior leadership course and one developmental assignment, perhaps mimicking exactly what the current CEO did. The key point is that the approach has changed from one of providing training to fill jobs to one of providing experiences to realize leadership potential. The most common development methods are promotions, job rotations, special assignments and action learning, formal training and development, and coaching and mentoring.

Promotions

Promotion refers to an employee's upward advancement in the hierarchy of an organization and usually involves increased responsibilities and compensation. Traditional models of management development saw managers moving up a pyramid, managing larger and larger units until they reached their appointments at the top. Each organization had its favourite route to the top, some through sales, others through operations. These paths became worn over time, and few succeeded by using other paths, such as an HR track. However, this all changed in the mid-1970s, when the oil crisis made unlimited growth of the pyramid more difficult: the baby boomers were bunching up at the bottom; rough economic times delayered the pyramid, making it flatter; and the development of generalists became more popular, reducing the use of the few footpaths to the top.[18] One organization used a system of temporary rotations, resulting in a win-win combination. Senior executives nearing retirement were given the option of a week's vacation in every month, which they welcomed, and were replaced by high-potential employees who could try new leadership skills in a safe setting. In flat organizations, where promotions are rare, a preferred developmental method is job rotations—developing managers horizontally rather than vertically.

promotion an employee's upward advancement in the hierarchy of an organization

Job Rotations

Job rotations are lateral transfers of employees between jobs in an organization. Rotations involve a change in job assignments but not necessarily more responsibility or money. For example, one way of orienting a new employee

job rotations a process whereby an employee's upward advancement in the hierarchy of an organization is achieved by lateral as well as vertical moves

quickly is to place him or her in a new department every few weeks, thus providing the employee an overview of the organization. The CEO of Maritime Life Insurance believes that rotation is the best indicator of whether an employee is ready for a top position. To avoid costly placement decisions, staff with potential are placed in a variety of roles across the organization. Succeeding at rotation is a prerequisite for a top-level position.[19]

Rotations have several motivational benefits for employees, including the reduction of boredom and fatigue. Trying out new jobs also benefits employees who have reached a career plateau. The development of additional skills may increase an employee's job and career prospects. Almost all the research suggests that job rotation makes employees more satisfied, motivated, involved, and committed.[20]

From the organization's standpoint, rotations are useful for orientation and career development. Rotations allow an employee to increase his or her experience. A common use of job rotation is to take a functional specialist, such as an accountant, and rotate this specialist through both HR and operations in preparation for management positions. An information technology specialist, before a rotation in sales, might try to sell his idea to management by saying, "We have to invest in a multiprotocal router," and might be met with complete incomprehension. After a rotation through the sales department, the same specialist might sell the same program by explaining, "We're building an infrastructure so salespeople can get access to product or inventory information from anywhere." The technician has learned business skills.[21] Jet Form, an Ottawa-based business with about 650 employees, uses cross-functional mobility as a key part of its strategic planning.[22] The results are encouraging, and employees are regularly rotated between functions to increase their knowledge and skills.

Besides the additional knowledge of the functional areas, such as sales, and management areas, such as business knowledge, the rotated employee is making contacts and establishing a network that might prove useful in the future. Learning new ways of doing things, with different co-workers and bosses, also might make employees more adaptable in their managerial jobs. The research shows that rotation improves an employee's knowledge of the organization (e.g., of business, strategy, and contacts) and improves his or her ability to cope with uncertainty. Furthermore, employees who have tried out several jobs gain a better insight into their own strengths and weaknesses. However, job rotation produces generalists and should be supplemented by training for any specific skills needed.

Of course, the downside of employee rotations includes the increased time needed to learn the new jobs, the cost of errors while learning, and the loss of efficiency that otherwise is gained through repetition and specialization.[23] In other words, workload may increase for the employee while productivity decreases. The manager and the team into which the employee is rotated experience additional work and stress as they attempt to socialize, orient, and train the newcomer.

At the managerial level, employers should be concerned about producing a short-term orientation in its leadership ranks. Employees in six-month jobs may well do more to create fast results, which might hurt the unit in the long term. For example, employees with a short-run focus may neglect plant safety in a rush to exceed production quotas. Furthermore, the rotation of managers places new expectations on performance, new goals, and reassignment of work, producing stress on the unit managed by rotation.[24]

One approach is to give an employee a number of assignments within the company or a related sector. For example, the president of Zellers (now merged with Kmart) has worked as president of Kmart, at Zellers, at the Hudson's Bay Company (the parent company), and at Woodward's.

Ultimately, managers may be better formed by developing skills horizontally, throughout an organization, rather than by developing specialized skills vertically, up a career ladder.

Special Assignments

On-the-job learning is still a favoured path to the development of managerial skills. Most organizations test high-potential employees by giving them an assignment in addition to their regular duties. For example, the manager of corporate banking might be placed on a task force that is considering the acquisition of another bank. A manager who needs international experience might be sent to work in China with a vendor to the company. In another case, a team of managers might be given a special assignment, such as developing an equity plan for the organization or developing an e-commerce plan for the company. These types of special projects enable candidates for future executive positions to network and to test their skills in new environments. Mistakes must be tolerated, as candidates will quickly learn that these special assignments are synonymous with failure, fostering a culture of fear where no employee dare be innovative or take bold measures, and finally, derailment from the fast track. Remember the story about the executive who is called into his boss's office expecting to be fired, because of a business decision that cost the company a million dollars. The CEO instead gives him another special assignment, reasoning, "Why should we fire you? We just invested one million dollars in your development."

Formal Training and Development

Management training and education is big business. Hundreds of thousands of dollars may be spent preparing one executive to become the CEO of the organization. This cost appears relatively minor when it is estimated that the total career investment in an individual employee is 160 times the initial starting salary.[25] In this book, we use the term "management development," but others label a similar process "executive education" or "leadership training" or a combination of any of these words.

According to a study of U.S. organizations, 87% offer management development programs that were designed, developed, and delivered in-house.[26]

Only a small number used external vendors. The majority of companies use traditional and passive instructional techniques and rate them least effective, but they are fast and easy to use. Most use lectures, seminars, and discussion groups more often than behaviour modelling and experiential learning. (For a fuller discussion of these methods, see Belcourt et al., *Performance Management through Training and Development*, 2003.) Senior managers need the soft skills of delegation and motivation, rather than hard technical skills such as website development or benefits management. Thus we would recommend that role-playing, case studies, behaviour modelling, and action learning, which are effective techniques, be used as training methods for management development. In most cases, the effectiveness of the training method is evaluated by the "smile sheets"—course evaluation sheets in which participants rate the course and instructors—at the end of the program rather than the application of the learned skills on the job. Techniques for increasing the extent to which training is then applied to and endures in the performance of the job have been described by Belcourt and Saks.[27] Some feel that these training programs teach very specific skills that might not be robust enough to stand the test of time and successfully prepare managers for rapidly changing environments.

Many companies prefer an educational approach that broadens intellectual skills such as the ability to analyze. These companies turn to universities to teach their executives conceptual skills, which would be useful in many situations. Others create their own training centres, which they label corporate universities.

U.S. organizations, more than 1000 of them, have begun opening corporate universities—available only to the employees—because these organizations view training as a lifelong process, rather than as discrete courses taken occasionally. Most of these universities focus on building competencies and skills that are aligned strategically to meet both employee and corporate needs. Individual corporate universities offer a wide range of courses, which together constitute something resembling a mini-MBA. Through case studies and action learning, the courses offer managers a chance to practise and receive feedback. Unlike professional athletes or musicians, managers seldom get a chance to practise their skills and try out new ideas and methods. Sometimes, these corporate universities have mentors on staff, often with more than 20 years in the business, who coach and assist in the transfer of knowledge.

Mentoring and Coaching

Many very successful managers will explain that their success resulted directly from having been mentored. A senior executive took an interest in them and their careers at a critical time in their lives. **Mentors** are executives who coach, advise, and encourage junior employees. The mentor takes an active interest in the career advancement and the psychosocial development of the protégé. Career development aspects include examining approaches to assignments and learning how tasks should be handled, which conferences or networks have high career value, and which senior managers to emulate. Psychosocial con-

mentors executives who coach, advise, and encourage junior employees

siderations include building the self-confidence of the protegé, as well as offering counselling and friendship to make him or her aware of the political open doors and open pits of the organization.

Mentoring used to happen informally, but organizations have recognized the value of having a senior manager take a career interest in a junior employee and so have started formal mentoring programs. One survey showed that 70% of highly productive organizations have mentoring programs, and employees in these programs report greater career satisfaction and experience faster career growth.[28] These programs link executives who have the motivation and time to nurture managerial talent with employees who are motivated to advance quickly. Mentors are almost always more senior people who volunteer within an organization, while coaches tend to be paid counsellors from outside the organization. The advantages of external coaches are described in Box 10.9.

While it is necessary for discussion purposes to separate management development methods, all companies will use a combination of methods. Some focus on formal programs, such as a three-week leadership course followed by an assignment in a foreign country. Other companies, such as 3M, allow their employees to choose assignments and to work on ad hoc committees to manage new projects, as well as giving them free time to tinker and play with ideas. The choice of a method depends on the employee's learning style and the goals to be achieved. Learning about foreign cultures is best done by spending time in a foreign office or with representatives from overseas, not from a book. Nor is shadowing an IT employee the best way to learn about IT.

Another reason for using different methods is that the development of a senior executive may take 25 years. It is unusual to see a vice-president of a large company who is less than 40 years old. So some companies, such as Wal-Mart,

BOX 10.9 Benefits of External Coaches

For the organization:

- Retain high performers with incentives other than financial rewards
- Develop key employees for succession planning
- Guide individuals and organizations through transition
- Change skills and attitudes for long-term sustainable results
- Give new perspectives on business experience and practices

For the individual:

- Reconnect the individual with personal values or missions
- Provide clarity and focus to accelerate the achievement of goals
- Compress learning time to optimize skills by building competencies faster through one-on-one coaching
- Translate leadership theories and concepts into "useful insights" to affect communication, decision-making, and overall strategies

Sources: Adapted from L. Hyatt, "Best Practices for Developing Great Leaders," *Workplace Today* (January 2003), pp. 14–17; G. Voisin, "When to Use an Internal or External Coach," *HR Professional* (June/July 2001), pp. 30–33.

start early, grooming the store managers under a mentoring system to take on more and more responsibility.

5. Monitor Succession Management

Some succession plans are placed on an executive's top shelf, ready to be dusted off to prepare for the annual discussion. In no way do they form part of a strategic plan, nor are they used to guide employee development. They are not effective. How do you measure the effectiveness of succession management? Succession planners used to count the number of predicted "high-potential replacements" with the actual number of those placed in the position. If the needs of the business change dramatically, this may be a poor way of measuring.

One expert asked, "If this process worked perfectly and everything happened the way it was supposed to happen, what would the results look like?"[29] The answer? Employees would receive regular feedback based on the assessment process and would participate in development plans. The best result would be an organization with skilled employees prepared to contribute to the goals of the organization under changing conditions. Organizations measure their success not only by the percentage of positions filled by designated high-potential employees, but also by attitude surveys of these employees, and exit interviews if these "hi-pots" leave the organization. The word "success" in succession is illuminating, in that studies are starting to show that corporations with strong succession management programs are higher performers measured by revenue growth, profitability, and market share.[30]

Until this point, we have examined succession management from the organizational perspective. No consideration has been given to the employee perspective.

Employee Role in Succession Management

A top-down, organization-directed approach to succession management assumes that employees are ready and willing to be prepared for the next generation of leadership. A top-down approach treats employees as pieces in a chess game. But employees are not pawns. Their voices need to be heard.

The first consideration is that an employee's relationship with any organization is not permanent. The employee can quit, or the employer can terminate him or her. Today's new employment contract does not guarantee jobs to anyone, even to those performing competently. The former contract was built on an implied promise of a long-term, mutually satisfying relationship. However, market forces create turbulence that sometimes causes companies to restructure or fail. These changes have resulted in a change in the psychological contract that an employee has with the employer. The traditional employment contract with the organization was built on an implicit understanding that the employee would work hard, develop additional skills provided mainly by the employer, and, in return, would be promoted on a regular basis. At a minimum, the employer would reward the loyalty and efforts of employees with job security. This contract is dead. Today's career model may be perceived as a transactional one in which benefits and contributions are exchanged for a short period.[31]

The new contract, transactional in nature, lists the responsibilities and rights of each party in the employer–employee relationship, and employees want this contract stated explicitly in writing. If loyalty to any organization still exists, it is to the professional organization, to a network of peers and to certifiable credibility that confers collegiality and respect. Box 10.10 contains a comparison of the two concepts of career management.

This transactional view of employer–employee relationships suggests that, as organizations develop employees, they must take into consideration employee aspirations and goals. Employees will participate in management development programs more eagerly if their goals match the succession plans of the company. Employees will enthusiastically engage in self-development if they are aware of the strategic goals of a company, thus enhancing their own job security or marketability. If employees of *The Globe and Mail* knew that the company was changing from a newspaper publishing business to an international information marketing business, employees would undertake, on their own time and at their own expense, to study languages or marketing. Managerial preferences cannot be the sole determinant in employee development. Career counselling and discussions at performance appraisal time will help ensure that

BOX 10.10 Comparing Traditional and Emerging Career Management Concepts

Characteristics	Traditional	Emerging
Employment contract	Implicit	Explicit
Duration	Long-term	Short-term
Career responsibility	Employer	Self-directed
Career identity	Organization	Profession/occupation
Benefits	Focus on security	Focus on learning
Loyalty	To the organization	Profession, friends, family
Mindset	Inward, political	Outward, entrepreneurial
Development	Formal training	Work experiences
Career progression	Vertical	Horizontal
Employment stability	Job security	Employability
Career goal	Corporate success	Psychological success

Source: Adapted from D. Hall and J.E. Moss, "The New Protean Career Contract: Helping Organizations and Employees Adapt," *Organization Dynamics* (Winter 1988), pp. 22–37.

the employee's voice is heard. While organizations cannot promise lifetime employment, competition for leadership talent is so intense that high-potential employees must be given a reason for staying with an organization.

An added benefit of listening to employees is the opportunity to customize the development plan. Employees are very aware of their strengths and weaknesses and their preferred learning styles. One employee might suggest that she could learn decision-making by being given a leadership role; another might prefer a seminar on decision-making. Some organizations like Ford Financial, which has 20 000 employees around the world, provide information to employees that enables them to make their own career plans. Ford Financial has a sophisticated skill- and competency-based learning program with direct links to the company's three core businesses and job requirements. Employees can determine the skills and competencies needed for any job within the organization, then undertake a self-development plan to master any of the 15 knowledge domains, 80 functional areas, and 800 separate skills.[32]

By creating a process that invites employee participation, succession managers are more likely to gain employee commitment to and ownership of the plans. We turn now to a discussion of the limitations of succession management.

SUCCESSION MANAGEMENT'S SOFT SPOTS

So far, we have discussed the many benefits of succession management and introduced a way to manage succession effectively. However, there are challenges to the implementation of a succession management program; these challenges include the creation of an elite corps of employees, the managerial risk encountered in spotlighting the best employees, the perennial problem of selection bias, and, finally, the very human inability to predict the future.

ELITISM

Management development programs, particularly if they support the training of selected employees for specific senior positions, may lead to the perception that there is an elite group on the one hand and the "unwashed masses" on the other. There are several advantages to preparing a limited number—a select group of the elite—including the reduced costs of training. However, many managers fear that by publicly identifying those who will be promoted, a cadre of "crown princes" will be created. Those who are on the list (and expect to be the next vice-president) may coast in their careers, as they know that their contribution has already been recognized and the reward is in the near future. The organization, too, may relax and not invest sufficiently in the further development of these promotable employees. A bigger problem will occur (and it happens frequently) when the star on the chart is not chosen to be the successor. At that point, the person who expected to be the "winner" feels publicly humiliated and will either leave the organization or not fully support the new candidate. Sometimes, things do not happen as quickly as first expected. As Prince Charles, another crown prince, will testify, sometimes the head never dies or departs, leaving the heir apparent to wait forever.

Employees can be "demotivated" by succession planning in several ways. The attitudes of the elite may create discontent among other employees with uncertain futures. Suppose the successors were identified on organizational charts and these charts were made public. Those not on the successors list may consider leaving the organization for another where their career prospects are brighter. Managers may ignore the development of other employees who, with some training and assignments, would become likely contenders.

These disadvantages—the demotivating effects on those not chosen, the disappointment and withdrawal if the employee's succession plans are not realized—have resulted in about two-thirds of companies not telling employees that they are on a fast track.[33] By not telling employees this, companies risk having employees leave the organization for one that offers better opportunities, and they also risk having to groom someone who may not want the job. (However, most employees realize their special status through the frequency of their promotions, assignments, and training.) Employers must avoid promises such as "you will become CEO in five years"; such promises are an implicit contract that may be judged to be binding.

Does identifying many successors solve these problems? Surely competition between successors will ensure that the best candidate wins by trying harder and demanding better training. Furthermore, if one successor does not develop to the potential that was anticipated or quits the organization, then others are willing and ready. But this approach has problems too. One is that candidates might sabotage each other, by not sharing important information or by raiding key employees to improve their own track records. As well, many might engage in managing impressions and performing for short-term results in order to be evaluated more highly. This strategy does not encourage team playing, which is a force in organization culture.

There is no easy solution to these problems. At NCR, the management development plan is labelled Project 64K because it is meant for all 64 000 employees, not an elite group. At Johnson & Johnson, the focus is on the top 700 managers.[34]

Risk of the Spotlight

Another problem with succession management is that executives may be reluctant to shine the spotlight on their most talented employees. Such executives may fear that if they identify their top performers, other units will grab these talented employees, necessitating the onerous task of finding and developing other talented employees. Managers may fear that by developing their own replacements, they will be replaced sooner than desired. However, managers have to know that this talent represents an organizational resource, not a departmental hidden asset. An effective succession program would force managers to identify backfill candidates. Ask these managers, "Who can do your job?" If they are unable to provide names, then ask, "What can I expect to be different next year?" This question leads to a developmental action plan.[35] A manager who does not identify and develop talent is like a high school coach who plays the most senior players to win this year's game with no thought of winning games in the years that follow.

Highly developed professionals and managers make good recruitment targets for competitors, suppliers, and even customer organizations. Increased attrition is a risk, especially if the job offers are attractive. Should companies not develop employees and thereby avoid this risk? The riskier proposition might be to not develop managers and then be unable to find them on the open labour market when the company badly needs their skills.

Selection Bias

Asking senior executives to determine the high potentials ("hi pots") poses three problems: (1) the criteria for selection is not clear; (2) evaluation strategies may vary by department; and (3) rating errors, such as those of recency, contrast, and leniency or strictness, can occur. Leaving the identification and development of the next generation of managers in the hands of the current one often leads to a "similar-to-me" selection bias. Managers have a tendency to select as their successors those who seem similar to themselves and who work in styles that are comfortable: the heirs apparent fit in, they look like the rest of the family members. Despite decades of employment equity, most key executives-in-waiting are white males.

Unpredictable Futures

Organizational careers are no longer guaranteed, if indeed they ever were. However, there seems to be a greater state of uncertainty and chaos today, and even those who have given exemplary service are subject to layoffs and job loss.

Organizational executives are not psychic; they cannot predict the future accurately. There is a tendency to clone the incumbent executives and to plan the future as a continuation of the present. But as Wayne Gretzky says, "Pass the puck not to where the player is, but to where he is going to be."[36] This is the challenge for organizations—determining where the play is going to be.

These kinds of problems may be the reason that only 40% of companies surveyed had a formal succession plan.[37] After a decade of restructuring, many organizations saw no point in planning for the future when survival and downsizing occupied all their thoughts. Now that growth is a primary objective for many companies, succession management is increasingly on the agenda, as can be seen in the situation at Air Canada.

Succession Management at Air Canada

In this case study, the steps in succession management are applied in the real world.

1. Link Succession Management with Strategic Goals of the Organization

During the early 1990s, Air Canada was in a survival mode primarily because of the economic recession. The HR planning role was to restructure the organization and downsize from 2500 managers in the early 1990s to 1200 in the next decade. Managers were released through a combination of early retirements, buyouts, and terminations. The strategic goal was survival.

In 1992, Hollis Harris was brought in as the new CEO, and his goal was to return the airline to profitability. The board of directors also wanted to ensure that there were strong successor candidates for the CEO position and for the next levels of management. The board gave Harris a strong mandate to build management strength. A key focus was succession planning at the executive level. One of Harris's first steps was to supplement the internal team by bringing in a few key outsiders to fill the senior management positions and achieve a balance of internal and external resources.

2. Identify the Competencies Needed

The second phase was to identify internal candidates. Branches were asked to think of their business and the issues that would arise in the future. They were asked if the business would change significantly and, if it did, would they then have the skills needed.

Identifying the requisite competencies was a particularly difficult area of succession management. Core competencies were identified but were not used systematically to select the high-potential employees. Jim Aldham, manager of Organization and HR Planning, admitted that predicting the skills of the future is the weakest part of succession management.

3. Identify the High-Potential Employees

A significant number of employees with growth potential had left the organization in the massive restructuring of the 1980s and early 1990s. As Jim Aldham said, "In hindsight, we should have been more selective about who went out the door. But we were losing $1 million a day; we were in survival mode. A lot of grey-haired experience went out the door, and we were left with very bright people with limited managerial experience."

Managers were asked to identify three candidates who would be their potential successors and to rate them as "A: ready now," "B: ready in 18 months," or "C: ready with development." The managers discussed these candidates with their executives. The executives then presented their lists to other executives in a group session. The purpose of these discussions was to validate the branch's perception of potential and to obtain other potential candidates (i.e., in a cross-functional approach). Both senior executives and the board of directors approved the succession plans. Unlike most organizations, Air Canada went a step further, using the succession management process as a vehicle to assess all employees. Thus, they also identified the following:

Reassignments: These were employees who needed to be reassigned to other jobs either because they were in the wrong job, given their skill sets, or because they needed a different experience for developmental purposes after staying in one job too long.

Supply gaps: These were positions for which immediate backfills were not available. At the senior level, these positions were key to the success of the organization and needed to be protected from gaps in succession. Managers were asked to develop an action plan, including steps for rectifying this replacement problem.

Marginal contributors: The employees whose performance was below standard and would be monitored for eventual improvement or termination were identified as marginal contributors.

Developmental requirements: These were employees who needed development opportunities to become more effective for current and future positions.

Expatriate candidates: Employees who had been moved to assignments in Europe and then brought back to more senior positions at Air Canada were considered expatriate candidates. These employees were assigned special status because of the huge expense involved in their relocations and the fast development curve they experienced as global managers.

There remained the issue of identifying high-potential employees (for management positions) among the 21 000 nonmanagement employees. Could they be identified through self-nomination—that is, by applying for posted jobs?

4. Develop the High-Potential Employees

In the delayered Air Canada (where 50% of the managerial jobs were eliminated), there was little opportunity for employees to acquire managerial skills, although their functional skills were well developed. Therefore, the emphasis then was on the rapid development of managerial bench strength. The company had several methods for doing this:

Developmental assignments: The candidate was given a special task on a team or was given an assignment to develop a part of a new venture such as Star Alliance.

Corporate learning: This method entailed training courses, workshops, and seminars. An example of one such training program was the International Airline Management Training program, in which employees were given the opportunity to run a fictitious company on the verge of bankruptcy. The team, composed of employees from various functional areas, had to save the company and present their action plan to a fictitious board of directors.

Job shadowing: This method involved a junior employee trailing a senior employee from another branch on an informal and as-needed basis. The goal was to expose the junior employee to other functions. Job shadowing sometimes led to a job in that other branch.

5. Measure the Results

Air Canada had monitored the results of this new foray into succession management. The company measured the degree to which the plan identified high-potential employees, marginal contributors, reassignments, senior positions with no backfill, developmental positions, and new hires. They tracked the stock of people and the flow of these people through the organization via promotions, resignations, retirements, and so on.

As of 2003, Air Canada's success at succession management was still open for debate. Environmental factors such as fear of terrorism and the price of oil continued to influence strategic planning. At the time this text was written, Air Canada had filed for bankruptcy.

Summary

In this chapter, we defined succession management and contrasted it with personnel planning. The five-step model of effective succession management includes these steps: (1) align succession management plans with strategy; (2) identify the skills and competencies needed to meet strategic objectives; (3) identify high-potential employees; (4) provide developmental opportunities and experiences through promotions, job rotations, special assignments, formal training and development, and mentoring and coaching; and (5) monitor succession management. The employee's role in the process must be considered. The limitations of the succession management process include the creation of an elite corps of employees, the managerial risk incurred by spotlighting the best employees, the possibility of selection bias, and the difficulty of predicting the future. The Air Canada case study showed how the succession management process can be applied.

Key Terms

competencies, 239

job rotations, 245

mentors, 248

promotion, 245

replacement planning, 235

succession management, 232

Suggested Websites

www.workforce.com/archive/article/22/03/20.php Showcases the leadership development program of the Metropolitan Transportation Authority, New York City.

www.entrepeneur.com Insights on job rotation.

www.jobquality.ca/indicator_e/des001.stm Job rotations trends in Canada.

Discussion Questions

1. Well Point Health Networks meets the health-care needs of more than 50 million members through subsidiaries such as Blue Cross and Healthlink. Their Human Resources Planning System (HRPS) won the Optimas Award in 2002 for its succession plan. Read why WellPoint was so successful in the article by P.J. Kiger, "Succession Planning Keeps WellPoint Competitive," *Workforce*, Vol. 81, No. 4, April 2002, pages 50–54. Compare their system to the model presented in this chapter.
2. Do you plan to align your career goals and developmental experiences with your employer's goals and needs? If so, how will you do this? If not, why not?

Exercise

Consider the following three scenarios:

(a) Lee Ki Chung managed all the operating systems for 8 Star Manufacturing Company. Always reliable and never absent, Lee was indispensable. One day, Lee phoned to say that he had been diagnosed with cancer and had to enter treatment immediately and did not know when he would return to the office.

(b) The president of Overseas Banking Corporation, the second largest bank in the country, had chosen as his successor the vice-president of Finance. However, as the president's retirement date approached, he began to worry that this star employee could no longer handle the stress and long hours of banking. The VP was absent for extended periods as he tried to deal with his son, who had been arrested for drug abuse, which in turn caused problems in his marriage.

(c) Hi Tech Corp was a company created by the next generation of Bill Gates clones. They had succeeded in attracting the best and the brightest to help them build a billion-dollar company developing the ultimate in software applications. On Tuesday, October 10, the entire design team announced they were quitting to start a rival company and recapture that entrepreneurial culture of the early years.

Could succession management have mitigated the impact on the organization of any of these situations? How could succession management mitigate the seriousness of the consequences?

CASE: ACCELERATION POOLS AT PEPSICO

PepsiCo is a world leader in convenient foods and beverages, with revenues of about $27 billion and over 143 000 employees. The company consists of the snack businesses of Frito-Lay North America and Frito-Lay International; the beverage businesses of Pepsi-Cola North America, Gatorade/Tropicana North America, and PepsiCo Beverages International; and Quaker Foods North America, manufacturer and marketer of ready-to-eat cereals and other food products. PepsiCo brands are available in nearly 200 countries and territories.

PepsiCo replaced its traditional personnel planning model with a system to groom high-potential employees for organizational levels, not jobs. PepsiCo found that 25 000 hours a year were spent discussing replacement plans and filling out forms. There was little return on this investment of executive time, so changes were needed. Under the new system, employees were no longer hand-picked as replacements for specific positions. Talent pools by both level and business unit have been created. For example, there might be a supervisory/professional level pool and a plant management pool. Once pool members were targeted, their development needs are diagnosed in a number of ways: through use of an acceleration centre, 360-degree feedback instruments, and interviews. Their skills are assessed in four areas:

- Organization knowledge (what the employee knows about functions, processes, products, etc.);
- Job challenges (what the employee has done, such as preparing a budget);
- Competencies (what the employee is capable of based on his or her knowledge, behaviour, technical skills, and motivations important to senior management such as change leadership); and

- Executive derailers (the personality traits that might cause failure, such as arrogance or low tolerance for ambiguity).

Those in the talent pool are given difficult assignments and are assigned to task forces, two methods that offer the best opportunities for intensive learning and the highest visibility. Each candidate is assigned a mentor and receives training, coaching, and developmental opportunities such as university executive education programs.

The Executive Resource Board (made up of the CEO/COO and senior line managers) is responsible for the pool and meets twice a year to review talent development; they then meet with the candidate, the manager, and the mentor. Discussions might focus on how to gain a new skill or effectively deal with a derailer. The focus is on measurable results, not just the process. Thus, a candidate who attended a training program is not given credit for taking the course, until there is proof of changes made as a result of the program. Each candidate creates and maintains a Career Development Portfolio, which includes a current CV, completed appraisal forms, and a development plan with progress reports. This portfolio is accessible by the Executive Resource Board.

Sources: "A New Look at Succession Management," by William C. Byham, Reprint #9B02TC03, *Ivey Business Journal*, May/June 2002, Vol. 66, No. 5, pp. 10–12. Copyright © 2002 Ivey Management Services Inc.; www.pepsico.com.

QUESTION

Analyze the effectiveness of PepsiCo's succession management program. Include in your report the strengths and weaknesses of the model and suggestions for increasing its effectiveness.

REFERENCES

Beeson, J. 1998. "The CEO's Checklist." *Across the Board* (June): 41–42.

Belcourt, M., and A.M. Saks. 1998. "Benchmarking Best Training Practices." *Human Resource Professional* (December 1997/January 1998): 33–41.

Belcourt, M., A.M. Saks, and R. Haccoun. 2000. *Performance Management through Training and Development*, 2nd ed. Toronto: ITP Nelson.

Belcourt, M., and S. Taggar. 2002. *Making Government the Best Place to Work: Building Commitment*. IPAC New Directions, Report No. 8.

Black, B. 2002. "CEO's Talk." *Canadian HR Reporter* (October 7, 2002): 17.

Borwick, C. 1993. "Eight Ways to Assess Succession Plans." *HRM Magazine*, Vol. 38, No. 4: 109–114.

Byham, W.C. 2002. "A New Look at Succession Management." *Ivey Business Journal*, Vol. 66, No. 5 (May/June): 10–12.

Butyn, S. 2003. "Mentoring Your Way to Improved Retention." *Canadian HR Reporter* (January 27): 13.

Campion, M.A., L. Cheraskin, and M.J. Stevens. 1994. "Career-Related Antecedents and Outcomes of Job Rotation." *Academy of Management Journal*, Vol. 37, No. 6 (December): 1518–1525.

Catano, V. M., S.F. Cronshaw, W.H. Wiesner, R.D. Hackett, and L.L. Methot. 2001. *Recruitment and Selection in Canada*, 2nd ed. Toronto: ITP Nelson.

Chereskin, L., and M.A. Campion. 1996. "Study Clarifies Job Rotation Benefits." *Personnel Journal* (November): 31–38.

Church, E. 1998. "New-Style CEOs Follow Zig-Zag Path." *The Globe and Mail* (February 20): B23.

Dahl, H.L. 1997. "Human Resource Cost and Benefit Analysis: New Power for Human Resource Approaches." *Human Resource Planning*, Vol. 11, No. 2: 69–78.

Drucker, P. 1998. "Management's New Paradigms." *Forbes* (October 5): 152–177.

Eichlinger, B., and D. Ulrich. 1996. "Are You Future Agile?" *Human Resource Planning*, Vol. 11, No. 2: 30–41.

Francis, K. 2001. "CEO's Talk." *Canadian HR Reporter*, Vol. 14, No. 11 (June 4): 17.

Fulmer, R.M. 1997. "The Evolving Paradigm of Leadership Development." *Organizational Dynamics* (Spring): 59–72.

Greengard, S. 2001. "Make Smarter Business Decisions: Know What Employees Can Do." *Workforce*, Vol. 80, No. 11 (November): 42–46.

Gore, N. 2000. "Managing Talent Replaces Static Charts in a New Era of Succession Planning." *Canadian HR Reporter*, Vol. 13, No. 15 (September 11): 12.

Guptil, D. 2003. "HR Leaders Talk." *Canadian HR Reporter* (February 10): 16.

Hall, D., and J.E. Moss. 1988. "The New Protean Career Contract: Helping Organizations and Employees Adapt." *Organization Dynamics* (Winter): 22–37.

Horwitt, L. 1997. "It's Your Career: Manage It." *Network World* (March 17): 39–43.

Joinson, C. 1998. "Developing a Strong Bench." *HRM Magazine* (January): 92–96.

Lawler, E.E. III. 1994. "From Job-Based to Competency-Based Organizations." *Journal of Organizational Behaviour*, Vol. 15: 3–15.

Lear, R. 1998. "Making Succession Succeed." *Chief Executive* (March): 14.

Leibman, M., R. Bruer, and B.R. Maki. 1996. "Succession Management: The Next Generation of Succession Planning." *Human Resources Planning*, Vol. 19, No. 3: 16–29.

Lenz, S.S., and S. Wacker. 1997. "Career Development in an Uncertain World." Unpublished paper presented at the Human Resource Planning Society Symposium, Ithaca, New York.

Newell, E. 2001. "CEO's Talk." *Canadian HR Reporter*, Vol. 14, No. 17 (October 8).

Pieperl, M., and Y. Baruch. 1997. "Back to Zero: The Post-Corporate Career." *Organizational Dynamics* (Spring): 7–22.

Rothwell, W.J. 2001. *Effective Succession Planning*. New York: Amacom.

Walter, G. 1996. "Corporate Practices in Management Development." *Conference Board*, Report No. 1158-96-RR. New York: Conference Board Inc.

Willins, R., and W. Byham. 2001. "The Leadership Gap." *Training*, Vol. 38, No. 3 (March): 98–106.

Yancey, G.B. 2001. "Succession Planning Creates Quality Leadership." *Credit Union Executive Journal*, Vol. 41, No. 6 (November/December): 24–27.

ENDNOTES

1. Belcourt and Taggar, 2002.
2. Drucker, 1998.
3. Willins and Byham, 2001.
4. Leibman et al., 1996.
5. Byham, 2002, pp. 10–12.
6. Ecihlinger and Ulrich, 1996.
7. Lawler, 1994.
8. Catano et al., 2001.
9. Ibid.
10. Joinson, 1998.
11. Lenz and Wacker, 1997.
12. Gore, 2000, page 17.
13. Guptil, 2003.
14. Yancey, 2001.
15. Newell, 2001.
16. Walter, 1996.
17. Church, 1998.
18. Peiperl and Baruch, 1997.
19. Black, 2002.
20. Campion et al., 1994.
21. Horwitt, 1997.
22. Francis, 2001, p. 17.
23. Horwitt, 1997.
24. Chereskin and Campion, 1996.
25. Dahl, 1997.
26. Walter, 1996.
27. Belcourt and Saks, 1998.
28. Butyn, 2003.
29. Borwick, 1993.
30. Willins and Byham, 2001.
31. Hall and Moss, 1998.
32. Greengard, 2001.
33. Joinson, 1998.
34. Fulmer, 1997.
35. Beeson, 1998.
36. Lear, 1998.
37. Rothwell, 2001.

Part 3

Strategic Options and HR Decisions

DOWNSIZING AND RESTRUCTURING

This chapter was written by Professor Terry H. Wagar, Department of Management, Faculty of Commerce, Saint Mary's University, Halifax, Nova Scotia.

CHAPTER GOALS

"IBM begins cutting jobs!" "Fiat shakeup will cost 6000 jobs!" "Sweeping cutbacks hit Ford." "British Airways to cut staff 12% as cost saving!"[1] No, these are not sample headlines from the downsizing era of the 1990s. Rather, they are but a small sample of employee cutbacks announced in 2001 and 2002. While some observers argued that downsizing was a thing of the past, there is growing evidence that this is not the case.

This chapter provides a discussion of a number of key issues relating to downsizing and restructuring. After describing the downsizing phenomenon and providing a definition of downsizing, we explore why organizations engage in downsizing. Considerable attention is paid to the downsizing decision, the impact of downsizing on the survivors and the organization, and the components of an effective downsizing strategy. The chapter concludes with an overview of the linkages between downsizing and HRM issues.

After reading this chapter, you should be able to do the following:

1. Appreciate the importance of defining "downsizing."
2. Be familiar with the complexity of the downsizing decision.

3. Recognize the need to address concerns of both the victims and survivors of downsizing.
4. Be aware of the consequences of downsizing.
5. Understand what downsizing strategies are effective in enhancing organizational performance.
6. Comprehend the concept of the "psychological contract."
7. Develop an awareness of the importance of HRM in managing the downsizing process.

THE DOWNSIZING PHENOMENON

downsizing activities undertaken to improve organizational efficiency, productivity, and/or competitiveness that affect the size of the firm's workforce, the costs, and the work processes

downsizing strategies strategies to improve an organization's efficiency by reducing the workforce, redesigning the work, or changing the systems of the organization

In the 1990s, organizations became obsessed with reducing the workforce and operating in a "lean and mean" fashion. However, there is growing evidence that a number of firms became too "lean" and **downsizing** cut into the muscle of the organization. Furthermore, a number of the reductions have been characterized as "mean"—destroying the lives of victims of cutbacks and leaving a demoralized and frightened group of "survivors." In today's environment, downsizing and restructuring are critical components of HR planning.

Until the 1990s, the focus of many organizations was on growth or the "bigger is better" syndrome. As a result, managers responsible for developing a **downsizing strategy** often had little experience in effectively managing the HR planning process and very little guidance from the management literature. Although the last 10 to 15 years has seen a considerable volume of articles on downsizing and restructuring, the suggestions they contain often are based on a single experience, are not supported by research, and frequently are in conflict. For instance, should cuts be targeted or across the board? Will the firm's stock price increase or decrease when the firm announces a major layoff or restructuring? Should an employer carry out all the cuts at once or stage them over a period of time?

Downsizing is not simply a Canadian phenomenon. Organizations around the world are striving to improve their competitive position and respond to the challenges of a global economy. Furthermore, downsizing is not restricted to the private sector—governments intent on trimming deficits and managing costs reduced public service employment in dramatic ways, and cutbacks in traditionally secure industries such as education, health care, and government became very common over the past decade.[2]

DEFINING DOWNSIZING AND RESTRUCTURING

It is important to clarify what is meant by the word *downsizing*. Managers and academics use it to mean a number of different activities: some examples of words used as synonyms for downsizing include building-down, de-hiring, de-recruitment, reduction in force, resizing, and rightsizing (for a summary of words used to describe downsizing, see Box 11.1). Obviously, it is difficult to understand the effect of downsizing if we do not understand clearly what it means.

Kim Cameron, a leading scholar in the area of organizational change, has defined downsizing in the following way: "Downsizing is a set of activities undertaken on the part of management and designed to improve organizational efficiency, productivity, and/or competitiveness. It represents a strategy implemented by managers that affects the size of the firm's workforce, the costs, and the work processes."[3]

Cameron identifies three types of downsizing strategies:

- ***Workforce reduction:*** Typically a short-term strategy aimed at cutting the number of employees through such programs as attrition, early retirement or voluntary severance packages, and layoffs or terminations. While a number of these approaches allow for a relatively quick reduction of the workforce, the problem is that their impact is often short term, and, in many instances, the organization loses valuable human resources.

workforce reduction a short-term strategy to cut the number of employees through attrition, early retirement or voluntary severance packages, and layoffs or terminations, etc.

- ***Work redesign:*** Often a medium-term strategy in which organizations focus on work processes and assess whether specific functions, products, and/or services should be changed or eliminated. This strategy, which is frequently combined with workforce reduction, includes such things as the elimination of functions, groups, or divisions; the reduction of bureaucracy; and the redesign of the tasks that employees perform. Since some planning is required, this strategy takes somewhat longer to implement and gets away from the problem of the organization simply doing what it always has done but with fewer people.

work redesign a medium-term strategy in which organizations focus on work processes and assess whether specific functions, products, and/or services should be changed or eliminated

It is possible to rank the work activities of the organization based on their importance to the business strategy. In carrying out this task, it is important to examine more carefully those activities within the business. Work can be classified into four categories: (1) competitive advantage work—core work processes; (2) strategic support work, which assists in completing competitive advantage work; (3) essential support work, which is not a source of competitive advantage but must be completed if the firm is to continue to operate (e.g., completing tax or zoning forms); and (4) non-essential work, which does not add value and is not required for the firm to operate but continues to be done because of past organizational practices.[4] The elimination of non-essential work often produces significant benefits for the organization.

- ***Systematic change:*** Long-term strategy characterized by changing the organization's culture and the attitudes and values of employees with the ongoing goal of reducing costs and enhancing quality. By its very nature, this strategy takes considerable time to implement. The thrust of the strategy is to consider downsizing as an evolutionary part of an organization's life with the goal of continuous improvement—employees assume

systematic change a long-term strategy that changes the organization's culture and attitudes and values of employees with the goal of reducing costs and enhancing quality

responsibility for cutting costs and searching for improved methods and practices. Because of the human and financial commitment to this strategy, the impact on the organization's bottom line is rarely immediate, and, consequently, the approach is less than appealing to firms that focus on short-term profits or budget goals.

Although a number of the downsizing efforts of the 1990s were limited to reducing the size of the workforce, many employers discovered that merely cutting back the number of people in the organization was not sufficient to achieve organizational goals. Consequently, some firms began placing more attention on "rightsizing" or "restructuring" the workplace.

There are three types of restructuring: (1) portfolio restructuring, which involves changes to the business portfolio of the organization; (2) financial restructuring, which may include such financial changes as reducing cash flow or increasing levels of debt; and (3) organizational restructuring, which is "any major reconfiguration of internal administrative structure that is associated with an intentional management change program."[5] While portfolio and finan-

BOX 11.1 Examples of Words Used to Describe Downsizing

Axed	Rationalized
Building-down	Reallocated
Chopped	Rebalanced
Compressed	Redeployed
Consolidated	Redesigned
Declining	Reduction-in-force
De-grown	RIF'd
De-hired	Redundancy elimination
De-massed	Re-engineered
De-recruitment	Reorganized
De-staffed	Reshaped
Disemployed	Resized
Dismantled	Resource allocation
Displaced	Restructured
Downshifted	Retrenched
Downsized	Rightsized
Fired	Slimmed
Involuntarily separated	Slivered
Personnel surplus reduction	Streamlined
Ratcheted down	Workforce imbalance correction

Sources: These examples are taken from various sources including K. Cameron, "Strategies for Successful Organizational Downsizing," *Human Resource Management*, Vol. 33 (1994), pp. 189–211; M. Moore, *Downsize This*, New York: Harper Perennial, 1996; and L. Ryan and K. Macky, "Downsizing Organizations: Uses, Outcomes and Strategies," *Asia Pacific Journal of Human Resources*, Vol. 36 (1998), pp. 29–45.

cial restructuring are important, the emphasis in this chapter will be on organizational restructuring.

It is important, when considering downsizing, to distinguish an approach involving a reduction in the number of employees with one based on a strategically oriented organizational redesign or restructuring.[6]

How Common Is Workforce Reduction and Restructuring?

One issue that comes up regularly involves how common workforce reduction is in Canada. In a national study of major Canadian organizations conducted in 1992 and in 1997–98, it was found that 56% of respondents permanently reduced the workforce over a two-year period ending in 1992, while 50% cut back the number of employees during the two-year period prior to 1997–98. About 31% of employers reduced the workforce in both 1992 and 1997–98 and 25% of organizations did not engage in workforce cutbacks in either period.[7]

Three recent studies (conducted in 2001 and 2002)[8] found that between 40 and 45% of participants reported that their organization permanently reduced the workforce over a two-year period. Moreover, when we consider the size of the workforce reduction, we are not talking about a small percentage of employees losing their jobs. Among organizations reducing the workforce, the average reduction was around 15% of the workforce. Similarly, when investigating how the workforce reductions were carried out, combining the results from the studies revealed that about 35% of the reductions were by attrition, 25% by voluntary severance or early retirement, and 40% by layoffs. Compared with the 1990s, these results suggest that organizations are relying less on layoffs and more on voluntary severance or early retirement programs as a means of reducing the number of employees.

There also appears to be a movement away from targeting higher-paid, more senior employees in workforce reduction efforts. For example, in 1999 the average tenure of those individuals terminated from employment was 9.8 years, but for 2001, the average tenure was only 4.8 years. The results suggest that employers are now more likely to discharge new hires and retain more experienced workers.[9]

In order to provide more information on the extent to which employers are restructuring the workplace and introducing organizational change, the results of three surveys conducted in 2001–2002 were merged; the findings are presented in Figure 11.1. Overall, about 15% of Canadian organizations are involved in an extensive restructuring program. The most common activities include eliminating unnecessary tasks, redesigning jobs, increasing collaboration among functional areas, and increasing the use of cross-functional teams. However, there is considerable variation across organizations with respect to restructuring and change efforts.

FIGURE 11.1 RESTRUCTURING AND ORGANIZATIONAL CHANGE

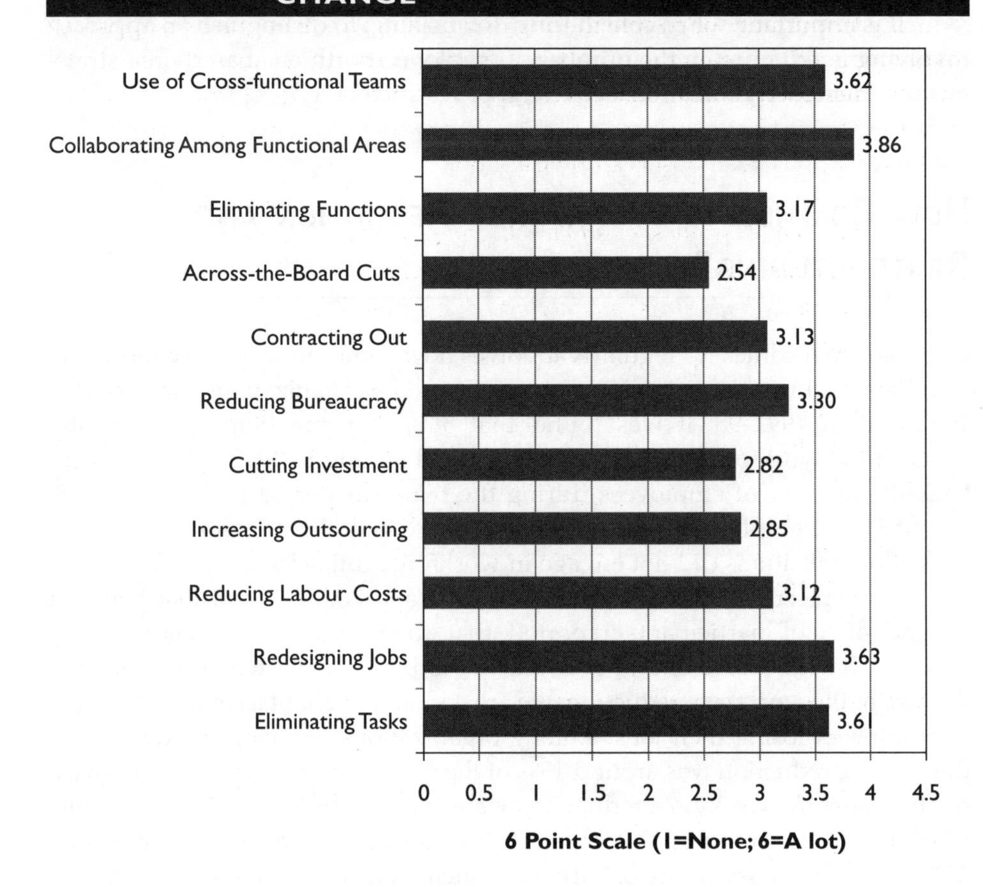

Why Do Organizations Downsize?

There are several reasons why organizations decide to downsize the workforce. Some of the factors most commonly mentioned include the following:

- Declining profits
- Business downturn or increased pressure from competitors
- Merging with another organization, resulting in duplication of efforts
- Introduction of new technology
- The need to reduce operating costs
- The desire to decrease levels of management
- Getting rid of employee "deadwood"

Simply put, many organizations engage in downsizing because managers believe that cutting people will result in reduced costs (with costs being more predictable than future revenues) and improved financial performance. In addition, labour costs are often seen as easier to adjust relative to other expenditures (such as capital investment). Although executives often perceive that reducing the number of people in the organization will lead to lower overhead costs, reduced bureaucracy, better communications, improved decision-making, increased innovative activity, and higher productivity, there is considerable evidence that workforce reduction programs often fail to meet their objectives, as has been observed by Cascio:[10]

> *Study after study shows that following a downsizing, surviving employees become narrow-minded, self-absorbed, and risk averse. Morale sinks, productivity drops, and survivors distrust management.*

Some organizations drastically reduce the workforce and employ a severe reduction strategy despite increasing demand and a favourable competitive environment.[11] This development, which has been mentioned by HR managers in personal interviews, may be due to a variety of reasons, including a decision to follow the lead of other firms engaging in cutback management and an increasing awareness of the need to operate in a lean and mean fashion.

The Downsizing Decision

For many organizations, going through a downsizing is a very painful and difficult experience. A 1994 article in *Business Week* profiled Robert Thrasher, executive vice-president at Nynex and the individual responsible for cutting 16 800 jobs. While he would prefer to be considered a change agent, he has been labelled the "corporate assassin." In speaking about downsizing, Thrasher commented,[12] "This is tough, ugly work. The stress is palpable. I'm vilified throughout the company ... that's a tough thing to carry around."

More recently, Robert Burton of Moore Corporation, when discussing his role in a cost-cutting plan at a previous company, stated: "I don't get frustrated any more. I just fire people."[13]

Too often, organizations embark on a downsizing program without careful consideration of whether there are feasible alternatives to downsizing. Study after study reveals that many downsizings are not well planned, frequently ignore the linkage between downsizing and the strategic direction of the organization, and underestimate the impact of downsizing on the organization and its human resources.

Alternatives to Downsizing

Downsizing can be a costly strategy for organizations to pursue, and, as a result, it is desirable to investigate whether alternatives to downsizing exist. In a number of instances, organizations discover that pursuing different alternatives to downsizing may eliminate the need to reduce the workforce or allow for a less severe downsizing strategy.

Some of the alternatives include (1) cutting nonpersonnel costs (e.g., through energy conservation, planned capital expenditures, leasing of capital equipment, reductions in travel or club memberships); (2) cutting personnel costs (e.g., through a hiring freeze, job sharing, a reduction in work hours, reduced benefits, wage concessions); and (3) providing incentives for voluntary resignation or early retirement.[14] Although this list is not complete, it emphasizes the need to consider other ways to manage costs within an organization.

One organization, High Road Communications Inc., asked each member of its staff to take one week of unpaid leave during the summer months. According to senior partner Mia Wedgbury, "It let us keep our core team together while reducing costs. And it went over well with the staff because it precluded layoffs."[15] Another organization, Acxion Corporation, cut the pay of each employee earning more than $25 000 by 5% but also gave the employee the option to buy company stock that would be matched one-for-one by the firm.[16]

Inplacement and Outplacement Issues

inplacement reabsorbing excess or inappropriately placed workers into a restructured organization

outplacement providing a program of counselling and job-search assistance for workers who have been terminated

In examining the downsizing decision, it is necessary to consider both inplacement and outplacement issues.[17] **Inplacement** refers to a career management approach aimed at reabsorbing excess or inappropriately placed workers into a restructured organization, while **outplacement** focuses on the provision of a program of counselling and job-search assistance for workers who have been terminated. In making career management decisions, organizational decision-makers may opt for an inplacement program or termination with outplacement.

In a survey of Canadian manufacturing firms completed in 2000, organizations that had gone through downsizing were asked to report on the benefits they provided to displaced workers. These results are provided in Figure 11.2. The most common benefits were severance pay, continuation of employee benefits, outplacement counselling, and an extended notice period. A minority of firms provided retraining assistance or family counselling.

Planning for Downsizing

Assuming the organization has decided to embark on a downsizing strategy, planning is essential. Some key issues include the following:

- Determining how many people will lose their jobs
- Determining who will be let go. For example, will the decision be made on the basis of seniority, performance, or potential?
- Determining how the reduction will be carried out. For example, to what extent will the organization use attrition, early retirement or voluntary severance programs, and layoffs or termination? It is possible to consider the

FIGURE 11.2 BENEFITS TO DISPLACED WORKERS

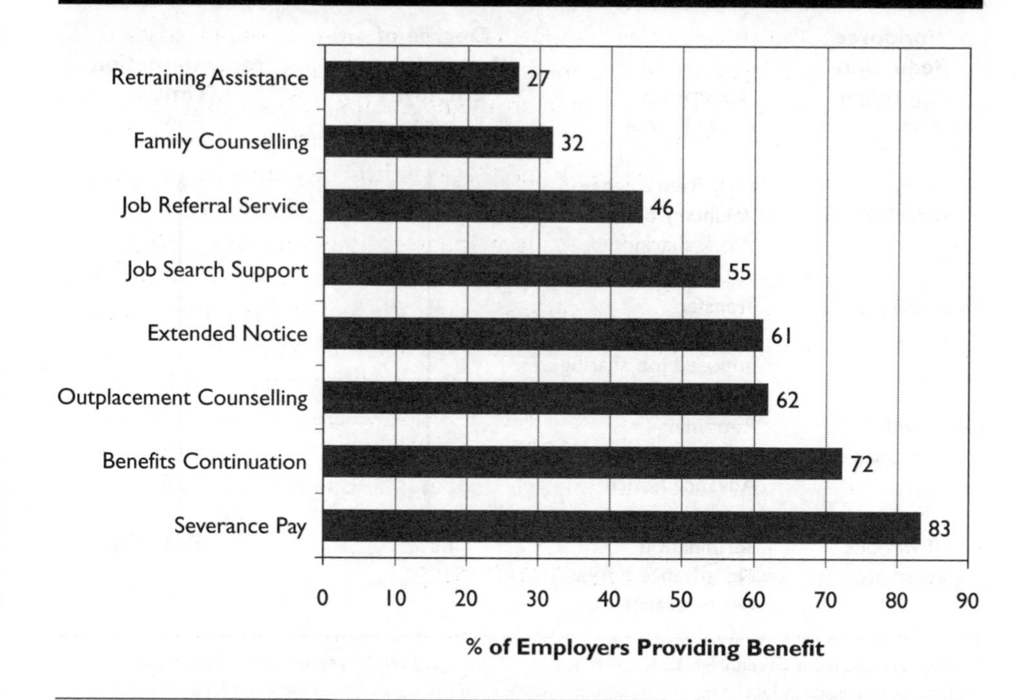

Note: The data from this figure are from Terry H. Wagar, Managing Change and Human Resources: Results from a Canadian Study of Employers in Manufacturing, Saint Mary's University, 2000.

approach to workforce reduction from the perspective of the employee? As indicated in Figure 11.3, the approaches to workforce reduction vary in the degree of protection to employees and the cost to employers.

- Determining the legal consequences. For example, organizations often ignore or are unaware of legal requirements when downsizing the workforce. Some areas of law to be aware of include the law of wrongful dismissal, employment standards legislation, trade union law, existing collective agreement provisions, and human rights legislation. For instance, there may be a very narrow line between voluntary and involuntary termination, and with the termination of older workers, there exists a possibility of an age discrimination claim.[18]
- Designing current and future work plans. This issue represents a key challenge for the organization and is frequently neglected.
- Implementing the decision. Implementation includes such elements as severance payments, outplacement counselling, the communication of the termination decision, the timing of the decision, security issues, and communications with remaining employees.
- Performing follow-up evaluation and assessment. Although this step is critical, it is often ignored in many organizations.[19]

FIGURE 11.3 APPROACHES TO WORKFORCE REDUCTION

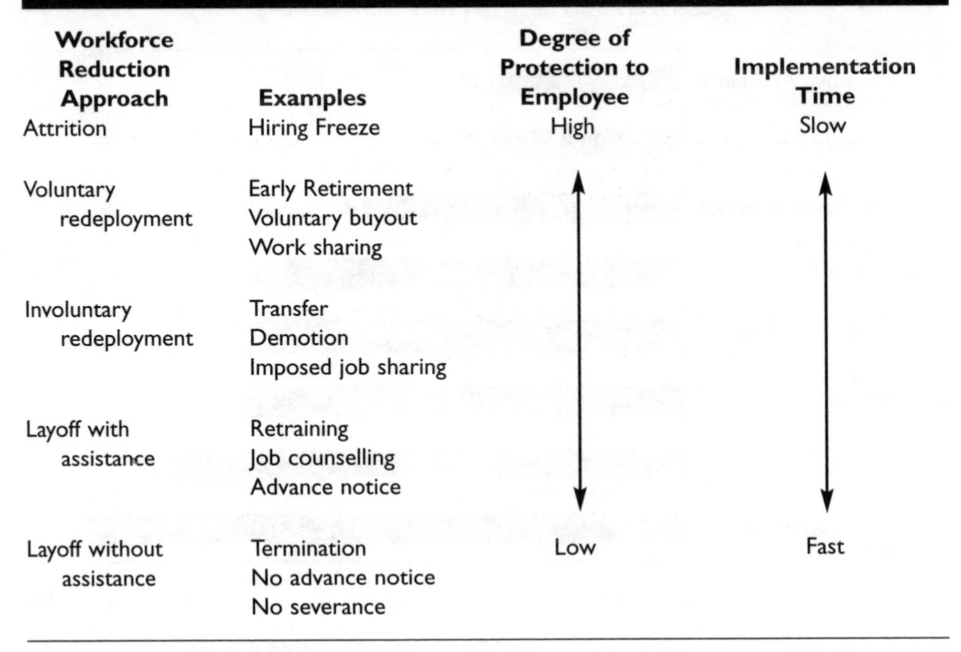

Workforce Reduction Approach	Examples	Degree of Protection to Employee	Implementation Time
Attrition	Hiring Freeze	High	Slow
Voluntary redeployment	Early Retirement Voluntary buyout Work sharing		
Involuntary redeployment	Transfer Demotion Imposed job sharing		
Layoff with assistance	Retraining Job counselling Advance notice		
Layoff without assistance	Termination No advance notice No severance	Low	Fast

Source: Adapted from Greenhalgh, L., A. Lawrence, and R. Sutton. 1988. "Determinants of Workforce Reduction Strategies in Declining Organizations," *Academy of Management Review*, Vol. 13, pp. 241–254.

ADJUSTING TO JOB LOSS

Workers who have lost their jobs frequently experience tremendous pain. As well, job loss can be very difficult for family members (see Box 11.2). Furthermore, many downsized employees are very bitter and angry with their former employer. A U.S. study of downsized workers revealed that 67% would never work for their former company again, 54% would not recommend that others purchase the organization's products or services, and 11% considered going to the media and talking about their layoff experiences.[20]

A number of organizational interventions and practices have been identified as helping previously employed workers adjust to job loss and secure new employment.[21] They include the following:

- Advance notification of layoffs, which gives employees time to deal with the reality of job loss and to seek future employment
- Severance pay and extended benefits, which provide an economic safety net
- Education and retraining programs, which give individuals time to acquire marketable skills
- Outplacement assistance to inform employees of new job opportunities and to improve their ability to "market" themselves

BOX 11.2 Parents' Job Insecurity and Children's Work Beliefs

Does the job insecurity of parents influence the work beliefs and attitudes of their children? Three researchers at Queen's University collected data from undergraduate students, their mothers, and their fathers in seeking to answer this question.

The results of the study indicated that children who observed their parents experiencing layoffs and job insecurity were able to perceive that insecurity and develop negative work beliefs that in turn predict their work-related attitudes. In other words, family stressors result in negative consequences for children.

Source: Adapted from J. Barling, K. Dupre, and C. Hepburn, "Effects of Parents' Job Insecurity on Children's Work Beliefs and Attitudes," *Journal of Applied Psychology*, Vol. 83 (1998), pp. 112–118.

- Clear, direct, and empathetic announcement of layoff decisions
- Consideration of HR planning practices that represent alternatives to large-scale layoffs

The "Survivors" of Downsizing

Although we see media accounts of people rebounding from downsizing and starting a new life for themselves, the reality is that for many individuals, the pain of being downsized is very severe. The impact on family life, career plans, and personal esteem are devastating and the social costs can be enormous.

What about the survivors of a downsizing? How do employees that remain with an organization react? Here is a description of a typical response:[22]

> *The initial anger and pain are often followed by fear and cynicism. Stress, bred of uncertainty and the necessity of doing more with less, skyrockets. Trust in the company and its management plummets. Employees who remain spend their days juggling more work and avoiding anything that approaches risk taking or innovation.*

Although surviving a downsizing can be traumatic, there is growing evidence that perceptions of **job insecurity** (even in the absence of a downsizing) may be associated with negative consequences for employees and employers. Job insecurity has been defined as "an individual's expectations about continuity in a job situation" or "overall concern about the future existence of a job."[23] In other words, employees in organizations that have not downsized may have perceptions of job insecurity, which has been related to impaired well-being, increased stress, mental distress, and lower job satisfaction.[24]

job insecurity feeling of concern about the continuing existence of a job

Perceptions of Justice

Perceptions of fairness and equity play a key role in understanding how survivors of a downsizing react to the experience. In examining the survivors of downsizing, three types of justice warrant consideration:[25]

procedural justice procedures or rules that determine which employees will be downsized

interactional justice the interpersonal treatment employees receive during the implementation of the downsizing decision

distributive justice the fairness of the downsizing decision

- ***Procedural justice:*** This focuses on the procedures (or "decision rules") used to determine which employees will leave or remain with the organization.
- ***Interactional justice:*** This addresses the type of interpersonal treatment employees receive during the implementation of the downsizing decision.
- ***Distributive justice:*** This deals with the fairness of the downsizing decision. For example, responses from employees may include feelings of guilt after seeing co-workers lose their jobs, support for the downsizing decision as necessary for the firm, or feelings of unfairness and concern that further layoffs may place their own jobs in jeopardy.

Survivor Reactions

There is considerable evidence that downsizing may produce a number of dysfunctional behaviours among the employees who remain with the organization. Some of these impacts are discussed below:[26]

- *Negative attitudes and behaviours:* In a number of downsizings, employees who retain their jobs report increased job insecurity, fear, stress, and burnout. They may also experience lower self-confidence and self-esteem, reduced job satisfaction, and lower commitment to the organization. Not surprisingly, these factors may lead to increased turnover, absenteeism, and lateness.
- *Reduced performance capabilities:* There is growing evidence that it is not necessarily the poor performers who leave the downsized organization. Of particular concern to organizations is the fear that the best employees will leave, since quality workers are more attractive to other firms. This result, which has been experienced by several organizations, undermines the HR activities of the organization.
- *Lower organizational productivity:* Negative employee attitudes and behaviour, in conjunction with lower performance capabilities, may destroy or markedly harm team activities and result in lower productivity.

Few studies have focused specifically on managers' reactions to downsizing. One exception is a study interestingly entitled "Voices of Survivors: Words That Downsizing CEOs Should Hear."[27] The authors conducted interviews with middle managers who had survived a downsizing in their organization (a large financial services firm). The managers were trying to come to grips with what happened, attempting to figure out their new roles as change agents and mentors in the new organization, and struggling to make sense of what had happened. Among the emotions that emerged were the following:

- *Anger:* For instance, one manager stated, "Stop telling us to work smarter. Show us how.... Stop blaming us! We've been loyal to the company. We've worked hard and did everything we were told."
- *Anxiety:* Comments included "We don't know who we are anymore." "We talk about empowerment, but we've still got shackles on people. We have to go to senior managers for permission."
- *Cynicism:* There is often very little trust in upper management.
- *Resentment:* Employees frequently compare their rewards with those of others, and even small symbols of inequity trigger emotional responses.
- *Retribution:* There is a need to redress past problems and then move on with the business of improving the new organization.
- *Hope:* While negative feelings often dominate in a downsizing environment, there are occasional voices of hope and expressions of a desire to enhance quality and productivity and rebuild the organization. However, those who are hopeful also believe it is essential that organizational structures not get in the way of rebuilding the organization.

Impact on the "Downsizers"

Although there has been a fair bit of research on the survivors of downsizing, what about the individuals who are responsible for carrying out the downsizing and actually terminating members of the workforce? In a recent study, detailed interviews were conducted with ten managers responsible for implementing the

BOX 11.3 White-collar Reactions to Job Insecurity

Are insecure white-collar employees less committed to their organizations and more concerned about their own careers? A recent study of more than 400 white-collar workers examined the relationship between job insecurity and a variety of employee and employer-oriented outcomes.

The results of the study indicated that a higher level of job insecurity was associated with the following:

- Less effort to ensure that the quality of the individual's work was higher than his or her peers,
- A lower score on "organizational citizenship behaviour" (which involves engaging in activities such as volunteering for things not required by the organization or helping out new employees),
- Lower organizational loyalty (commitment to the organization),
- Higher levels of career loyalty (a focus on the individual's career), and
- More job search behaviour (seeking alternative employment).

Source: Adapted from J. King, "White-Collar Reactions to Job Insecurity and the Role of the Psychological Contract: Implications for Human Resource Management," *Human Resource Management*, Vol. 39 (2000), pp. 79–92.

downsizing. The results showed that participating in the downsizing process was very difficult for a number of the managers. Of particular note was the experience of social and organizational isolation, a decline in personal health and well-being, and an increase in family-related problems.[28]

A number of downsizers begin speaking in less personal terms when talking about their job—for instance, a workforce reduction may be described as a realignment or "revectoring." According to Nora Spinks, a workplace consultant, "The more impersonal it gets, the easier it is on an emotional level. In the early nineties, executives tried to justify job reductions by using terms such as downsizing and rightsizing. Now, they talk of realigning or repositioning, which emphasizes broad strategic objectives."[29]

Financial Performance and Downsizing

Do organizations that have reduced their workforces perform better than other firms? This is an important question—one would anticipate that organizations engaging in downsizing expect that their financial performance will improve.

While some analysts suggest that downsizing will improve the value of a firm's stock, investors generally respond negatively to the announcement of a layoff, particularly if the reduction is due to financial factors or involves a large-scale permanent cutback of employees. A Canadian study that examined the effect of a layoff announcement on stock market prices found that shareholders generally reacted negatively to the announcement, particularly when a large percentage of the workforce was let go.[30]

When we look at financial performance outcomes, the research results do not paint a very clear picture. One study of the financial performance of Fortune 100 firms revealed that firms engaging in layoffs continued to perform much more poorly than organizations not laying off employees.[31] Another study, involving major Canadian firms, found no consistent relationship between downsizing and profitability.[32] A third study, of 250 large U.S. corporations, indicated that workforce reduction was associated with improved financial performance, particularly in the short term.[33]

Why the conflicting results? In examining the various studies, it is difficult to make comparisons because authors don't use similar measures of performance and each defines downsizing somewhat differently. In addition, the research tends to look at workforce reduction behaviour without considering the overall downsizing strategy.

However, there is some U.S. evidence supporting the position that improved return on assets and common stock may be related, at least in part, to the downsizing strategy employed by the organization.[34] Firms following a "pure employment" downsizing (a workforce cutback of at least 5% but little change in plant and equipment expenditure) did not outperform other firms in their industry. However, "asset downsizers" (firms that cut at least 5% of the workforce accompanied by a decline of at least 5% in expenditures on plant and equipment) generated higher returns relative to other industry competitors.

Consequences of Downsizing

There is growing evidence that many downsizing efforts fall well short of meeting organizational objectives. Moreover, many workforce reductions are carried out with little strategic planning or consideration of the costs to the individuals and the employer.[35] More often, job cuts represent a short-term reaction to a much more complex problem. Senior executives often focus on financial issues during a reorganization, but the benefits of restructuring frequently fail to transpire if HR issues are not carefully thought out and resolved appropriately.

Despite the guilt associated with permanently reducing the workforce, a growing number of firms are willing to downsize but are discovering that workforce reduction can lead to many unwanted consequences.[36] Some of these consequences include the high human costs, psychological trauma experienced both by those let go and the survivors, reduced employee commitment, lower performance among employees due to job insecurity, greater attention by management to the downsizing process while ignoring customer and client needs, loss of valuable employees, a shift from innovation to protection of one's turf, lower morale, and potential litigation by employees who believe that they are victims of discrimination.

Some Canadian Evidence

One study of almost 1300 major Canadian organizations investigated the relationship between permanent workforce reduction and a number of organizational outcomes.[37] Employers experiencing a workforce reduction were more likely to report that expenses had been cut as low as possible and that the organization was better able to control operating expenses. In addition, employers experiencing a workforce reduction perceived that the downsizing had a negative impact on the firm's reputation. Furthermore, the downsizing firms were more likely to perceive problems relating to financial performance.

The most dramatic results were found when investigating employee relations issues. There was a strong relationship between permanent workforce reduction and eight of the nine "people outcomes" examined in the study.

Organizations engaging in employee cutbacks were more likely to experience more employee resistance to change, lower employee morale, more critical employee perceptions of top management, more conflict within the organization, higher turnover, more feeling of job insecurity, greater stress among managers, and loss of credibility among top management.

Two other studies also shed light on the effect of downsizing on the workplace and its people. One study of almost 2000 Canadian workplaces indicated that establishments reporting employee cutbacks also had lower overall employee satisfaction and less favourable employer–employee relations.[38] The second study examined "serial downsizers" (that is, firms that had downsized the workforce both when the study began and five years later). The serial downsizers had the poorest scores when considering changes in employee satisfaction (for instance, poorer morale, quality of work life, commitment to the organization). While the "late downsizers" also had negative scores on the employee satisfaction measures, the scores for "early downsizers" did not significantly differ from those of employers that did not downsize throughout the period of the study. In other words, it appears that the negative consequences on employees that were associated with the early downsizing had dissipated over the five-year period.[39]

Workforce reduction has a more immediate impact on the people in the organization—the effect on performance and efficiency outcomes may be more long term. However, the degree to which this poses a problem is open to question. If a single organization acting alone decided to engage in workforce cutbacks, the employees would have the option of seeking alternative employment; however, in an economy in which several firms are downsizing, frustrated employees have few alternative employment opportunities and survivors may be unwilling to engage in negative behaviour for fear that they would lose the jobs they currently hold.[40] Still, firms that have not treated employees well may encounter difficulties in attracting and keeping quality employees when the demand for workers is high.

Effective Downsizing Strategies

Some organizations are not lean and mean, and downsizing may be an appropriate strategic response. However, cutting the number of people in an organization is not a "quick fix" remedy: prior to embarking on any workforce reduction effort, firms should carefully consider the consequences. Considerable care and planning must go into the decision, and the reasons for the reduction must be effectively communicated to employees. Organizations tend to focus on workforce reduction while ignoring the critical aspects of redesigning the organization and the implementation of cultural change. In addition, managers frequently have little experience or training with regard to downsizing and restructuring.

From a strategic perspective, an important decision involves answering such questions as these: Should we downsize? When should we do it? How should we do it? The focus should be on *rightsizing,* which involves establishing a shared vision of the organization and a clearly stated strategy supported by management, understood by employees, and involving a sense of "ownership" by members of the firm.[41]

It is critical that the HR department play a very active role in the early stages of formulating a downsizing strategy. There is evidence that negative outcomes associated with downsizing could be mitigated by increased communication and employee participation and systematic analysis (in advance) of tasks and personnel requirements.[42] In addition, senior management must take an aggressive, visible, and interactive role in formulating the downsizing strategy. However, the identification, development, and implementation procedures should involve the employees. In many instances, the identification of inefficiencies and areas where improvements are possible is best left to employees, who typically are in a better position to make such judgments.

Strategic Downsizing

Why do so many workforce reduction programs fail to meet expectations? More than half the organizations engaging in downsizing had no policies or programs to address problems associated with cutting human resources, and several organizations failed to anticipate the dramatic impacts workforce reduction has on the work environment, employees, customers, and clients. Furthermore, many downsizing efforts were not carefully thought out or integrated as part of the organization's overall strategic plan.

In a number of instances, organizations embarking on a downsizing strategy are also going through considerable organizational change. As indicated in Box 11.4, there are several change issues to be considered by organizations seeking to remain competitive in today's economy.

An effective downsizing is dependent on comprehensive planning for change; proper communication of the plan; credibility of the organization with employees, customers, suppliers, and other stakeholders; and consideration and compassion for both employees who are terminated and those remaining with the organization.[43] Moreover, firms engaging in downsizing typically focus only on workforce reduction aspects of the strategy and ignore the more time-consuming but critical strategies of redesigning the organization and developing a systematic strategy predicated on massive cultural change within the firm. Research in both Canada and the United States indicates that while almost all organizations engaging in downsizing focus on the first component (workforce reduction), only about one-half make some attempt at work redesign and less than one-third implement a systematic change strategy.

One study compared the effect of the three downsizing strategies (workforce reduction, organizational redesign, and systematic change) on two performance outcome measures (cost reduction and quality improvement).[44] It was found that the workforce reduction strategy was negatively related to organizational performance while the organizational redesign and systematic change strategies were associated with improved performance. In other words, firms that simply focus on reducing the number of employees typically will find the results fail to meet organizational objectives. Moreover, mutual trust between employees and senior management plays an important role in the success of

BOX 11.4 Organizational Change and Downsizing

Characteristic	Old Approach	New Approach
Organizational structure	Functional specialization	Matrix/cross-functional teams
Operational focus	Internal (production)	External (customer/client)
Decision-making	Top down	Bottom up
Response to change	Centralized	Decentralized
Communication	Slow	Fast
Career paths	Downward	Multidirectional
Recognition	Hierarchical	Lateral/diagonal
	Individual	Teamwork

Source: Adapted from N. Mathys and E. Burack, "Strategic Downsizing: Human Resource Planning Approaches," *Human Resource Planning*, Vol. 16 (1993), pp. 71–85. Reprinted with permisson by the Human Resource Planning Society, 317 Madison Ave., Suite 1509, New York, NY 10017, Phone: (212) 490-6387, fax: (212) 682-6851.

organizational redesign and systematic change strategies. The creation of a culture of trust is essential prior to embarking on a downsizing strategy.

It has been noted that an effective downsizing strategy requires a consideration of

1. the tactics used to reduce the workforce (for instance, the time over which downsizing will take place, the use of harsh tactics such as layoff, and the provision of outplacement assistance),
2. the implementation processes used during downsizing and the redesign of work (for example, employee participation in the change process, communication issues, and the degree to which the organization engages in a systematic analysis of structure, work, and human resource needs), and
3. the changes to or impacts on structures and processes within the organization.[45]

Of particular relevance is whether the organization follows a strategy in which downsizing drives redesign (that is, getting the work done with fewer people) or whether redesign drives downsizing (in other words, what is key is changing the way the work is done). While either of the approaches can be use proactively or reactively, the redesign-drives-downsizing strategy will see much greater changes within the organization and a dominant focus on restructuring.

Effective and Ineffective Downsizing Strategies

A number of studies have pointed out downsizing strategies and practices that do not work. For instance, one study identified nine ineffective downsizing practices (most of which have been identified in other studies):

1. Offering voluntary early-retirement programs
2. Instituting across-the-board layoffs
3. Eliminating training programs
4. Making personnel cutbacks that are too deep
5. Placing survivors in jobs for which they lack the necessary skills and hoping that they will learn by experience
6. Emphasizing employee accountability instead of employee involvement
7. Expecting survivors to "row harder"
8. Implementing layoffs slowly in phases over time
9. Promising high monetary rewards rather than careers[46]

One set of studies attempted to identify the practices that distinguished successful and unsuccessful workforce reduction efforts.[47] Five key issues associated with more successful downsizings were as follows:

1. *An expressed higher commitment to job security:* A number of successful organizations met with survivors of workforce reduction and assured them that they were an important component of the restructured organization.
2. *An ideology based on progressive decision-making and a culture that focuses on human resources:* Again, organizations with these attributes were overwhelmingly more likely to have higher economic performance and overall employee satisfaction scores. A progressive decision-making ideology is characterized by participative decision-making, explanations of proposed changes to those affected, open channels of communication, and employee input into the decision-making process.
3. *An entrepreneurial spirit within the organization:* Organizations that performed better after a workforce reduction were more likely to underscore the importance of both innovation in the development of new products or services and the presence of an entrepreneurial culture.
4. *Investment in training, new technology, and a quality management/customer/client focus:* While there is often a tendency to cut training and investment in new technology, organizations with lower investment in these two areas tended to be less successful in their workforce reduction strategies. Similarly, moving away from a focus on quality and the customer leads to a number of negative consequences.
5. *The manner in which the workforce reduction was carried out:* While there was little evidence that aspects of the severance arrangement provided to employees who were let go was associated with enhanced performance, the results indicated that more successful reductions were characterized by the following:
   - The reasons for the reduction were clearly explained to employees.
   - The employees perceived that the cuts were necessary.
   - Employee input into the decision-making process was fair.

- The methods used to select which employees to let go were communicated to employees.
- Employees perceived that the assistance provided to workers who were let go was fair.
- Cuts were targeted rather than across the board.
- Downsizing was part of the strategic management process.

The role of communications in the downsizing decision cannot be overemphasized. Consider the experience of one receptionist in a dot-com firm—"They called us down for a meeting and told us the dream was over. They laid everyone off. The company is gone."[48]

It is important to (1) attend to rumours, (2) provide survivors with available information on the downsizing, (3) ensure that survivors are aware of the new organizational goals, (4) make expectations clear, (5) tell survivors that they are valued, and (6) allow time for grieving.[49] Box 11.5 contains a summary of some key points of effective downsizing.

BOX 11.5 Some Key Issues in Effective Downsizing

Approach

Envision downsizing as a long-term strategy.

Treat the organization's human resources as assets.

Develop early warning signals to identify HR needs.

Establish HR planning systems that focus on redeployment of the organization's human assets.

Prepare in advance for downsizing.

Downsizing Strategy

Formulate strategy based on the future mission of the organization and its core competencies.

Communicate in a direct, honest, and empathetic manner with employees.

Involve employees in the design and implementation of worker assistance programs.

Carefully consider the impact of downsizing on employees, the organization, customers, and the community.

Cooperate with relevant organizations, agencies, and institutions (such as labour unions, government agencies, community groups, and educational institutions).

Ensure that organizational leaders are visible, accessible, and interacting with the individuals affected by downsizing.

Smooth the transition for employees losing their jobs by providing safety nets (such as advance notice of layoff, severance pay, outplacement counselling, and job skills training).

Don't neglect to evaluate the impact of the downsizing strategy.

Sources: Adapted from K. Cameron, S. Freeman, and A. Mishra, "Best Practices in White Collar Downsizing: Managing Contradictions," *Academy of Management Executive*, Vol. 5 (1991), pp. 57–73; D. Feldman and C. Leana, "Better Practices in Managing Layoffs," *Human Resource Management*, Vol. 33 (1994), pp. 239–260; B. Kane, "Downsizing, TQM, Re-engineering, Learning Organizations and HRM Strategy," *Asia Pacific Journal of Human Resources*, Vol. 38 (2000), pp. 26–49.

Summary of Best Practices

A list of six best practices in downsizing firms has been developed:

1. Downsizing should be initiated from the top but requires hands-on involvement from all employees.
2. Workforce reduction must be selective in application and long-term in emphasis.
3. Special attention should be paid both to those who lose their jobs and to the survivors who remain with the organization.
4. Decision-makers should identify precisely where redundancies, excess costs, and inefficiencies exist and attack those specific areas.
5. Downsizing should result in the formation of small, semi-autonomous organizations within the broader organization.
6. Downsizing must be a proactive strategy focused on increasing performance.[50]

HRM Issues

A critical issue revolves around the impact of downsizing on an organization's HRM initiatives. In light of the growing evidence that HRM practices do matter and are related to organizational performance, it is essential that any downsizing decision be made with consideration of the impact on HRM initiatives.[51]

Managing the Changing Psychological Contract

An important part of the employment relationship is the **psychological contract** (those unwritten commitments between employers and employees). Over the past decade, the psychological contract between employers and employees has changed dramatically. Historical notions of job security and rewards for loyal and long service to the organization have, in many instances, been replaced by ongoing change, uncertainty, and considerable shedding of employees. Associated with such developments are the considerable pain, stress, and hardship inflicted on employees, including both workers who have lost jobs and those survivors who remain with an organization.

psychological contract an unwritten commitment between employers and their employees that historically guaranteed job security and loyalty

A number of organizations try, as part of their HR planning and development activities, to hire from within the firm (where possible). Such organizations develop internal labour markets in which new employees are hired at specific "ports of entry," and other positions are filled through internal transfers and promotions. Historically, employers and employees often had an implicit contract that was based on the notion that there was a mutual commitment by both employers and workers to long-term employment, and job hirings were viewed as "implicit contracts" in which employees are given certain assurances regarding security of wages and employment. However, such contracts have been radically altered or have ceased to exist in many organizations.

The "New Deal" in Employment

In recent years, many organizations have been unwilling to promise job security and continued employment to loyal senior employees. Rather, a new employment arrangement between employees and a number of employers is emerging. This "new deal" has been described in the following way:

> *You're expendable. We don't want to fire you but we will if we have to. Competition is brutal, so we must redesign the way we work to do more with less. Sorry, that's just the way it is. And one more thing—you're invaluable.... We're depending on you to be innovative, risk-taking, and committed to our goals.*[52]

What does this mean for employees? In many organizations, we have moved away from the expectation of lifetime employment.[53] Rather, workers should prepare for a "multiorganizational career" and recognize that it is highly unlikely that they will remain with the same organization throughout their working lives.

Although nonmanagerial employees have been the victims of downsizing for years, the trend toward cutting huge numbers of managers is a recent phenomenon. However, the massive cutbacks of management personnel are more than simply a response to competitive pressure or to the introduction of new technology. They demonstrate that we are experiencing a dramatic change in the employment relationship characterized by a movement away from paternalism and a community of loyalty to the new order of "community of purpose," which focuses on completion of the task or mission rather than on loyalty to the organization.[54]

Altering the Psychological Contract

How does an organization go about changing the psychological contract with its employees? There are two different approaches that may be taken:

- *Accommodation:* This approach involves working with the existing contract and changing parts of the agreement over time. For example, there may be a change in hours of work, job duties, or benefits. Although this approach is preferable in a number of instances since workers do not experience dramatic changes, it requires a positive relationship between the employer and employees.

- *Transformation:* This approach involves establishing a new employee mindset and requires workers to *radically* change the old way of doing things. Examples include moving from individual to team-based work or learning to operate new technology. There are four steps in implementing transformational contract change:
  1. *Challenge the old contract:* An organization that wants to introduce major changes to the employment contract and yet still retain valued employees needs to provide solid reasons for the changes. Without effective communication and trust, workers simply are not going to buy into the changes.
  2. *Prepare for change:* This involves creating credible signs of change (that is, that the organization is committed to change and is going to follow through), reducing losses associated with change (such as loss of authority, emotional distress, and increased uncertainty), and establishing transition structures (such as phased-in change or the setting up of task forces to help employees adjust to change).
  3. *Generate the new contract terms:* It is critical that managers communicate the new expectations and secure employee acceptance of the terms.
  4. *Live the new contract:* Organizations must make it clear that the old contract is over and there is no going back. Too often, managers send mixed messages to employees who then may try to cling to the old agreement. Training for all organization members is critical.[55]

Can flexible employment contracts be the source of product and process innovation? Despite the growth in contingent work arrangements, most organizations make relatively little use of short-term contracts. Among those employers that were using such contracts, it was rare that the primary focus was as a strategic lever to increase innovation. Rather, the major reasons for using short-term contracts were to cut labour costs and address fluctuations in product or service demand. Contracting out of key functions may negatively affect the innovation potential of an employer.[56]

Downsizing and "High-Involvement" HRM

Although it has taken some time, a growing number of organizations are introducing programs such as total quality management or continuous quality improvement, self-managed work teams, joint labour–management committees, and incentive compensation. However, a number of these same firms have also undertaken (or are planning to undertake) large-scale restructurings. From the perspective of the employee, these strategies appear to be in competition—if human resources are so valuable and worthy of development, why is the organization getting rid of its assets? Management credibility is destroyed since employees view the notion of progressive HRM practices as diametrically opposed to the shedding of workers—employee involvement and empowerment programs require employee attachment and commitment while downsizing programs focus on organizational detachment.

Can high-performance work practices exist in an environment of layoffs and restructuring? It has been argued that downsizing may be incompatible with the introduction of high-performance work practices because team-based work requires relatively stable membership of team members and high-performance work practices are based on the notion of substantial employee commitment to the organization. Research has found that the use of high-performance work practices was associated with work reorganization and a *greater* reliance on layoffs in later years.[57]

When considering the implications of downsizing from an HRM perspective, six key issues have been identified:

1. The shifting of responsibility for employment security away from the organization to the employee
2. The paradox of laying off some employees while simultaneously hiring from outside to match employer needs and employee skills
3. Movement from traditional hierarchical career paths to ones in which promotions may be lateral
4. The development of training programs so that employees and managers are able to survive and function at a high level in the new workplace
5. Compensation packages with a larger component consisting of variable pay
6. A focus on the learning organization and continuous improvement[58]

HR experts have a considerable role to play in downsizing and restructuring. Some considerations are as follows:

- Advising on restructuring the organization (including work groups, teams, departments, and so on) to maximize productivity and retain quality performers
- Developing skill inventories and planning charts to evaluate the impact of a downsizing on HR needs and projected capabilities
- Communicating the downsizing decision effectively
- Evaluating the downsizing program after completion. This includes an assessment of who left the organization and who remains. Some key issues include job design and redesign, worker adjustment to change, the need for employee counselling, organizational communication, and a review of the appropriateness of HRM policies and programs (such as training, compensation and benefits, and orientation of employees into the "new" organization)[59]

Labour Relations Issues

Practitioners in unionized organizations often face additional challenges when participating in the restructuring process. In any downsizing involving a union, it is critical that management representatives *read* the collective agreement—while this should go without saying, in many instances practitioners do not follow this advice. The collective agreement often outlines the procedures to be followed in the event of a reduction of bargaining unit employees. Of particular relevance are clauses addressing notice period requirements in the event of a layoff and provisions dealing with seniority.

There has been a movement in labour relations toward greater cooperation between labour and management and the emergence of new employment relationships. However, changes in managerial attitudes and behaviours are necessary if cooperation between labour and management is going to succeed—unfortunately, many downsizing programs have destroyed positive labour relations programs. Securing commitment to joint labour–management initiatives is, not surprisingly, very difficult when an organization is also cutting the number of employees. One recent study of workforce reduction in the unionized environment revealed that the labour–management climate was poorer for those bargaining units that experienced a reduction of the workforce. Of note was that this result was consistent when considering *both* employer respondents and union officials.[60]

Should unions participate in management-initiated restructuring efforts? A recent case study documented the experiences of three union locals involved in the process of restructuring. Each union local negotiated with the employer over the issue of workplace restructuring but the substance of the bargaining as well as the level of involvement by the union and its members varied noticeably. However, it is possible to identify two distinct union responses. The *interventionist* response was characterized by early involvement in the restructuring process and the involvement of a broad cross-section of the union membership in the development and implementation of the new form of work organization. On the other hand, the *pragmatic* response was one in which the union relied on the employer to make workplace changes and then negotiated with management over the impact of such changes. While this response is not surprising, the study results indicate that it may not be the optimal response—in redesigning

BOX 11.6 Unionized Employees' Perceptions of Role Stress and Fairness During Downsizing

Do union members who survive a downsizing have lower job satisfaction and less favourable attitudes toward the union? Very little research has examined the effects of downsizing on union members' attitudes and perceptions. A recent study of unionized workers in a Swedish hospital sheds some light on the consequences of downsizing in a unionized environment.

Downsizing was associated with reduced levels of job satisfaction and perceptions of poorer health but was not related to union members' satisfaction with their union. However, union members who perceived that their union treated employees fairly during the downsizing reported higher levels of job satisfaction and well-being.

Source: Adapted from J. Hellgren and M. Sverke, "Unionized Employees' Perceptions of Role Stress and Fairness During Organizational Downsizing: Consequences for Job Satisfaction, Union Satisfaction and Well-Being," *Economic and Industrial Democracy*, Vol. 22 (2001), pp. 543–568.

the work, management has limited information about the work itself and workplace norms, the change does not proceed through a series of steps in which union input is sought, and the lack of involvement in the process leads to lower commitment to change on the part of the union and its members.[61]

It remains to be seen how true cooperation can exist when the job security of employees is threatened. By way of example, union leaders frequently report that joint committees and employee-involvement programs are designed to get workers to make suggestions that increase productivity at the cost of job security. Although a positive labour climate is often associated with favourable organizational outcomes, achieving such a climate is very difficult, and several good relationships have been destroyed when firms embark on a program of cutting jobs.

Summary

HR planning plays an important role in the development and implementation of an effective downsizing strategy. The "job for life" approach has been radically changed in the past decade, resulting in a number of new challenges for both employees and employers. It does not appear that the downsizing phenomenon is over, and, consequently, HR professionals must have a solid understanding of how to manage the downsizing process.

There is considerable evidence that many downsizings fell far short of achieving the goals that senior management expected. In a number of organizations, downsizing was followed by lower morale, greater conflict, reduced employee commitment, and poorer financial performance. Moreover, many downsizings were carried out without considering the strategic objectives of the organization, and many employers failed to assess how downsizing would affect its victims, surviving employees, the organization, customers, or society. Managing human resources in a time of cutback management presents several unique challenges to the HRM professional.

Key Terms

distributive justice, 276
downsizing, 266
downsizing strategies, 266
inplacement, 272
interactional justice, 276
job insecurity, 275
outplacement, 272
procedural justice, 276
psychological contract, 285
systematic change, 267
work redesign, 267
workforce reduction, 267

Suggested Websites

www.isma.org.uk/stressnw/hospnurse1.htm Describes the effect of restructuring and job insecurity on the job satisfaction of nurses.

www.theworkfoundation.com/pdf/5110000038.pdf Deals with the issue of "reflective" restructuring and how organizations can be smarter when they go through downsizing and restructuring.

www.employmenttown.gov.sg/MOM/LRD/others/Restructuring.pdf Focuses on responsible restructuring strategies.

http://faculty-gsb.stanford.edu/oyer/wp/whostays.htm A case study on the effects of downsizing/restructuring on employees.

Discussion Questions

1. What can managers embarking on an organizational downsizing do to minimize the impact of the process on the "survivors" of downsizing?
2. In light of the negative consequences often associated with downsizing, why do organizations downsize? Why do so many downsizings fail to meet organizational objectives?
3. What are the challenges facing an organization deciding to pursue Cameron's three downsizing strategies?
4. What is the "psychological contract"? Why has it changed over the past 25 years? When considering the next 10 years, what changes to the psychological contract do you envision?
5. Can a high-involvement human resource management strategy succeed in an organization that is also going through a downsizing?

Exercises

1. Discuss the following statement: "Downsizing is unavoidable. Firms that want to survive and prosper in the global economy need to engage in downsizing strategies."
2. Interview three classmates, friends, or family members who are currently working. Ask them to describe their perception of the psychological contract that exists between the organization and its members.
3. Meet with an HRM professional or a senior management official whose organization has gone through a downsizing. Ask the individual to describe the downsizing strategy employed by his or her organization.

4. Consider Cameron's three downsizing strategies of workforce reduction, work redesign, and systematic change. To what extent did the organization use any or all of these strategies?

Case: A Downsizing Decision at the Department of Public Works

Kathleen Pool is a human resources officer with a municipal government in a town of just over 25 000 people. A well-known consulting firm, in cooperation with senior government officials, recently completed a detailed audit of government operations. As a result of the audit, selected government departments (including the Department of Public Works) were targeted for restructuring. The consultants made it clear in their report that they believed the budget allocation for the Department of Public Works was adequate and recommended that the department not expect any increase in funding for the next two years. Note that operating costs for the department are projected to increase at a rate of about 3.0% annually.

Kathleen has been given the responsibility of managing the restructuring at the Department of Public Works. Rather than directing the department to cut a specific number of jobs, Kathleen has been asked to develop a restructuring strategy that will meet the town's mission of "providing quality service to its residents in a cost-effective manner." She is currently reviewing the department's operating policies.

The Department of Public Works is responsible for such tasks as garbage collection, basic sidewalk and road maintenance, maintaining city parks and arenas, installing street signs and parking meters, and snow removal. At the present time, employees work in one of three sub-units—garbage collection, parks and recreation, or city maintenance. Each of the sub-units is housed in a separate building, has its own equipment and supplies, and has its own operating budget. As well, while employees can formally apply to transfer to a different sub-unit, this has to be agreed on by the managers of the sub-units involved and the director of Public Works (who is responsible for the overall operation of the department). Unless a vacancy at one of the sub-units arises, it is rare that any employee transfer will be approved.

In 1997, the Department of Public Works underwent a considerable downsizing and 5% of its permanent positions were cut. In addition, the department stopped its practice of hiring summer students from local high schools and universities in an effort to cut costs. Prior to this, students were employed over the summer to help with special projects and to cover vacation periods for full-time employees. In 2000, a smaller cutback of 2% of the workforce took place.

In 2002, the municipality brought back the practice of hiring summer students. This decision was welcomed by the full-time employees at the department, in particular because it allowed the employees much more flexibility in selecting their vacation time. From 1997 to 2001, management placed considerable restrictions on when employees could go on vacation—employees with 10 or more years of service could have a maximum of one week's vacation in the months of July or August while employees with less than 10 years of service were not permitted to go on vacation during these two months. Under the collective agreement, management has the right to determine the vacation schedule of unionized employees.

In reviewing turnover data for the Department of Public Works, Kathleen found that very few full-time employees quit their jobs to pursue other employment opportunities. In addition, dismissals for cause were rare—over the past 10 years, only two employees were terminated for cause. In both cases, the union lost the discharge grievance at an arbitration hearing.

Since the early 1990s, the municipality has had a local consulting firm conduct surveys of both municipal employees and the users of government services. A summary of the findings from the employee survey (for Department of Public Works employees only) is contained in Table 1. Note that each of the items (such as employee morale) is measured using a five-point scale (1 = very low; 5 = very high). Similarly, Table 2 contains summary information from the survey of municipal residents concerning the performance of the Department of Public Works. Again, respondents were asked to reply using a five-point scale (1 = very low; 5 = very high). Note that on both the employee survey and users of government services survey, there were only minor differences in the results when the data were broken down by sub-unit (garbage collection, parks and recreation, or city maintenance).

QUESTIONS

1. Outline the issues that Kathleen should consider prior to designing a restructuring strategy.
2. Design a strategy to restructure the Department of Public Works. Be sure to provide support for the decisions or recommendations you propose.

TABLE 1 SUMMARY RESULTS FROM A SURVEY OF PUBLIC WORKS EMPLOYEES

Year	Employee Morale	Employee Commitment to Department	Overall Employee Job Satisfaction	Intention to Stay with the Municipality
1996	3.89	3.72	4.02	4.77
1997	2.21	1.99	2.34	4.11
1998	2.36	2.22	2.87	3.77
1999	2.65	2.62	3.22	3.99
2000	2.38	2.33	2.66	4.44
2001	2.88	3.01	2.99	4.50
2002	3.54	3.52	3.88	4.72

TABLE 2	SUMMARY RESULTS FROM A SURVEY OF MUNICIPAL RESIDENTS	
Year	**Level of Satisfaction with the Board of Public Works**	**Quality of Service Provided by the Board of Public Works**
1996	3.95	3.88
1997	3.22	3.01
1998	3.34	3.24
1999	3.65	3.66
2000	3.56	3.49
2001	3.78	3.72
2002	4.01	3.98

3. A recent newspaper editorial suggested that the town contract out the collection of garbage. What are the advantages and disadvantages of contracting out services that had been provided by government?

REFERENCES

Adamson, B., and M. Axmith. 1983. "Managing Large Scale Staff Reductions." *Business Quarterly*, Vol. 48: 40–52.

Armstrong-Stassen, M. 1993. "Survivors' Reactions to a Workforce Reduction: A Comparison of Blue-Collar Workers and Their Supervisors." *Canadian Journal of Administrative Sciences*, Vol. 10: 334–343.

Becker, B., and B. Gerhart. 1996. "The Impact of Human Resource Management on Organizational Performance." *Academy of Management Journal*, Vol. 39: 779–801.

Byrne, J. 1994. "The Pain of Downsizing." *Business Week* (May 9): 60–63, 66–69.

Cameron, K. 1994. "Strategies for Successful Organizational Downsizing." *Human Resource Management*, Vol. 33: 189–211.

Cameron, K., S. Freeman, and A. Mishra. 1991. "Best Practices in White Collar Downsizing: Managing Contradictions." *Academy of Management Executive*, Vol. 5: 57–73.

Cappelli, P. 1995. "Rethinking Employment." *British Journal of Industrial Relations*, Vol. 33: 563–602.

Cascio, W. 1993. "Downsizing? What Do We Know? What Have We Learned?" *Academy of Management Executive*, Vol. 7: 95–104.

Cascio, W., C. Young, and J. Morris. 1997. "Financial Consequences of Employment-Change Decisions in Major U.S. Corporations." *Academy of Management Journal*, Vol. 40: 1175–1189.

Challenger, J. 2002. "Short-term Staff Face the Axe, While Loyalty Pays Off." *Canadian HR Reporter* (February 25, 2002): 4.

Dalton, G., L. Perry, J. Younger, and W. Smallwood. 1996. "Strategic Restructuring." *Human Resource Management*, Vol. 35: 433–452.

Davy, J., A. Kinicki, and C. Scheck. 1997. "A Test of Job Security's Direct and Mediated Effects on Withdrawal Cognitions." *Journal of Organizational Behavior*, Vol. 18: 323–349.

DeMeuse, K., P. Vanderheiden, and T. Bergmann. 1994. "Announced Layoffs: Their Effect on Corporate Financial Performance." *Human Resource Management*, Vol. 33: 509–530.

Dunlap, J. 1994. "Surviving Layoffs: A Qualitative Study of Factors Affecting Retained Employees After Downsizing." *Performance Improvement Quarterly*, Vol. 7: 89–113.

Feldman, D., and C. Leana. 1994. "Better Practices in Managing Layoffs." *Human Resource Management*, Vol. 33: 239–260.

Ford, R., and P. Perrewe. 1993. "After the Layoff: Closing the Barn Door Before All the Horses Are Gone." *Business Horizons* (July/August): 34–40.

Freeman, S. 1999. "The Gestalt of Organizational Downsizing: Downsizing Strategies as Packages of Change." *Human Relations*, Vol. 52: 1505–1541.

Frost, A. 2001. "Reconceptualizing Local Union Responses to Workplace Restructuring in North America." *British Journal of Industrial Relations*, Vol. 39: 539–564.

Heckscher, C. 1995. *White Collar Blues: Management Loyalties in an Age of Corporate Restructuring*. New York: Basic Books.

Hitt, M., B. Keats, H. Harback, and R. Nixon. 1994. "Rightsizing: Building and Maintaining Strategic Leadership and Long-term Competitiveness." *Organizational Dynamics*, Vol. 23: 18–32.

Kane, B. 2000. "Downsizing, TQM, Re-engineering, Learning Organizations and HRM Strategy." *Asia Pacific Journal of Human Resources*, Vol. 38: 26–49.

Lam, H., and Y. Reshef. 1999. "Are Quality Improvement and Downsizing Compatible? A Human Resources Perspective." *Relations Industrielles*, Vol. 54: 727–747.

LaReau, J. 2001. "Firm Picks Pay Cuts Over Pink Slips." *The Globe and Mail*, April 11, p. B13.

Latack, J. 1990. "Organizational Restructuring and Career Management: From Outplacement and Survival to Inplacement." In G. Ferris and K. Rowland, eds., *Research in Personnel and Human Resources Management*. Greenwich, Conn.: JAI Press.

Lee, C. 1992. "After the Cuts." *Training*, Vol. 29: 17–23.

Mason, M. 2001. "The Other Dot-com Workers." *The Globe and Mail*, April 17, p. B15.

McKinley, W., and A. Scherer. 2000. "Some Unanticipated Consequences of Organizational Restructuring." *Academy of Management Review*, Vol. 25: 735–752.

Mentzer, M. 1996. "Corporate Downsizing and Profitability in Canada." *Canadian Journal of Administrative Sciences*, Vol. 13: 237–250.

Mishra, A., and K. Mishra. 1994. "The Role of Mutual Trust in Effective Downsizing Strategies." *Human Resource Management*, Vol. 33: 261–279.

Mone, M. 1994. "Relationships between Self-Concepts, Aspirations, Emotional Responses, and Intent to Leave a Downsizing Organization." *Human Resource Management*, Vol. 33: 281–298.

O'Neill, H., and J. Lenn. 1995. "Voices of Survivors: Words That Downsizing

CEOs Should Hear." *Academy of Management Executive*, Vol. 9: 23–34.

O'Reilly, B. 1994. "The New Deal: What Companies and Employees Owe One Another." *Fortune* (June 13): 44–52, at p. 44.

Osterman, P. 2000. "Work Reorganization in an Era of Restructuring: Trends in Diffusion and Effects on Employee Welfare." *Industrial and Labor Relations Review*, Vol. 53: 179–196.

Pitts, G. 2001. "Pick Up Your Pink Slip on the Way Out—You've Been Revectored." *The Globe and Mail*, September 4, p. B1.

Rosenblatt, Z., and A. Ruvio. 1996. "A Test of a Multidimensional Model of Job Insecurity: The Case of Israeli Teachers." *Journal of Organizational Behavior*, Vol. 17: 587–605.

Rousseau, D. 1996. "Changing the Deal While Keeping the People." *Academy of Management Executive*, Vol. 10: 50–59.

Storey, J., P. Quintas, P. Taylor, and W. Fowle. 2002. "Flexible Employment Contracts and Their Implications for Product and Process Innovation." *International Journal of Human Resources Management*, Vol. 13: 1-18.

Sverke, M., and J. Hellgren. 2002. "The Nature of Job Insecurity: Understanding Employment Uncertainty on the Brink of a New Millennium." *Applied Psychology: An International Review*, Vol. 51: 23–42.

Swimmer, G. 2000. *Public Sector Labour Relations in an Era of Restraint and Restructuring*. Toronto: Oxford University Press.

Tomasko, R. 1990. *Downsizing: Reshaping the Corporation of the Future*, 2nd ed. New York: AMACON.

Tomlinson, A. 2002. "Did They Really Want to Retire?" *Canadian HR Reporter* (February 11): 1, 16.

Ursel, N., and M. Armstrong-Stassen. 1995. "The Impact of Layoff Announcements on Shareholders." *Relations Industrielles*, Vol. 50: 636–649.

Wagar, T. 1996. "What Do We Know About Downsizing?" *Benefits and Pensions Monitor*, Vol. 6: 19–20, 69.

———. 1997. "Organizational Outcomes and Permanent Workforce Reduction: An Exploratory Analysis." *Research and Practice in Human Resource Management*, Vol. 5: 1–15.

———. 1998. "Exploring the Consequences of Workforce Reduction." *Canadian Journal of Administrative Sciences*, Vol. 15: 300–309.

———. 2001. "Consequences of Work Force Reduction: Some Employer and Union Evidence." *Journal of Labor Research*, Vol. 22: 851–862.

———. 2002. *Human Resource Management, Strategy and Organization Change: Evidence from Canadian Employers*. Report to study participants, July 2002.

Wagar, T., and K. Rondeau. 2002. "Repeated Downsizing, Organizational Restructuring and Performance: Evidence from a Longitudinal Study." Proceedings of the Administrative Sciences Association of Canada (HRM Division), Winnipeg, Manitoba.

Wayhan, V., and S. Werner. 2000. "The Impact of Workforce Reductions on Financial Performance: A Longitudinal Perspective." *Journal of Management*, Vol. 26: 341–363.

Wood, S. 1999. "Human Resource Management and Performance."

International Journal of Management Reviews, Vol. 1: 367–413.

Worrell, D., W. Davidson, and V. Sharma. 1991. "Layoff Announcements and Shareholder Wealth." *Academy of Management Journal*, Vol. 34: 662–678.

Wright, B., and J. Barling. 1998. "The Executioner's Song: Listening to Downsizers Reflect on Their Experiences." *Canadian Journal of Administrative Sciences*, Vol. 15: 339–355.

ENDNOTES

1. The sources of these headlines are "IBM begins cutting jobs," *The Globe and Mail*, May 24, 2002, p. B7; "Fiat shakeup will cost 6,000 jobs," *The Financial Post*, December 11, 2001, p. FP3; "Sweeping cutbacks hit Ford," *The Globe and Mail*, January 11, 2002, p. B1; and "British Airways to cut staff 12% as cost saving," *The Financial Post*, February 14, 2002, p. FP3.
2. Swimmer, 2000.
3. Cameron, 1994.
4. Dalton et al., 1996.
5. McKinley and Scherer, 2000.
6. Kane, 2000.
7. Wagar and Rondeau, 2002.
8. Wagar, 2002.
9. Challenger, 2002.
10. Cascio, 1993.
11. Tomasko, 1990.
12. Byrne, 1994.
13. *The Financial Post*, June 30, 2001, p. C2.
14. Adamson and Axmith, 1983.
15. "Better Than Downsizing," *National Post Business*, December 2001, p. 29.
16. LaReau, 2001.
17. Latack, 1990.
18. Tomlinson, 2002.
19. This material is adapted from Adamson and Axmith, 1983.
20. "If You Must Layoff," *Canadian HR Reporter*, April 22, 2002, p. 4.
21. Feldman and Leana, 1994.
22. Lee, 1992.
23. See Davy et al., 1997; Rosenblatt and Ruvio, 1996.
24. Sverke and Hellgren, 2002.

25. Armstrong-Stassen, 1993.
26. Mone, 1994.
27. O'Neill and Lenn, 1995.
28. Wright and Barling, 1998.
29. Pitts, 2001.
30. See Ursel and Armstrong-Stassen, 1995. Similar results from the United States are found in Worrell et al., 1991.
31. DeMeuse et al., 1994.
32. Mentzer, 1996.
33. Wayhan and Werner, 2000.
34. Cascio et al., 1997.
35. Cameron, 1994.
36. Tomasko, 1990.
37. Wagar, 1997.
38. Wagar, 1998.
39. Wagar and Rondeau, 2002.
40. Cappelli, 1995.
41. Hitt et al. 1994.
42. Cameron, 1994.
43. Ford and Perrewe, 1993.
44. Mishra and Mishra, 1994.
45. Freeman, 1999.
46. Hitt et al., 1994.
47. Wagar, 1996.
48. Mason, 2001.
49. Dunlap, 1994.
50. Cameron et al., 1991.
51. Two excellent reviews are found in Becker and Gerhart, 1996; and Wood, 1999.
52. O'Reilly, 1994.
53. Cappelli, 1995.
54. Heckscher, 1995.
55. Rousseau, 1996.
56. Storey et al., 2002.
57. Osterman, 2000.
58. DeMeuse et al., 1994.
59. Mone, 1994.
60. Wagar, 2001.
61. Frost, 2001.

12

STRATEGIC INTERNATIONAL HRM

This chapter was written by Dr. Xiaoyun Wang, I.H. Asper School of Business, University of Manitoba, Winnipeg, Manitoba; and by Dr. Sharon Leiba-O'Sullivan, Department of Management, Faculty of Commerce and Administration, University of Ottawa, Ottawa, Ontario.

CHAPTER GOALS

Globalization has created opportunities for Canadian companies to enter foreign markets. When a firm decides to open a subsidiary or a joint venture in a foreign country, an essential job for the HR manager is to help staff and develop an HR system for the local affiliate. The key and first step to successful accomplishment of this task is to find, attract, and retain competent global managers who not only understand the local business milieu, but also can combine that understanding with the home company's strategies and existing HR systems.

After reading this chapter, you should be able to do the following:

1. Understand the definition of strategic international human resource management (SIHRM).
2. Realize the importance of international human resource management (IHRM) for the implementation of a firm's international strategies.
3. Recognize the significance of having a long-term career development plan for global managers, and of having the international assignment represent an important step in a broader plan of global competence development.

4. Recognize the kind of recruiting and selection techniques that might help to predict expatriate success.
5. Understand the rationale behind testing for expatriate trainability.
6. Recognize the various methods of cross-cultural training, as well as their advantages and disadvantages.
7. Be able to discuss the strategic issues involved in compensating expatriates' performance.
8. Recognize the potential opportunities of learning from repatriates.
9. Recognize critical strategic issues that may arise when employing labour from around the globe.

Strategic International Human Resource Management

Attracting and retaining managers who are competent to represent the company in a global arena have been rated as the most critical goals of international HRM by multinational corporations (MNCs).[1] However, complex and dynamic local factors make it difficult and challenging to attract and retain these global managers. Cultural values and political, economic, and legal systems vary from country to country and change over time. The global environment is extremely complex. This complexity makes international HR planning challenging and at the same time crucial. **Strategic international HR planning** typically involves projecting global competence supply, forecasting global competence needs, and developing a blueprint to establish global competence pools within companies, so that the supply of global managers worldwide will be sufficient to meet with the MNC's global strategies.

strategic international HR planning projecting global competence supply, forecasting global competence needs, and developing a blueprint to establish global competence pools within companies

Moreover, international HR planning needs to fit with both the internal factors, such as a firm's strategies, competencies, and existing HR system; and the external factors, such as local economic, political, social, cultural, legal, and HR systems. It also needs to be flexible; to respond to any changes in these internal and external factors. A fit and flexible IHRM system is critical for firms to successfully implement their international strategies and to gain competitive advantage. Studies found that MNCs implement their home HR practices in their subsidiaries abroad on some issues, such as pay systems, management development, or employee communications. However, with other issues, such as wage determination, hours of work, forms of job contract, and redundancy procedures that are subject to local laws and convention, MNCs tend to follow the local practices,[2] although the extent to which IHRM practices fit with the local environment or with home headquarters varies from company to company and from country to country. Strategic thinking is needed for IHRM to project HR supply and to forecast HR needs for the foreign subsidiaries.

Therefore, **strategic international HRM** is defined as "human resource management issues, functions, and policies and practices that result from the strategic activities of multinational enterprises and that impact the international concerns and goals of those enterprises."[3]

strategic international HRM human resource management issues, functions, policies, and practices that result from the strategic activities of multinational enterprises and that affect the international concerns and goals of those enterprises

Corporate International Business Strategies

Generally, as multinational corporations evolve, four stages of growth will occur: domestic, multi-domestic, multinational, and global.[4] At each stage, different strategic objectives exist, and each presents planning implications for international HRM.[5]

- **Domestic strategy:** At the domestic stage, MNCs usually begin to become international by exporting goods abroad as a means of seeking new markets.[6] At this stage, the firm is focusing on domestic markets and exporting their products without altering the products for foreign markets. An export manager may be assigned to control foreign sales. Management at this stage usually adopts an ethnocentric attitude, as well as a short-term perspective.[7]

domestic strategy internationalizing by exporting goods abroad as a means of seeking new markets

- **Multi-domestic strategy:** As the firm develops expertise in the international market and as the foreign market grows in importance for the success of the organization, a subsidiary is typically set up,[8] which signals the start of the multi-domestic stage. Employees working in the subsidiary will have a range of tasks, concentrating on the development of foreign markets by selling to foreign nationals. Depending on the scale of the operations, one or more managers may be required to manage the global subsidiary.[9] Management at this stage realizes that there are "many good ways" to do business and that cultural sensitivity is important to be successful in the local market. A polycentric perspective is a trademark of this stage and firms use the multi-domestic strategy to develop culturally appropriate products for local markets.[10]

multi-domestic strategy a strategy that concentrates on the development of foreign markets by selling to foreign nationals

- **Multinational strategy:** When more and more MNCs enter the same market, the competition from other multinationals forces management to shift its strategy, resulting in the standardization of its products and services around the world to gain efficiency. This marks the start of the multinational stage. At this stage, a price-sensitive perspective is popular and cultural differences are less emphasized.[11]

multinational strategy standardizing the products and services around the world to gain efficiency

- **Global strategy:** At last, along with the globalization process, many MNCs start to enter the final stage of international business evolution, which is the global stage. At this stage, companies are striving to introduce culturally sensitive products, with the least amount of cost. To accomplish this, resources and materials within regional branches are reallocated globally to make quality products at the lowest cost. A geocentric perspective is taken by the company management at this stage.

global strategy a strategy that aims to introduce culturally sensitive products in chosen countries with the least amount of cost

The above four strategies are usually adopted by MNCs. The company may not practice one strategy exclusively at any one time and it might simultaneously implement the four strategies for different products at the same time.

Strategic IHRM Fits with Corporate International Business Strategies

fit the degree to which the needs, demands, goals, objectives, and/or structure of one component are consistent with the need, demands, goals, objectives, and/or structure of another component

As mentioned in previous chapters, HR planning should fit with the overall business strategies of the firm. This principle should apply to international human resource management as well. **Fit** is defined as "the degree to which the needs, demands, goals, objectives and/or structure of one component are consistent with the need, demands, goals, objectives and/or structure of another component."[12] Based on this principle, the IHR approaches and policies will be influenced by the overall corporate international strategies (*internal fit*). At the same time, it is important to fit with the local legal, political, economic, and cultural factors (*external fit*). The internal and external fits of IHRM are vital to the effective implementation of corporate strategy. Basically, three IHRM approaches would match with *multi-domestic*, *multinational*, and *global* corporate strategies. They are the *adaptive* approach, *exportive* approach, and *integrative* approach.[13] These IHRM approaches are differentiated based on the extent to which the HR practices in the foreign subsidiaries follow local practices or headquarters' ways of management.

At the domestic stage, since this is an initial stage of going international and there is no subsidiary in foreign countries, there is very little demand on the HR department to conduct its practices any differently than domestic HR practices. Usually, an export manager is appointed by headquarters to take charge in the exporting business. When the firm enters the multi-domestic stage, international HR planning becomes strategically important. Usually, at this stage, HR managers will take *adaptive* IHRM orientation, which means HRM systems for foreign subsidiaries will be consistent with the local economic, political, and legal environment. When the firm enters the multinational stage, along with the price-sensitive perspective, an *exportive* IHRM approach will be taken, which means that the MNC management will wholly transfer its home HRM systems to its foreign subsidiaries without modifying or adapting to the local environment. Finally, when the firm enters the global stage, an integrative IHRM approach will be developed to select the most qualified people for the appropriate positions no matter where these candidates come from. Details of these three IHRM approaches follow, showing how HR policies and practices will vary from different IHRM approaches.

1. Adaptive IHRM Approach

With this approach, local cultural, political, and legal issues will be considered and local HR practices will be adopted. For example, the French lodging giant

ACCOR (www.accor.com) is taking this approach and has adopted many local HRM practices in its U.S. subsidiaries in order to attract and retain local employees. Following an adaptive IHRM approach, a local executive is usually hired to take charge of the subsidiaries' HR management. The advantage of this method is that the local HR manager for the subsidiaries is familiar with local issues, and there is no language barrier between the HR manager, local partners, and employees. Hiring a local HR manager can also guarantee the consistency of the HR practices with the local legal system and environment. The disadvantage of this approach could be the fact that the local HR manager does not know the corporate culture well enough to reflect the overall corporate strategies and the corporate principles in the subsidiary HR system. Nevertheless, because HRM is very sensitive to local legal and economic systems, compared to other business functions, such as finance and manufacturing, HRM has mostly adhered to local practices in many multinational corporations.[14]

2. Exportive IHRM Approach

With an exportive approach, MNCs will have standardized HR systems across their subsidiaries all over the world. Quite a few MNCs, such as Ernst & Young (www.ey.com), have adopted this approach to reduce transaction costs, ensure the consistency of their corporate policies all over the world, and gain control over their subsidiaries.[15] The advantage of this approach is that the HR managers at headquarters have a "tried and true" HR system and can readily implement it efficiently in subsidiaries in other countries. The disadvantage of this approach is that the local environment will not have been considered in the HR system, and the fit with the local system will be missing, which may cause some problems for the subsidiaries' management. Even though some companies are using the exportive approach, this ethnocentric perspective needs a strong internal corporate culture to hold and may result in some problems caused by incompatibilities within the local environment.

3. Integrative IHRM Approach

An integrative approach combines home HR practices with local practices. The best HR policies and practices will be chosen for the foreign subsidiaries. For example, some Japanese companies have transferred some of their HR practices, such as job flexibility, intensive on-the-job training, teamwork, and cooperative relations between management and employees, to North America, but abandoned other practices, such as the use of uniforms.[16] With this approach, not only can the best context-free HR practices be transferred to subsidiaries, but also sound foreign practices can be learned and transferred to headquarters. The decision-making regarding HR policies and practices will be jointly in the hands of headquarters and foreign subsidiaries. Therefore, this approach usually goes along with the global strategy and is recommended for the purpose of mutual learning between headquarters and subsidiaries. The challenge of using this approach is that the HR managers in the headquarters need to have a geocentric or global perspective, be culturally sensitive, and be able to strategically move HR resources around the subsidiaries and headquarters.

Of these approaches, it is not difficult to see that the adaptive approach has the highest external fit, the exportive approach has the highest internal fit, while the integrative approach has the maximum fit both internally and externally. The integrated approach is highly recommended, since as mentioned above, both internal factors and external factors are important to successfully implement corporate international strategies.

Strategic IHRM Flexibility

flexibility the ability to respond to various demands from a dynamic competitive environment

Flexibility is another issue in IHRM. **Flexibility** is defined as "a firm's abilities to respond to various demands from a dynamic competitive environment."[17] In an international context, the changes are dramatic and fast paced, though they are different from country to country. In such a dynamic global competitive environment, IHRM systems need to be flexible to quickly adjust their policies and practices to respond to the changes.

Obviously, it is very challenging for the MNC's HR manager to keep the corporate IHRM system both fit and flexible, even though it is necessary to have both abilities in the same HR system.[18] No matter how capable the HR manager is, it is impossible to expect him or her to know every internal and/or external factor and follow all the changes in the international competitive environment. However, the MNCs can obtain a high level of fit and flexibility by consummate planning and by developing a large global competency pool with a wide range of KSAOs (knowledge, skills, abilities, and other characteristics).[19] From this pool, the MNC HR managers can choose the global managers who know both the local environment and the corporate structure. This sophisticated and flexible global competency pool can be further enhanced by consistent global career development and other well-planned HR practices, such as selection and training.

International Staffing and Career Development

When MNCs staff their overseas subsidiaries, employees from the home country or from a third country are assigned and sent abroad (to the local country) to get the job done. These employees, who are assigned to work overseas on a temporary basis, are called expatriates. The well-being of these expatriates and their families in the local country, as well as the expatriates' career arrangements following the overseas assignment, should be considered strategically by the MNC's IHRM policies. An international staffing without a strategic plan would jeopardize not only the MNCs' profitability, but also the individual employees' careers. A knee-jerk reaction to international expansion should be avoided.[20] However, a study by the National Foreign Trade Council revealed that less than 20% of the MNCs link international staffing with assignee preparation, and few MNCs would focus on career development and succession planning for global managers.[21]

Predicting international staffing needs should be based on the MNCs' short- and long-term strategies. After the needs for international assignments are identified, the headquarter's HR manager should look for potential candidates and attract them into the international career development program to develop their global competency. Many MNCs have already implemented global leadership development programs to prepare for their international expansion.[22]

Each specific assignment might have different job descriptions and require different knowledge, skills, and abilities (KSAs), which are similar to domestic assignments. However, general KSAs are also required to carry out these assignments in a foreign context. Caligiuri and Di Santo's[23] empirical study identified a list of abilities, knowledge, and personality characteristics that are essential for global managers with different positions in diverse cultures (see Box 12.1). This list can be used as a set of goals for a global competency development program. We now turn to a discussion of specific IHRM practices to illustrate what a headquarter's HR manager can do to develop global competence in selection, training, compensation, and retention.

BOX 12.1 The Eight Developmental Goals of Global Competence

Category	Proposed Developmental Goal
Ability	Increase an individual's ability to transact business in another country.
	Increase an individual's ability to change leadership style based on the situation.
Knowledge	Increase an individual's knowledge of the company's worldwide business structure.
	Increase an individual's knowledge of international business issues.
	Increase an individual's network of professional contacts worldwide.
	Increase an individual's openness.
	Increase an individual's flexibility.

Source: P. Caligiuri and V. Di Santo, "Global Competence: What Is It, and Can It Be Developed Through Global Assignments?" *Human Resource Planning* (July 2001), pp. 27–35.

Selection of Global Manager Candidates

Selecting the right candidates for global assignments is crucial for the long-term success of both the MNCs and the individual managers. Increasing numbers of firms have realized the importance of this issue and started to initiate programs with better selection and preparation to improve their return on investment (ROI) (see Box 12.2).

1. Personality as a Selection Criterion

The five-factor personality model (FFM)[25] has been demonstrated crucial to expatriate adjustment.[26] These five factors are emotional stability, extraversion, openness, agreeableness, and conscientiousness (see Box 12.3 for a detailed explanation). Expatriates who scored high on these five dimensions were found to be better adjusted in overseas assignments.[27] This personality model should be used for selecting the potential global managers. The instrument for measuring these dimensions of personality can be found at www.parinc.com.

BOX 12.2 International Selection

A survey called the 2001 Global Relocation Trends Survey was conducted by Windham International GMAC GRS, the National Foreign Trade Council (NFTC), and the SHRM Global Forum. It revealed that among organizations that planned major expatriate and family-support initiatives for 2002 to improve their expatriate ROI, 32% planned to have better candidate assessment and selection, 26% used career path planning and cross-border skills upon the expatriates' return, 24% wanted to be more effective in communicating assignment objectives, 20% would do better assignment preparation, 17% were instituting a company-sponsored monitoring program, 10% were introducing mandatory cross-cultural preparation, 7% were going to develop or expand the company's intranet for expatriates, 6% would become more communicative and provide more recognition during an assignment, 5% were using web-based cross-cultural training, and 4% installed mandatory destination-support services. The large number of verbatim comments from organization respondents indicates a high level of interest in this topic.

Verbatim Comments: Programs to Improve ROI

The following are some of the comments companies repeatedly gave when discussing what they planned to do to improve initiatives to support expatriate employees and their families:

- We are improving the planning of the assignments.
- There are no support initiatives. It's only been a recent initiative to even standardize our approach to an international program. The global human resources department that created the program probably will not review the process for some time. They are dealing more with downsizing issues and outsourcing.
- Our company made significant progress in clearly identifying goals upfront and finding suitable candidates to fill specific roles overseas. The number of "failed" assignments has been significantly reduced over the last three years due to better expatriate preparation and selection.
- For most expatriates, assignments are part of a budgeted project execution plan with clear objectives.

Source: Global Relocation Trends 2001 Survey, February 2002, www.windhamint.com.

BOX12.3 Five-Factor Model of Personality

Emotion stability: Individuals who score high on emotion stability are usually calm, even-tempered, and relaxed, and they are able to face stressful situations without becoming upset or rattled.

Extraversion: Individuals who score high on extraversion are sociable, like people, and prefer large groups and gatherings; they are also assertive, active, and talkative. They like excitement and stimulation and tend to be cheerful in disposition. They are upbeat, energetic, and optimistic.

Openness to experience: Individuals who score high on openness are curious about both inner and outer worlds, and their lives are experientially rich. They are willing to entertain novel ideas and unconventional values, and they experience both positive and negative emotions more keenly than do closed individuals.

Agreeableness: Individuals who score high on agreeableness are fundamentally altruistic. They are sympathetic to others and eager to help them and believe that others will be equally helpful in return.

Conscientiousness: Individuals who score high on conscientiousness are purposeful, strong-willed, and determined.

Source: P.T. Costa, Jr., and R.R. McCrae, *Revised Neo Personality Inventory*. Odessa, Florida: Psychological Assessment Resources, Inc., 1992.

2. Trainability as a Selection Criterion

Research so far appears to have presumed that cross-cultural training (CCT) is the panacea for most expatriate ills.[28] Yet it is quite possible that some individuals are simply more cross-culturally adaptable than others, and that, accordingly, CCT will have a more positive effect on them. Other researchers have also observed that there is a synergistic relationship between selection and training.[29] If you select someone who is "ready to hit the ground running," you are less likely to need to invest costly training dollars in that person. Therefore, the question of selecting for trainability is an important one. **Trainability** refers to an individual's ability to acquire certain skills to a desired level of performance.[30] Preliminary conceptual research on expatriate trainability[31] has observed that the various cross-cultural KSAs may be classified according to their stable properties (e.g., personality) versus their dynamic properties (e.g., knowledge, skills). Put simply, we may be able to gain incremental success in our selection efforts if we select expatriates who possess a minimum level of the stable characteristics (e.g., extraversion) because such individuals may be better able to acquire the interpersonal skills (e.g., developing and maintaining relationships with culturally different others) that contribute to that success.

trainability an individual's ability to acquire certain skills to a desired level of performance

3. Other Personal Characteristics

Many other different antecedent factors of cross-cultural adjustment have been identified in the literature. These include cultural knowledge, stress-management skills, conflict resolution skills, communication skills, and cognitive flexibility.[32] Several authors[33] have simplified the above lengthy list into the following three dimensions of cross-cultural competencies:

- Self-maintenance competencies, which refer to the capability to substitute sources of reinforcement when necessary and deal with alienation and isolation;
- Relationship competencies, which refer to the capability to develop and maintain relationships with home-country nationals (HCNs); and
- Perceptual competencies, which refer to the capacity to understand why foreigners behave the way they do, to make correct attributions about the reasons or causes of HCNs' behaviour, and to correct those attributions when they prove to be incorrect.

The above three competencies can be used as selection criteria for potential global managers. The challenge, though, is that the instruments used to measure these various competencies have not been formalized in the literature.[34]

Select the Best Potential Global Manager

home-country nationals (HCNs) individuals from the subsidiary country who know the foreign cultural environment well

parent-country nationals (PCNs) individuals from headquarters who are highly familiar with the firm's products and services, as well as with its corporate culture

third-country nationals (TCNs) individuals from a third country who have intensive international experience and know the corporate culture from previous working experience with corporate branches in the third country

In the domestic context, one of the key strategic decisions in recruitment is the internal recruitment versus the external recruitment decision. This two-option decision has a three-option parallel in the international domain: three types of employees (PCNs, TCNs, and HCNs) each have their own strategic advantages and disadvantages.[35] **Home-country nationals (HCNs)** are individuals from the subsidiary country who know the foreign cultural environment well. **Parent-country nationals (PCNs)** are individuals from headquarters who are highly familiar with the firm's products and services, as well as with its corporate culture. **Third-country nationals (TCNs)** are individuals from a third country who have intensive international experience and know the corporate culture from previous working experience with the corporate branches in the third country. The advantages and disadvantages of selecting among the above three groups of candidates is discussed below.

- *Select PCNs.* If you choose to staff the management positions in your subsidiaries entirely with PCNs (what the researchers term an ethnocentric approach), you have the advantage of having employees who are well versed in your company's needs and norms, but the disadvantages of (1) having employees who may be unfamiliar with the cultural norms of the host country (including norms of supervision), (2) potentially blocking HCNs' career progression within the firm, and (3) the considerable costs of relocating many employees abroad. MNCs taking a strong exportive SIHRM approach tend to send PCNs to their foreign subsidiaries.
- *Select HCNs.* If you choose to staff the management positions in your subsidiaries entirely with their own HCNs (a polycentric approach), you have the advantage of using employees who are familiar with the host-country culture. However, the disadvantages are that (1) the employees may be less familiar with your firm's own operations, (2) the PCNs at headquarters may lack sufficient understanding of the subsidiary's needs, and (3) corporate strategy for the subsidiary may suffer as a result. MNCs taking a strong adoptive IHRM approach tend to hire HCNs for their foreign subsidiaries.

- *Select TCNs.* As a third option, you may choose to staff the management positions in your subsidiary with TCNs as well. With this approach, you would have the following advantages: (1) you would be using employees who may be more familiar with the host-country culture than your PCNs would be (if, that is, the TCNs come from a proximal nation) but whose loyalty will be to the firm (rather than to the host country per se); (2) the relocation costs would be lower than for PCNs; (3) you would be allowing employees from the various subsidiaries to move to other subsidiaries, and perhaps even to headquarters, thereby enhancing career development opportunities; and (4) TCNs positioned in headquarters, be it regional or corporate headquarters, would have the opportunity to interact with PCNs, thereby improving the corporation's understanding of the subsidiaries' needs and vice versa. However, this mixed approach would also involve several disadvantages: (1) you would be using employees who will still be considered cultural outsiders, so some degree of cross-cultural preparation may still be required; (2) unless the TCNs have worked for your company before, in another subsidiary, they will also suffer from a lack of knowledge of the corporate culture; (3) because the use of TCNs is often part of a strategy that entails the use of employees from many nationalities (including HCNs and PCNs), the overhead for expatriate relocation across the entire firm will be considerable; and (4) if you are using TCNs to the exclusion of HCNs, you may create the same problem of blocked career advancement that occurs when PCNs are used in this manner.

It is recommended that the best way to select the global manager candidates is by combining and taking advantage of the above three sources and selecting candidates based on their true potential. In other words, the best potential global managers should be selected because of their personality, trainability, interpersonal skills, and attitudes, regardless of whether they are PCNs, HCNs, or TCNs. A capable global manager should be able to work in different countries to successfully implement his or her headquarters' strategies. This is usually the integrative approach, which seeks, for the most part, to place the best-qualified person in the position, regardless of the nationality of that person. In order to select the best person at the right time for the right place, you should start with identifying the best potential global managers, then putting them through training and helping them develop their global careers. With this resultant group of managers available around the world, you will be able to recruit one of them for any global position that comes along.

Cross-Cultural Training (CCT)

Studies have consistently found that cross-cultural training positively influences expatriate self-development, interpersonal skills, and cross-cultural perception. Training was also found as having a major impact on the adjustment and effectiveness of expatriate managers.[36] Researchers have been calling for firms to conduct more formalized CCT for years. However, in reality, many firms still fail to heed this call,[37] even though the situation has been improved (see Box 12.4). Part of the problem could be a lack of coordination with HR planning activities; many firms find that expatriates are often selected too quickly,[38] which precludes a lengthy training process. Because of the improper usage of expatriate training, companies have not benefited from the training.[39]

Strategic HR planning is needed for training in order to meet the goals of the career development for global managers and to focus on the development of global competencies as defined previously. Ptak et al.[40] interviewed professionals who were experienced in expatriate training. These professionals were asked to suggest some useful guidelines for overseas training. They found that effective training should emphasize five points: (1) assess and evaluate the needs of training for expatriates; (2) clarify the purpose and goals of training that are relevant and applicable to participants' daily activities; (3) plan and design the training programs to meet training goals; (4) implement the training plan; and (5) use several techniques to increase the effectiveness of training programs. Based on the work of Ptak et al., the following four steps are provided for guiding the effective training:

- *Training planning.* Assess and evaluate the needs of training for every selected potential global manager. Clarify the purpose and goals of training that are relevant and applicable to global managers' daily activities. Plan and design the training programs to meet training goals.

BOX 12.4 Cross-Cultural Training

Cross-Cultural Program Availability

Most companies (69%) provide cross-cultural preparation of at least one day's duration—up from 57% in 2000 and compared to a historical average of 62%. Forty-four percent provide training for the entire family, 21% for expatriate and spouse, and 4% for expatriates alone. In addition, 50% of these cross-cultural programs extend to two days, and they are most commonly offered as a pre-departure service.

Effectiveness of Cross-Cultural Programs

When cross-cultural preparation is available, 67% of expatriates participate. When asked if cross-cultural preparation is mandated for all employees going on international assignments, only 30% responded yes, compared to 41% in 2000. When asked to rate the value of cross-cultural preparation with regard to expatriate success, 80% of companies report that it has great or high value, compared to a historical average of 84%. Only 2% indicate that it has little or no value.

CD-Based and Web-Based Cross-Cultural Programs

When asked if their formal cross-cultural programs include CD-based or web-based alternatives, only 22% of respondents make these alternatives available. Of those who provide CD-based and web-based alternatives, 58% use them as additional pre-move and post-move support to reinforce in-person cross-cultural programs, 33% use them as standalone alternatives to in-person programs, and 20% rely on CD-based or web-based alternatives as the only type of cross-cultural preparation offered.

Source: Adapted from Global Relocation Trends 2001 Survey Report, February 2002, www.gmacglobalrelocation.com. The fall 2002 Global Relocation Trends Survey report and reports from previous years can be accessed from www.gmacglobalrelocation.com.

- *Training contents.* Training can cover many areas depending on the needs of individual managers, ranging from technical training, managerial training, interpersonal skills training, to cultural training. Typically, cultural training involves the following aspects[41]: (1) area studies programs that include environmental briefings and cultural orientations; (2) culture assimilators—essentially multiple-choice questions about cultural characteristics (each answer choice has a paragraph associated with it, describing why that answer was correct or incorrect; until the right answer is picked, the reader is asked to read the paragraph and then return to the question for another guess); (3) language training; (4) sensitivity training (which could include role-playing exercises and behavioural modelling videos designed to raise awareness of cultural differences in behaviour); and (5) field experiences, such as visits to the restaurants of the target nationality or actual visits to the host country itself. These cultural training activities are not only useful for the global managers, but also helpful for their spouses and children. Box 12.5 illustrates the importance of spousal assistant programs.
- *Training approaches.* Several training approaches have been used in reality, ranging from (1) an information-giving approach (such as lecture-based area briefings), to (2) behavioral modelling videos or case studies that offer vicarious learning, and (3) the most experiential forms (e.g., training based on role-playing and immersion in the form of field experiences).[42] These three methods should be encompassed in the training plan based on the training needs. An information-giving approach will increase the knowledge competency of the global managers; the other two approaches will increase the trainees' other skills, such as interpersonal and analytical skills. All methods will be effective if they are planned properly to meet the training needs of the global managers, but the experiential methods are usually considered more "rigorous" (i.e., as having a greater degree of trainee involvement).[43]

BOX 12.5 Frustrated Spouses

The 1999 Global Relocation Trends Survey conducted by Windham International GMAC GRS, the National Foreign Trade Council (NFTC), and the International Institute of Human Resources (IIHR) reveals that 69% of expatriates are married, with spouses accompanying them abroad 77% of the time. Of those spouses, 49% were employed before an assignment and only 11% were employed during an assignment. And if you don't think this is a negative factor in relocating, think again. The most common reason listed for assignment failure is lack of partner satisfaction (27%), which is directly tied to their work.... So, what are companies doing about this problem? Not enough. About 37% provide education assistance to spouses; 36% provide education assistance to spouses; 36% establish spousal networks; 21% reimburse educational expenses; 20% assist with career planning; and 20% help to find jobs when possible. And 30% provide no spousal assistance at all.

Source: Charlene Marmer Solomon, "Unhappy Trails—What Can Ruin an Overseas Relocation? Dual-Career Dilemmas and Frustrated 'Trailing Spouses'," *Workforce* (August 2000), pp. 36–40.

- *Treating the international assignment as on-the-job training.* Global experience has been found to be the best way to help employees gain global competence. For example, Warner-Lambert has its Global Leadership Associates Program (GLAP), which is designed to rotate potential global mangers through various foreign Warner-Lambert businesses. By gaining experience in different cultures and functions, these managers will gain skills, ability, and knowledge to lead anywhere in the world.[44] To treat the international assignment as merely one step in an overall career development plan, one must consider the issues and principles involved in job rotation in general.[45] More specifically, the employee should remain on the rotation long enough to attain a level of proficiency that enhances context-specific knowledge and self-efficacy. The rationale for this is as follows: if one of the objectives of the expatriate's assignment is to acquire cross-cultural interpersonal skills that are available only in the subsidiary, then ample time should be allowed for the expatriate to develop these skills; similarly, if an objective of the assignment is to learn, from headquarters, how the organization works, ample time should be allowed for this to happen. The point is that removing the employee from the assignment prior to some degree of mastery being achieved may be detrimental to his or her self-efficacy (and, hence, to the actual expertise you sought to cultivate in the first place because self-efficacy is closely related to performance outcomes of various kinds).[46] In addition, on-the-job training and mentoring at the host-country site should also be arranged.[47] This could be provided by other expatriates at the host-country site or by HCNs. Moreover, to fully regard the international assignment as part of a long-term career development process, a plan must be in place for the expatriate's return to the home country (presuming, that is, that the PCN is to remain a PCN or to become a TCN). This, unfortunately, is where a lot of organizations fall short, and it has led to what has become known as the "repatriation issue."

The Repatriation as a Step of Career Development

repatriation the PCNs, TCNs, or even HCNs return to their home headquarters or home subsidiaries

Repatriation usually means that the PCNs, TCNs, or even HCNs (working in headquarters as part of a career development plan) finish their overseas assignment and come back to their home headquarter or home subsidiaries. It is somehow expected that one will encounter "culture shock" when moving to another country. That one might experience culture shock upon return from abroad is usually not a concern. Yet research[48] suggests that the "big picture" of the cross-cultural adjustment process is that it is not just a U-curve process (i.e., the high of the post-arrival honeymoon, the low of the cultural shock experience, and the eventual regained high of adjustment and mastery), but rather a W-curve process, with the last "V" of the "W" happening in the form of "reverse culture shock" on return to the home country.[49]

It has been argued that reverse culture shock upon repatriation leads to several serious consequences for the employee and the organization.

- Prior to the return home, the employee may become anxious at the thought of having no appropriate position to return to; this anxiety can affect productivity abroad and work adjustment shortly after repatriation.[50]
- The employee may become dissatisfied with his or her standard of living upon return, having become accustomed to the special status that accompanied the expatriate position.[51]
- Co-workers may not be interested in hearing about the repatriate's experiences—lots of things have gone on in their own lives over the last few years, and they've had their own preoccupations and focus.[52]
- The repatriate's job may not make as much use of internationally acquired KSAs as it could.[53] In this case, "ought of sight, out of mind" is the operative phrase.[54] Box 12.6 illustrates how this attitude can create "perpetual expatriates" and deprive a firm's headquarters of badly needed international competencies.
- There is a high rate of turnover among repatriates, ranging from 20% to 25% for U.S. repatriates;[55] comparable figures are not available for Canadian repatriates.

Clearly, a career development plan for global managers will minimize these negative consequences; the MNCs can also make the most of the repatriate's internationally developed KSAs by treating them as candidates for global managers. The career planning for repatriates will also let the soon-to-be-repatriated individual have a clearer idea of what's in store, which will go a long way toward minimizing these negative consequences.

BOX 12.6 Once Abroad, Always Abroad?

A study by CIGNA International Expatriate Benefits, the National Foreign Trade Council (NFTC), and WorldatWork suggests that employers and employees hold significantly different opinions on the success of expatriate assignments. Forty-four percent of employees who had returned from an assignment reported leaving their employers within two years of their expatriate experience. A major problem of repatriation was the employees' status upon return. Twenty-one percent of employers implied that there was a commitment to have a job for the employee upon their return, according to the survey. More often, there was no commitment and employees found a troubling situation upon their return. Sometimes, expatriates like the overseas experience so much that they seek another assignment. Seventy-seven percent of those surveyed reported they are more likely to accept an international position with another employer than a domestic position with their current employer. Eighty-seven percent would accept another overseas assignment with their current employer.

Source: Jeremy Handel, "Out of Sight, Out of Mind," *Workspan* (June 2001), pp. 54–58.

Making the Most of Your Repatriate's International KSAs

Two issues are of great importance for the long-term career development of global managers. The first is to regard the international assignment as merely one step in an overall career development plan. The second is to ensure that the next step (i.e., the candidate's subsequent assignment) makes good use of the KSAs developed internationally, as these will serve as a source of competitive advantage to the firm. There are a number of ways to incorporate KSAs acquired internationally into the repatriates' subsequent career development. The repatriate could serve as a mentor or formal trainer to future expatriates or provide input into the CCT process by recounting critical incidents experienced abroad. (This could have the benefit of giving the repatriate an appropriate forum in which to discuss his or her experiences.) Alternatively (or as well), the repatriate can apply his or her understanding of the subordinate's needs by eventually serving as a long-distance supervisor to other expatriates. Another option is for the expatriate not to be repatriated but instead to join the pool of global managers and remain an international employee for the duration of his or her career, rotating from subsidiary to subsidiary. Box 12.7 provides anecdotal evidence of how consideration of the repatriation issue proved to be effective for the Colgate-Palmolive Co.

Other Issues in Strategic IHRM

1. International Performance Appraisals

Two broad categories of global assignments exist: technical/staff specialist and managerial.[56] The managerial expatriate may perform technical/staff specialist roles as well (usually at a low- or mid-level managerial position) or may hold a

BOX 12.7 An Effective Repatriation Policy

Colgate-Palmolive Co. recognized the wealth of information it already had on expatriate skills—in a system not originally designed for that purpose. Coleen Smith, New York-based vice-president for global people development, says that the company began putting together a global succession-planning database almost 10 years ago. "It has taken a variety of forms over the years," she says. While Colgate-Palmolive's database is primarily for succession planning, it also contains data on each manager's experience with or awareness of particular cultures. The information is made available throughout the company's worldwide network. "Senior leaders," Smith says, "have come to expect a certain level of information, which we really manage through our global succession-planning database."

Source: Robert O'Connor, "Plug the Expat Knowledge Drain," *HR Magazine* (October 2002), pp. 101–107.

higher level managerial position, such as being the general manager of the entire subsidiary itself. Performance criteria should be developed ahead of time and the criteria will vary according to the particular international assignment under consideration.

This may sound straightforward—after all, the job has objectives, and the objectives become criteria for evaluation. But, in the international realm, several additional environmental factors combine to make the choice of criteria significantly more complex than they would first appear.

- One such factor is the extent of interaction that the position requires.[57] A technical position in one context may demand greater interaction with HCNs than would a similar position in another context. For example, a computer specialist charged with the task of resolving a computer database problem may have relatively greater isolation when performing the task than would, say, a marketing manager charged with establishing a local distribution network. The greater the amount of interaction demanded, the greater the extent to which performance is contingent on the expatriate's cross-cultural skills. Expatriates hired in operational element positions may face a different kind of challenge. Such individuals, particularly those with managerial responsibilities, will often be faced with tasks that may both be novel and require considerable interaction with the environment. Such cross-cultural contextual factors will need to be incorporated into the performance targets set (either as criteria, or as a moderator of the level at which other targets are set). Otherwise, the set of criteria used may not be truly valid in content.
- Expatriates sent abroad to serve as upper-level managers, such as the general manager of a subsidiary, are often evaluated on the basis of the subsidiary's bottom-line results. But how comparable are these results internationally? Differences in accounting systems and financial reporting across countries can often lead to misinterpretation of results.[58] For example, Peruvian accounting rules count sales on consignment as firm sales.[59] Can this measure of sales performance be reliably and fairly used as an indicator of successful performance if none of the firm's other subsidiaries count their sales figures in this way?
- Another complicating factor is the volatility of the foreign labour market. If labour costs are high in a particular host country (e.g., Hong Kong) but not in any of the other countries in which the firm's subsidiaries operate, is it fair to penalize the general manager operating in the country with high labour costs for lower returns because of costs that are beyond his or her control? Or, if the skill level of HCNs is fairly low, but the host-country government requires the firm to employ a minimum percentage of locals in their operations, can the resultant lacklustre productivity levels (as compared to other subsidiaries of the firm) be justly blamed on the general manager?
- In addition, telecommunication and transportation infrastructures are severely lacking in many host countries, which adds to the time inefficiencies

(and hence, costs) of doing business in these places.[60] Sometimes the infrastructure may exist, but it may operate in a way that is thoroughly foreign to the expatriate. Performance may be fairly slow until the expatriate has reached a more advanced level in his or her learning curve regarding "the way things are done around here" (i.e., in the host country). All of the above must be taken into consideration when setting target levels for performance.

Therefore, the international performance appraisal should be conducted within the contextual considerations mentioned above. Everything we know about performance appraisals says that measuring observable behaviour (e.g., using behaviourally anchored rating scales, or BARS) is the most valid and reliable means of assessing performance. When using this standardized instrument (BARS) for an international assignment, it is recommended to have both host-country supervisors and subordinates and home-country supervisors and subordinates perform the appraisal.[61] When taking the bottom-line financial results as appraisal criterion, the targets should be set in accordance with the environmental considerations mentioned above.

2. International Compensation

Expatriates and their families will usually incur the following categories of cash outlays:[62] (1) goods and services (food, personal care, clothing, household furnishings, recreation, transportation, and medical care); (2) housing (major costs associated with the employees' principal residence); (3) income taxes (payments to federal and local governments for personal income taxes); (4) reserve (contribution to savings, benefits, investments, education expenses, social security taxes, etc.); and (5) shipment and storage (major costs associated with shipping and storing personal and household effects). Employees working in any particular subsidiary may come from a multitude of countries; consequently, the first three of these outlay categories are where the greatest discrepancies can arise if the firm does not take careful action.

The multinational firm has several choices to make regarding how to cover these expenses. For example, salary can be paid at the home rate rather than the local rate or in the home currency rather than local currency. Ceilings can be established for payment of certain expenses (or certain expenses can be completely prohibited if excessive). The expatriate candidate should be informed of these ceilings in advance. The firm can also alter the combination of the package according to its direct and indirect compensation components to alleviate the effects of tax discrepancies across borders.[63] Finally, benefits such as home leave allowances (trips home) are commonly offered.[64]

By having a policy for the firm's strategic approach to international compensation, the firm will increase the likelihood that the above choices will be made in a fairly consistent manner and that there exists some incentive to be posted abroad. Three common policy options typically are considered: (1) a home-based policy, (2) a host-based policy, and (3) a region-based policy.[65]

- The home-based policy approach links the expatriate's and TCN's base salary to the salary structure of the relevant home country. For example, a Canadian executive transferred to Mexico would have his or her compensation package based on the Canadian base salary level rather than that of the host country, Mexico. The advantage is that this policy (1) creates equity with home-country colleagues and (2) can be cheaper when some home countries have lower wages than the host country (e.g., if a Mexican employee was stationed in a Canadian subsidiary for a while). The key disadvantage is that international staff performing the same function in a given subsidiary may be paid at different base salaries merely due to an accident of birth location. This option can become a problem when the expatriate has been bouncing around from subsidiary to subsidiary over many years and no longer identifies himself or herself as a birth-country national.
- The host-based policy approach links the base salary to the salary structure in the host country but retains the home-country salary structure for other international supplements (e.g., cost-of-living adjustment, housing, schooling, and other premiums). The one advantage of this approach is that it attracts PCNs or TCNs to a higher-paying location. Disadvantages are that it does not eliminate inequities between PCNs and TCNs unless the home-country supplements are phased out over time (something that would apply primarily to expatriates who are unlikely to be repatriated to their country of origin).
- Finally, the region-based policy compensates expatriates working in their home regions (e.g., Canadians working in North America) at somewhat lower levels than those who are working in regions far from home. This approach has the advantages of (1) providing incentives for distant foreign relocation and (2) allowing significant cost savings, since those stationed in neighbouring countries will not receive the same premiums as those travelling farther away, and so it remains a promising option.[66]

3. International Labour Relations

Knowledge of the types of unions that exist in a country (i.e., the union structure) and the rate of unionization in that country can be critical to international HR managers. This is because union activities can influence the HR practices that may be implemented and how implementation may proceed. In short, such knowledge can influence international HR strategy.

At least four types of unions can be identified:[67] industrial, craft, conglomerate, and general. Industrial unions represent all grades of employees in an industry; craft unions are based on skilled occupations across industries; conglomerate unions represent members in more than one industry; and general unions are open to all employees in the country. This diversity of types of unions can be found to varying extents in different countries.[68] For example, Canada's union structure is industrial, craft, and conglomerate. In Australia, the United Kingdom, and the United States, all four types of union structures exist, although the United States has white-collar unions as well. Germany's union structure is primarily industrial and white collar, and Norway's is both industrial and craft. Japan's union structure consists of enterprise unions, which operate within the enterprise and have the employees of this enterprise as its members.

In addition to the diversity in types of unions, nations vary in their rates of unionization:[69] The United States has the lowest unionization rate, at 17%. Japan's rate is slightly higher, at 29%. Canada's unionization rate is tied with Germany's, at 38%. Australia's rate is 46%, while the United Kingdom's is 52%. One of the highest rates of unionization exists in Norway, where it is 65%.

Awareness of practical differences in labour relations, while laudable, is by itself insufficient. International HR managers need to translate this awareness into practice. Labour relations activities can constrain MNCs' abilities to influence wage levels (perhaps even to the extent that labour costs become noncompetitive).[70] Such activities may also limit the ability of MNCs to vary employment levels at will and may hinder or prevent global integration of the operations of the MNC.[71]

Accordingly, international HR managers must devise strategies to improve the fit between their labour relations activities and the external environment. Strategic compensation might be limited in countries with strong governmental or union wage interference. Firms operating in such countries may need to find other ways of maintaining low costs. Staffing may be affected in countries that limit the firm's ability to implement redundancy programs.[72] In such countries, worker retraining may be important because of the economic necessity to cross-train and retain workers to adapt to environmental and technological changes affecting the firm rather than lay off workers.[73] In short, the presence of unions need not be disastrous for the international firm; rather, the wise international HR manager will simply learn the constraints posed by the local union conditions and devise an effective strategy to plan accordingly.

Summary

This chapter has addressed many of the strategic issues and decisions that must be taken into consideration in the context of managing international employees. Organizations seeking to expand their businesses internationally would do well to do the following: first, recognize the strategic decision issues inherent in managing the HR function in an international context; second, strive to make these decisions in ways that take into account their firm's strategic objectives rather than in ways that neglect the added complexity that the international context brings; and third, the continuous career development of global managers should be arranged starting from the point of expatriate selection, followed by on-going training and career arrangement after repatriation. Overall, all IHRM practices and issues should be implemented strategically and a global competence pool should also be developed strategically.

Key Terms

domestic strategy, 301
fit, 302
flexibility, 304
global strategy, 301
home-country nationals (HCNs), 308
multi-domestic strategy, 301
multinational strategy, 301
parent-country nationals (PCNs), 308
repatriation, 312
strategic international HRM, 301
strategic international HR planning, 300
third-country nationals (TCNs), 308
trainability, 307

Suggested Websites

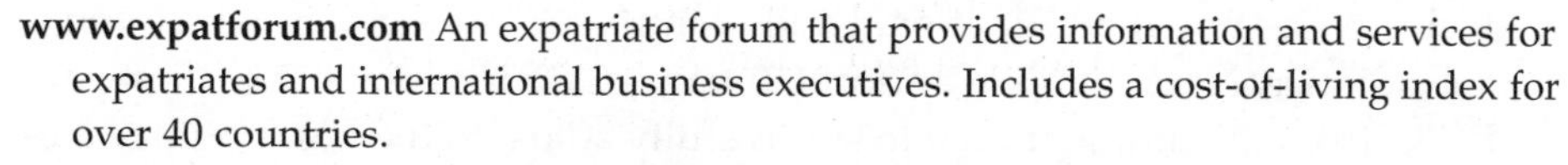

www.expatforum.com An expatriate forum that provides information and services for expatriates and international business executives. Includes a cost-of-living index for over 40 countries.

www.globescope.com/portfolio.html Embassy contacts—provides addresses and other information about consulates around the world.

www.windhamint.com Provides global relocation services.

www.expatexchange.com Offers good information on two forums: a tax and finance forum and an international career page. Publishes a monthly newsletter from the Middle East. The focus is primarily on Americans working abroad.

www.aarp.org/cyber/sd5_1.htm Lists and has links for on-line newspapers from around the world.

www.conference-board.org A powerful research organization supported by leading companies. The Conference Board's website contains lots of information regarding the latest research and thinking on all types of business issues, including a special council focus on HRM.

Discussion Questions

1. Your company will adopt a global strategy in the near future. As an HR director/manager, what kind of HR policy are you going to adopt and how are you going to plan your HR practices to align with this strategy?
2. What are global competencies and how can they be established in multinational organizations?
3. This chapter introduced three international HRM approaches. Discuss the ways in which these different approaches will (or should) influence the selection, training, and compensation of global managers.

EXERCISES

1. Go to the library and collect current articles about five companies in one functional area of international HRM. Articles can be found in journals such as *International Executive, Personnel, Human Resource Management,* and other practitioner journals in HRM. Summarize these articles. Then compare and contrast the practices used by these companies with the kinds of principles and issues raised in this chapter. Do the companies appear to be successful at what they are trying to do? Do they appear to be adhering to the prescribed theoretical approaches for managing these international HR functions? Comment on the similarity and differences between practice and theory. If real-life companies are not managing in the ways that are recommended by theory, which deviations from the text theory appear to be having the greatest impact, and what is it about the firm and its particular circumstances that appears to be causing certain deviations to be more significant than others?
2. Pick a well-known multinational and identify the countries in which it has subsidiaries. Next, compile a short (10-page) CCT module that will prepare PCNs from the multinational to successfully adjust to the host-country culture of one of the firm's subsidiary countries. Using both pre- and post-tests, have your classmates evaluate the module based on its impact on their self-efficacy for interacting with HCNs from that culture.

CASE: AN INTERNATIONAL CAREER MOVE

John Markham is a biochemist who now works as a manager with Drugs From Bugs (DFB), an innovative international pharmaceutical firm. John has been with DFB for the past 10 years. He is married and has two children (a daughter in high school and a son in kindergarten). His wife, Anya, is a certified general accountant who works for a major accounting firm in the Toronto area. Their combined household income amounts to $150 000. The president of DFB has asked John to become the managing director of DFB's operations in Israel. The government there has just offered a number of incentives to international pharmaceutical firms that make Israel a highly desirable location in which to operate.

John is keen on increasing the business in Israel, but he has concerns about his future with the company. He has heard that life in Israel can be fascinating but also quite difficult for someone who has never lived outside Canada.

John has received a memo from Anne Monty, DFB's vice-president of HR: "John, I hear there are quite a few good websites about Israel. You might want to check them out. Meanwhile, I have asked the Israeli Tourist Board to forward some material to you. Are you free for lunch next week? I look forward to hearing your thoughts. Cheers, (signed) Anne."

QUESTIONS

1. Discuss the various issues that John should be concerned about regarding the transfer.
2. What additional information should John seek from the HR department?
3. Suggest the types of financial and nonfinancial incentives that DFB might offer to John to induce him to accept the transfer.
4. Using the material discussed in this chapter, what issues should DFB consider when setting John's performance objectives for the international assignment?

REFERENCES

Abe, H., and R.L. Wiseman. 1983. "A Cross-cultural Confirmation of the Dimensions of Intercultural Effectiveness." *International Journal of Intercultural Relations*, Vol. 7: 53–67.

Adler, N.J. 1997. *International Dimensions of Organizational Behavior*, 3rd ed. Cincinnati, Ohio: South-Western College Publishing.

Adler, N.J., and F. Ghadar. 1990. "Strategic Human Resource Management: A Global Perspective." In R. Pieper, ed., *Human Resource Management in International Comparison*. Berlin: de Gruyter: 235–260.

Anderson, J.B. 1990. "Compensating Your Overseas Executives, Part 2: Europe in 1992." *Compensation and Benefits Review* (July/August).

Beck, J.E. 1988. "Expatriate Management Development: Realizing the Learning Potential of the Overseas Assignment." In F. Hoy, ed., *Best Papers Proceedings, Academy of Management 48th Annual Meeting* (August 1988). Anaheim, Ca.: 112–116.

Beechler, S., and J. Yang. 1994. "The Transfer of Japanese-Style Management to American Subsidiaries: Contingencies, Constraints, and Competencies." *Journal of International Business Studies*, Vol. 25: 467–491.

Belcourt, M., and P.C. Wright. 1996. *Managing Performance through Training and Development*. Toronto: Nelson Canada.

Bishko, M.J. 1990. "Compensating Your Overseas Executives, Part I: Strategies for the 1990s." *Compensation and Benefits Review* (May/June): 33–34.

Black, S., and H.B. Gregersen. 1991. "When Yankee Comes Home: Factors Related to Expatriate and Spouse Repatriation Adjustment." *Journal of International Business Studies*, Vol. 22, No. 4: 671–694.

Black, J.S., and M. Mendenhall. 1990. "Cross-cultural Training

Effectiveness: A Review and a Theoretical Framework for Future Research." *Academy of Management Review*, Vol. 15, No. 1: 113–136.

———. 1991. "The U-Curve Hypothesis Revisited: A Review and a Theoretical Framework." *Journal of International Business Studies*, Vol. 22, No. 2: 225–247.

Bonache, J. 2000. "The International Transfer of an Idea Suggestion System." *International Studies of Management and Organization*, Vol. 29, No. 4: 24–44.

Briscoe, D.R. 1998. "What Matters Most: Integrating Business and HR Strategies in the Selection of International Assignees." Paper presented at What Matters Most in the Management of Expatriates, a symposium chaired by D. Ondrack at the annual meeting of the Academy of Management, San Diego, Ca.

Caligiuri, P., and V. Di Santo. 2001. "Global Competence: What Is It, and Can It Be Developed Through Global Assignments?" *Human Resource Planning*, Vol. 24, No. 3: 27–35.

Costa, P.T., and R.M. McCrae. 1992. *Revised NEO Personality Inventory* [NEO-PI-R] *and NEO Five-Factor Inventory* [NEO-FFI] *Professional Manual.* Odessa, Fla.: Psychological Assessment Resources, Inc.

Cuthill, S. 2000. "Managing HR Across International Borders." *Compensation and Benefits Management*, Vol. 16, No. 3: 43–45.

Deller, J. 1997. "Expatriate Selection: Possibilities and Limitations of Using Personality Scales." In Z. Aycan, ed., *Expatriate Management: Theory and Research*, Greenwich, Conn.: Jai Press: 93–116.

Deshpande, S.P., and C. Viswesvaran. 1992. "Is Cross-cultural Training of Expatriate Managers Effective: A Meta Analysis." *International Journal of Intercultural Relations*, Vol. 16: 295–310.

Dowling, P.J., R.S. Schuler, and D.E. Welch. 1994. *International Dimensions of Human Resource Management*, 2nd ed. Belmont, Ca.: Wadsworth Publishing Company.

Feldman, D. 1989. "Relocation Practices." *Personnel*, Vol. 66, No. 11: 22–25.

Ferner, A. 1997. "Country of Origin Effects and HRM in Multinational Companies." *Human Resource Management Journal*, Vol. 7, No. 1: 19–37.

Garland, J., R.N. Farmer, and M. Taylor. 1990. *International Dimensions of Business Policy and Strategy,* 2nd ed. Boston: PWS-Kent.

Gist, M.E., C. Schwoerer, and B. Rosen. 1989. "Effects of Alternative Training Methods on Self-Efficacy and Performance in Computer Software Training." *Journal of Applied Psychology*, Vol. 74: 884–891.

Gist, M.E., C.K. Stevens, and A.G. Bavetta. 1991. "Effects of Self-Efficacy and Post-Training Intervention on the Acquisition and Maintenance of Complex Interpersonal Skills." *Personnel Psychology*, Vol. 44: 837–861.

Gomez-Mejia, L.R., and L.E. Palich. 1997. "Cultural Diversity and the Performance of Multinational Firms." *Journal of International Business Studies*, Vol. 28, No. 2: 309–335.

Groh, K., and M. Allen. 1998. "Global Staffing: Are Expatriates the Only Answer?" *HR Focus*, Vol. 75, No. 3: S1–S2.

Handel, J. 2001. "Out of Sight, Out of Mind." *Workspan* (June): 54–58.

Harvey, M.G. 1982. "The Other Side of Foreign Assignments: Dealing with the Repatriation Dilemma." *Columbia Journal of World Business*, Vol. 17, No. 1: 52–59.

Ioannou, L. 1995. "Unnatural Selection." *International Business* (July): 54–57.

Katz, J.P., and S.W. Elsea. 1997. "A Framework for Assessing International Labor Relations: What Every HR Manager Needs to Know." *Human Resource Planning*, Vol. 20, No. 4: 16–25.

Katz, J.P., and D.M. Seifer. 1996. "It's a Different World Out There. Planning for Expatriate Success Through Selection, Pre-Departure Training, and On-site Socialization." *Human Resources Planning*, Vol. 19, No. 2: 32–47.

Leiba-O'Sullivan, S. 1999. "The Distinction Between Stable and Dynamic Cross-cultural Competencies: Implications for Expatriate Trainability." *Journal of International Business Studies*, Vol. 30, No. 4: 709–725.

McEnery, J., and G. Des Harnais. 1990. "Culture Shock." *Training and Development Journal*, Vol. 44, No. 4: 43–47.

Mendenhall, M., E. Dunbar, and G. Oddou. 1987. "Expatriate Selection, Training, and 'Career-Pathing': A Review and Critique." *Human Resource Management*, Vol. 26: 331–345.

Mendenhall, M., and G. Oddou. 1985. "The Dimensions of Expatriate Acculturation." *Academy of Management Review*, Vol. 10: 39–47.

Milliman, J., M.A.V. Glinow, and M. Nathan. 1991. "Organizational Life Cycles and Strategic International Human Resource Management in Multinational Companies: Implications for Congruence Theory." *Academy of Management Review*, Vol. 16, No. 2: 318–339.

Nadler, D., and M. Tushman. 1980. "A Model for Diagnosing Organizational Behavior." *Organizational Dynamics*, Vol. 9, No. 2: 35–51.

Nicholson, N. 1984. "A Theory of Work Role Transitions." *Administrative Science Quarterly*, Vol. 29: 172–191.

Ondrack, D., and S. Leiba-O'Sullivan. 1998. "Staffing a New International Operation." Paper presented (by Ondrack) in the Applied Research Track at the annual conference of the Human Resources Professionals Association of Ontario, February. Toronto: 18–20.

Ones, D.S., and C. Viswesvaran. 1997. "Personality Determinants in the Prediction of Aspects of Expatriate Job Success." In Z. Aycan, ed., *Expatriate Management: Theory and Research*. Greenwich, Connecticut: Jai Press, pp. 63-92.

Parker, B., and G.M. McEvoy. 1993. "Initial Examination of a Model of Intercultural Adjustment." *International Journal of Intercultural Relations*, Vol. 17: 355–379.

Phatak, A.V. 1989. *International Dimensions of Management*, 2nd ed. Boston: PWS–Kent Publishing Co.

Pinder, C.C., and K.G. Schroeder. 1987. "Time to Proficiency Following Job Transfers." *Academy of Management Journal*, Vol. 30, No. 2: 336–353.

Ptak, C.L., J. Cooper, and R. Brislin. 1995. "Cross Cultural Training Programs: Advice and Insights from Experienced Trainers." *International Journal of Intercultural Relations*, Vol. 19, No. 3: 425–453.

Rhinesmith, S. 1996. *A Manager's Guide to Globalization*, 2nd ed. New York: McGraw-Hill.

Rosenzweig, P.M., and N. Nohria. 1994. "Influences on Human Resource

Management Practices in Multinational Corporations." *Journal of International Business Studies*, Vol. 25: 229–251.

Sanchez, R. 1995. "Strategic Flexibility in Product Competition." *Strategic Management Journal*, Vol. 16, Special Issue: 135–159.

Tannenbaum, S.I., and G. Yukl. 1992. "Training and Development in Work Organizations." *Annual Review of Psychology*, Vol. 43: 399–441.

Taylor, S., S. Beechler, and N. Napier 1996. "Toward an Integrative Model of Strategic International Human Resource Management." *Academy of Management Journals*, Vol. 21, No. 4: 959–985.

Thaler-Carter, R.E. 2000. "Whither Global Leaders?" *HR Magazine*, Vol. 45, No. 5: 83–88.

Thomas, D.C. 1998. "The Expatriate Experience: A Critical Review and Synthesis." *Advances in International Comparative Management*, Vol. 12: 237–273.

"Trends in Expatriate Compensation." *Bulletin to Management* (October 18, 1990): 336.

Tung, R.L. 1981. "Selecting and Training of Personnel for Overseas Assignments." *Columbia Journal of World Business*, Vol. 16: 68–78.

———. 1982. "Selection and Training Procedures of U.S., European, and Japanese Multinationals." *California Management Review*, Vol. 25, No. 1: 57–71.

———. 1988. "Career Issues in International Assignments." *Academy of Management Executive*, Vol. 2, No. 3: 241–244.

Walton, S.J. 1990. "Stress Management Training for Overseas Effectiveness." *International Journal of Intercultural Relations*, Vol. 14: 507–527.

Welch, D., T. Adams, B. Betchley, and M. Howard. 1992. "The View from the Other Side: The Handling of Repatriation and Other Expatriation Activities by the Royal Australian Airforce." In O. Yau and B. Stening, eds., *Proceedings of the AIB Southeast Asia Conference*. Brisbane, Australia.

Wexley, K.N., and G.P. Latham. 1991. *Developing and Training Human Resources in Organizations*, 2nd ed. New York: Harper-Collins.

Wright, P.M., and S. A. Snell. 1998. "Toward a Unifying Framework for Exploring Fit and Flexibility in Strategic Human Resource Management." *Academy of Management Review*, Vol. 23, No. 4: 756–772.

ENDNOTES

1. Cuthill, 2000.
2. Ferner, 1997; Rosenzweig and Nohria, 1994.
3. Taylor et al., 1996, p. 961.
4. Adler, 1997; Adler and Ghadar, 1990.
5. Ondrack and Leiba-O'Sullivan, 1998.
6. Adler, 1997; Phatak, 1989.
7. Milliman et al., 1991; Adler and Ghadar, 1990; Dowling et al., 1994.

8. Dowling et al., 1994.
9. Briscoe, 1998.
10. Adler and Ghadar, 1990.
11. Ibid.
12. Nadler and Tushman, 1980, p. 40.
13. Taylor et al., 1996.
14. Rosenzweig and Nohria, 1994.
15. Bonache, 2000; Gomez-Mejia and Palich, 1997.
16. Beechler and Yang, 1994; Bonache, 2000.
17. Sanchez, 1995, p. 138.
18. Wright and Snell, 1998.
19. Caligiuri and Di Santo, 2001.
20. Ioannou, 1995.
21. Groh and Allen, 1998.
22. Caligiuri and Di Santo, 2001; Rhinesmith, 1996; Thaler-Carter, 2000.
23. Caligiuri and Di Santo, 2001.
24. Dowling et al., 1994.
25. Costa and McCrae, 1992.
26. Deller, 1997; Ones and Viswesvaran, 1997.
27. Ones and Viswesyaran, 1997.
28. Leiba-O'Sullivan, 1999.
29. Wexley and Latham, 1991.
30. Tannenbaum and Yukl, 1992.
31. For example, Leiba-O'Sullivan, 1999.
32. Mendenhall and Oddou, 1985; Walton, 1990; Black and Mendenhall, 1990; Abe and Wiseman, 1983; Parker and McEvoy, 1993.
33. For example, Black and Mendenhall, 1990; Mendenhall and Oddou, 1985.
34. Phatak, 1989.
35. Dowling et al., 1994.
36. Black and Mendenhall, 1990; Deshpande and Viswesvaran, 1992.
37. Belcourt and Wright, 1996; Feldman, 1989; McEnery and Des Harnais, 1990.
38. Mendenhall et al., 1987.
39. Black and Gregersen, 1991; Thomas, 1998; Tung, 1981.
40. Ptak et al., 1995.
41. Tung, 1981.
42. Black and Mendenhall, 1990.
43. Tung, 1982.
44. Caligiuri and Di Santo, 2001.
45. Nicholson, 1984; Pinder and Schroeder, 1987.
46. Gist et al., 1989; 1991.

47. Katz and Seifer, 1996.
48. Welch et al., 1992.
49. Black and Mendenhall, 1991.
50. Black and Gregersen, 1991.
51. Ibid.
52. Harvey, 1982.
53. Beck, 1988; Tung, 1988.
54. Dowling et al., 1994; Handel, 2001.
55. Adler, 1997.
56. Dowling et al., 1994.
57. Ibid.
58. Ibid.
59. Garland et al., 1990.
60. Dowling et al., 1994.
61. Ibid.
62. Ibid.
63. Bishko, 1990.
64. "Trends in Expatriate Compensation," 1990.
65. Anderson, 1990.
66. Dowling et al., 1994.
67. Katz and Elsea, 1997.
68. Ibid.
69. Ibid.
70. Ibid.
71. Ibid.
72. Ibid.
73. Ibid.

13

MERGERS AND ACQUISITIONS

Chapter Goals

This chapter examines the role that the HR function can play in mergers and acquisitions. We start by examining the reasons that organizations want to merge, how they merge, and the success rate of these mergers. Culture management is the key to successful mergers. Then we examine the impact of a merger on each HR function.

After reading this chapter, you should be able to do the following:

1. Understand the various types of mergers and acquisitions.
2. Explain why organizations merge and the methods used to achieve a merger.
3. Identify the financial and human impacts of mergers.
4. Describe the issues involved in blending cultures.
5. Discuss how a merger affects HR planning, selection, compensation, performance appraisal, training and development, and labour relations.

Big Is Beautiful

The biggest IT merger in the history of Canadian mergers occurred in 2001 when Hewlett-Packard and Compaq merged. In 2002, the merged organization placed third in the *Report on Business*'s ranking of Canada's top employers. Much of the credit for this successful merger can be given to the HR team, which managed the integration of systems and people coming from two different cultures. Another example of a successful merger occurred when Beatrice Foods and Alt Foods merged to become Parmalat, a multinational food company with 10 000 employees in over 30 facilities in North America. Key to the success was the development of vision, mission, and guiding principles, which were introduced throughout the organization via a two-day training program for groups of 20 employees over six weeks.[1]

Mergers and acquisitions (M&As) play a critical part in a corporation's survival, growth, and profit strategies. "Big is beautiful" is the belief. In 1999 Petro-Canada in Calgary bought Veba Oil and Gas GMBH for $3.2 billion, which made Petro-Canada the largest integrated oil and gas company in Canada. The number of mergers appears to be holding steady at about 1400 transactions a year. However the value of these deals is dropping dramatically (approximately 65%), primarily because of the disappearance of high-ticket technology deals.[2]

Before we embark on a discussion of the motives for mergers, readers are encouraged to become familiar with the terms used to describe them.

Definitions

merger the combination of two organizations to create a third organization

A **merger** is a combination of two corporations in which a new corporation arises and the previous ones cease to exist. Within mergers, there are three categories:

horizontal merger the merging of two competitors

- A **horizontal merger** is the merging of two competitors. The competitors combine to increase market power. These mergers typically are subject to review by regulators who fear monopoly power in the marketplace. The merging of Coles Books and Smith Books to form Chapters (which was then acquired by Indigo), is an example of competitors uniting to achieve economies of scale and to withstand the attack from American megabookstores. Box 13.1 describes a merger of two big competitors.

vertical merger the merger of a buyer and seller or supplier

- A **vertical merger** occurs when a buyer and a seller (or supplier) merge to achieve the synergies of controlling all factors affecting a company's success, from the production of raw goods to manufacturing to distribution

BOX 13.1 A Rough Ride

One of the mergers that attracted a great deal of attention was the multi-billion-dollar merger of Chysler and Daimler-Benz. There are always problems merging two cultures, but this merger posed additional problems because the rivals were also from two different countries. Behaviours based in national differences are very difficult to identify and describe. For example, the Daimler-Benz German culture is strong on formality, which the Americans judged as brutal and harsh, whereas to the Germans it meant respect. Likewise, the Germans saw the American informal or casual way of doing business as "goofy" and "acting like a game show host." Added to this mix were the two fiercely competitive organization cultures with each "rival" trying to establish who was best at what.

Source: D. Brown, "Everything's Fine, and Then…" *Canadian HR Reporter* (October 22, 2001), p. 1.

and retail sales. A real estate agency might merge with a real estate developer, for example.

- A **conglomerate merger** occurs when one company merges with another but the two companies have no competitive or buyer-seller relationship. In other words, they are in different businesses competing in different markets.

conglomerate merger the merger of two organizations competing in different markets

An **acquisition** is the purchase of an entire company or a controlling interest in a company. The purchase of Federated Department Stores by Robert Campeau is a highly public example. By purchasing Federated Department Stores for $6.6 billion, Campeau, a Canadian, became the fourth-largest retailer in the United States.

acquisition the purchase of a company

A **consolidation** occurs when two or more companies join together and form an entirely new company. In this case, the assets and liabilities of both companies are taken on by the third company, usually after the original companies are dissolved. Burroughs and Sperry, two computer manufacturers, consolidated to form UNISYS. Three hospitals in Toronto—York Finch, Humber Memorial, and Northwestern General—merged in response to budget cutbacks.

consolidation two or more organizations join and form a new organization

A **takeover** occurs when one company seeks to acquire another company. Usually, a takeover refers to a hostile transaction, but it can mean a friendly merger as well. A hostile takeover refers to the acquisition of a company against the wishes of its management. ClubLink, known for operating 18-hole golf courses, received a hostile takeover bid from Tri-White Corp. The ClubLink management team campaigned actively to win the support and votes of more than 50% of the outstanding shareholders.

takeover one company acquires another company

For the purposes of this chapter, M&As will be treated as one category, that of two or more companies joining together. Box 13.2 describes the merger and acquisitions activity of the TD Financial Group over a decade. Why do companies wish to join together? The next section examines three motives for merging.

BOX 13.2 Merger History

The TD Financial Group has 51 000 employees and 13 million customers, and a track record of mergers and acquisitions:

2002	Acquired Stafford and LETCO	2000	TD Waterhouse acquired DealWise of the United Kingdom
2001	Acquired direct access broker R. J Thompson	1999	Acquired CT Financial Services in the largest acquisition in Canadian banking history
2001	Acquired 96% of Harrowston shares	1999	Acquired Trimark Trust (Retail Branch)
2001	Joint venture with DBS Group, the largest banking group in Southeast Asia	1996	Acquired Waterhouse, a U.S. self-service brokerage company
2000	Acquired Canada Life Company		
2000	Acquired Newcrest Capital		

Source: www.td.com/fastfacts/html.

The Urge to Merge

Companies merge for three reasons: strategic benefits, financial benefits, or the needs of the CEO or managing team.

Strategic Benefits

Companies that have growth as a strategic objective can expand in many ways: leveraging current customers, opening new markets internationally, corporate venturing, and M&As. The first three are slower methods. Acquisitions of companies in different regions or serving different markets is much quicker than internal expansion. Compaq and HP both sell computers but target two different markets: home offices and home entertainment customers. Their merger will create more sales than two single brands.

Another strategic rationale that can be achieved through mergers and acquisitions is the strengthening of competitive position. Pfizer, a pharmaceutical company, took over its competitor, Warner-Lambert, in order to obtain the powerful cholesterol drug Lipitor.

Companies may acquire or merge with others to achieve complementarities. Different types of synergies can be achieved through M&As. (*Synergy* is a term taken from the physical sciences and refers to the type of reactions that occur when two substances or factors combine to produce a greater effect together than would result from the sum of the two operating independently. More simply stated, synergy can be described as two plus two equals five.) **Operating synergy**, which usually is referred to as economies of scale (decreases in per-unit costs), is the cost reduction produced by a corporate com-

operating synergy the cost reductions achieved by economies of scales produced by a merger or acquisition

bination. Compaq and HP can renogotiate contracts with suppliers for memory chips and hard drives to save a total of $3 billion annually.[3] These gains are achieved by the spreading of overhead, the increased specialization of labour and management, and the more efficient use of capital equipment. Closely related to the economies-of-scale benefit is the economy-of-scope advantage. This is the ability of a firm to use one set of inputs to produce a wider range of products and services.[4] Banks, for example, would like to use their bank tellers (now called financial consultants) not only to do banking, but also to do mortgage financing, insurance selling, and so on. Another type of synergy may occur when the acquiring firm believes that it can manage the target firm better and could increase its value. For example, a small firm may benefit significantly by using the larger firm's distribution networks and experienced management.

Companies may merge to gain access to new markets. For example, Air Canada was facing a domestic market that was mature, with little likelihood of growth. Therefore, Air Canada joined with several other carriers, including Thai Airways, Lufthansa, SAS, and United Airlines, under the Star Alliance banner, to pool costs, revenues, and destinations. More importantly, the merger allowed Air Canada, Canada's largest airline, to serve foreign markets such as Asia and northern Europe, which it was forbidden to access under bilateral agreements.

Diversification may be another strategic motive. A company may wish to reduce its dependency on a market that is cyclical in nature to capitalize on excess plant or employee capacity. For example, a ski resort may acquire a golf course in order to fill its hotel rooms and restaurants during the stagnant summer months. General Electric pursued this diversification strategy. Not wanting to depend entirely on electronics, the company became a diversified conglomerate by acquiring insurance businesses, television stations, plastics manufacturing businesses, credit card businesses, and so on over a 10-year period.

Companies may even wish to redefine their businesses through acquisitions. Nortel Networks made a series of acquisitions in the 1990s to move from being a supplier of switches for traditional voice networks to a supplier of technology for the Internet.

Companies may also wish to achieve the benefits associated with vertical integration and horizontal integration. **Vertical integration** refers to the mergers or acquisitions of companies that have a buyer–seller relationship. Such a move may ensure either a dependable source of supply or control over quality of the service or product. PepsiCo acquired KFC, Taco Bell, and Pizza Hut and thus ensured the distribution of its products in these restaurant outlets. (However, Coke then convinced Wendy's and other fast-food chains that selling Pepsi in their outlets would indirectly benefit their competitors.[5])

vertical integration the merger or acquisition of two organizations that have a buyer–seller relationship

Horizontal integration refers to the increase in market share and market power that results from M&As of rivals. Western Canada's BC Telecom and Telus merged to become a stronger regional telephone company that was better able to compete against Bell Canada's launch of a new national company.

horizontal integration the merger or acquisition of rivals

Financial Benefits

Organizations look to M&As to achieve some financial advantages. Among these are the following:

- Organizations expect to reduce the variability of the cash flow of their own business. An organization lowers its risk by putting its "eggs in different baskets." However, a counterargument suggests that executives cannot manage unrelated businesses and must focus on and protect the core business from competitive and environmental pressures. The suggested wisdom is to put eggs in similar baskets.[6]
- Organizations expect to use funds generated by their own mature (or cash cow) businesses to fund growing businesses. However, some experts argue that the advantages of using one division to fund another division may be risky in the long run. Labelling one business in the portfolio a "cash cow" and another a "star" results in negative effects. Employees in the "mature" business may feel neglected, as resources are poured into the star, and may reduce their commitment to production and innovation. Management may misjudge which businesses have potential for market share increases and which do not. For example, most industry observers viewed the piano market as having slow or no growth. However, Yamaha saw the industry quite differently: the company looked worldwide for market share, saying, "Anyway, we are not in the piano business, we are in the keyboard business."[7] Sometimes slow-growth, highly competitive industries offer stable (not risky) returns.
- There may be tax advantages to the takeover, which vary by country. Considerable tax losses in the acquired firm may offset the income of a parent company.
- Astute corporations may analyze the financial statements of a company and decide that the company is undervalued. By acquiring the company, and sometimes by merging it with the administration already in place, a company can achieve financial gains.

The overriding goal is to increase the shareholder's wealth.

Managerial Needs

Some argue that corporate life is a game, and managers love to play it. The theory here is that managers seek to acquire firms for their own personal motives, and economic gains are not the primary consideration.[8] This hypothesis may help explain why some firms pay questionably high premiums for their takeover targets.

One theory examines the "incentives" or payoffs to the CEOs if they engage in acquisition behaviour. Managers may pursue their personal interests at the expense of stockholders. For example, there is a positive correlation between the size of the firm and management compensation, and so CEOs can expect higher salaries for managing larger firms.[9] Other indirect incentives may include the prestige or status of owning larger firms or companies in fashionable sectors, such as the entertainment or sports sectors.

Another perspective examines the unconscious motives of CEOs. Robert Campeau's takeover of Allied Stores and Federated Department Stores has been subject to "armchair" analysis because he overpaid for his acquisitions and ultimately went bankrupt servicing the debt. Speculation on his motives ranges from the simple need to prove himself to complex theories espoused by psychoanalysts. But does the research support the theory that managers make decisions based on Freudian or unconscious motivators?

Most of the work in this area analyzes the role that a manager's unconscious desires or neuroses play in formulating corporate strategy or decision-making.[10] Some research is based on the intensive analyses used by therapists to explore motives. A few studies attempt to link personality characteristics, such as the need for power, with growth strategies.[11] One study found that the greater the ego of the acquiring company's CEO—as reflected in the CEO's relative compensation and the amount of media attention given to that CEO—the higher the premium the company is likely to pay.[12] However, few studies arrived at helpful conclusions that would explain the behaviour of executives.

Merger Methods

How do companies merge? The process, in a friendly environment, is relatively simple. The management of one company contacts the management of the target company. Sometimes an intermediary is used, such as an investment banker or, in smaller firms, a colleague who makes an introduction. During the first tentative talks, the boards of directors are kept informed of the procedures, and, ultimately, they approve the merger. Friendly deals can be completed quickly. Hostile takeovers become dramatic, with management pushing for "poison pills" and seeking "white knights" to protect themselves. (The term *poison pills* refers to the right of key players to purchase shares in the company at a discount—around 50%—that makes the takeover extremely expensive. *White knights* are buyers who will be more acceptable to the targeted company.) There is even a "Pac-Man" defensive manoeuvre, by which the targeted company makes a counter-offer for the bidding firm.

The Success Rate of Mergers

Many studies have established that about 50% of M&As ultimately fail.[13] Acquisitions of related businesses fare better than acquisitions of businesses unrelated to the parent business.[14] The novice M&A management team does as poorly as the experienced team. Why? Perhaps because each merger is different, with different synergies and cultures.

Not only is the merged firm at risk, but the subsidiaries may also be at risk. There is some indication that a merger occupies so much management time, attention, and other resources that the original businesses are neglected.

Executives of HP and Compaq spent more than one million person-hours planning for the integration.[15] There are enormous challenges in joining two companies. The problems include integrating computer systems, eliminating duplication, re-evaluating supplier relationships, reassuring clients, advising employees, and reconfiguring work routines.

The success rate may also vary by sector and by size. The manufacturing sector, for example, differs from the service sector. In the manufacturing sector, much more is fixed, with capital investments already made, with technology controlling process, and with lower job skills. The service sector, in contrast, relies on social-control mechanisms, which are highly subject to culture management. As such, the risk is greater with acquisitions in the service sector.

Size appears to influence success rates. A large firm can absorb a small firm in a relatively inconsequential fashion. The merger of two large firms generates more problems.

Financial Impact

For many reasons, the financial returns are rarely those that were envisioned. Sometimes, a premium price was paid, and the company is unable to service the debt or recover the investment. At other times, the forecasted economies of scale or complementarities are not achieved. The market may have changed, resulting in revised forecasts.

During the merger of two health-care facilities in the United States, chaos was created in the resulting company by the collapsing of 525 branches into 350, the attempt to standardize the two facilities' computer systems, the termination of a tenth of the workforce, an attempt at a second acquisition, and the defence of the company against a barrage of lawsuits.[16] The result was that outstanding bills jumped 30% in one year, payment times increased from 109 days to 131 days, earnings were down substantially, revenues were less than those of previous years, and the stock price dropped.

Overall, studies by consulting company McKinsey & Co. reported that only 23% of mergers end up recovering the costs incurred in the deal, and about half of those analyzed by the American Management Association resulted in profit reductions.[17] Four out of five fail to produce any shareholder value.[18] Most devastating of all for merger maniacs was the analysis that demonstrated that non-acquiring companies (i.e., those that made no acquisitions) outperformed acquiring companies on Standard & Poor's industry indices.

Many mergers fail because the buyer overextends itself financially.[19] The buyer borrows heavily and then must engage in cost-cutting to service the debt. Assets are spun off, employee numbers are reduced, and the new company is left in a financial shambles.

Even if the overall financial picture of the merged company appears rosy, there are indications that different functional areas suffer. For example, a firm that has to use cash to pay for the debt incurred in acquiring another business now has less to spend on certain projects that can be postponed, such as research and development.

The specialists in post-integration mergers at PricewaterhouseCoopers have conducted research that compares the goals of mergers to their success rates (see Box 13.3).

However, there are some winners, namely the merger advisors. The Campeau-Federated Department Stores deal alone generated approximately $500 million (U.S.) in fees for M&A advisory firms.[20]

Impact on Human Resources

The real costs of a merger may be hidden—that is, not evident when analyzing financial records. Takeovers result in human displacement. The cost of losing the best sales rep, who either is anxious about her job or does not wish to work for the acquired company, cannot be measured in accounting terms. The time involved in replacing this employee with a new one represents a cost to the employer.

Another study showed that nearly half of the senior executives in large acquisitions leave within a year of the takeover and 75% leave within three years.[21] Add to this the thousands of jobs that are lost in the restructuring or downsizing of the merged companies. That is a national effect. The organizational effects are that it takes from 6 to 18 months for an organization to assimilate the results of an M&A, and the productivity loss is estimated to be 15%.[22] The loss of employee productivity stems from many sources:

- Employees go underground, afraid to make themselves visible or do anything that may put their jobs at risk.
- Overt sabotage occurs when employees deeply resent the turmoil the merger is causing in their lives.

Box 13.3 Goals of Mergers and Achievement Rates

Goals	Rationale for deal (%)	Rate of achievement (%)
Access to new markets	76	74
Growth in market share	74	60
Access to new products	54	72
Access to management/tech talent	47	51
Enhanced reputation	46	48
Reduction in operating expenses	46	39
Access to distribution channels	38	60
Access to new technologies	26	63
Reduction in number of competitors	26	80
Access to new brands	25	92

Source: K. Frers and A. Chaday. 2000. "Why You Can't Create a Purple-Footed Booby," *Canadian HR Reporter* (November 20), p. 16. Adapted by permission of Carswell, a division of Thomson Canada Limited.

- Self-interested survival tactics emerge, including hiding information from team members to accumulate a degree of power (the employee feels that he or she is "the only one who really knows how things work around here").
- A resigned attitude appears, stemming from the belief that no amount of work will prevent one from being fired.[23]
- Employees spend at least one hour a day dealing wirh rumours, misinformation, and job-search activities.[24]

But the real cost is to the thousands of employees who lose their jobs. Those who survive are affected in different ways. Most experience stress and anxiety, with the resultant loss of productivity.

To summarize, the feeling among those experienced in M&As is that, while mergers are forged for strategic and financial reasons, they succeed or fail for human reasons. The next section examines what many consider to be the greatest challenge of M&As—the blending of corporate cultures.

Cultural Issues in Mergers

In an effort to increase the probability that the merger will work, many managers are turning to the principal reason that they fail: the meshing of cultures. The friendly merger of TransCanada Pipelines Ltd. and Nova Corp. was described as GI Joe meets the Care Bears.[25] The nearly $10-billion (U.S.) merger of Nortel and Bay Networks was greeted with sceptism about its possible success, principally because of a predicted clash between the clutures[26] of a traditional telephone equipment manufacturer with a brash upstart newcomer. **Culture** is the set of important beliefs that members of an organization share. These beliefs are often unspoken and are shaped by a group's shared history and experience. Culture can be thought of as the "social glue" that binds individuals together and creates organizational cohesiveness.[27] Cultures, growing slowly over time, are not easy to describe, and employees are often aware of their corporate culture only when they try to integrate with people from another organization that has a different culture.

culture the set of important beliefs that members of an organization share

It is estimated that one-third of all merger failures are caused by the faulty integration of diverse operations and culture.[28] The longevity of an organization's culture cannot be underestimated. Canadian Airlines International was formed by merging about half a dozen different airlines. A decade after the merger, employees still referred to themselves as veterans of Wardair or Canadian Pacific Airlines—that is, they retained their original cultures. Integrating two cultures is a difficult process. Early on, the merger executives have to decide if one company's culture will be grafted onto the other company's, or if the two cultures will merge to create a third culture.

In some cases, firms that are aware of the difficulties of merging cultures attempt to negotiate, in the form of a contract, many aspects in advance. The assignment of positions or the acceptance of a culture, such as one of empowerment, seems like good advance planning. But those who have been through this process liken it to a marriage. The couple may agree, in writing, on who will do the dishes and how many children they want, but the day-to-day living may be quite different, and the assumptions change over time. Recognizing this, some employees may choose to leave the corporation rather than endure the pain of culture mergers.

Anthropologists have something to say about the blending of cultures. According to researchers, there are four options open to those involved in M&As:[29]

Assimilation: Assimilation occurs when one organization willingly gives up its culture and is absorbed by the culture of the acquirer or the dominant partner.

Integration: Integration refers to the fusion of two cultures, resulting in the evolvement of a new culture representing (one hopes) the best of both cultures. This form rarely occurs because the marriage is rarely one of two equals, and one partner usually dominates.

Deculturation: Sometimes the acquired organization does not value the culture of the dominant partner and is left in a confused, alienated, marginalized state known as deculturation. This is a temporary state, existing until some integration or separation occurs.

Separation: In some instances, the two cultures resist merging, and either the merged company operates as two separate companies or a divorce occurs.

Merging two cultures is difficult. How can a rule-bound, bureaucratic organization such as the Bank of Montreal merge with the "cowboys" of the brokerage firm Nesbitt Burns? To complicate this issue, the acquiring company typically wants to retain the entrepreneurial spirit of the target company and to infuse this spirit into its own troops. Instead, the entrepreneur is squashed by the rules and rigid decision-making of the parent company. For example, Novell purchased WordPerfect (currently owned by Corel) and managed to stifle the innovative talent it had bought.

The level of difficulty in merging two cultures is increased when the merger is one between companies from two different countries—i.e., an international M&A. For example, Canadians tend to look to employee task forces and committees to provide input on decisions; people from other countries expect their managers to provide direction. Mexicans want more structure and definition of roles and responsibilities than do Canadians. In one case, a merger was stalled because Mexicans needed this information but would not ask for it as it was seen as questioning management's authority.[30] Similarly, basic concepts of time can make international mergers more difficult. Long term in Canada means three years; in Japan, long term is thirty years.

The blending of cultures can take years. As in all organizational change programs, a process must be undertaken. The first step is to identify the differences, to ensure that employees are aware of the differences and can verbalize or label them. Is one company entrepreneurial and the other risk averse? Does one have programs of team building while the other rewards individual achievements? Later, we recommend that a team of "sprinters" be appointed to deal with urgent matters. Likewise, we suggest that a team of "long-distance runners" be appointed to address broad issues of mission statements, the creation of culture to achieve the strategic goals, and similar matters. Part of their mandate would be to measure current attitudes, solicit opinions, and give the employees a voice in the process.

Here is an example of how this is done. Two hospitals that merged had very different cultures, which did not blend. One had a culture of controlling employees; the other, a culture of encouraging employees.[31] The hospitals began the culture-blending process by conducting a comprehensive audit, using a paper-and-pencil diagnostic tool. The results were terrible, and the only positive finding was that *everyone* wanted a change. Two teams were appointed, one to change the culture of both hospitals to a culture of employee development and the other to help form this new culture.

Sometimes, cultural characteristics that are common to both merging companies can be identified. For example, two very different firms found out that they both placed top priority on customer service, and this common focal point became the link for their merger. Sometimes a superordinate goal can be created.

The formation of task forces or one-off projects has integration as a subgoal. As is the case when warring nations are forced to fight together against an alien force, the ways in which two corporate cultures are more similar than different are apparent when a superimposed goal becomes the catalyst. American Express uses this technique regularly. Managers from merging firms work together on projects to develop new products or services, for which the merged firms can claim ownership. Besides integration, such projects have other benefits: they develop in-house talent, provide an opportunity to solicit broad perspectives, and facilitate transfers as the project ends.[32]

While all of this seems time-consuming, it may, in fact, save time in the longer term. Organizational change experts realize that time spent ensuring employee buy-in will speed implementation. If time is not spent ensuring that employees are committed to the changes, employees will resist the changes.

Another approach is to "seed" the company with experienced managers who "walk the talk" and can facilitate the adoption of the new culture. However, just transferring personnel from one company to another may only increase the differences between them and promote subcultures or cliques. "Living together" before the marriage may also help ease merger shock. Japanese companies usually have worked on a joint venture or a collaborative project, designed to assess cultural fit, before they acquire another company. Turf battles are a problem unless companies establish the new structure, including the reporting relationships, early in the merger process.

Consultants specializing in post-merger integration practices at PriceWaterhouseCoopers believe that two cultures cannot be merged by just waving the common-vision banner above the employees. They suggest these specific steps be undertaken:

- Deploy role models—those in highly visible positions of authority should exemplify the new and desired behaviours.
- Provide meaningful incentives—shower the role models and employees who replicate the desired behaviours with quick and visible rewards.[33]

More radical measures may be necessary. Some companies force into early retirement or some other exit option employees who are opposed to the merger or cannot adapt to the new culture.

A more positive story is that of the merger of Lotus and IBM, discussed in Box 13.4.

HR Issues in M&As

Experts in HRM have much to say about increasing the success rate of mergers. The impact of a merger on HRM is discussed below, using the familiar functional areas of HR.

BOX 13.4 The Blending of Cultures

IBM and Lotus had agreed to merge, but many Lotus employees were worried about the impact of the IBM culture on the Lotus culture. Lotus employees were used to a culture known for its quality-of-life programs. Lotus had won awards for its willingness to accommodate the needs of its employees through spousal benefits programs, job sharing, allowing employees to work from home or at remote sites, on-site child care, summer camp programs, a lunch-and-learn wellness series, tuition reimbursements, and so on. Lotus employees were understandably worried that IBM would challenge these programs. But IBM was intrigued by the Lotus culture and chose to adopt Lotus's innovative approach to quality of working life. The result was that the Lotus employees who left before the merger phoned a year later asking to be rehired.

Successful mergers may result from an analysis of the cultures. Each firm could identify its strengths, such as empowered employees, and the merged firm could attempt to retain this aspect and build on it. For example, in the Lotus–IBM merger, the senior manager of HR reports:

> *What's been unique to Lotus is that IBM, in the past, has absorbed companies it has bought and found that total absorption can actually put people at risk. With us, it has tried to figure out what we do well that it could do better; it has tried to figure out in what ways to leave Lotus alone so that it retains its unique culture, and it has also tried to figure out how to leverage us so that the merged company can become stronger in the market.*

These culture audits provide an objective means to identify differences, provide a basis for discussion, and track merger progress.

Source: Adapted from V. Frazee, "Winning Ideas Prove Timeless," *Workforce Magazine* (November 1996), pp. 48–57. Reprinted with permission.

HR Planning

In a merger, planning moves beyond the traditional concepts of HR planning for several reasons. HR planning in an M&A situation has several dimensions that are not part of the normal planning process outlined in Chapters 5 to 10.

1. The Contingency Plan

Strategic planners must be aware of the board of directors' interest in M&As. Based on this expressed interest, a contingency plan that can be implemented when a deal is in play should be prepared. The plan should identify the contact person and the merger coordinator, who should have received training in effective merger management. The contact person should develop a plan, similar to emergency plans developed for fires or gas leaks. The plan should outline the chain of command, methods for communicating, procedures to follow during a takeover, and negotiation skills training and media response training for the senior team, and should identify a transition team.[34] Some companies even keep lists of compatible white knights (in cases of being targeted for acquisition) and prepare lists of consultants who are experts in negotiation techniques or productivity enhancement methods.

2. HR Due Diligence

The second element of HR planning in an M&A situation is the need to conduct a due diligence review.[35] The first question to be asked is how the transaction is structured as this affects the treatment of employees, as described in Box 13.5.

From an HR perspective, the due diligence would include a review of the following:

- collective agreements;
- employment contracts;
- executive compensation contracts (particularly golden parachutes);

BOX 13.5 Share or Asset Purchase

Share purchase—the purchaser acquires the shares of a company. The corporate entity continues to exist, and employees are retained.

Asset purchase—the purchaser acquires all or some of the company's shares, but there is a different corporate entity that continues the management of the business. Employees of the company are transferred to the purchaser (i.e., no longer work for the seller) and a new employment relationship must be worked out with the purchaser. In general, the purchaser has no legal obligation to hire all or some of the employees or provide them with the same working conditions and terms. But in practice, most purchasers do so in order to carry on with business and to limit liability for terminations.

Source: D. Corbett, "HR Issues in M & A," *HR Professional* (August/September 2002), pp. 18–21.

- benefit plans and policies;
- incentive, commission, and bonus plans;
- pension plans and retirement policies;
- WSIB statements, claims, assessments, and experience rating data;
- employment policies; and
- complaints about employment equity, health and safety, wrongful dismissal, unfair labour practices, and applications for certification and grievances.

Sometimes these liabilities (e.g., an enriched retirement plan) or obligations (e.g., an incentive plan) may kill the deal. Once the legal obligations have been thoroughly assessed, the level of employees' KSAs must be evaluated. The HR planning team would address the suitability of current management talent and cultural fit. A deal may be aborted if talent shortfalls are extreme or if the cultures are seriously incompatible. Despite the obvious benefits of involving the HR team in due diligence, only four out of ten companies do so.[36]

3. Transition Team

A third dimension is the need to appoint a transition team. This team is necessary because of the urgency of the M&A situation and the information gaps and employee stress that characterize it:

- *Urgency:* Staffing decisions, such as terminating, hiring, evaluating, and training, become urgent. Planners don't have the luxury of planning in three-year periods, during which orderly succession proceeds as predicted. Job analyses must be conducted immediately to identify duplicate positions and new work processes. Soon after the merger is announced, decisions about the retention of employees and the reassignment of others have to be made and executed humanely. At the same time, marketable employees are finding jobs elsewhere and customers are re-examining their business relationships. The uncertainty impedes productivity and new business development.
- *Information gaps:* While both companies may have excellent plans for employees and reams of documentation, these plans have to be adjusted to the merged needs. For example, the targeted company may have prepared succession plans for its finance department, but now most of these positions (and people) are redundant because the bidder may have its own finance department. Furthermore, the merged company may use its combined resources to seek businesses in new countries (with different financial reporting or tax laws), and neither of the merged companies has that expertise. Thus, the information accumulated to date may have to be updated rapidly and revised in light of the new needs. The loss of capable employees, those who are marketable and can easily find other jobs, also results in the need to update plans continuously during a merger. Upon the announcement of its merger, AOL Time Warner immediately created an online tutorial that explained the reasons for the merger, how it affected employees, and career opportunities under the new regime.[37]

- *Stress:* The moment that the companies go "into play," employees are stressed. They are aware of the traditional fate of employees in merged companies. Most employees realize that most positions are duplicated. A transition team, whose sole concern is HR issues in the merger, must be appointed. The transition team may be the most important determinant of merger success. The role and responsibilities of the transition team are outlined in Box 13.6.

The goals of the transition team are to retain talent, maintain the productivity (both quantity and quality) of employee performance, select individuals for the new organization, integrate HR programs (e.g., benefits, incentive plans), and take the first steps toward the integration of cultures. Some have adopted a 100-day strategy. The anxiety felt by employees and other stakeholders is lessened when the merger team announces that within 100 days of closing, all job decisions will have been made.

BOX 13.6 The Transition Team

Senior vice-presidents of HR who have had a lot of experience in mergers recommend that a transition team be appointed to deal with the concerns of employees in mergers. These vice-presidents cite the need to deal with employee stress before the stress renders employees incapable of working. In addition, it is known that employees who have access to information about their future are less likely to begin a job search and leave the organization. Communication is critical, and employees should be the central focus of communication efforts. The transition team should be composed of employees from both companies and union representatives (if there is a union in either company).

Here are some elements of a good merger management process:

- *A formal announcement:* When a merger or acquisition is announced, the CEO should issue a statement containing the following items of information:

  The rationale for the merger—that is, its intended benefits

  General information about both companies

  Information about changes in the corporate name and structure, particularly changes in key management positions

  Plans for employee reductions

  Plans for recognizing and working with the union

  Plans for changes in products or services

  Detailed information about changes in benefits, or the date for decisions about such changes
- *A merger hotline:* When Inland Gas purchased Mainland Gas, creating BC Gas, the company immediately set up a hotline so that employees could call the vice-president of HR and ask direct questions. E-mail and voice-mail make the management of this process easier.
- *A newsletter or web page:* Experts agree that the formation of communication channels must be swift and consistent and all communication must be honest. One company created a fictional employee (called Frank) who, on behalf of the workforce, asked questions about the merger and reported back to the employees, from their perspective.[39]

As the transition team is handling the urgent matters, the HR planners can undertake the revisions necessary to prepare HR plans. Employee skills inventories must be updated and succession plans revised. If the business enters new sectors and they require new labour pools, these labour pools have to be identified and the need for them assessed. Employment equity data have to be revised and, perhaps, resubmitted to the relevant agencies. Based on the revised strategic plans, the HR department must revise and align its plans and produce a new forecast for HR requirements.

A review of the HR policies will likely reveal three types of situations:

- *complementary*—one company may focus on career development, while the other focuses on benefits
- *duplicated*—both companies have identical HRIS
- *contradictory*—one organization uses the performance management system for career development while the other uses its system to support incentive pay programs.[38]

Selection

Retention and reduction, paradoxically, are two critical areas that must be addressed immediately. Duplicate positions and redundant employees must be terminated while highly qualified employees in critical positions must be motivated to stay. The first critical question is, How many employees does the merged company need? The answer is not to eliminate the most jobs possible in an attempt to operate a lean and mean corporation; the result would be work overload and stress. The answer may lie in benchmarking statistics. Increasingly, HR professionals are developing benchmark data, by sector. For example, one merged hospital, which employed six full-time workers per occupied bed, reduced the number of employees to match the benchmark of four full-time workers per occupied bed.[40]

Key workers must be identified and offered retention bonuses and employment agreements. Employees are offered incentives to stay at least until the deal closes and, often, for periods after the closure. The superstar financial brokers at Merrill Lynch were offered a one-time retention bonus of 110% of their take-home pay (more than $1 million a year) by CIBC in order to retain them. The retention bonus was structured as a five-year loan, so that each year 20% of the loan was forgiven.[41]

Reductions might be necessary. The dismissal process can be heartbreaking, as is described in one merger case.[42] In the rush to terminate quickly, some employees were notified by voice-mail or e-mail or in hurried and short meetings with strangers. A supervisor was forced to fire three of his employees before being fired himself. His termination was particularly difficult to understand, as his performance reviews were excellent. As wave after wave of salespeople were laid off, customers became confused about their contacts. Departing employees took advantage of this and went to the competition, taking the business relationships with them.

Chapter 11 covered this aspect of restructuring in detail. A number of decisions need to be made immediately. Employees will want to know if they will be offered employment in the merged company; if not, they will want to know what the severance packages contain. If jobs are offered, can employees choose not to accept them? For those wary of the new owner or who fear being dumped once the sale closes, will there be a safety net? For those who are terminated, will assistance such as financial planning, job relocation, and career planning be offered? Will benefits continue for a short adjustment period? One organization, which could not promise job security to its employees, did promise to position them for work in the new organization or outside of it.[43] This pledge was kept. Employees were trained, at organizational expense, for other positions. Part of the training included seminars in which employees were taught to be responsible for their own development and were given assistance to develop a survival kit called Making Me Marketable. Jobs were reanalyzed to focus on basic skills. For example, the job specifications for a patient-care technician stated that a high school diploma was required, but a review showed that certain skills, and not a high school diploma, were needed to do the job. Managers used their contacts and networks to assist departing employees. Employees were encouraged to work on cross-functional teams to expand their horizons and skills. The result was that productivity did not diminish dramatically, as occurs in most mergers. Furthermore, the downsizing and exodus were orderly, lessening the stress on remaining employees. The culture was changed, and employees were rewarded.

Those who stay with the newly acquired or merged company face several fates:

- *Demotion:* Under the new organizational structure, some employees are given less responsibility, less territory, or fewer lines due to amalgamation.
- *Competition for the same job:* Some companies force employees to compete for their old jobs by having to apply as new candidates for a position.
- *Termination*: If not successful in the competition, employees are then let go. Sometimes, the acquiring firm waits until it can obtain its own appraisal of employee capabilities and has a chance to determine fit.

The survivors have adjustments to make, and these were detailed in Chapter 11. Like employees involved in a restructuring, the survivors of a merger are dealing with their loss of identity as the company changes, a lack of information and the resultant anxiety, a lack of protection from adverse effects over which they have no control, the loss of colleagues, and a change in their jobs.[44] Those remaining with the corporation will need to know about compensation plans.

Compensation

Two companies with two different compensation systems have to either merge their systems, adopt one, or create a new one. AOL Time Warner replaced the straight salary system of Time Warner with the AOL system of salary plus stock options.[45] Incentive plans have to be aligned to support the merger strategy. But consideration can be given to incentives to make the merger work. BC Gas gave each employee 50 free shares and introduced an attractive stock purchase plan to promote commitment to the new company.[46]

In a merger, a major issue for the HR department is the integration of benefit plans. Which company's plan should be adopted? Employees obviously wish for the most favourable benefits, but organizations are concerned with cost. When benefits are removed or reduced in the integration of companies, employees may experience loss of morale. Thus, for employees in the process of considering their futures with the organization, the resolution of the benefits package may affect their decision.

The best resolution of this problem would be to conduct a cost–benefit analysis of the benefits, package by package. For example, child-care centres or health and wellness centres may seem to be costly benefits. But if the number of sick days and mental health days taken is reduced or employee turnover is diminished, then the benefits may outweigh the costs. Pension concerns will be high. Although there are regulations governing certain pension credits, different approaches to pension plan transfers must be analyzed, as variances can run into the millions of dollars.

For employees who are being terminated, retaining certain benefits during the months or years after the merger may be a humane way to soften the adverse effects of the merger. Companies may wish to offer extended medical and dental coverage, modified retirement plans, and some counselling to deal with unemployment and with career plans.

Performance Appraisal

During a merger, employees undergo stress, and productivity can be expected to drop. Focusing on long-term goals may be difficult and so short-term goals should be substituted. Business is not as usual. The role of the manager may change from one of supervisor to one of coach. Employees may play it safe and may require constant positive reinforcement for the work they do accomplish under the new house rules.

One model constructs employee behaviour during a merger as falling into one of three categories: not knowing (remedied by more communication), not able (the solution is training), or not willing (a strong case for performance management through feedback and incentives).[47]

Performance appraisals for development purposes may have to redone. The merged company may be larger or engaged in different businesses, allowing for more or different promotion paths and developmental experiences. Employee intentions and aspirations under the new regime will have to be redocumented.

Stress levels may necessitate a relaxation of the rules and more counselling and coaching. Personal problems (such as financial or marital difficulties), rather than performance problems, may surface as the stress begins to affect employees.

Training and Development

Once the strategic plan has been developed, an inventory of the KSAs needed to align with the strategy should be undertaken. Information based on previous needs analyses may have to be revised in light of the new strategy, which may create new jobs.

Managers and peers may need some additional training in the role of coach and counsellor. Every employee might benefit from stress reduction or relaxation programs. Developmental programs, such as overseas assignments or executive exchanges, or long-term educational opportunities may be put on hold while the new organization establishes long-term plans.

Labour Relations

Unionized employees are covered by a collective agreement, which is a legally binding document. Typically, these agreements set out the conditions under which job changes must occur. Various issues will need to be considered. For example, will unionized employees continue with the same working conditions and benefits, as negotiated, or will the contracts be renegotiated? At a minimum, the collective agreements must be read to determine what provisions exist for job security and what the notification periods are for layoffs and terminations. Merger experts say that unions should be informed and involved from the outset of the merger so that they can make valuable contributions.

As you can see, HR plays a pivotal role in the success of M&As.

Summary

The focus of this chapter was on the HRM implications of M&As. Mergers are undertaken to provide a strategic benefit or a financial benefit, or to fulfil the psychological needs of the managers. The financial and other results of mergers are not always as positive as expected and the effect on staff can be devastating, whether they stay with the merged company or not. The culture of the previously separate companies and the new merged company is the area that experts say is the most important predictor of merger success. The merger has an impact on each of the functional areas—HR planning, selection, compensation, performance appraisal, training and development, and labour relations.

Key Terms

acquisition, 329
conglomerate merger, 329
consolidation, 329
culture, 336
horizontal integration, 331
horizontal merger, 328
merger, 328
operating synergy, 330
takeover, 329
vertical integration, 331
vertical merger, 328

Suggested Websites

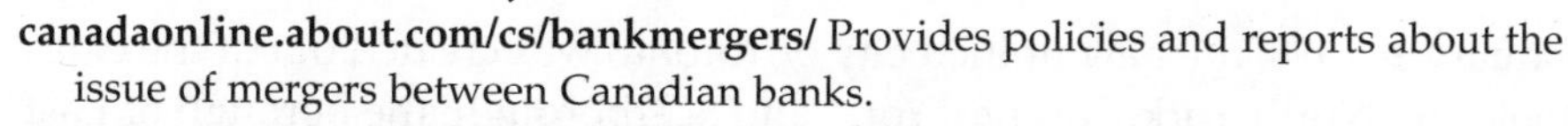

canadaonline.about.com/cs/bankmergers/ Provides policies and reports about the issue of mergers between Canadian banks.

www.crosbieco.com/M&A.html The annual directory of mergers and acquisitions in Canada.

www.canadiandimension.mb.ca/archive/murdock.htm An article on the merger of unions to create super-unions.

www.calipercanada.com/mergers.htm An article on the people issues in mergers.

Discussion Questions

1. Prepare a list of all the reasons why an organization would want to acquire a competitor.
2. Describe the effects that a merger may have on employees. What can management do to lessen the more negative effects of a merger? What can employees do to protect themselves when they start to hear rumours of a merger?
3. One of the urgent issues facing executives immediately after the merger is announced is the retention of key employees. How would you define or describe a key employee? What methods would you use to identify key

employees? Describe some programs that you could use to retain your key employees, during and after the merger.

EXERCISE

"WHAT'S GOING TO HAPPEN TO ME?"

The treatment of employees during a merger is critical. Employees will be asking lots of questions. If you are currently working, imagine that your company is going to merge with a competitor. In groups, prepare a list of questions that you would like management to answer. If you are not working, imagine the merger of your university or community college with another, and prepare a list of questions that you would like answered regarding your status in your program.

CASE: THE CITY OF TORONTO—COURAGE IN THE FACE OF CHAOS

On January 1, 1998, the new unified city of Toronto was created out of the cities of Etobicoke, North York, Toronto, York, and Scarborough; the borough of East York; and the municipality of Metropolitan Toronto. Few mergers have attempted to integrate seven organizations. The goal was to integrate the policies, practices, and systems of municipalities as large as Toronto (with a staff of 11 000) and as small as East York (with a staff of 430) and to achieve savings from the overlapping of administrative and staffing costs of the seven municipalities. Toronto is now the fifth-largest city in North America, with 2.5 million residents. Its budget of $6 billion and staff of 26 000 are larger than those of several Canadian provinces. More than 800 municipal staff from all seven jurisdictions worked on the integration project, developing a vision, a mission, and a governance structure. About 70% to 95% of departmental budgets cover staffing costs.

An important position, particularly in the merger process, was that of the executive director of Human Resources and Amalgamation, a position that was filled through an internal and external search. Brenda Glover, formerly the HR commissioner of the city of Etobicoke, was chosen for the position of executive director. Ms. Glover had the critical task of designing an HR strategy that would accomplish the integration in a seamless fashion by building a new vision and culture. She noted, "If HR was not organized, then the rest of the city is in chaos. The first goal is to have all people in place."

Ms. Glover discussed the staffing, labour relations, compensation, benefits, and culture issues in this very large public-sector merger:

Staffing: An HR transition team focused first on staffing. On January 1, 1998, only six new employees were working for the merged city. The goals, which were met, were to have separation programs ready by February 1, all HR directors in place by March 1, and all managers in place by April 1. Every municipal employee had the opportunity to compete for the "new" jobs, his or her former job, and jobs two levels down. Within one year, from March 1998 to March 1999, the HR department had posted 900 jobs, and an average of 12 candidates competed for each job. The priority was to hire internally, but the HR staff also looked at 16 000 résumés from external candidates during this period.

About 10% of the total number of jobs (or 2500) were to be eliminated. Attrition and voluntary exit packages were the primary basis for workforce reduction. Those facing termination were given counselling, retraining opportunities, incentive programs for early retirement, and assistance in the job search process.

Labour relations: The seven cities operated with 56 collective agreements. The unions were given time to work through their members to determine who would be the bargaining agent. It might have been faster to force the Labour Relations Board to make this decision, but urgency was subordinated to longer-term issues of trust and collaboration.

Compensation: Working with the seven municipalities, the transition team developed an interim salary schedule. It had problems and, in hindsight, a compensation consultant should have been hired to design a completely new salary schedule. There were significant integration problems, such as the case of two people who were doing the same job for which one employee was earning $20 000 more than the other.

Benefits/payroll: The goal was to harmonize the benefits and move from seven systems to one benefits policy. This was not easy, as the new city wanted to achieve savings and rationalize benefits whereas employees rarely want to give up their "rights" to achieved benefits. So the decision made was to go neither to the lowest nor the highest standard but to benchmark, creating a new standard.

Culture: When mergers occur between just two partners, cultural issues are a challenge. Imagine a merger between seven partners. Here are some of the cultures, without naming names, that had to be harmonized:

City A: Cheap, fiscally prudent; has meagre compensation and resources; has a history of downsizing and little job security

City B: Politically correct; an advocate for change

City C: Bureaucratic, process oriented

City D: Quick, entrepreneurial, rich; does little research or analysis; has good job security

As could be predicted, early encounters were filled with comments such as "I am from Etobicoke, and we think ..." or "The way we do things ..." The goal was to create new values and a new mentality that was not wedded to old ways of doing things.

Lessons Learned

When asked what she would have done differently, Ms. Glover mentioned several lessons learned:

1. *Communication:* "We had websites, brochures, hotlines, everything to inform employees about emerging policies. But we found that unless and until a policy impacts an employee personally, it is not heard or absorbed. So we found we were answering the same questions over and over again. We learned that timing, frequency, and repetition are very important."
2. *Training:* "It became obvious very early that the transition team needed skills, and employees needed unique skills, to integrate the seven municipalities. For example, the move to City Hall required new skills, such as enhanced project management. We should have realized this earlier."
3. *Profile:* Mergers in the public sector are particularly difficult because they tend to be high profile, and many of the merger decisions are made public. For example, the separation packages, which had to be approved by Council, were leaked to the press before there was time to inform employees.
4. *Services:* The integration was accomplished in such a way that the public saw no disruption in services. Ms. Glover states, "Not one heartbeat was missed in service, even when management was in chaos, with some managers leaving and others coping with loss [of employees] and organizational memory. The frontline employees deserve a lot of credit."

What was done right? Ms. Glover reports, "No merger works without a sense of urgency. We met deadlines. We balanced urgency against fairness. We had to create teams, which is a slow process, while balancing the need to deal with immediate issues. We communicated, with lots of meetings, updates, answering questions personally. But a merger presents incredible opportunities to create a culture, handpick staff ... basically a blank sheet to do things right."

Questions

1. Compare the process used by the city of Toronto with the prescriptions for an effective merger as outlined in this chapter.
2. What do you see as the differences?
3. Would you have handled the merger of the cities any differently?

REFERENCES

Adams, M. 2002. "Making a Merger Work." *HR Magazine*, Vol. 47, No. 3: 52–57.

Alphonso, C. 2002. "Top Staff Gain Clout in Mergers." *The Globe and Mail*, May 29, 2002, C1.

Anand, J. 2000. "A Match Made in Heaven." *Ivey Business Journal* Vol. 64, No. 6 (July/August 2000): 68–73.

Bernhut, S. 2000. "Bridging Cultures Adding Value in a Merger." *Ivey Business Journal*, Vol. 64, No. 3: 53–58.

Berry, J.W. 1990. "Social and Cultural Change." In H.C. Triandis and R.W. Brislin, eds., *Handbook of Cross-cultural Psychology*, 5th ed. Boston: Allyn & Bacon.

Buchanan, R., and M. Daniell. 2002. "The Leadership Testing Ground." *Journal of Business Strategy*, Vol. 23, No. 2: 12–17.

Cartwright, S., and C.L. Cooper. 1993. "The Role of Culture Compatibility in Successful Organizational Marriage." *Academy of Management Journal*, Vol. 7, No. 2: 57–70.

Edwards, C., and A. Park. 2002. "HP and Compaq: It's Showtime." *Business Week*, June 17, 2002: 76–77.

Fisher, A. 1994. "How to Make a Merger Work." *Fortune*, Vol. 129, No. 2 (June 24): 64–66.

Frers, K., and A. Chada. 2000. "Why You Can't Create a Purple-Footed Booby." *Canadian HR Reporter*, Vol. 13, No. 20: 16.

Galpin, T.J., and M. Herndon. 2000. *The Complete Guide to Mergers and Acquisitions*. San Francisco, Ca.: Joss-Bassey.

Gaughan, P.A. 1996. *Mergers, Acquisitions, and Corporate Restructuring*. New York: John Wiley & Sons.

Hamel, G., and C. Prahalad. 1989. "Strategic Intent." *Harvard Business Review*, Vol. 3: 73.

Harshbarger, D. 1990. "Mergers, Acquisitions, and the Reformatting of American Businesses." In D.B. Fishman and C. Cherniss, eds., *The Human Side of Corporate Competitiveness*. Newbury Park, Ca.: Sage Publications.

Hollister, M. 1996. "Competing Corporate Cultures Can Doom Acquisition." *Human Resource Professional* (January/February): 7–10.

Hood, S.B. 2003. "Do You Know What Your CEO Really Wants?" *HR Professional* (February/March): 38–40.

Howes, C. 2001. "There Is More to a Merger than Making a Buck: Making Cultures Fit." *Financial Post*, February 2: C5.

Kadlec, R.E. 1990. "Managing a Successful Merger." *Business Quarterly* (Autumn).

Kemp, A., and P. Lytwyn. 2002. "Merging HR Departments: How to Make It Work." *HR Professional* (August/September): 29–30.

Kets de Vries, M.F.R. 1991. "Introduction: Exploding the Myth That Organizations and Executives Are Rational." In M.F.R. Kets de Vries and Associates, *Organizations on the Couch: Clinical Perspectives on Organizational Behavior and Change*. San Francisco, Ca.: Jossey-Bass.

Koeth, B. 1985. "Expressly American: Management's Task Is Internal Development." *Management Review* (February): 24–29.

Kroll, M., P. Wright, L. Toombs, and H. Leavell. 1997. "Form of Control: Determinant of Acquisition Performance and CEO Rewards." *Strategic Management Journal*, Vol. 18, No. 2 (February): 85–96.

Laroche, L., G. Gitelson, and J. Bing. 2001. "Culture Shock." *CMA Management*, Vol. 75, No. 1: 40–44.

Lubatkin, M.H., and P.J. Lane. 1996. "Psst—The Merger Mavens Still Have It Wrong." *Academy of Management Executive*, Vol. 10, No. 1 (February): 21–39.

Madell, I., and R. Piller. 2000. "Merger Mania: The Financial Risks of Mergers and Acquisitions." *CMA Management*, Vol. 74, No. 3: 25–29.

Master, L.J. 1987. "Efficient Product of Financial Services: Scale and Scope Economies." *Federal Reserve Bank of Philadelphia* (January/February): 15–25.

Riddel, A., and F. Lipson. 1996. "Bankrupt Hospital Lands on Its Feet." *Personnel Journal* (August): 83–86.

Roll, R. 1986. "The Hubris Hypothesis of Corporate Takeover." *Journal of Business*, Vol. 59, No. 2 (April): 197–216.

Rovenpor, J.L. 1993. "The Relationship between Four Personal Characteristics of Chief Executive Officers and Company Merger and Acquisition Activity." *Journal of Business and Psychology*, Vol. 8, No. 1 (Fall): 27–55.

Schonfeld, E. 1997. "Have the Urge to Merge? You'd Better Think Twice." *Fortune* (March 31): 114–116.

Shrivastava, P. 1986. "Postmerger Integration." *Journal of Business Strategy* (Summer): 65–79.

Slain, L. 2003. "Strategic Emphasis." *HR Professional* (February/March): 42–45.

Stuart, P. 1993. "HR Actions Offer Protection during Takeovers." *Personnel Journal* (June): 84–95.

"Value of Mergers and Acquisitions Drops 64%." *Daily Commercial News*, Vol. 74, No. 247 (2002): A7.

Walker, J. 1992. *Human Resource Management*. New York: McGraw-Hill.

Zwieg, P.L. 1995. "The Case against Mergers." *Business Week* (October 30): 122–130.

ENDNOTES

1. Slain, 2003; Hood, 2003.
2. "Value of Mergers and Acquisitions," 2002.
3. Edwards and Park, 2002.
4. Master, 1987.
5. Anand, 2000.
6. Lubatkin and Lane, 1996.
7. Hamel and Prahalad, 1989.
8. Roll, 1986.
9. Kroll et al., 1997.
10. Kets de Vries, 1991.
11. Rovenpor, 1993.

12. Zweig, 1995.
13. Madell and Piller, 2000.
14. Gaughan, 1996.
15. Edwards and Park, 2002.
16. Schonfield, 1997.
17. Fisher, 1994.
18. Laroche et al., 2001.
19. Kadlec, 1990.
20. Harshbarger, 1990.
21. Galpin and Herndon, 2000.
22. Laroche et al., 2001.
23. Hollister, 1996.
24. Laroche et al., 2001.
25. Howes, 2001.
26. Bernhut, 2000.
27. Cartwright and Cooper, 1993.
28. Shrivastava, 1986.
29. Berry, 1990.
30. Laroche et al., 2001.
31. Riddel and Lipson, 1996.
32. Koeth, 1985.
33. Frers and Chadha, 2000.
34. Stuart, 1993.
35. Walker, 1992.
36. Galpin and Herndon, 2000.
37. Adams, 2002.
38. Kemp and Lytwyn, 2002.
39. Galpin and Herndon, 2000.
40. Riddel and Lipson, 1996.
41. Alphonso, 2002.
42. Schonfield, 1997.
43. Riddel and Lipson, 1996.
44. Walker, 1992.
45. Buchanan and Daniell, 2002.
46. Kadlec, 1990.
47. Galpin and Herndon, 2000.

14

OUTSOURCING

CHAPTER GOALS

Outsourcing has existed for a very long time. In villages in medieval times, a family may have "outsourced" its baking to a village bakery. Parents today "outsource" child and elder care, activities that were once provided in-house.

Outsourcing refers to a contractual relationship for the provision of business services by an external provider. In other words, a company pays another company to do some work for it. Currently, outsourcing is being promoted as one of the most powerful trends reshaping management. However, organizations have always outsourced some functions. For decades, most organizations hired firms to operate their cleaning or restaurant functions. What is different now is the scale. Firms are outsourcing everything from information technology management to entire functions such as human resources.

After reading this chapter, you should be able to do the following:

1. Define outsourcing.
2. List the reasons why organizations outsource functions and programs.
3. Identify the advantages of outsourcing.

4. Cite the risks and limitations of outsourcing.
5. Develop the criteria necessary for managing the outsourcing relationship.

Outsourcing

outsourcing the practice of one organization contracting with another organization to provide services or products

Outsourcing occurs when an organization contracts with another organization to provide services or products of a major function or activity.

Work that is traditionally done internally is shifted to an external provider, and the employees of the original organization are often transferred to the service provider. Outsourcing differs from alliances or partnerships or joint ventures in that the flow of resources is one-way, from the provider to the user. Typically, there is no profit sharing or mutual contribution.

Outsourcing HR Functions

Surveys continue to show that nearly all organizations have outsourced parts of their HR functions.[1] Over half of these organizations plan to outsource even more functions. IBM outsourced its entire HR department, which was called Workforce Solutions, a profit centre that produced gains in flexibility, accountability, competitiveness, and profitability. Box 14.1 provides examples of other companies that outsourced parts of their HR functions.

In HR, the functions most likely to be outsourced are temporary staffing, payroll, training, recruiting, and benefits administration. Box 14.2 lists the functions within HR that are likely to be outsourced.

HR departments are under increasing pressure to produce deliverables, not just do-ables, and so are searching to determine which activities add value and who can best do these. Outsourcing is also a response to the demand from executives that HR reduce costs for its services. Outsourcing to service providers with

BOX 14.1 HR Outsourcing Examples

Many organizations outsource their HR functions. Gow Corp., a 90-employee Alberta organization that processes livestock for institutional and restaurant clients, teamed with its vertical partners (a distributor and a supplier) to outsource and share two HR professionals who would handle payroll, training, health and safety, etc. The United Church of Canada outsourced job evaluation, recruitment, and compensation, in order to tap a wealth of experience that was not available in-house. Pratt & Whitney Canada outsourced its training function to DDI (Development Dimensions International). Pratt & Whitney executives wanted a partner that could handle the tactical level in managing administrative tasks, but also the strategic level in matching learning solutions to business needs.

Sources: Adapted from A. Patel, "Vertical HR: Will the Experiment Work," p. 14; L. McKibbin-Brown, "Who Is Outsourcing What?", p. 32; P.J. Labrie and J. Bedard, "Outsourcing Training at Pratt & Whitney Canada," p. 42—all from *HR Professional*, Vol. 10, No. 3 (June/July 2002).

BOX 14.2 HR Functions That May Be Outsourced

Compensation
- Payroll
- Benefits
- Compensation administration
- Pension

Training
- Program delivery
- Program design and development
- Training consulting to line departments
- Training needs analysis
- Program Evaluation
- Strategic Planning for T & D
- Administration
- Developing training policy

Recruitment and Selection
- Advertisements
- Screening of applications
- Testing
- Reference checking
- Preliminary interviews
- Salary negotiations—at the executive level
- Exit interviews

Health and Safety
- Employee assistance programs
- Wellness programs

international expertise also allows HR departments to harmonize employee packages for a global workforce, while complying with local laws.

While smaller firms might outsource all HR functions, most large firms retain the critical components. Box 14.3 describes the reasons that small businesses outsource HR. Larger organizations rarely engage in 100% outsourcing for three reasons. As has been argued throughout this text, the HR function is

BOX 14.3 Small Business and HR Outsourcing

Most businesses do not hire an HR professional until the employee numbers reach about 100, or even 400. But legislated HR functions, such as payroll and benefits, are necessary for every organization, regardless of size, so small businesses turn to other small businesses specializing in HR. The advantages are the following:

- Lessens the handling of routine, transactional HR work (payroll) by in-house staff
- Offers access to experts who may provide advice in atypical situations (employee fraud)
- Provides the management of one-off services (such as computer training)
- Ensures that the company is complying with current legislation

Outsourcing is not the same as using consultants who may provide assistance on a project-by-project basis. Small businesses are looking for a long-term relationship with a provider who understands small business in general and their business in particular.

so critical to the culture and strategic objectives of an organization that it must be closely managed by the organization itself. Second, situations arise that are impossible to predict, such as industrial relations disputes, and this unpredictability makes it difficult to develop a contractual arrangement with a vendor. Timeliness of response is crucial. The final reason is the lack of providers of total HRM services. The field of outsourcing is replete with hundreds of small companies specializing in market niches. One company might do an excellent job of benefits counselling, another might specialize in employee assistance, but few can do everything from training to managerial succession to payroll. These competencies have to reside within the firm.

The Rationale for Outsourcing

Almost all organizations outsource, and the trend is growing. In a study conducted by the American Management Association, 94% said of those surveyed said that they had outsourced one or more HR functions.[2] CIBC's decision to outsource is explained in Box 14.4.

If the organization needs experts and cannot afford to hire or train them, outsourcing may be a solution. Most organizations want to achieve cost savings or improved services or access to experts or technology as the basis for their

BOX 14.4 Outsourcing at CIBC

One of Canada's largest companies has outsourced major portions of its HR functions. CIBC employs about 44 000 people, about 450 in HR. In 2001, CIBC outsourced payroll processing, benefits administration, a call centre for employment enquiries, occupational health and safety services, and HR technology to a company specializing in HR services, EDS, in a seven-year, $227-million deal. Two hundred CIBC HR employees have been transferred to EDS, cutting the bank's HR department nearly by half. CIBC's vice-president of HR commented, "I don't think that in today's world, power is about the number of employees you have working for you. HR should get its power from how much it helps the business units meet their goals."

The reasons for outsourcing included the desire to improve service, to increase automation, and to have the HR department focus on the strategic issues of making a contribution to the company. CIBC does not add value by administering pension plans; EDS does. The HR department is freed from routine transactions and can focus on policy, providing advice and programs to move the business forward.

The CIBC–EDS deal was unique as an outsourcing arrangement for several reasons. CIBC arranged with EDS to introduce best practices back into its organization and to update the bank on industry trends on a regular basis. CIBC searched for a vendor that would be a cultural fit with its organization. The main attribute the bank was looking for was "adapting to client needs." As the CIBC vice-president of Strategic Alliance Management said, "You can't put everything in a contract, so it is important to choose a company you can work with. You should be as clear as possible in terms of defining roles and responsibilities, but you cannot possibly think of all eventualities up front.... It is important to have a process built into the contract to manage these issues."

Sources: D. Brown, "CIBC HR Department Halved as Non-strategic Roles Outsourced," *Canadian HR Reporter*, Vol. 14, No. 11 (2001), pp. 1 and 6; S. Geary and G. Coffey-Lewis, "Are You Ready to Outsource HR?" *HR Professional* (June/July 2002), pp. 26–29.

decision to outsource. However, many managers approach outsourcing as a solution without first defining what the problem is.[3]

There are at least six major reasons that organizations outsource: financial savings, strategic focus, access to advanced technology, improved service levels, access to specialized expertise, and organizational politics.

FINANCIAL

The first reason cited for the outsourcing decision is to save money. Organizations believe that costs can be reduced by outsourcing a function such as payroll. Economies of scale can be achieved when the provider, such as Ceridien, which specializes in providing benefits administration, concentrates on one area and provides this service to many corporations. Specialized vendors are more efficient because they can spread the costs of training personnel and undertaking research and development across more users. Studies of outsourcing arrangements of at least two years' duration showed that outsourcing resulted in cost savings ranging from 0 to 40%, with an average of 15%.[4] About 50% of the firms felt that their cost savings objectives had been met, and labour productivity had improved.

Related to the issue of saving money is cost control. Company users of a service may be more cautious when the contractor charges them for each service, as opposed to the "free" in-house service. Training is a good example. If in-house training is free and training provided by an external vendor costs $1000 per day, then managers are more stringent about requiring employees to prove that the training is needed and that there would be measurable benefits. Sometimes, when an organization is just starting to offer a service, such as fitness training for employees, it is cheaper to contract this out than to make the capital investments in a gym and specialized staff. This capital can then be redirected to other initiatives that have a higher rate of return. Outsourcing also makes sense when usage of a service is variable or unpredictable. An organization may recruit on an irregular basis for IT staff; in this case, retaining an in-house IT recruiter is not economically viable.

STRATEGIC FOCUS

Employers recognize that they cannot pursue excellence in all areas. Therefore, they decide to focus on their **core competence**, such as customer service or innovation, and move secondary functions, such as benefits administration, to firms in which these functions are a core competence.

core competence an internal activity critical to organizational success, which creates a competitive advantage and influences future growth

How is core defined? There are four meanings:[5]

- Activities traditionally performed internally.
- Activities critical to business success. Core work contributes directly to the bottom line; non-core work doesn't.
- Activities creating current or potential competitive advantage.
- Activities that will influence future growth or rejuvenation.

The notion of core competencies was created by Prahalad and Hamel, who argued that the real sources of competitive advantage were not products but management's ability to consolidate skills and technologies into competencies to adapt to changing circumstances.[6] A competence is a combination of technology, management, and collective learning.

Executives will decide to concentrate on what the organization does best, and contract everything else out to vendors. Core functions that should not be outsourced are orientation, leadership development, employee relations, final selection, performance management, and succession management, as these depend on an understanding of organizational culture, a long-term orientation, consistency, trust, and confidential information.

By outsourcing non-core activities, managers hope to be able to focus on value-added roles. For example, CIBC outsourced the design of training programs and development and delivery, allowing the company to focus on planning, needs analyses, and coaching after program completion.[7] The firm Avenor Inc. of Montreal outsourced all pensions, benefits, and payroll administration. As James Merchant, CHRP, vice-president of Human Resources at Avenor explained,

> *Outsourcing allowed us to get out of low value-added administrative work and become more strategic. We now focus on health and safety, leadership development, total compensation, and employee and labour relations. Our department at head office has 12 staff today compared to 40 in 1994. But, with our change in focus, our performance within the organization has taken a quantum leap.*[8]

Technical

Another driver of this trend has been technology. Many functions are outsourced because organizations want to improve technical service, or they cannot find technical talent, or they need quick and reliable access to new technologies.[9] Much of traditional HR service has involved answering employee inquiries about benefits or making changes to employee files. These kinds of tasks can be handled easily by interactive voice responses and managed by companies that specialize in this service. Technology also enables a company to reduce transaction time (the time it takes to handle a request).

Improved Service

Quality improvement is cited as another benefit of outsourcing. Performance standards can be written into the contract more tightly than may be possible with current and long-tenured employees. Managers can choose the "best-of-breed" vendors that have outstanding track records and more flexibility in hiring and rewarding their employees.

HR departments are often criticized for being overly bureaucratic. When using a service provider whose focus is service, clients of HR see a marked improvement in flexibility, response, and performance.

Confidentiality is also a good reason to outsource. An employee with a drinking problem, for example, is more likely to seek assistance from an external counsellor, than an in-house employee assistance officer.

Specialized Expertise

Another reason cited by some companies for outsourcing is that they find the laws and regulations governing HR so complex that they decide to outsource to firms that have the specific expertise required. The motto is "Outsource when somebody can do it better than you."

Employees who are outsourced to the service provider may see opportunities for career development in their disciplines. In an organization specializing in training, for example, employees would have greater access to expert colleagues to use them as sounding boards, and to career paths and opportunities to upgrade their knowledge and skills.

The use of experts also reduces the risks and liabilities for organizations. Specialists know the legislation better than anyone and can assure the user organization that all their practices comply with legislation.

Access to leading practices is another motivator to outsource.

Organizational Politics

An outsourced function is not as visible as an in-house department performing the same tasks. Some organizations make the decision to outsource to get rid of a troublesome department, such as one where employees are underperforming. Outsourcing a function also reduces the head count. Head counts are important in the public sector; the fewer civil servants on payroll, the happier the taxpaying public. The contractor is often able to justify and negotiate technology improvements and other investments more easily than in-house managers.

Risks and Limitations

As with any major decision, there are positives and negatives to outsourcing. The decision to outsource carries risks and has limitations. Are the anticipated benefits realized? What are the risks to service levels? What is the effect on employee morale? Does outsourcing reduce the value of the organization? These four questions are discussed below.

Projected Benefits vs. Actual Benefits

For organizations with experience in outsourcing functions, there are hints that the process is not as cost-effective and problem-free as expected. Surveys have indicated that about half of the respondents found that it was more expensive to manage the outsourced activity than originally expected and that service levels were not as good as expected.[10] About 40% reported problems with higher costs. The reasons for the cost overrides include system incompatibilities and client demands outside the standard vendor package. Outsourcing compares poorly to other processes designed to save costs. For example, re-engineering can generate cost savings over 50%; outsourcing savings seem to be, on average, 10 to 15%.[11] Over 30% of outsourcing arrangements were not renewed because the cost savings were not achieved.[12]

Service Risks

The vendor will provide services as specified in the contract. If the needs of the user organization change, contracts will have to change. The flexibility of adding new features or enhancing or reducing service is reduced. Furthermore, it is possible that the vendor may enter the market and become a competitor. For example, Schwinn, a U.S. manufacturer of bicycles, outsourced the manufacture of its bicycle frame to a Taiwanese organization, Giant Manufacturing. A few years later, Giant entered the bicycle market and damaged Schwinn's business. Companies can lessen this risk by erecting strategic blocks—terms in the contract that limit the replication of certain competitive advantages, such as propriety technology—or spreading the outsourcing among many vendors. Nike, for example, outsources all manufacturing but keeps its core competencies (branding, marketing, and R & D) in-house.[13]

Employee Morale

One of the primary risks in outsourcing is the effect on employee morale and performance.[14] Outsourcing is a form of restructuring that always results in displaced employees. Organizations provide employees with a sense of identification and feelings of security and belonging. When these are disrupted, employees, as stakeholders, may feel resentful and retaliatory.

In an outsourcing arrangement, employees are transferred to the outsourcing firm, transferred internally to other functions, outplaced, and/or offered voluntary retirements. Despite all these options, redundancies and layoffs of staff do occur. In certain cases, the service provider employs the entire displaced workforce but may negotiate higher fees to accommodate what is perceived to be surplus or inefficient labour. Employees are resentful of these arrangements, with their connotations of "serfdom" in which the "serfs" are sold as capital equipment.[15]

Outsourcing can lead to the disintegration of an organization's culture. Instead of empowering and valuing employees, an outsourcing decision alienates and "deskills" employees. The transferred employees will experience emotional loss and a change in culture. The outsourced function may have served as a developmental site for managers and this is now lost, unless arrangements can be made with the vendor.

In most cases, negotiated arrangements of pay and job security are not transferrable. The vendor is able to offer cost savings because of reduced wages and increased work intensity.[16]

Organizations that attempt to outsource face a backlash. The City of Toronto endured a three-week strike by garbage workers over the issue of outsourcing. Citizens lived with rotting garbage on the streets during a heat wave while the strike was under way. Members of CUPE were demanding job security ("lifelong employment") for employees, but the city won a public relations battle by saying that the demands were unreasonable because no working and tax-paying citizen enjoyed this right.

Once rumours of outsourcing arrangements are started, HR managers can expect talented employees to start job searches and all employees to suffer anxiety resulting in lost production. Managers will have to deal with the reactions of displaced employees and survivors and allow for a period of mourning.

Reduced Value

Extreme levels of outsourcing hollow out a company, leaving it a shell. There may be unintended consequences of outsourcing the organization's knowledge and skills to outsiders. The vendor may even sell the acquired know-how and company secrets to a competitor. Organizations can find that outsourcing employees' skills limits these organizations' ability to learn and exploit changes.

The organization experiences a reduced capacity to generate profits or innovate. Even a non-core activity, such as IT, may be tightly linked to other functions such as HR, so outsourcing IT reduces the firm's capability for cross-functional synergies and creativity. The vendor cannot know your organization's special needs, nor can it distinguish your high-profile customer (the president of the company that outsourced the function) from any other customer. When HR functions are outsourced, the internal image of HR may deteriorate as there is less interaction with internal customers, and less and less HR work is performed by the HR department.[17]

Management of Outsourcing

Managing the outsourcing well is critical. First, outsourcing must be subjected to a cost–benefit analysis. Can the contractor do a better job, faster, while maintaining service levels and meeting legislative requirements? How will this be measured? The following sections describe ways of selecting vendors, negotiating the contract, and monitoring the arrangement.

Selecting the Vendor

Once a decision is made to explore outsourcing a function, the organization should

- inform the staff of the affected function,
- prepare an **RFP (request for proposal)**,
- invite internal and external bids, and
- establish a team to evaluate these bids.

See Box 14.5 for a summary of the key information that should be contained in a response to an RFP.

Request for proposal (RFP) describes the responsibilities to be outsourced and invites potential providers to present their proposal for carrying out the job

BOX 14.5 Response Requirements to a Request for Proposal for Outsourcing

In a response to a request for proposal, the potential provider should do the following:

- Explain how the provider is uniquely qualified to accomplish the measurable objectives that are described in the request.
- Describe actual situations in which the provider is currently providing the services that are proposed for this operation.
- Identify the challenges that the provider expects to encounter while improving the operation.
- Explain how these challenges will be met and present a proposed timetable for meeting them.
- Describe the economic model that is proposed for the operation.
- Specify the fee that the provider believes to be reasonable compensation for its services.

Source: Moneta, L., and W.L. Dillion. 2001. "Strategies for Effective Outsourcing." In *New Directions for Student Services*, No. 96 (Winter), John Wiley & Sons, p. 42. Copyright © 2002. Reprinted with permission of John Wiley & Sons, Inc.

The point at which the staff should be informed about the potential outsourcing is hotly debated. If informed early in the process, the most talented and marketable employees may leave, and the stress and anxiety among those remaining affects productivity. However, employees will find out sooner than management might like, and it is far better to keep them in the loop of communication; they may even play a vital role in the development of the RFP.

The items to be included in an RFP vary by the service to be outsourced. Typical details include activity levels, errors, response rates, deliverables, and goals.[18] Costs are never included.

Companies that have had successful outsourcing arrangements always started by comparing vendor bids against bids newly submitted by in-house functional experts.[19] The internal group may have had ideas to reduce costs or improve services, but were thwarted for many reasons. Once it's clear that outsourcing is the preferred route because the same service cannot be provided in-house, the organization can proceed with its outsourcing plans, secure that every avenue has been explored.

The evaluation team should include the technical experts, including a manager who will not be affected by the outcome, procurement officers who can qualify suppliers, and even customers who can check out the suppliers' track records and personnel.[20] This team sets the evaluation criteria, analyzes bids against the criteria, and chooses the vendor. The process should be as obsessive and detailed as the due diligence undertaken with mergers and acquisitions. Examples of evaluation criteria can be found in Box 14.6.

BOX 14.6 Outsourcing at Autoglass

Autoglass, a company in the business of repairing and replacing automobile windows, uses and weights ten criteria in choosing a vendor:

Criterion	Weight
1. Commitment to implement urgently needed system	10
2. Software competency	10
3. Cultural fit	9
4. Contract conditions	9
5. Hardware competency	8
6. Knowledge of user requirements	7
7. International capability	7
8. Cost	7
9. Client references	6
10. Contract length	5

Source: M. Milgate, *Alliances, Outsourcing, and the Lean Organization*. Copyright © 2001 Michael Milgate. Reproduced with permission of Greenwood Publishing Group Inc., Westport, CT.

Negotiating the Contract

Experts advise organizations looking to outsource to not work with the contract the vendor will offer because these contracts typically do not include performance standards or penalty clauses if the vendor does not meet requirements.[21] Payment provisions in these standardized contracts also tend to favour the vendor. The vendor also has a tendency to want to start the service before the contract is signed and "take care of the details later." Anything not provided at the beginning is then subject to excess fees.

An essential first step that the user organization must undertake is the establishment of benchmark levels with current services. The goal is to document baseline services currently being provided, using criteria such as response time, response cost, and customer satisfaction ratings. Thus, a performance standard might read that "90% of benefits enquiries must be answered within 24 hours." Of course, everyone forgets about the other 10%, so that too must be specified (e.g., "The remaining 10% must be answered within three working days"). Quality measures have to be included—for example, "Clients rate the service satisfactory or excellent 98% of the time." Failure to meet these levels must result in penalties, such as reduction in the costs or payments to the user. On the other hand, if service is superior, incentives should be built into the contract. It may be necessary to include clauses for severe fluctuations in demand. Finally, any contract should include a termination clause.

The negotiations tend to be imbalanced, with the vendor having employed many technical and legal experts in order to prepare the agreement. The user organizations should do likewise and hire an expert to protect their interests. A technical expert can help develop performance standards and a legal expert ensures that the customer's wishes are expressed in the contract.

Monitor the Arrangement

The work is managed by results—in other words, there are targets or objectives such as "All calls answered within 90 seconds"—not necessarily by time expended to generate the results. A person will need to be assigned to monitor that the results are as expected; in complex arrangements, it may take a team to do this monitoring. The outsourced project or function must be clearly defined. If the terms are fuzzy, however, the contractor might be invited to brainstorm and help generate the guidelines and standards.[22] A relationship with the firm must be established to ensure that the outsourcer acts in the firm's best interests and has knowledge of its unique needs. References must be checked, just as they are when hiring any employee. Demand frequent and accurate reporting. Conduct internal and external client satisfaction surveys.

When managed according to these guidelines, organizations can maximize the benefits of outsourcing while mitigating the risks.

Summary

Outsourcing refers to the contractual arrangement wherein one organization provides services or products to another. There is a growing trend to outsource HR functions. The advantages of outsourcing include the reduction of costs, the increased energy and time to focus on an organization's core competencies, access to technology and specialized expertise, which both result in increased levels of service, and the political advantages of removing a troublesome function or reducing headcount. But there are disadvantages. The anticipated benefits may not be realized. Service levels may decrease. Employee morale and commitment may be reduced, as well as the value of the organization. Managing the contractual arrangement with the service provider is the key to optimizing the benefits and minimizing the risks.

Key Terms

core competence, 359

outsourcing, 356

Request for proposal (RFP), 363

Suggested Websites

www.outsourcing.com Links to content on benefits of outsourcing.

www.hrmsbook.com Provides a selection system for choosing an HRMS consultant.

www.peoplesoft.com Provides a series of tools to conduct a needs analysis and a means to calculate return on investment.

www.gartner.com Provides suggestions and readings on outsourcing.

Discussion Questions

1. Experts suggest that core functions should never be outsourced. Make a list of all the services and products that a large HR department in a large organization would provide. Prepare a definition of core. On a scale of 1 to 10, assign a weight to each HR service or product to assess if it is core or non-core.
2. Canadians have experienced several strikes over outsourcing. Identify these, and focus on the most recent strike. Analyze the media reports, and consult the employer and union websites to determine the perspectives of each on the issue of outsourcing. Have one team prepare the arguments against outsourcing from the union perspective; have another group prepare the arguments for outsourcing from the employer's perspective. Have each group write a two-page message to be given to the media.
3. Using a search engine, determine which public companies have made major outsourcing decisions. List the value of their shares one year before the announcement, one day before, one day after, and one year later to calculate the impact of an outsourcing decision on shareholder value.

Exercise

Most of you reading this text are students at a community college or university. Using your educational institute's directory, make a list of all organizational functions. In groups, determine which functions are possible candidates for outsourcing. Choose one and establish a business case for the president to outsource the function. Identify one or two service providers, and consult with them about the benefits of outsourcing. Choose another function and establish a case for retaining the function internally.

Case: Calgary Health Region

In November 2001, the Calgary Health Region issued an RFI (Request for Information) to suppliers interested in forming a partnership to finance and deliver an HRIS and provide certain human resources functions. A steering committee, composed of the vice-president, Human Resources; executive director, Human Resources; vice-president, Finance; executive director, Finance; director of Compensation, Benefits and HR Systems; and executive director, Information Technology, was formed to steer the project and screen the responses to the RFIs. The steering committee selected three of the responses and issued an RFP (Request for Proposal). Each supplier was given six weeks to provide a systems solution and shared-service outsourcing arrangement reflecting best HR practices, expertise, and financial arrangements. They were given detailed specifications and asked to bid on identified HR and payroll functions (e.g., payroll, benefit administration, pension) as a core service and bid on options such as recruitment services and occupational health and safety services.

The Evaluation and Selection team reviewed the submissions, and all met most of the requirements. Each consortium of suppliers was invited to present their proposals and respond to questions during a one-day presentation. All consortiums included a change management consultant and an information systems consultant. A detailed scoring system was developed that included an emphasis on service delivery and the impact on the current HR staff. The Evaluation and Selection team conducted site visits and reference checks on organizations in Boston, Vancouver, Edmonton, Toronto, and Calgary. The consortium chosen comprised Telus (providing the lead with an investment in the software application People Soft 8.8), PriceWaterhouseCoopers (for change management and implementation support), together with additional individual advisors. Due diligence was conducted in the fall of 2002. The negotiations continued for weeks in an attempt to craft a detailed proposal and a shared service contract that would result in the creation of a new organization and service provider.

The advantages of this potential partnership to the Calgary Health Region would be that their HRIS needs would be met by a state-of-the-art HRMS with no capital outlay. The region's current cost of "business as usual" for the staff and associated expenses transferring to the new organization would be paid to the provider throughout the term of the contract. In turn, the new organization would benefit from efficiencies generated by new systems and processes as well as revenue generated by building the client base. Additionally, the Calgary Health Region would potentially benefit from any new business generated. Each current HR employee would be guaranteed a job for at least one year, with the same or better compensation, benefits, and performance bonus plan as well as additional perquisites such as stock options. Some employees seemed to be excited by the possibility of working in an organization whose core business is HR and not always competing for funds with the dominant health-care divisions.

The consortium saw a benefit from a long-term contract and the possibility of generating revenues from increasing the business and client base. Indeed, the major expectation was that this service could be provided to other organizations, particularly in the health-care and educational sectors, where there is limited capital available for investment in human resources services and associated systems.

However there were some risks. The service delivery may not have met expectations despite standards such as "99.9% accuracy in payroll," and financial penalties would occur for failure to meet these standards. There may have been some loss of control related to the direct supervision of the service, although there would be contract managers in both organizations. The separation of groups of employees who normally worked together, such as the recruitment consultants and the recruitment assistants, may have posed problems (i.e., what is the impact of splitting strategic and transactional functions?). Finally, several groups of employees might have had to relocate to the new company; some were unionized, others exempt. There might have been a fight for successorship rights and the possibility of labour board challenges.

Source: Duncan Truscott, Acting Vice-President, HR; and Diane Pollo, Director, Compensation, Benefits, and HR Systems, Calgary Health Region. Courtesy of Calgary Health Region.

Questions

1. If you had been a member of the Calgary Health Region, what conditions would you have insisted be included in the contract with the vendor?
2. Prepare a report for management on the advantages of outsourcing, and the risks of this decision and your recommendations for managing each risk.

References

Albertson, D. 2000. "Outsourcing Shows Limited Impact for Strategic HR." *Employee Benefit News*, Vol. 14, No. 10: 70.

Alexander, M., and D. Young. 1996. "Strategic Outsourcing." *Long Range Planning*, Vol. 29, No. 1: 116–119.

Bryce, D.J., and M. Useem. 1998. "The Impact of Corporate Outsourcing on Company Value." *European Management Journal*, Vol. 16, No. 6: 635–643.

Burn, D. 1997. "Outsourcing: Transforming the role of Human Resource Professionals." *HR Professional*, (February/March): 26–33.

———. 1998. "To Outsource Training or not to Outsource Training: That Is the Question." *Human Resources Professional*, Vol. 15, No. 1(February/March): 18–23.

Cook, M. 1999. *Outsourcing Human Resources Functions*. New York: AMACOM.

The Economist Intelligence Unit. 1995. *New Directions in Finance: Strategic Outsourcing*. New York: The Economist Intelligence Unit.

Elmuti, D., and Y. Kathawala. 2000. "The Effects of Global Outsourcing Strategies on Participants' Attitudes and Organizational Effectiveness." *International Journal of Manpower*, Vol. 21, No. 2: 112–128.

Geary, S., and G. Coffey-Lewis. 2002. "Are You Ready to Outsource HR?" *HR Professional*, Vol. 19, No. 3 (June/July): 26–29.

Greer, C.R., S.A. Youngblood, and D.A. Gray. 2002. "Human Resource Management Outsourcing: The Make or Buy Decision." In J.A. Mello, *Strategic Human Resource Management*. Cincinnati, Ohio: South Western Thompson Learning.

Laabs, J. 2000. "Are You Ready to Outsource Staffing." *Workforce*, Vol. 70, No. 4: 56–60.

Labrie, P.J., and J. Bedard. 2002. "Outsourcing Training at Pratt & Whitney Canada." *HR Professional*, Vol. 10, No. 3 (June/July): 42.

LaCity, M.C., and R. Hirschheim. 1995. *Beyond the Information Systems Outsourcing Bandwagon*. Toronto: John Wiley & Sons.

McCauley, A. 2000. "Know the Benefits and Costs of Outsourcing Services." *Canadian HR Reporter*, Vol. 13, No. 17 (October 9): 18–19.

McKibbin-Brown, L. 2002. "Who Is Outsourcing What?" *HR Professional*, Vol. 10, No. 3 (June/July): 32.

Milgate, M. 2001. *Alliances, Outsourcing and the Lean Organization*. Westport Conn.: Quorum Books.

"Outsourcing and the Implications for Human Resource Development." *Journal of Management Development*, Vol. 19, No. 8 (2000): 694–699.

Patel, A. "Vertical HR: Will the Experiment Work." *HR Professional* Vol. 10, No. 3 (June/July): 14-14.

Petrick, A.E. 1996. "The Fine Art of Outsourcing." *Association Management* (December): 42–48.

Prahalad, C.K., and G. Hamel. 1990. "The Core Competence of the Corporation." *Harvard Business Review*, Vol. 68, No. 3: 79–91.

Sullivan, J. 2002. "The Case Against Outsourcing." *IHRIM Journal* (July): 38–41.

ENDNOTES

1. Greer, et al., 2002.
2. Cook, 1999.
3. McCauley, 2000.
4. Bryce and Useem, 1998.
5. Alexander and Young, 1996.
6. Prahalad and Hamel, 1990.
7. Burn, 1998.
8. Burn, 1997.
9. LaCity and Hirschheim, 1995.
10. Albertson, 2000.

11. Bryce and Useem, 1998.
12. Geary and Coffey-Lewis, 2002.
13. Milgate, 2001.
14. Elmuti and Kathawala, 2000.
15. "Outsourcing and the Implications for Human Resource Development," 2000.
16. Bryce and Useem, 1998.
17. Sullivan, 2002.
18. The Economist Intelligence Unit, 1995.
19. LaCity and Hirschheim, 1995.
20. Laabs, 2000.
21. LaCity and Hirschheim, 1995.
22. Petrick, 1996.

INDEX

A&P, 47
Ability, 113
Absenteeism, 86
Academic journals, 56
Acceleration centre, 244
Acceleration pools (PepsiCo), 259–260
Accenture, 106
Accommodation, 286
ACCOR, 303
Acquisition, 329
Acxion Corporation, 272
Adaptive IHRM approach, 302–303
Agreeableness, 307
Air Canada, 3–4, 13, 255–257
Alcatel, 200
Aldham, Jim, 255
Aldo Shoes, 19
Aligning HR with strategy, 21–51
  differentiation strategy, 48–51
  HR strategy by division, 35
  low-cost-provider strategy, 45–48
  strategic HRM. *See* Strategic HRM
Alvares, Ken, 177
American Institute of Certified Public Accountants, 127
Analyzer, 16
AOL Time Warner, 345
Assessment centres, 244
Asset purchase, 340
Assimilation, 337
AT&T, 237
Attitudes, 84
Attrition, 174
Audit, 93–94
Augmented HR system, 140
Autoglass, 365

Baby boomers, 58, 65
Baby busters, 65
Balanced scorecard, 90
Bank of Montreal, 95
Bankruptcy, 9
BARS, 124
Basic personnel system, 139
Bay, The, 16
Bayer Group AG, 119
BC Gas, 342, 345
BCG growth matrix, 14–15
Behaviourally Anchored Rating Scales (BARS), 124
Bell, 48
Benchmark, 117
Benchmarking, 94–95
Best-cost provider strategy, 16
Best practices, 96
BMO Financial Group, 95
BMW, 48
Boston Consulting Group model, 14–15
Bowey, John, 206
Broad differentiation strategy, 16
Budget, 190–191
Burger King, 16
Burton, Robert, 271
Business strategies, 12–17

Calgary Health Region, 368–369
Cameron, Kim, 267
Campeau, Robert, 329, 333
Campeau-Federated Department Stores deal, 329, 333, 335
Canada Bread, 155–156
Canadian Airlines International, 336
Canadian Imperial Bank of Commerce (CIBC), 106–107, 358, 360
Canadian Public Service Commission, 168
Cantor Fitzgerald, 235
Cara Operations, 12
Career management concepts, 251
Case studies
  Aldo Shoes, 19
  Calgary Health Region, 368–369
  Canada Bread, 155–156
  downsizing, 292–293
  faculty shortage, 226–228
  international career move, 320–321
  madness at Moosehead U, 131–132
  new version of HR, 40–41
  PepsiCo, 259–260
  recruiting, 200
  Sun Microsystems, 177
  Toronto (creation of mega-city), 348–350
  Wells Fargo, 99–100
  work–life balance, 73–74
Cash cows, 15
Catano, Victor, 80
Cause and effect models, 172
Chain effect, 208
Chapters, 328
Childless couples, 58
CIBC, 106–107, 358, 360
Cigarette smoking, 87
Cisco Systems, 193
City of Richmond, 231
Clearnet, 15
Client satisfaction, 81–84
Clients, 67
Club Managers Association of America, 127
ClubLink, 329
Coach, 249
Coca-Cola, 21
Colgate-Palmolive, 314
Compensable factors, 114

Compensation
differentiation strategy, 50
international, 316–317
low-cost-provider strategy, 46–47
M&As, 345
Competencies, 239–240
Competency, 126
Competency models, 126–128
Compliance, 81
Comprehensive and interactive HRMS, 140
Concurrent strategy formulation, 29
Conferences and seminars, 55
Conglomerate merger, 329
Conglomerate unions, 317
Conscientiousness, 307
Consolidation, 329
Consumers Distributing, 26
Contamination, 115
Contingency plans, 168
Contingent workers, 59
Contracting out, 287. *See* Outsourcing
Contribution, 87–90
Core competencies, 126, 240, 359
Corel, 48
Corporate international business strategies, 301
Corporate scorekeeping, 78
Corporate strategies, 8
Cost–benefit analysis, 91
Cost control, 85–87
Craft unions, 317
Critical incident method, 83
Critical incidents technique, 124
Cross-cultural training (CCT), 309–312
Crown princes, 252
Cuddy, A. Mac, 233
Culture, 84, 336
Culture management, 84–85
Culture shock, 312
Current forecast, 167
Customers, 67

Daimler-Chrysler merger, 329
Data security, 142
Decision support system (DSS), 144
Deculturation, 337
Defender, 15
Deficiency, 115
Dell Computer, 193
Delphi technique, 57, 185–188
Demand forecasting. *See* HR demand
Demographic factors, 65–66
Demographics, 65
Designated groups, 164
Deutsche Bank, 80
Diaries, 118
Dictionary of Occupational Titles (DOT), 117
Differentiation strategy, 48–51
Direct costs, 91
Disengaged workers, 58
Distributive justice, 276
Divestiture, 9
Division of labour, 62
Dogs, 15
Domestic strategy, 301
DOT, 117
Dow Chemical, 66, 106
Downsizing, 265–298
adjusting to job loss, 274–275
alternatives to, 271–272
best practices, 285
case study, 292–293
communication, 284
consequences of, 279–280
decision to downsize, 271
defined, 266
financial performance, and, 278–279
high-performance work practices, 288
HRM issues, 285–290
impact on downsizers, 277–278
inplacement/outplacement, 272
labour relations issues, 288–290
organizational change, 282
planning for, 272–273
psychological contract, 285–287
strategic, 281–282
strategies, 280–284
survivors, 275–277
why done, 270–271
Downsizing strategy, 266
Drucker, Peter, 50, 232, 243
DSS, 144

Early retirement, 234
East Side Mario's, 16
Eaton's, 15, 232
Economic climate, 61–62
Effective HRM strategy, 35–36
Efficiency, 85
Efficiency measures, 85–86
Egalitarian pay structures, 50
Electronic monitoring, 65
Elitism, 252–253
Emergent strategy, 7
Emotion stability, 307
Employee requirement ratio, 183
Employee retention programs, 220–224
Employee value proposition (EVP), 242
Employees
differentiation strategy, 49
high potential, 241–243
low-cost-provider strategy, 45–46
stakeholders, as, 69
strategic resources, as, 24–25
succession management, 250–252
Envelope, 167
Envelope/scenario forecasting, 191–193
Environmental influences, 53–76
demographic factors, 65–66
economic climate, 61–62
environmental scanning, 54–60
example, 70, 71
globalization, 62
labour market, 62–63
political/legislative factors, 63–64
social/cultural factors, 66
stakeholders, 67–70
technological factors, 64, 65
Environmental scanning, 54–60
e-recruiting, 193
Ernst & Young, 303

Ethics, 64
Evaluation of HR programs, 77–108
    5C model of HRM impact, 81–90
    auditing, 93–94
    benchmarking, 94–95
    case study (Wells Fargo), 99–100
    challenges in measuring HRM, 96–97
    client satisfaction, 81–84
    compliance, 81
    contribution, 87–90
    cost–benefit analysis, 91
    cost control, 85–87
    culture management, 84–85
    importance, 78–79
    rationale, 79–80
    resistance to, 79
    utility analysis, 91–93
Event-based forecasting, 160
EVP, 242
Execution of strategy, 6
Executive compensation, 59
Expert forecasts, 184–185
Exportive IHRM approach, 303
External coaches, 249
External fit, 36, 302
External supply, 170
Extraversion, 307

Faculty shortage, 226–228
Family businesses, 206
Fast-food businesses, 16
Federated Department Stores, 329, 333, 335
Financial restructuring, 268
Fire Department of New York, 235
Fit, 35–36, 302
5C model of HRM impact, 81–90
Five-factor personality model (FFM), 306, 307
Five Ps of strategy, 5
FJA, 125
Flexibility, 304
Focused strategy, 16–17
Ford, 62
Forecasting. *See* HR forecasting
Four Seasons Hotels, 48
Frost, Inc., 34
Functional job analysis (FJA), 125

Gen X, 65
Gen Y, 66
General Electric (GE), 35, 50
General Motors (GM), 62
General unions, 317
Giant Manufacturing, 362
GIGO, 146
Global strategy, 301
Globalization, 62
Glover, Brenda, 348, 350
Goal optimization, 89
Goldman Sachs, 233
Gordon Capital, 233
Gow Corp., 356
Grant, Philip, 122
Gretzky, Wayne, 254
Growth strategies, 10–12
Guptil, David, 242

Hard competencies, 239
Harris, Hollis, 255
Hathcock, Bonnie, 30
Hay system, 125–126
HCNs, 308
Hewlett, Bill, 29
Hewlett-Packard, 29, 48, 193
Hewlett-Packard–Compaq merger, 328, 330
High-potential employees, 241–243
High Road Communications, 272
Hiring freeze, 174
Historical costs model, 104
Home-country nationals (HCNs), 308
Honda, 48, 50
Horizontal integration, 331
Horizontal merger, 328
Hostile takeovers, 333
Hot issues, 58–59
HR accounting methods, 104–107
HR alignment. *See* Aligning HR with strategy
HR budget, 190–191
HR deficit, 174
HR demand, 168–170, 181–202
    Delphi technique, 185–188
    envelope/scenario forecasting, 191–193
    e-recruiting, 193
    expert forecasts, 184–185
    HR budgets, 190–191
    index/trend analysis, 182–184
    nominal group technique, 188–190
    regression analysis, 194–197
HR forecasting, 159–179
    activity categories, 160–161
    benefits, 161–163
    defined, 159
    environmental factors, 166
    forecasting models, 172
    HR demand, 168–170. *See also* HR demand
    HR supply, 170–171. *See also* HR supply
    HR surplus/deficit, 173–174
    net HR requirements, 168–175
    organizational factors, 166
    personnel analyses, 163–166
    time horizons, 166–167
HR intranets, 150
HR management systems, 137–158
    core data elements, 147–152
    data inclusion, 146–147
    future expansion, 145–146
    how used, 141
    implementation time, 149
    intranets, 150
    possible add-on modules, 145–146
    selection/design criteria, 141–146
    stages of HRMS development, 139–141
    strategic HR planning, 147
    succession management, 244
    system costs/service support, 143–144
    system security/access control, 141–142
HR planning
    differential strategy, 49
    M&As, 340–343
HR role assessment survey, 83
HR strategy and corporate strategy, 28–29

HR strategy by division, 35
HR supply, 170–171, 203–230
 linear programming, 213–214
 Markov models, 210–213
 movement analysis, 214–218
 retention programs, 221–224
 skill and management inventories, 204–205
 succession/replacement analysis, 205–210
 vacancy model, 218–221
HR surplus, 173, 174
HR system implementation, 163
HRIS, 137
HRM. *See* Human resource management
HRM impact. *See* Evaluation of HR programs
HRMS, 137. *See also* HR management systems
Hudson Institute, 56
Human asset accounting approach, 104–105
Human capital, 23
Human capital metrics, 80
Human resource management
 defined, 22
 future of, 58
 sources of information, 55–56
Human resources management systems (HRMS), 137. *See also* HR management systems

IBM, 237
Identification and personal record, 147–148
Impact analysis, 57
Incremental growth, 10
Index/trend analysis, 182–184
Indirect costs, 91
Industrial unions, 317
Informal feedback, 82
Information sources, 55–56
Information systems. *See* HR management systems
Inplacement, 272
Integrated systems, 145
Integration, 337
Integrative IHRM approach, 303–304
Integrative linkage, 32
Intellectual capital, 105
Intellectual capital approach, 105–106
Intended strategy, 7
Interactional justice, 276
Internal fit, 36, 302
Internal labour markets, 213
Internal supply, 170
International career move, 320–321
International compensation, 316–317
International growth, 10
International HRM. *See* Strategic international HRM
International labour relations, 317–318
International performance appraisals, 314–316
Interviews, 118
Intranet, 150
ithink, 168

Jet Form, 246
Job, 112
Job analysis, 111–135
 competency-based approaches, 126–128
 constituent elements, 114
 defined, 112
 feedback, 123
 job description, 112, 113, 119–122
 job specification, 112, 119–120, 122
 problems, 115–116
 process of, 116–123
 reward system, 123
 scientific management, 114
 step 1 (determine job to be analyzed), 116–117
 step 2 (determine methods/analyze job), 117–120
 step 3 (examine recorded data), 120
 step 4 (define new methods/performance standards), 120–122
 step 5 (ensure usage of new methods), 122–123
 techniques, 124–126
 time measurement, 114
Job analysis techniques, 124–126
Job insecurity, 275, 277
Job loss. *See* Downsizing
Job rotations, 245–247
Job sharing, 174
Johnson & Johnson, 253
Journals, 118
Judgmental models, 172
Justice, 276

Kimberly-Clark, 13
Knowledge, 113
KnowledgePoint, 121
Krispy Kreme, 10, 11
KSAs, 113

Labour hoarding, 28
Labour market, 62–63
Labour relations
 differentiation strategy, 51
 downsizing, 288–290
 international, 317–318
 low-cost-provider strategy, 48
 M&As, 346
Labour shortages of highly qualified workers, 59
Labour wastage, 221
Large vs. small organizations, 69
Layoffs. *See* Downsizing
Legislative factors, 63–64
Leiba-O'Sullivan, Sharon, 299
Linear programming, 213–214
Linearity, 194
Liquidation, 9
Logical incrementalism, 7
Long-run forecast, 167
Long-term succession, 205
Lotus–IBM merger, 339
Low-cost-provider strategy, 16, 45–48
Lumenon, 200

Magna International, 233
Maintenance strategies, 11–12

Management development methods, 245–250
  job rotations, 245–247
  mentoring/coaching, 248–250
  promotion, 245
  special assignments, 247
  training and development, 247–248
Management information system (MIS), 144
Management inventories, 205
Managerial competencies, 240
Market niche strategy, 16–17
Markov chains, 211
Markov models, 210–213
M&As. *See* Mergers and acquisitions
McCain's, 232
McDonald's, 9, 27, 45, 48
Measuring HRM practices. *See* Evaluation of HR programs
Medium-run forecast, 167
Mentor, 248–250
Mercedes-Benz, 48
Merchant, James, 360
Merger, 328
Merger hotline, 342
Mergers and acquisitions, 327–353
  case study (Toronto mega-city), 348–350
  compensation, 345
  cultural issues, 336–338
  definitions, 328–329
  financial benefits, 322
  financial impact, 334–335
  goals, 335
  HR issues, 339
  human resources, and, 335–336
  labour relations, 346
  managerial needs, 322–333
  merger methods, 333
  performance appraisal, 345–346
  planning, 340–343
  post-merger integration practices, 338–339
  selection, 343–344
  strategies benefits, 330–331
  training and development, 346
  transition team, 341–343
Merrill Lynch, 343
Microsoft, 15, 62
Miles and Snow's organizational types, 15–16
Minacs Worldwide, 11
MIS, 144
MNCs. *See* Strategic international HRM
Morals, 64
Movement analysis, 214–218
Multi-domestic strategy, 301
Multinational corporations (MNCs). *See* Strategic international HRM
Multinational strategy, 301
Multiplier effect, 212
Multivariate regression analysis, 194

National Occupational Classification (NOC), 117
NCR, 253
Nestlé, 62
New deal, 286
New version of HR (case study), 40–41
NGT, 188–190
Nicotine addiction, 87
Nike, 362
NOC, 117
Nominal group technique (NGT), 188–190
Nortel, 200
Nortel–Bay Networks merger, 336

Objectives, 6
Observation, 118
Online recruiting sites, 193
Ontario Hydro, 236
Openness to experience, 307
Operating synergy, 330
Organizational restructuring, 268
Outplacement, 272
Outsourcing, 355–371
  case study (Calgary Health Region), 368–369
  defined, 356
  employee morale, 362–363
  example (CIBC), 358
  HR functions, 356–358
  management of, 363–366
  monitoring the arrangement, 366
  negotiating the contract, 365–366
  reasons for, 358–360
  RFP, 363, 364
  risks/limitations, 361–363
  selecting a vendor, 363–364
  service risks, 362
  small business, 357

Packard, David, 29
Pac-Man defensive manoeuvre, 333
PAQ, 124–125
Parent-country nationals (PCNs), 308
PepsiCo, 21, 259–260
Performance appraisal. *See* Performance evaluation
Performance evaluation
  differentiation strategy, 50–51
  international, 314–316
  low-cost-provider strategy, 47
  M&As, 345–346
  succession management, 244
Performance Management through Training and Development (Belcourt et al.), 248
PERSIM, 168
Personal identification number (PIN), 142
Petro-Canada, 328
Pfizer–Warner-Lambert takeover, 330
PIN, 142
Plans, 6
Poison pill, 333
Policies, 6
Political/legislative factors, 63–64
Polo Ralph Lauren, 48, 68
Porter, Michael, 16, 24
Porter's model of business strategy, 16
Portfolio restructuring, 268
Position Analysis Questionnaire (PAQ), 124–125
Positions, 112
Pratt & Whitney, 356
Prediction, 167

Present value of future earnings model, 105
PriceWaterhouseCoopers, 95
Probabilistic models, 210
Procedural justice, 276
Process-based forecasting, 160
Procter & Gamble, 10, 48
Professional associations, 55
Professional consultants, 55–56
Projection, 167
Promotion, 245
Prospector, 15
Psychological contract, 285
Public Service Commission of Canada, 241
Publications, 55, 56

Question marks, 15
Questionnaires, 118

Reactor, 16
Realized strategy, 7
Recruitment and Selection in Canada (Catano et al.), 240
Red Lobster, 16
Regression analysis, 194–197
Relational database, 140
Renewal model, 218
Repatriation, 312–314
Replacement charts, 241
Replacement costs model, 104
Replacement planning, 235–238
Request for proposal (RFP), 363, 364
Research, Measurement and Evaluation of Human Resources (Saks), 93, 95
Research journals, 56
Restructuring, 268. *See also* Downsizing
Restructuring strategies, 8–10
Retention programs, 220–224
Return on equity (ROE), 89
Return on investment (ROI), 89, 90
Reverse culture shock, 312
Review/react linkage, 32
RFP, 363, 364
Rightsizing, 280. *See also* Downsizing
Ripple effect, 208
ROE, 89
ROI, 89, 90
Role of specific competencies, 240
Rolex, 48
Rotations, 245–247

SaskTel, 223
Scandia, 106
Scenario, 168
Scenario forecasting, 191–193
Schwinn, 362
Scientific management, 114
Scorecard measures, 78
Sears, 25
Selection
- differentiation strategy, 49–50
- M&As, 343–344

Selection bias, 254
Separation, 337
September 11 terrorist attacks, 235
Sequencing model, 218
Share purchase, 340
Shareholders, 67
Short-run forecast, 167
Short-term emergency replacement, 205
Short-term employment contracts, 287
Simple regression, 194
Simple regression prediction model, 195–197
Size of organization, 69
Skill, 113
Skill and management inventories, 150–152
Skills determine strategy outlook, 28
Skills inventory, 170, 204–205
Skills shortage, 222
Small vs. large organizations, 69
Smith, Coleen, 314
Smoking, 87
Soft competencies, 239
Sources of information, 55–56
Southwest Airlines, 242
Special assignments, 247
Specialist programs, 145
Specific competencies, 126
Spinks, Nora, 278
Stakeholders, 67
Stars, 15
Stochastic models, 210
Strategic downsizing, 281–282
Strategic HR planning model, 37–38
Strategic HRM, 22–33
- defined, 22
- employees as strategic resources, 24–25
- HRMS, 147
- importance, 23–24
- improved goal attainment, 25–26
- linking HR processes to strategy, 27
- need for, 4–5
- risks, 26–27
- traditional HR, contrasted, 33
- ways to become involved, 32–33

Strategic IHRM flexibility, 304
Strategic intent, 6
Strategic international HR planning, 300
Strategic international HRM, 299–326
- adaptive approach, 302–303
- case study (international career move), 320–321
- corporate business strategies, 301
- cross-cultural training, 309–312
- defined, 300
- exportive approach, 303
- flexibility, 304
- HCNs/PCNs/TCNs, 308–309
- integrative approach, 303–304
- performance appraisals, 314–316
- repatriation, 312–314
- selection of global management candidates, 306–309
- spouses of global managers, 311

Strategic partnering, 30–31
Strategic plan, 6
Strategic planning, 6
Strategic replacement, 241–242
Strategic types, 8–12
Strategy, 5
Strategy formulation, 6

Strategy implementation, 6
Stronach, Belinda, 233
Succession management, 231–262
  defined, 232
  employee perspective, 250–252
  example (Air Canada), 255–257
  importance, 232–234
  internal vs. external candidates, 237
  problems/soft spots, 252–254
  reasons for, 234
  replacement planning, compared, 238
  step 1 (align plans with strategy), 238–239
  step 2 (identify skills/competencies), 239–240
  step 3 (identify high-potential employees), 241–243
  step 4 (provide developmental opportunities), 243–250
  step 5 (monitor succession management), 250
Succession planning, 205
Succession readiness codes, 208
Succession/replacement analysis, 205–210
Succession/replacement chart, 207–208
Succession/replacement table, 208–210
Sumitomo Metals, 49
Sun Microsystems, 28, 177
Suppliers, 68
Supply forecasting. *See* HR supply
Surrey Metro Savings Credit Union, 32
Survey instruments, 118
Surveys, 82–83
Survival, 88–89
Syncrude Canada, 243
Synergy, 330
System security, 141–142
Systematic change, 267

Taco Bell, 87
Taggar, Simon, 80
Takeover, 329
Talent management culture, 242
Talent Network, The, 200
Taylor, Frederick, 114
TCNs, 308, 309
TD Financial Group, 330
Technological factors, 64, 65
Telecommuting, 65
Temporary replacement, 241
Third-country nationals (TCNs), 308, 309
Thomson, David, 233
Thomson, Ken, 233
Thomson Corporation, 233
Thrasher, Robert, 271
3M, 49, 249
360-degree evaluation, 118, 241–242
Time series models, 172
Timex, 45
Toronto (creation of mega-city), 348–350
Toyota, 45
Trainability, 307
Training and development
  differentiation strategy, 50
  low-cost-provider strategy, 47
  M&As, 346
  succession management, 247–248
Transaction-based forecasting, 160
Transformation, 287
Transitional probabilities, 211
Trend analysis, 57, 182
Turnaround strategy, 8
Turnover, 86–87

Unions, 68–69, 317. *See also* Labour relations
Unique or distinctive competencies, 240
UNISYS, 329
United Church of Canada, 356
United Food and Commercial Workers (UFCW), 47
United Parcel Service (UPS), 34
Utility analysis, 91–93

Vacancy model, 218–221
Vertical integration, 331
Vertical merger, 328–329
Violence in the workplace, 66
"Voices of Survivors: Words That Downsizing CEOs Should Hear," 276

Wagar, Terry H., 80, 265
Wal-Mart, 13, 61, 67–68, 249
Wang, Xiaoyun, 299
Warner-Lambert, 312
Wedgbury, Mia, 272
Wells Fargo, 99–100
Whale, Elliot, 244
White knight, 333
Woodward's, 232
Work history, 148
Work–life balance, 66, 73–74
Work redesign, 267
Workforce reduction, 267
Workplace violence, 66

Yamaha, 332

Zellers, 45